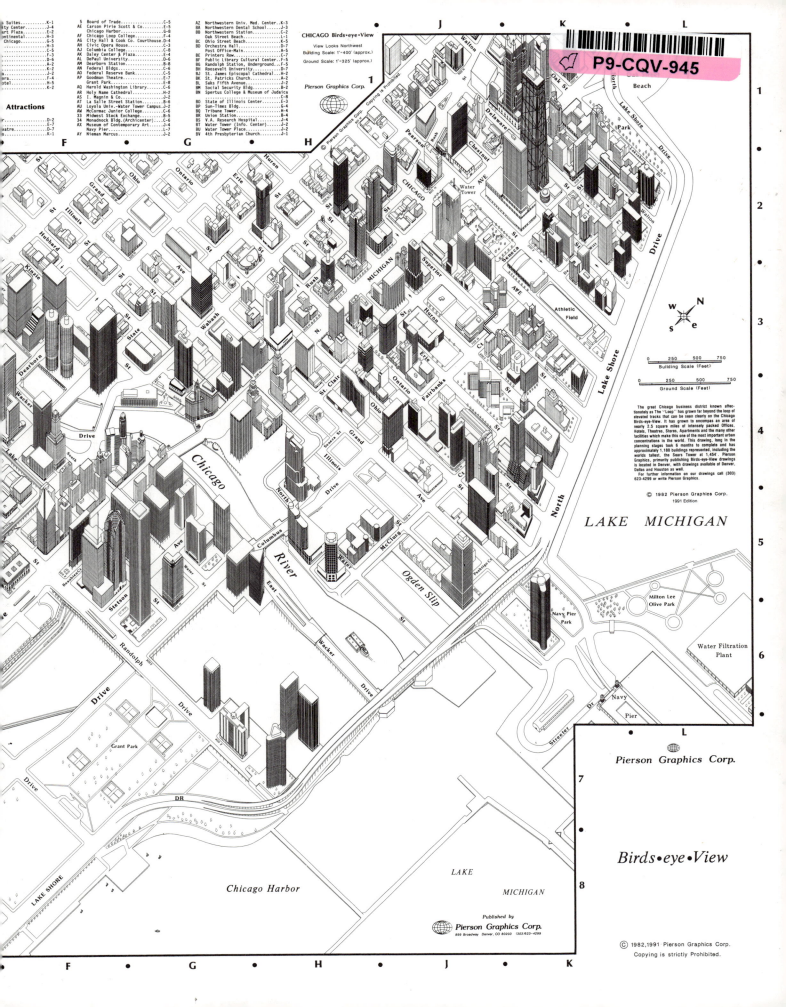

THEY BUILT CHICAGO

Entrepreneurs Who Shaped a Great City's Architecture

Miles L. Berger

Bonus Books, Inc., Chicago

96 95 94 93 92   5 4 3 2

Library of Congress Catalog Card Number: 91-77990

International Standard Book Number: 0-929387-76-7

Bonus Books, Inc.
160 East Illinois Street
Chicago, Illinois 60611

Printed in the United States of America

To the memory of my father
Albert E. Berger
One who made a difference

CONTENTS

LIST OF
ILLUSTRATIONS

FOREWORD

James R. Thompson

In the 1940s my family lived in a succession of workingmen's flats in the neighborhood of Garfield Park, on Chicago's West Side. My parents, products of rural and small-town life in DeKalb County, Illinois, had been the only members of their families to leave the tranquillity of life in the Corn Belt to seek a new opportunity to marry, raise a family, and work in the challenging and growing city that was then bursting at the seams with defense workers and urban migrants like themselves.

My life in Chicago was very much involved with the streets and neighborhoods of the city. The vast acreage of Garfield Park and its lagoons, pools, and gardens were my front yard. We played baseball and "King of the Hill" on the vacant lots or "prairies" of the park, stalked the fascinating jungles and deserts of the Garfield Park Conservatory and (strictly against parental cautions) walked the railroad tracks that were the city's arteries of commerce.

But the irresistible lure—the magnet that pulled at my playmates and me—was "Downtown." It was high adventure to accompany my parents to the Loop as a special treat on weekends or to sneak off occasionally on my own to ride the Madison Street streetcar or the "El" (a first solo escapade at the age of seven!) into these fascinating canyons lined with skyscrapers built on a grand scale for commerce, entertainment, and retailing. Those were days when "Marshall Field's Downtown" was one word, Harry Blackstone and other entertainers competed on the stage of baroque movie palaces, and lakefront and architecture merged—then as now—to produce the most dramatic urban landscape in America.

In later years, as governor of Illinois, I had the opportunity to lend the support of state government to Chicago's development and redevelopment in projects and programs that included replacing the Sherman House Hotel with Helmut Jahn's futuristic State of Illinois Center; building McCormick Place II; funding the Oceanarium at the Shedd Aquarium; rehabilitating the Burnham-designed State of Illinois Building; funding the reconstruction and redevelopment of Navy Pier; acquiring the Pullman Works and Hotel Florence for rehabilitation by the State of Illinois as a major transportation museum; building a new Comiskey Park; and setting the stage for development of the new Chicago Stadium. After retiring as governor in 1991, I moved to a forty-sixth-floor office at the law firm of Winston and Strawn, a coanchor tenant in John Buck's Leo Burnett building at 35 West Wacker Drive—a building that, along with the State of Illinois Center, anchored and accelerated Chicago's North Loop redevelopment.

In all of these years, I have, as a citizen and resident, shared a pride in living in the most "livable" large city in America. On trade missions to Europe and Asia I hustled for Chicago and championed its central location, political and business leadership, commerce, beauty, art, music, theater, and, of course, its architecture. "Chicago," I would say in my stump speech to foreign business investors, "is the world's capital of modern architecture." And no one would disagree.

But as Miles Berger demonstrates in this book, the real story of Chicago—its rise and constant renewal, its strength of commerce, and its urban beauty—is the story of those Chicagoans who *developed* the city. These are the men who assembled and captained the teams of architects, builders, financiers, and business and community leaders to give life to the combination of spaces and ideas that we experience collectively as Chicago's great architecture. Men who gave flesh to their dreams include the likes of Paul Cornell, who created Hyde Park and brought it to the status of Chicago's most famous neighborhood; Ferd Kramer, who helped build Lake Meadows, Prairie Shores, and Dearborn Park; and Phil Klutznick, who invented a new American life-style when he built Park Forest and a new urban retail form when he created Water Tower Place. Magic names in Chicago architecture, Dankmar Adler and Louis H. Sullivan, are forever linked with the city's famed Auditorium Building and Theater, but it was a young Chicago developer, Ferdinand W. Peck, who acquired the land, the financing, and the services of Adler and Sullivan to give shape to his vision of a multiuse center that would provide a home for opera, symphony, and other entertainments as well house businesses and a great hotel.

Once you accept the notion that our love for Chicago and its architecture may have obscured the role of the developers who gave birth to this city, it is clear that no one is better qualified to tell their story than Miles Berger, who for more than four decades has been active in Chicago's real estate, development, banking, investment, and planning communities. Through his service on the Chicago Plan Commission, he was in a unique position to understand how development—especially post-World War II activity—depended upon firing the imagination of public officials such as mayors and governors, as well as tapping into the resources of federal, state, and local programs designed to spur construction of housing and commercial structures. Berger's love for his city and his unrelenting passion for uncovering the personal histories, the dreams, and the motivations of its builders come through on every page of this volume. His meticulously researched account is told with the knowledge and insight of the quintessential insider, but without the ego that so often was the moving force behind the enormous accomplishments of his subjects.

Miles Berger's story of the development of Chicago is both engaging and encompassing, no doubt because his curiosity about his subject and his imagination continuously pulse. Invited to a Christmas housewarming party at the Lincoln Park penthouse of an acquaintance, he was found clambering over the boxes and catering paraphernalia that had been stacked in the twenty-degree cold of the apartment's rear terrace so that he could experience the apartment's "best view" and marvel at the sight of many of the neighborhoods and structures described in this book. And, of course, he disappeared to the terrace twice more during the course of the evening to renew and expand his observations.

In all the history of this great city, and of all the treatises and tomes that have described, analyzed, and exclaimed over it, no book quite like *They Built Chicago* has ever been written. And, clearly, no one but Miles Berger could have told this engrossing tale as it is told here—with the same passion as that which seized the men who saw the opportunity of this mighty confluence of prairie and water, and who, through dreams brought to life with imagination, hard work, and luck, made of this the reality that is Chicago.

PREFACE

For a good part of my lifetime I have been an appreciative observer of the never-ending process that is the building of Chicago. For more than forty of these years I have been involved to some extent in that process—as a real estate investor, developer, consultant, and as a member, vice chairman, and chairman of the Chicago Plan Commission.

I found myself wondering about the widely held perception that Chicago's great buildings and magnificent skyline were the sole creation of the city's architects. Where were the developers in this story? After all, it is the developer who—through the force of his vision, his energy, his capital, and his daring—gives a project its life and then its support system. The developer conceives the idea for a structure, acquires a suitable location, selects an architect, secures the financing, and, finally, arranges for the sale or management of the building after it is completed.

The brilliance of Chicago's architects notwithstanding, the fact remains that the architect works as a participant in what essentially is a team effort. The developer's requirements and the purpose for which he commissions a project directly affect both the appearance and ultimately, I believe, the significance of a building. The architect's work reflects not only his own creativity but the intent and vision of the building's developer.

It seemed paradoxical to me that buildings that are given life and substance by developers perpetuate the names of their architects, but very seldom the names—or perhaps more important, the intentions—of their creators. I was surprised to find that, for all the volumes written on Chicago's great architecture, there was no work singularly recognizing the contribution of the developer to the growth of the city and to the distinctive character of its buildings. Intrigued by what seemed an almost implausible oversight in the otherwise generously documented history of Chicago, I began my own search for the rest of the story.

I started the research for this book with the idea of compiling an anthology highlighting the careers of nineteenth- and twentieth-century Chicago developers. As my interest heightened and my files outgrew first the space allotted on my dining room table and then my library, I realized that I could not reduce the personal histories of such larger-than-life individuals to a bloodless catalogue of dates and addresses. Nor, given the remarkably creative climate that still characterizes Chicago development, could I limit my inquiry to the early periods. The search I had undertaken as a brief historical inquiry soon became a massive research project. The work took on a life of its own.

As the pieces began to fall into place, I found common patterns and some distinctive traits in the personalities of men who dare to be developers. While the developer is often portrayed in media stereotypes as a greedy and insensitive individual interested only in reaping the greatest financial reward for himself, the personal histories of the men themselves present another, far more intriguing, picture. Chicago developers, like the architects they commission, have been men of great imagination and creativity, willing to risk all for the purpose of creating a new structure—sometimes as a monument, sometimes as a legacy, very often for the purpose of expressing a uniquely individual vision.

It interests me in retrospect to see that although I began my project with the intention of running up the banner of the developer, I found that as the research and interviews proceeded I was gaining new respect for the very significant role that the architect plays in the development process. Time and again I was told by developers of the special character of that relationship, and witnessed it myself in my research. It is a relationship to which the partners—architect and developer—of necessity bring both identical and highly divergent characteristics and talents.

The book has been organized into four major periods, spanning more than 150 years of Chicago history: 1830 to 1879; 1880 to 1899; 1900 to 1929; and the years from the end of World War II to the present. Although the distinction in terms of dates is somewhat arbitrary, each of these periods presented its own opportunities and challenges and each manifested a characteristic development style. The four sections are introduced by a brief overview defining significant development issues in the period, and each developer profiled is placed within the period during which he was most active. Throughout the book, both in the profiles themselves and in an introductory chapter, I have made an effort to identify the vision of the developers, to illuminate their character and personal styles, and to touch on how they perceived themselves and were perceived in the communities and the times in which they lived and worked. In my search for insight into the lives and motivations of the developers of the early periods—and indeed in some cases for the names of the developers themselves—I turned of necessity to archival sources. These included public records, newspaper accounts, reports of real estate transactions, correspondence, and other unpublished materials.

I found two not unrelated problems in seeking information on the early developers. The first is that, with a few flamboyant exceptions, developers for various good reasons did not seek either fame or public recognition. Architects, always on the lookout for the next commission, were far more committed to publicizing their efforts. A second factor tending to obscure the developer's role is that a developer's ideas and his instructions to his architect often were (and still are) exchanged verbally. A real estate developer's files have never been considered as important to posterity, nor as likely to belong to the public, as an architect's drawings. As a consequence, most of these records have long since been destroyed, often by the developer himself.

Sources covering the period from the end of World War II to the present are far more available and accessible. In profiling the developers of the modern period, I tried to maintain focus on the man himself, leaving evaluations or critiques of his work to other writers in other contexts. In this regard, my primary sources have been conversations with the developers themselves or with members of their families. I have, of course, relied heavily on my own experience and observations, drawn particularly from the years in which I served on the Chicago Plan Commission. To this extent I have taken the liberty of adding commentary to many of these chapters, specific to my own perspective, in the form of author's notes. In an effort to reduce reference notes citing sources, and at the same time to suggest to the reader the resources I have drawn upon and that are available to future researchers, I have added a bibliographical appendix.

By far the most difficult task in completing this book has been to narrow the group of some one hundred developers whose work was researched, and whose work I know personally, to the collection of forty-four individuals profiled in this volume. In making a selection, I tried first to identify those who, in my judgment, had made the greatest difference in the development process and who had the most significant impact on their times. I then tried, through the selection of developers profiled, to provide a glimpse of the range and types of development activity and techniques prevalent in a given period.

My regret is that space did not permit the inclusion of many other individuals, both in the past and in the present, whose work and contribution to the growth of Chicago readily met the criteria I set. It is important to note that there are many whose work was not covered in this book who are making continuing contributions to the development of the city, and still others, just starting, whose names will be part of the myth and substance of Chicago in the twenty-first century.

My purpose in writing this book has been to add an additional perspective, one too long neglected, to our knowledge of men who built Chicago. My hope is that readers may find the subject as fascinating as I have and that their interest might inspire further research into the role played by the developer in the continually unfolding story of this extraordinary city.

Miles L. Berger

ACKNOWLEDGMENTS

Although my name is on the cover, this book could not have been created without the assistance of Ann Paden and Diane Ruscitti, who worked with me at every stage of its development, from primary research through the final rewrite and editing process. This was truly a team effort. The work in its present scope would not have been possible without their energy, encouragement, and belief in the value of the project. I am grateful to Rex Olsen, my editor at Bonus Books, for his knowledgeable and astute comments and recommendations in the final stages of manuscript preparation. Doug Montgomery's assistance as a photo researcher has been invaluable in assembling the broad range of photographs that appear in this book, including many that have never appeared in print before. I want to thank the staff of the Chicago Historical Society, the Art Institute of Chicago, and the Newberry Library for making seldom-seen documents and manuscript collections available to us, as well the developers and families who shared with us their records and their memories. The assistance and cooperation of numerous organizations, institutions, and government offices is gratefully acknowledged. These include the City of Chicago Municipal Reference Library; the Cook County Recorder of Deeds; the Chicago Public Library; the University of Illinois at Chicago; and the Elmhurst, Villa Park, Lake Forest (Illinois), Lake Geneva (Wisconsin), and Medford (Massachusetts) libraries and historical societies.

INTRODUCTION

In 1991 the American Institute of Architects recognized Chicago as architecturally the most important city in the United States. The announcement did not come as a surprise. Nor did the AIA's further observation that Chicagoans have been in the business of "designing a city like none built before in America" for well over a hundred years.

Some say that Chicago's predilection for innovative architecture and construction was a product of the Great Fire of 1871, which swept away every old structure in the central business district, inspiring Chicagoans to rebuild their city—bigger and better than before. Others say that the unique geographic and economic conditions that made Chicago a natural center of transportation and trade—and the scarcity of land in the downtown area—necessitated the invention and continual refinement of the skyscraper. Both explanations, of course, are true, but both lack the human ingredient—that ineffable energy—that for more than a century has made Chicago different from any other of America's great cities. That difference may well be accounted for by the nature of the men who were—and still are—drawn to Chicago: bold, dynamic, creative entrepreneurs. These included those men of vision who in the aftermath of the Great Fire conceived building projects the likes of which had not been seen before, risked massive capital, and hired the architects and engineers who would execute their vision.

But the phenomenon is by no means limited to the nineteenth century. Chicago's development climate in the 1850s was as dynamic in the rush to build as in the postwar period of the 1950s. The golden age of Chicago development in the 1880s was mirrored in the building boom of the 1980s. Developers' varied responses to the financial panic of 1893 were paralleled by developers' responses to the business downturn of the early 1990s. In each of these periods, the lives and work of Chicago developers have been characterized by an irrepressible creative force. Their stories are the "story behind the story" of Chicago's great architecture.

The term *developer* has been loosely applied to anyone who owns or manages, buys, or sells a piece of real estate. In the proper sense, however, a developer is far more than an investor in real estate. A developer is that individual who takes on the responsibility—often at very great personal risk—for making something out of nothing, for adding value to land by creating a new structure or renovating an old one. By this definition, the role for the developer has remained consistent over the more than 150 years of Chicago's building history. It is the developer who, by his choice of site, land use, and building style, establishes the physical character of the city and in many respects shapes the quality of urban life.

Some believe that architects and developers are natural enemies—coexisting, but just barely, in a constant state of conflict. According to this interpretation, the architect claims that the developer brings only his capital to a project, while the developer gives the architect credit only for carrying out his wishes, and then at outrageous expense. The interaction is seen as a love-hate relationship similar to the conflicts and jealousies often seen in married couples. They acknowledge their need for one another, but each feels that he (or she) is making the major contribution, and each is sure that the other doesn't appreciate him (or her). The reality is quite different. Were it not for the developer's pursuit of his dream, there would be little opportunity for the architect to express his artistry. The reverse is equally true. Without the architect's ability to translate the developer's vision into steel and stone, the dream might not be realized. Developer and architect complement one another. When they work together, they create great works.

Memorable examples include the synergy created in the 1880s among Chicago property manager Owen Aldis, Boston investor Peter Brooks, and a pair of young architects named John Root and Daniel Burnham. From this partnership between developer and architect emerged an entirely new form of commercial building—the spare and functional style now known as the first Chicago school of architecture. Another notable partnership between developer and architect was the support offered by developer Edward Waller to a little-known architect named Frank Lloyd Wright. Even at the dawn of Wright's career, Waller understood the architect's genius and became his foremost patron, taking every opportunity to promote young Wright and his unconventional ideas. A more modern parallel is the extraordinary collaboration of developer Herbert Greenwald and Ludwig Mies van der Rohe, a pairing that significantly influenced the course of American architecture in the mid-twentieth century.

But what kind of person is this who would risk his capital, his credit, and his reputation to erect a building? The question becomes all the more intriguing when one begins to realize that developers typically are multitalented, versatile individuals who often have achieved considerable success in other fields. For example, the developer of Illinois center, Bernard Weissbourd, gave up a highly rewarding law practice to become a developer. A century earlier, Potter Palmer had proven himself as a resourceful and remarkably successful retailer before turning his hand to the development of State Street and the creation of Chicago's Gold Coast residential district.

Although financial return is among the objectives of those who go into development, it seems not to be the only factor that drives them. The risks are too great. The options for a more secure and often better livelihood are many for people with the range of abilities that developers possess. If not money alone, then what is the motivating force? A singular combination of personality traits emerges when one looks at the developer's mentality—historically and in the present.

The first and most obvious characteristic is that developers are risk-takers. They are also problem solvers. Time and again in interviews for this book, developers such as Dan Levin spoke of a fascination with the complexity of a project. Others, including individuals as different as Charles Shaw and Richard Stein, are living proof that development is a high-action activity. Paper-pushers need not apply. Some developers, such as John Mack and Eugene Golub, create the action through the pursuit of the "deal" that will make the building happen. Others, including a large number of the nineteenth-century developers, were, and are, equally active on the job site.

Developers are drawn to a challenge. That challenge is not necessarily to build bigger or better or higher, although in Chicago bigger and better has frequently been a by-product of their ambitions. Often, the challenge is in the application of new technologies, as in the case of Peter Brooks, who wrote in 1881 that "hereafter, high buildings will pay well if a way can be found to build them," and who then exploited the undeveloped potential of the elevator to prove his point. Or in the case of Robert Wislow, who recognized that the financial institutions of the 1980s needed twenty-four-hour, state-of-the-art communications facilities, and provided that capability in the One Financial Place complex.

Developers are people of considerable creativity and imagination. It was surprising to find how many—including Greenwald, Stein, and Golub—have commented on their wish to write poetry, paint, or produce a film. Some—including nineteenth-century home builder Samuel Gross, who wrote a critically acclaimed play in verse, and Al Robin, who is an accomplished abstract painter—have provided proof of their talents in such areas.

Other developers see their buildings as an expression in brick and mortar, steel and glass, of an artistic impulse—often a highly personal vision. Perhaps it is this kind of vision that drives Lee Miglin and Paul Beitler's dream for the 125-story spire they hope to create in the center of Chicago. At the turn of the century, Ben Marshall was another of the artist-developers who realized a vision—and popularized a new lifestyle for Chicagoans—when he created his Gold Coast luxury apartments, calling them "mansions in the sky."

Developers are tenacious. We see the end result of their efforts, but we are seldom given insight into the path taken to get there. Potter Palmer saw every one of his grand State Street buildings reduced to rubble in the Great Chicago Fire. His buildings uninsured, his talent and his good credit his only remaining assets, Palmer despaired, but came back and rebuilt, better than ever. The development process can include years of negotiation and litigation, with a great deal of capital tied up over a long period of time, as in the case of the Illinois Center and One Financial Place developments. But the developers of these complexes stayed with their projects.

The road followed by developers may lead to financial loss and to great personal disappointment when the social promise of a project is not fulfilled, as in the case of the South Commons development on Chicago's Near South Side. It may, as it did for nineteenth-century developer Wilson K. Nixon, involve bankruptcy, precipitated by perilous economic cycles. Nixon persevered, repaying his creditors dollar by dollar. He became one of the most prolific developers of his day, but died impoverished.

Developers overcome formidable obstacles because they feel great passion for their projects. To understand the developer's motivation and the strength of his drive, often we need look no further than the purpose for which he builds. Ferdinand Peck was impassioned in his desire to bring grand opera to

Chicago and to make it available not only to the elite but to the working class. The result, accomplished with great energy through two long Chicago winters and at great personal cost, was the Auditorium Building and Theater. Edward C. Waller made a mission of creating well-designed, low- and middle-income apartment housing at the turn of the century, an unpopular and admittedly marginally profitable concept that was decades ahead of its time. Ferd Kramer, a driving force behind the Lake Meadows and Prairie Shores complexes, was similarly committed to solving the pressing problems of the post-World War II housing shortage and rescuing the inner city as a place where families would choose to live and work.

Developers share many characteristics, but they also defy stereotype. They come from educational backgrounds as diverse as particle physics (Illinois Center developer Weissbourd), psychometrics (industrial developer Marshall Bennett), and journalism (office tower developer Lee Miglin). And from occupations as varied as social work and teaching (Herbert Greenwald), professional sports (Charles Gardner), and public service and international diplomacy (Philip Klutznick).

The subjects chosen for this book were selected as representative of the period in which they worked or are working, and the list is by no means complete. But the observations recorded here about the characteristics of successful developers can be seen time and again in the scores of individuals who have made great contributions to Chicago real estate and development. Their talents often cluster in highly creative fields. Bertrand Goldberg, for example, the developer of Marina City—the "corncob" apartment towers that in the 1960s took their place among the symbols of modern Chicago—is an architect, engineer, inventor, and a philosopher of the urban community. Developers' business activities are diverse and may be quite unexpected. Jerry Reinsdorf is best known as the owner of the Chicago White Sox and the Chicago Bulls. But as a founder of the Balcor Corporation, Reinsdorf is a prominent leader in Chicago real estate, although not principally as a developer. Accomplishments of Chicago developers may be many and varied. Dempsey Travis, a social activist who expresses his interest in South Side communities through a wide range of real estate and development activities, is even better known to Chicagoans in his roles as a musician and author.

The contributions that some developers make in their roles as public servants are far-reaching. Nineteenth-century developer Robert A. Waller, for example, was an influential president of the Lincoln Park Commission and a righteous and reform-minded city comptroller. The role played by Phil

Klutznick, a former U.S. commissioner of public housing, in creating the postwar "new town" exemplified by south suburban Park Forest, cannot be understated. Harry F. Chaddick, a trucking executive who turned the shell of a World War II aircraft engine plant into the 242-acre Ford City industrial district and shopping mall, is also the father and architect of the monumental and innovative 1957 Chicago Zoning Ordinance, a code that was still in force more than thirty years after it was written.

Other investor-developers have played a major role in revitalizing Chicago development through their personal ability—based on reputation, talent, and sheer energy—to get buildings financed, built, and occupied in otherwise neglected sectors of the city. Most notable among these is Jerrold Wexler. Wexler is best known as one of the most active and prolific of the city's real estate deal makers. But Wexler and Edward Ross, his partner in Jupiter Industries and a subsidiary, Jupiter Real Estate Corporation, have also developed at least forty properties—one for every year they have worked together.

Wexler has pioneered many developments, and, while he may turn over properties fairly quickly, the Wexler presence has had a coattails effect in bringing other investment into an area. Wexler, for example, decided to build the high-rise Outer Drive East apartments in the early 1960s when there was nothing but railroad tracks east of Michigan Avenue. Similarly, he was one of the first to open up the Streeterville area north of the Chicago River for redevelopment when he built McClurg Court Center there in 1971, followed by the Holiday Inn Chicago City Centre. He headed the investment group formed to build River City on the South Branch of the Chicago River in 1977, and was an early investor in the Illinois Central air rights and in the North Loop Redevelopment district. As a buyer, seller, and owner-manager of properties, Wexler also has been a formidable force over the years in the redevelopment of North Michigan Avenue, although he has never developed a building there.

Similarly, another group of real estate entrepreneurs have made significant contributions to the real estate and development industry in Chicago, but in the strictest sense are primarily investors and assemblers of property. Ronald Berger and Robert Berger, for example, have developed some five million square feet of industrial space over the years, but are known principally not as developers but as real estate investors. In this respect, the story of Chicago real estate will not be told without consideration of the role played in the industry by Judd Malkin, Neil Bluhm, and Robert Judelson (later with Balcor), the founders of JMB Realty Corporation. JMB, which keeps its base in Chicago, led the way to the real estate syndication business in the 1970s and 1980s, and by the 1990s had become one of the largest real estate owners in America and the developers of 900 North Michigan Avenue.

Although the nature of ownership has changed and diversified over the last half-century, creating deals of sometimes astounding complexity, the developer's role as the central creative force in a project and as the individual responsible for putting together the financial package to execute it and the know-how to market it has remained the same. This was the case in the early 1980s when Bob Wislow put together the financial and creative team that turned an undesirable tract of railroad land south of Van Buren Street into the dazzling One Financial Place complex. And it was just as much of a challenge for Peter Brooks and Owen Aldis when, in the early 1880s, they set their minds to the task of creating the world's first office skyscraper—a project with dubious acceptability in the marketplace. In both cases most people said it couldn't be done.

One cannot stress too much the part played by the individual entrepreneur in the story of Chicago development. But the city's real estate history is also the history of significant corporate commitment to the community, both in the civic sense as benefactors of the cultural institutions of the city and as real estate developers or equity partners themselves. It is a tradition that dates back to the Montgomery Ward structures built on the North Branch of the Chicago River. In modern times, Sears sparked a revival of activity in the West Loop with the development of the world-famous Sears Tower. The American Medical Association development is changing the complexion of the State Street district north of the Chicago River. The Standard Oil, Equitable, Prudential, IBM, and AT&T buildings are other examples of contributions made by corporate entities to the vitality and leadership of Chicago architecture.

A number of Chicago families also played prominent roles in the financing of Chicago developments in the years after World War II. Among these are Pritzker family members who were early backers of Bennett and Kahnweiler's Centex Industrial Park development, and the Crown family, which has entered into equity partnerships and joint ventures with developers such as Metropolitan Structures, U.S. Equities, Romanek and Golub, and Tishman Speyer.

A single, common thread that runs unbroken through the history of Chicago development is the intermingling of the civic, the social, and the commercial commitments of the individuals and institutions whose stories are told in this book. It has been said that great architecture is not born in a vacuum, nor in the solitary minds of isolated practitioners. Similarly, Chicago's tradition of visionary and dynamic development was not born in a vacuum, but emerged as a response to the creative and innovative spirit that has characterized Chicago since its earliest days. Those singular individuals with the courage and passion to express that spirit in buildings of incomparable style and quality have left a great legacy. We owe it to ourselves and to the history of this great city to pause to consider their work.

SETTING THE STAGE

1830-79

If the little settlement called Chicago was born to greatness, that fact could not have been apparent to the few dozen residents who in 1830 clustered around the harsh and windswept frontier outpost of Fort Dearborn. It took another type of traveler to see the future of the rugged village on the lake. These were not the trappers who passed through the settlement to gather provisions, nor were they the farmers fanning out through the West in search of homesteads.

The men of vision were the speculators, men who had traveled the Northwest Territory, visiting hundreds of start-up towns in search of opportunity. They moved from settlement to settlement, where they would stay a year, or two, or three, then move on. Some, when they reached Chicago, saw something both extraordinary and obvious in the confluence of the river and the lake. Fired by promises of a harbor and canal that would link the lakes to the Mississippi and the auction of government lands to pay for it, the speculators quite rightly envisioned the settlement as a portal to the West. Here they chose to stay. Word of land to be had and fortunes to be made spread like wildfire.

Chicago in 1830 was hardly a town to write home about, especially if one had come from a great eastern city such as Boston, Philadelphia, or New York. Mired in mud, ravaged by disease and Indian wars, the settlement in 1830 was made up of no more than a dozen log structures, some within Fort

Dearborn, others spread over a half-square-mile area near the fork of the Chicago River. That was soon to change.

Geography may be destiny, but cities are built by men. From the earliest days, the development business in Chicago was characterized by unusual creativity. Reflecting the sense of urgency and the great vitality that prevailed from the outset, the old method of building that used heavy timber posts and beams secured by mortise-and-tenon joints was quickly supplanted by the faster technique of balloon frame construction, invented in Chicago in 1833. This technique of literally hanging a building on a light wood frame held together only with nails enabled a man and a helper to put up a house in a week's time or less. By 1834, some three hundred of the revolutionary new frame structures had sprung up in Chicago.

Commercial development and more substantial construction proceeded apace. The first warehouse was built in 1832. The city's second commercial structure was Philip F. W. Peck's dry goods store. A hotel named the Tremont House was built in 1833. A three-story brick office building and public hall was erected in 1836. When Chicago incorporated in 1837, with land speculator William B. Ogden as mayor, it had grown from a village of a little more than four hundred persons in 1833 to

Balloon framing. This construction technique, using studs, joists, and roof rafters joined by nails, was developed in Chicago in the early 1830s. The light framing, which "went up like a balloon," enabled builders to put up a two-story structure within a few days, thus keeping pace with rapid population growth. [Tom Hargis, David Hocker and Associates—Mark Bethel]

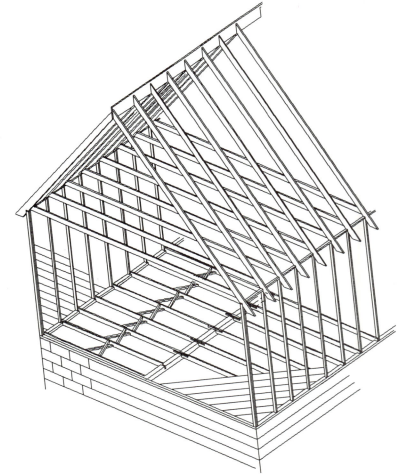

a turbulent town of more than four thousand. Many were attracted by the prospect of quick profits to be realized in the buying and selling of town lots or acreage. Each land sale brought speculators who bid up the prices of the land parcels, attracting even more bidders to the next sale. The speculative fervor heightened after the government land office opened in 1835. Real estate prices peaked in 1836, tumbling sharply when the national financial panic of 1837 struck. Recovery was slow. By 1842 nearly every leader of the early business community, including Ogden, was either ruined or close to ruin. Those who still believed in the dream stayed on. They had their work cut out for them.

Fulfillment of the town's potential as the hub of a water transportation network was the key to recovery, but the canal project moved slowly, plagued by the economic torpor that followed the panic of 1837 and by the vicissitudes of federal and state funding. When the Illinois and Michigan Canal was at last completed in 1848, the achievement was due largely to the energies of Ogden and other Chicago businessmen who took it upon themselves to borrow money to complete the project, with canal land and revenues pledged as collateral.

The timing was right. Demand for transportation to the West in the late 1840s and the need to move the myriad goods required to build a nation spurred the growth of the Great Lakes shipping industry. Chicago, emergent as the major terminus, developed a prosperous and diversified economy anchored in the meat packing, lumber, and grain shipment industries.

Ogden, who had refused to give up the dream of a canal, also saw the promise of the railroad. In 1836 he chartered the Galena and Chicago Union Railroad, a project that collapsed after the financial panic of 1837. Ten years later, Ogden traveled the length of the proposed route on horseback, soliciting private subscriptions to lay the first ten miles of track. Within twenty years, more than forty railroads served the Chicago area. The operation of the canal and the expansion of the railroads spearheaded unprecedented growth. Prairie farmers could send their produce to the growing commodities center in Chicago by water or rail or a combination of the two. Commerce brought a new surge of population: longshoremen to unload the cargo from barges, warehousemen to move the grain to elevators, millers to grind the wheat into flour, shopkeepers to sell the flour, and speculators to wager on the price and quantity of upcoming harvests.

In 1847 the city's population was slightly under seventeen thousand; by 1850, it had jumped to thirty thousand. The one-hundred-thousand mark was reached by 1860. Rapid growth was a mixed blessing, creating a vigorous economy on the one hand but tremendous overcrowding on the other. Neither builders nor the expanding city limits could keep pace with the population explosion.

Outbreaks of cholera and smallpox were common. The epidemic of 1854 claimed hundreds of lives, with some sixty people a day succumbing over the summer months of that year. Epidemic disease went hand in hand with the massive sanitation problems faced by a town built on marshy lowlands, unable to cope with drainage problems and the fetid stagnation of open sewers.

Plank roads offered little relief from this lake of mud. Loosened by the wear of heavy carriages and wagons, they had a tendency to float away after a rainfall. Some citizens, motivated by a concern for the safety of passersby as well as by the opportunity to express their frustration, would mark the plank-less places along the street with signs reading "No Bottom Here," or "The Shortest Road to China." Reminisced one early area resident, "A man could stand on a board and shake the ground all around him."

In 1855 a board of sewage commissioners declared that dry streets and adequate drainage could be achieved only if the streets were raised above the level of the marshlands—an astounding but obvious solution. City council members feared that the cost of so fanciful a project would bankrupt the city. Property owners, whose places of business would be left at the original grade, were vehemently opposed. Opponents did not prevail. To the wonderment of the world, the grade was raised in 1855 and again in 1857. Property owners responded as they had to, by raising their buildings to the new street level. One of the most successful of the raisers of buildings was George M. Pullman, who came to Chicago for that purpose and stayed on to revolutionize the railroad car industry.

The outbreak of the Civil War precipitated a run on Chicago banks, and cash became tight. The war ultimately accelerated the growth of manufacturing as Chicago began supplying the Union soldier and his family with everything from food and clothing to pianos. By the end of the decade, more than a thousand Chicago firms were producing tens of millions of dollars worth of goods.

Nowhere was growth so explosive as in the building industry. When the first census was taken in 1837, the city had fewer than five hundred buildings. By 1871 there were nearly sixty thousand. Real estate values also showed phenomenal increases in these years, checked only by the financial crises of 1837 and 1857 and by a wave of bank failures following the Civil War. In 1850 land in Chicago was worth almost $29 mil-

Marine Bank, northeast corner of La Salle and Lake streets, 1856. The four-story masonry bank building—set among new construction going up on the river, plank roads, and the board sidewalks of Lake Street—reveals both the aspirations of Chicagoans and the hard reality of life in the mid-nineteenth century. The State of Illinois Center now stands on the site of the two-story balloon-frame grocery and dry goods stores at lower right.
[Alexander Hesler—Chicago Historical Society]

lion. By the fall of 1871, the value of Chicago land was estimated at almost $481 million. South Side property was most highly valued. The area was home to the fashionable and affluent. The city's business and civic leaders erected mansions there as extravagant—or more so—as those of their counterparts in Boston, Philadelphia, and New York. Developers such as Paul Cornell created graceful subdivisions beyond the city limits as havens for affluent Chicagoans escaping the clamor of the city.

The recurrent financial panics of the nineteenth century and resultant roller-coaster real estate market were a scourge for the town's entrepreneurial spirit. Another was fire. Both were an inevitable cost of doing business in Chicago. Disastrous fires had ravaged the city in 1837 and 1857, but none equaled the fire of 1871. Nothing could stop the Great Chicago Fire. It swept the city for twenty-five hours, beginning on Sunday evening, October 8, 1871, raging over twenty-one hundred acres and destroying more than seventeen thousand buildings. The North Side was hardest hit. More than 70 percent of the burned area lay within this district. Property worth

almost $200 million was destroyed, less than half of it insured. Among those not insured was Potter Palmer, who cleared the rubble that had been his own street of dreams—the State Street retail district—dumping the debris on the shore of Lake Michigan. A new wedge of city land emerged at the waterfront, built from the fill created by the skeletons of the city's burned-out buildings.

The rebuilding effort began immediately. Within five weeks, five thousand homes had been built or were being completed. One year after the Great Fire, Chicago had ten thousand new buildings with an estimated value of just over $40 million—a tribute to the vitality, vision, commitment, and just plain stubbornness of the city's citizens. The postfire structures had some similarities to the old ones. Most were walk-ups, and most were imitations of their burned counterparts, differing only in that a new city ordinance prohibited construction of wooden structures within the city limits. The new buildings were built by the same Chicagoans who had taken the chances, invested their money, and put up the buildings before the fire struck. Palmer, who returned to rebuild State Street, was one such man. Banker William Coolbaugh was another. Coolbaugh's block of eighteen stores on Market Street had been finished just one week before the fire consumed them. He told his builder to start anew, as soon as the debris was cool enough to clear away. It was this resiliency that attracted the attention, admiration, and dollars of outside investors. New money flowed into the city, fanned by the old speculative fervor, the promise of vacant land, and the manifest commitment of Chicagoans to rebuild.

Not even another fire could derail the train of progress running through the city. A largely unpublicized fire of 1874 consumed another sixty acres of property southwest of Michigan Avenue and Van Buren Street, an area that had been spared by the fire of 1871. Nothing less than the national financial panic of 1873 could curb the massive rebuilding process. As the economy staggered, construction dwindled. By 1879 new construction was at its lowest level since the end of the Civil War. The development spirit was strong, however, and would rebound. Great plans were still generated, if only on paper. Soon capital began flowing back into the city. Chicago was poised for its golden age of development.

BOLD VISIONS

Potter Palmer
(1826-1902)

Potter Palmer.
[Chicago Historical Society]

As a real estate developer, Potter Palmer was a century ahead of his time. His genius was in seeing far beyond existing development and investment patterns. His talent was in doing what others said couldn't be done. His strategy was to determine the direction of growth and then mold development to his plan. He bought land in volume when prices were low and intensively developed it, in so doing creating not only new value but a torrent of additional development as new uses followed where he led.

Within a space of just three years after the Civil War, Palmer succeeded in rotating Chicago's retail district on its axis, redefining the spatial configurations of the city with the development of an entirely new commercial center on State Street. Ten years later, he staked a claim on a windswept lakefront sand hill north of the city center, creating the residential district known today as the Gold Coast. His investments in undeveloped land on Upper Michigan Avenue and the controls he asserted over development there fixed the location of Chicago's so-called Magnificent Mile a full quarter of a century before the Michigan Avenue bridge opened the Near North to commercial development.

Potter Palmer may be remembered as the founder of the great retail business that later became Marshall Field and Company. Or he may be remembered as a hotelier, the builder and proprietor of Chicago's internationally known Palmer House. He may even be remembered, to paraphrase another husband of a famous wife, as "the man who accompanied Bertha Honoré Palmer to Paris." He is probably least often remembered for his greatest accomplishment—indeed, his lifework— which was forging new paths in the development of great sections of the city, molding much of Chicago to his vision. Potter Palmer saw real estate development in the aggregate. He saw it in a way no other Chicagoan did.

Potter Palmer was born in 1826 near Rensselaerville, New York. The fourth of seven sons and daughters of the former Rebecca Potter and Benjamin Palmer, he left home at eighteen to enter the mercantile business. Soon he opened dry goods stores in the upstate New York communities of Oneida and Lockport. In the spring of 1852, Palmer sold out his interests in New York and, with $5,000 in working capital, made his move to Chicago.

Lake Street was then the town's business district—a hive of wholesale and retail businesses, banks, and seamen's hotels crowded along a rutted and muddy road near the Chicago River. Palmer rented the narrow ground floor and cellar of a four-story building on West Lake Street, arranged for the shipment of a stock of goods bought at auction in New York, and hung out his sign: "P. Palmer & Co." Palmer's strategy as a merchant was one that he would later carry over into his real estate investments. When dry goods prices collapsed in the aftermath of the 1857 national financial panic, Palmer bought stock in volume at panic prices, extensively advertised arrivals of new goods at his store, and continued to undersell his competitors. When other dry goods establishments were having distress sales, or closing their doors altogether, Palmer was expanding into larger space.

In 1860, with the clouds of war between the states gathering, Palmer anticipated demand for a single commodity. He bought cotton and cotton goods, and he bought them by the warehouseful. When supplies from the South were cut off, Palmer sold at scalper's prices. By war's end, he was hailed one of the most successful businessmen of the time. He was not yet forty.

In 1865 Palmer offered a controlling interest in his by then multimillion-dollar dry goods business to Marshall Field and Levi Z. Leiter and left Chicago for an extended European vacation. For a time, after his return from Europe, he established his home and commercial base in New York City, prompting Chicagoans to speculate that Palmer had decided to return to New York permanently and live off the profits of his labors in the West. Nothing could have been further from his mind. In this period, Palmer was formulating a venture in land-use planning that was without precedent in America's growing cities. It was investment with design. He had long considered the question of how Chicago might grow. He intended to direct that growth by buying well-positioned land in volume where it was still available at uninflated prices and improving it with attention-getting buildings to be offered for lease or sale. He reasoned, correctly, that property improvement on the scale he envisioned would draw new development in its wake.

Lake Street was in gridlock by the late 1860s. It could not grow east, west, or, at that time, up. Others who were watching real estate trends believed that Wabash Avenue would become Chicago's north-south commercial corridor. Palmer thought otherwise. Wabash was built up with homes and churches, a fact that he viewed as a barrier to development. He looked instead to State Street, a block west of Wabash. It was then little more than an alley, described by builder Henry Ericsson in his memoirs as "a wretched stretch of old frame houses and shanties." But the location was right, and the price was right. Even before his European trip, Palmer had begun to buy up land along State Street, at a tenth of the cost of property elsewhere in the central area. Within a short time, he owned nearly a mile of State Street frontage. Palmer was embarked upon a forceful, clear-eyed, and ultimately costly program to make over the moseying Old State Road into a first-class retail center.

State Street, looking south from Lake Street, late 1860s. Potter Palmer reoriented the city's retail district from its east-west axis on Lake Street to a new retail center on the north-south Old State Road. In 1871 all of Palmer's State Street buildings were reduced to rubble by the Great Chicago Fire.
[From a stereograph by J. Carbutt—Chicago Historical Society]

The business community ridiculed the apparent grandiosity of Palmer's designs and the expenditures he made in bringing in New York and Connecticut marble for buildings that rose up among the shanties of State Street. But this was not the first time in Palmer's career that his colleagues thought he was a mad dreamer, nor would it be the last. Palmer knew that to create an adequate commercial center, the street would need to be widened, and he built his own buildings with generous

The first Field, Palmer and Leiter Store. Known as "Potter Palmer's Marble Palace," the six-story showpiece was designed by Chicago's first architect, John M. Van Osdel, and stood at the northeast corner of State and Washington streets.
[From a stereograph, c. 1870, by Kopelin and Melander—Chicago Historical Society]

setbacks. The move met with strong opposition, both from the powerful Lake Street merchants, who had no wish to see Palmer's plan succeed, and from the existing State Street property owners, who had no wish to give up an inch of their own land. The night of the Great Chicago Fire would change all that, democratically reducing every building, whatever its setback, to rubble. The street widening and setbacks that Palmer had sought were made permanent when the city was rebuilt.

For his architect, he chose the best: John M. Van Osdel, the designer whom William B. Ogden had brought to Chicago in 1836 and who over the course of his long career would create such hallmark buildings as the Tremont House, the 1855 Courthouse, and eventually the 1885 City Hall and County Building. By 1870 Palmer had completed more than thirty high-quality buildings on State Street, at an estimated cost of $2 million. The flagship structure was the six-story retail store built to house the dry goods company that Palmer had sold to Marshall Field and Levi Leiter. The Van Osdel-designed Field, Leiter and Company store at the northeast corner of State and Washington quickly became known as "Potter Palmer's Marble Palace."

Palmer had returned from Europe a changed man, on the surface at least. No longer the serious, striving young merchant, he now dressed with flair, wintered in Florida, and was seen often at Saratoga and other fashionable racetracks. He drove a dashing four-in-hand, and as a bachelor millionaire was considered quite a catch by many young ladies and their ambitious mothers. But he had eyes only for Bertha Honoré, the elder of the two Kentucky-born daughters of Henry Hamilton Honoré and his elegant wife, Eliza Carr Honoré. Palmer was a close friend of "H. H." Honoré and had known the family since Bertha was in her early teens. The engagement of Bertha to Potter Palmer in 1870 and news of their July wedding was the talk of the town. The bride was twenty-one. Palmer was then forty-four.

Bertha Palmer was her husband's helpmate and supporter throughout the thirty-two years they would have together. Palmer's own reticent manner, Quaker work ethic, and fondness for his stables and gardens were complemented by Bertha's cosmopolitan interests, progressive philosophies, and political acumen. Mrs. Potter Palmer became in her own right the undisputed leader of Chicago society and a tireless advocate for social reform and the furtherance of the causes of working women. Her husband was proud of her accomplishments, as she was of his. She was a shrewd businesswoman who helped oversee Palmer's business and real estate interests toward the end of his life and who, with her sons' assistance, astutely managed his fortune after his death.

Palmer's plans for the development of State Street called for a fine hotel to anchor his commercial buildings. Work on the first Palmer hotel, at the northwest corner of State and Quincy streets, began in 1869. In 1871 Palmer started construction of a second hotel, to be located at the southeast corner of State and Monroe streets where the present Palmer House stands. On September 26, 1871, the hotel at State and Quincy was opened to the public. Thirteen days later, over the night of October 8, much of Chicago, including the hotel, was consumed by fire.

Palmer had been in New York attending the funeral of one of his sisters when he learned that his State Street buildings had been reduced to tangles of iron and stone. His fortune seemed also to have gone up in smoke. Uninsured, he lost not only his enormous investment in the State Street developments but also an estimated $200,000 annually in rental income from the properties. Chicagoans expected Palmer to make a new fortune in the frenzy of real estate speculation that followed the fire by selling his State Street properties to eastern investors and retiring to New York. The wags were wrong again. Palmer cleared the rubble of his buildings, moving the debris to the lakefront, where it became part of the landfill that is now Grant Park. He refinanced and proceeded to rebuild on State Street, making the district bigger and better than before.

Palmer put reconstruction of the second Palmer House at State and Monroe on a fast track, building on foundations laid just before the fire and using materials already ordered and en route to Chicago. But no corners were to be cut. The new Palmer House would be the largest and finest hotel in Chicago, perhaps even the finest in the nation, he declared. And so it was. Palmer again chose the venerable Van Osdel to design the building, assisted now by the younger C. M. Palmer. Palmer was no relation to Potter Palmer, but he became an architect that Palmer would hire again for other projects and whose name would become most closely associated with dozens of brownstone mansions that Palmer would build on the Near North Side lakefront. Potter Palmer and Van Osdel clearly had a productive working arrangement—one that must have been pleasing to the architect.

Palmer set high standards for his buildings and spared no effort or expense in providing the best available building materials. But like many developers then and now, he left nothing to chance. He involved himself in every detail of design and construction and was a constant presence on the construction site as the nine-story hotel went up. A Chicago publication reporting on the progress of the building in 1873 noted that "Mr. Palmer, with his usual energy and thoroughness, determined to master the difficulties of the construction himself, that he might guard against the mistakes which are often made under the supervision of the best architects." In the spring of 1873, work went on from dawn until nearly midnight. Construction by night was illuminated by calcium arc lights, a sight altogether new to Chicago. Every evening at dusk, sightseers flocked to the site by the hundreds. Palmer was seen every-

The first Palmer hotel, northwest corner of State and Quincy streets. By the time this hotel opened in September 1871, Palmer was already building the second Palmer House, at State and Monroe streets. Within two weeks, both buildings were leveled by the Great Fire. [Engraving, from *Chicago and Its Makers*]

where, carrying a lantern and supervising the hoisting of loads of iron beams.

When the new Palmer House was opened to its first resident in 1873, it was said to be the nation's first totally fireproof hotel. The Palmer House became renowned for the lavishness of its decoration and furnishings. Unique features of the building included a rooftop conservatory and greenhouse of Palmer's own design, planted with orange trees, a rose garden, trailing vines, and a variety of exotic camellias. It was never Palmer's intention that he himself should become the innkeeper. He planned to lease the hotel to another proprietor, just as he leased his other State Street developments. When no lessee appeared, Palmer took over the management himself and continued to run the hotel from the day of its opening until his death more than a quarter of a century later. The Palmers made their own home at the hotel for ten years, raising their two sons there. Bertha's niece Julia, the granddaughter of President Ulysses S. Grant, was a frequent visitor. The Palmers' intimate connection with General Grant, an American hero and the Palmer House's most celebrated guest, was not lost on Chicago society.

By 1881 Palmer had begun to think about building another kind of palace, specifically a home for his family. The logical

Working at night on the Palmer House during its construction by the use of calcium lights. Potter Palmer himself was a constant presence on the construction site when the third Palmer House was built on the foundations of the second at State and Monroe streets. When the new hotel opened in 1873, it was said to be the nation's first totally fireproof hostelry.
[Engraving, from a photo by Kaufmann and Fabry—Chicago Historical Society]

WORKING AT NIGHT ON THE PALMER HOUSE DURING ITS CONSTRUCTION, BY THE USE OF CALCIUM LIGHTS.

site would have been among the great mansions of South Michigan Avenue, where Mrs. Palmer's parents lived, or on Prairie Avenue, near Marshall Field. But characteristically, Palmer looked for a new area to develop. His choice was the lakefront north of Oak Street, an area described by the newspapers as a "frog pond" and an "unhealthy slough" where nobody could live even "had they desired to do so." The area was bounded on the north by Lincoln Park and extended south through the sandbars later claimed by the raffish George Wellington "Cap" Streeter. With Palmer's decision to put down his roots at the point where Banks Street now meets Lake Shore Drive, Chicago's Gold Coast was born.

Palmer bought half a mile of lake frontage and, even before pacing off the foundations for his own home, bought additional properties to the north, south, and west of the parcel he planned to build on. Under an agreement with the Lincoln Park commissioners, he brought in men and machinery to dredge sand from the lake as fill. In return, the park was promised riparian rights. Palmer would, in a matter of very few years, be living the Chicago land speculator's dream: selling by the front foot land he had bought by the acre, and then only to buyers of his choice. Palmer advanced his Near North lakefront development plans with the same strategy he had pursued in redefining the city's retail district. He bought large amounts of land before other investors saw the potential. He then proceeded to improve the property himself, adding significant value in a very short time. He selected sites where he could control, or at least strongly influence, the quality and type of development that would follow.

Work on the Palmer castle, a fortress looming in lonely splendor over the lakeshore between Banks and Schiller streets, went on for almost three years. In planning the house, Palmer had turned to architects Henry Ives Cobb and Charles Sumner Frost. The result of this collaboration between homeowner and designer was not altogether happy. Palmer intended to spend $90,000 on the three-story residence. Its cost eventually exceeded $1 million. When construction stalled after the first year, the Chicago *Tribune* reported that Palmer was deeply dissatisfied with the way the house looked, citing specifically the oddly matched limestone and granite that created discordant horizontal bands on the facade. The architects' cavalier response, according to the *Tribune,* was that Mr. Palmer himself had decided upon the combination of stone and had insisted on its use in the manner in which it had been applied—but that he had done so against their advice.

As was the case with his other ventures, most people thought Palmer was out of his mind to sink good money into sand dunes and marshlands so far north of the established South Side upper-class residential districts. As the oft-interrupted construction progressed, observers became sure that Palmer would never finish, much less occupy the house, citing both his rumored dissatisfaction with the building's appearance and the dangers of the presumably malarial swamp where it was being built. The strange facade and the unusual effect of its eighty-foot castellated tower notwithstanding, the completed mansion was recognized as—if not the most beautiful—certainly "the most imposing house in our city." The interiors were magnificent beyond anything seen outside of the palaces of Europe. The Palmers took up residence in the "Palmer Castle" in 1885, and a new era for Chicago society—and Chicago property development—began.

By 1893 Potter Palmer's North Side development had become the new center for the new residences of the city's new—and old—elite. As Chicago society deserted the upper-class areas of Prairie Avenue and South Michigan Avenue in the rush to North Lake Shore Drive (at one time called Palmer Boulevard), land values quadrupled. Those who came to scoff stayed to pay. Palmer had a vision, and he acted on it, transforming a desolate dune into Chicago's richest and most desirable residential district. Palmer subdivided and developed the remain-

Palmer House, ladies' entrance, 1903.
[Chicago Historical Society.]

der of his North Side land almost as rapidly as he had acquired it, building homes and apartment buildings that were both for sale and for rent. He built extensively on Huron, Cedar, Chestnut, Elm, Division, Ritchie Place, Goethe, Bellevue Place, Schiller, Astor, North State Parkway, and Pine. Many of these three- and four-story granite or brownstone residences are still standing and are easily identifiable as "Palmer houses" (a reference to both the Palmer style and to his architect, C. M. Palmer). A 1918 reckoning of the value of the Palmer estate acknowledged him as builder of as many as three hundred North Side houses and apartments.

In the mid-1890s Palmer began to concentrate his investments on the north end of Pine Street (now Michigan Avenue). By 1898 he owned frontage on both sides of North Michigan Avenue between Walton Street and Delaware Place and nearly all the frontage from Oak Street south to Pearson Street on the east side. The properties Palmer acquired in this period included land now occupied by the Drake Hotel, the Palmolive Building (later the Playboy Building and now 919 North Michigan), the Westin Hotel, the John Hancock Center, One Magnificent Mile, and 900 North Michigan.

Like his colleague in merchandising Marshall Field, Palmer was at root a Yankee trader, bred to stoic Northeast traditions. But unlike Field, Palmer had a flashier side, and had learned earlier how to enjoy his money, especially to the extent that it provided the backdrop for Bertha Palmer's social and civic activities. Palmer, however, was not indifferent to the life of the city. As one of the first commissioners of the Chicago South Park District, he fought for the land and assessment that made Chicago's great park system possible. He was among the promoters of the 1873 Inter-State Industrial Exposition and a developer of the huge, vaulted Exposition Building that stood at the present site of the Art Institute of Chicago. The architect for that building was William W. Boyington, whose work in Chicago also included the Water Tower, the first University of Chicago, and the Grand Pacific Hotel. Palmer was among the group of business leaders responsible for bringing the 1893 World's Fair to Chicago. And, on the lighter side, was also the first president of the Chicago Baseball Club.

Potter Palmer died of pneumonia on May 4, 1902, at the age of seventy-six. His death occurred exactly fifty years after his arrival in Chicago in 1852. Mayor Carter H. Harrison II, a childhood friend of Bertha Honoré Palmer and her family, summed up Potter Palmer's place in Chicago history with these words: "Potter Palmer was one of the men who made Chicago. His history is the history of the city."

HYDE PARK

Paul Cornell
(1822-1904)

Paul Cornell.
[Chicago Historical Society]

Paul Cornell set about developing the suburb of Hyde Park as systematically as if he were building a model village in a sandbox. He started with three hundred acres of virgin land, much of it actually sand hills and marshlands. Then he persuaded the Illinois Central Railroad to link his land to the city. He gave the site a fashionable name —Hyde Park—and put up a resort hotel to lure summer visitors. He built a nondenominational church. He added a public school, a park, and a post office. He even helped establish a cemetery. Paul Cornell saw his little village on the lakefront grow from a settlement of seven families in 1857 to a community of one hundred thousand people when the township was annexed to Chicago in 1889. Cornell left little to chance. Hyde Park and the communities that grew up with it in the 1860s have been characterized, even in this century, as "the greatest models for planning in the United States." The Hyde Park strategy was one that worked as well in the suburban boom of the 1950s and '60s as it did for Cornell in the 1850s and '60s. Very simply, Cornell had a talent for making his site both desirable and accessible and for accessing funds other than his own to make that happen. In this he worked his magic equally on the railroad, on Hyde Park's first home builders, and on the publicly funded park commission that he helped to create.

Born in New York State in 1822 and brought up in western Illinois near the Missouri border, Paul Cornell made his first trip to Chicago in 1845. He returned to stay in 1847. The man who would become known as the "Father of Hyde Park" was at that time twenty-five years old. His assets consisted of $1.50, the clothes he was wearing, and a license to practice law. Law was congenial to Cornell's exacting mind, and by 1851 he had become a partner in the firm that eventually became Cornell, Jameson, and Hibbard. Cornell moved in distinguished circles, including that of the famed Illinois senator Stephen A. Douglas. But Cornell's dreams included more than just the practice of law.

The growth of Chicago from a small settlement on the lake to a city of thirty thousand by 1850 left the city fathers with little time or inclination to attend to the amenities of urban life. The city had great commercial promise, but it was not necessarily a pleasant place to live, as Cornell soon perceived. Cornell imagined the lure that an elite residential suburb might have to the growing numbers of Chicago's upper middle class. He saw before him the examples of the North Shore town of Evanston, and its founding fathers John Evans and Orrington Lunt (Cornell would soon become related by marriage to the latter).

In 1853, on the advice of Douglas, who himself owned undeveloped land south of the city, Cornell invested his savings in the purchase of an uninhabited tract of land along the lakefront between what are now Fifty-first and Fifty-fifth streets. He continued to acquire land in this area until he was ready in 1856 to subdivide and market the property. He made his plans with great precision. After the land, the basic element of a residential suburb had to be transportation to and from the city. That link, Cornell speculated, would be provided by the new Illinois Central Railroad, chartered by an act of Congress in 1850. Senator Douglas lobbied hard to make sure that the line passed through Chicago, instead of through the center of the state as originally planned—a change of course that no doubt was as much to the benefit of the senator and his friends as it was to the city of Chicago. Cornell followed by giving the Illinois Central right-of-way across his property in exchange for a promise of passenger service between Hyde Park and the city.

True to its word, the railroad built a wood-frame station at what is now Fifty-first Street, commanding an unobstructed view of open prairie. On July 21, 1856, Chicago's first regular suburban passenger service was launched with trains called Hyde Park Specials. It was the only rail commuter service west of Philadelphia. As might be expected, it was not an immediate success; on its first regular round trip, the line did not carry a single passenger in either direction.

Cornell envisioned Hyde Park as a tranquil sanctuary for families seeking refuge from the city, and the railroad was the first critical ingredient. The second was a destination to which railroad passengers might travel. To this end, Cornell began work in 1856 on the first Hyde Park House, a hotel at Fifty-third Street and the lakeshore. The elegantly appointed resort hostelry opened in 1858 and, to Cornell's satisfaction, quickly became a fashionable summer gathering spot. Mrs. Lincoln stayed at Hyde Park House with her sons after the assassination of the president. The hotel was also a favorite of Mrs. Ulysses S. Grant.

With Chicagoans visiting Hyde Park in greater numbers, Cornell tackled the job of populating his town. Whereas a developer today might create excitement over a still barren subdivision by building a few well-appointed model homes, Cornell skipped that step. Ever the consummate salesman, Cornell persuaded family members and business associates to buy and build in Hyde Park. Thus, the ''model homes'' in Cornell's subdivision were the owner-built homes of the chosen few whom Cornell targeted to become pillars of the community. The first residents included his uncle, Hassan Hopkins; a brother-in-law, George Kimbark (later a founder of the community of Riverside); and a number of Cornell's current and former law partners, among them Homer N. Hibbard and J. A. Jameson. On the strength of his friends' reputations, he began to advertise Hyde Park in the Chicago newspapers as an ideal setting for the establishment of country estates by business and professional men.

Cornell was a fastidious subdivider. Contemporary historian Arthur T. Andreas reported that J. A. Jameson's first house was built, in 1857, on the wrong lot. The fact that the area at the time was ''nothing but sand hills, prairie, trees, and wild flowers'' apparently did not allow the new residents any special license. When Jameson rebuilt, in splendid isolation at the corner of Fifty-third Street and Cornell Avenue, he made sure that the house was set back precisely twenty feet from the property line in precise compliance with stipulations imposed by Cornell on all purchasers of lots. In 1858 Cornell added a third component to the community by building a nondenominational church at Hyde Park Avenue and Fifty-third Street. He eventually deeded the church and three adjacent lots to the First Presbyterian Church. Oak Woods Cemetery at Sixty-seventh Street had been incorporated in 1853 with Cornell as an officer of the company. The first school was opened in 1859. The character and spirit of a town was emerging just as Cornell had planned it.

In 1860 residents went to Springfield seeking a special act of incorporation. Cornell's subdivision, together with Kenwood just to the north and a number of other hamlets to the north and south, were incorporated as the Township of Hyde Park in

Hyde Park residence. The H. L. Fulton residence at 5742 Monroe Avenue [now Kenwood Avenue], 1887. [Chicago Historical Society]

1861. The remaining components of a town began to fall into place. A public school was erected in 1863 at the instigation of Cornell, Jameson, and Hibbard, with inhabitants protesting that "there would not be enough children to fill it in forty years." The town supervisors, headed by Cornell, occupied themselves with building sidewalks and improving streets, sewers, and drainage systems. By 1873 the community had its own waterworks and gas plant. Prominent Chicagoans, most of whom moved in the same business and social circles, began moving to Kenwood and Hyde Park, building expensive, spacious homes.

The plan was working. With the infrastructure in place, Cornell was eager to speed up the pace of migration to the South Side. In 1857, while building Hyde Park House, Cornell established a small park, called the Common, on the lakeshore at Fifty-third Street. From this beginning, Cornell saw his next step clearly. Suppose a network of parks could be built surrounding the new communities? Surely such an asset would make the area even more attractive to the city dwellers that Cornell hoped to lure to Hyde Park. It was a plan that ultimately led to the development of Chicago's extraordinary park system. In 1866 and again in 1867, Cornell and others spent the winter in Springfield lobbying the state legislature for a bill that would finance South Side parkland acquisition and the development of a boulevard system. Cornell proposed that the projects be financed through a multimillion-dollar bond issue supported by an annual tax. Despite public opposition—and there was a great deal of that—the referendum establishing a South Park Commission as an independent taxing body was approved on the second try. Those who had opposed Cornell and the park tax screamed even louder when the governor appointed Cornell one of the five commissioners of the Park District. (He would serve in that position for fourteen years, and, as an officer in 1878, even draw a salary of $2,120.)

Old Hyde Park Hotel, 1859.
Paul Cornell's Hyde Park House, a resort hotel at Fifty-third Street and the lakeshore, opened in 1858 and quickly became a fashionable destination for affluent Chicagoans seeking to escape the heat and grime of the city. In 1865 Mrs. Abraham Lincoln and her sons summered here. [From *Chicago and Its Makers*]

It is not surprising that the community that reaped the greatest immediate benefit was Hyde Park, one of three townships supporting the tax. The lands purchased under the act became North Park (Washington Park), which bordered Hyde Park on the west; South Park (Jackson Park), which bordered it on the South; and the Midway Plaisance, the spacious thoroughfare (originally planned as a lagoon) that connected the two. Famed landscape designer Frederick Law Olmsted was charged with laying out the South Park system. Although Cornell's commitment to the development of a publicly funded South Side park and boulevard system was expressed in terms of the welfare of the general populace, Cornell himself would not deny his underlying private interest. To paraphrase Chicago Mayor Richard J. Daley, what was good for Hyde Park development in this case also happened to be good for the people of Chicago.

At the time of the 1871 fire, Hyde Park had a population of about three thousand. The fire greatly accelerated population

movement out of the city, and Hyde Park, with its elite reputation and developing park system, became increasingly attractive, both to families seeking to relocate and to land
speculators. Property that had been selling for $100 an acre
just after the Civil War brought as much as $15,000 an acre af-
ter the Great Fire.

Hyde Park was not Paul Cornell's only South Side development. In order to keep Hyde Park a purely residential community, Cornell set out early on to acquire land outside the
village, but near it, for light industrial uses. To that end, he established the town of Grand Crossing southwest of Hyde Park,
at the heavily trafficked intersection of the Illinois Central and
the Lake Shore and Michigan Southern railroad tracks. There
he built another hotel and established a watch factory, creating
the base around which he hoped an industrial town would
grow. Cornell worked hard at marketing the Grand Crossing
subdivision. In a 1933 newspaper interview, John E. Cornell
recalled these days: "I well remember a feat of super salesman-
ship which my father performed in the spring of 1873, when,
unable to take a prospect over some real estate because it lay
under two feet of water, he took him to the top of the tower in
the Cornell watch factory at Seventy-ninth" and, John Cornell remembered, "sold two blocks at $300 a lot." In 1872 the
Village of Hyde Park became a corporate entity within Hyde
Park Township. It was said to be the largest village in extent of
territory in the world. And when the township was annexed
to Chicago in 1889, it was said to be the largest in population,
having more than 100,000 inhabitants.

Two events remained to complete Paul Cornell's grand
plan. From the beginning, he had hoped to locate a major institution, such as Evanston's Northwestern University, in
Hyde Park, but had not been successful. The dream was realized when the new University of Chicago opened its doors on
the Midway Plaisance in 1893. That same year, the careful
groundwork that Cornell had laid over three decades to provide rapid access to his development both by rail and by road
paid off in a way that even Cornell could not have anticipated:
Hyde Park's Jackson Park was selected as the site of the 1893
World's Columbian Exposition, drawing international attention to the Hyde Park community.

Paul Cornell died in 1904 at his residence at the new Hyde
Park House, which had been rebuilt at Hyde Park Boulevard
and Lake Park Avenue. Cornell had come to Chicago in 1847
equipped with a planner's mind and the idea of creating a
town. He lived to see Hyde Park grow in a mere forty years
from an all but forsaken railroad depot on a desolate prairie to
the status of Chicago's most famous neighborhood.

GOLDEN AGE OF DEVELOPMENT

1880-99

As the decade of the 1880s dawned, Chicago was no longer a frontier town. It was the heartland of the continent. The settlement on the lake had become the hub of the transcontinental railroad; a manufacturing and industrial colossus; the seat of great fortunes made and yet to be made in meatpacking, lumber, dry goods, and the grain trade. Chicago was also a survivor: of hard beginnings, a harsh climate, devastating financial crises, and a succession of terrible fires. Chicago deserved the 1880s. The city was primed for development. All the essential inputs—land, labor, capital, and building materials—were available at favorable prices. Breakthroughs in related technologies and new financing methods hovered on the horizon. The surge of innovative development that characterized the period was nourished by a creative spirit that was unique to this young city.

The age of the skyscraper was at hand, but the moment awaited the perfection of the passenger elevator. Elevators were not unknown in Chicago. The hydraulic elevator, a successor to the Otis brothers' mechanical lift, had been invented in Chicago in 1870 by C. W. Baldwin and tested in a building on Lake Street. After the Great Fire, the concept of the lift inspired construction of buildings higher than six stories. But the elevator had little appeal to passengers who preferred to go no higher than they were willing to walk. If used at all, elevators were used for freight. Upper floors remained difficult to

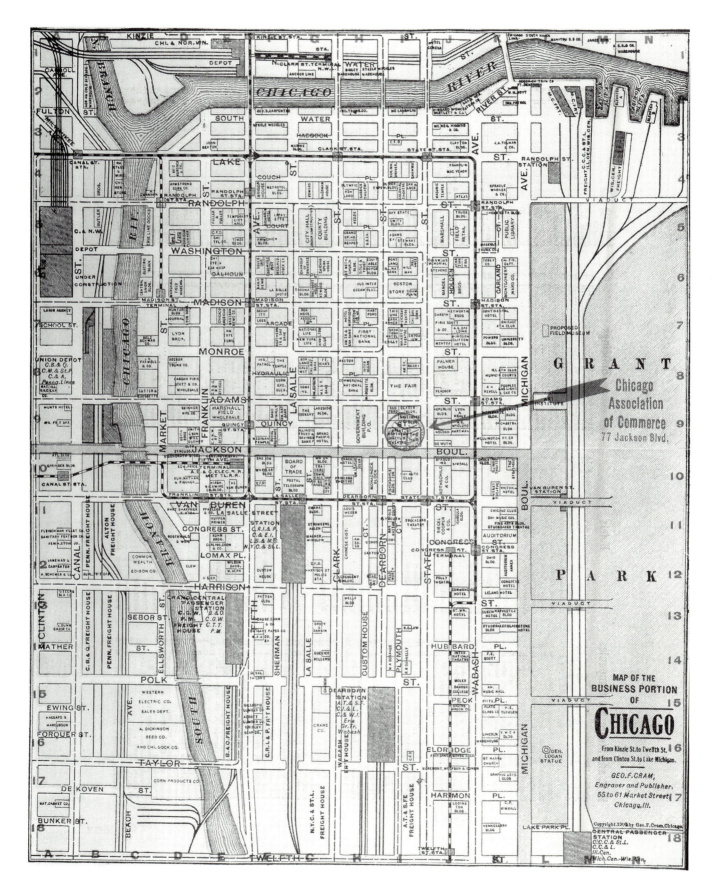

MAP OF THE
BUSINESS PORTION
OF
CHICAGO

From Kinzie St. to Twelfth St.
and from Clinton St. to Lake Michigan.

GEO. F. CRAM;
Engraver and Publisher,
55 to 61 Market Street,
Chicago, Ill.

Copyright, 1902, by Geo. F. Cram, Chicago

rent, and most of the space on these floors was used for storage.

A few entrepreneurs foresaw the tremendous rental income to be realized from tall buildings serviced by smoothly operating elevators transporting not just freight, but people as well. Developers, including Boston investor Peter C. Brooks, began to dream of taller structures. Building and profitably renting the tall buildings was another matter. In stone and masonry construction, the weight of additional stories could be supported only as the thickness of the walls at the base of the building was increased proportionately, a factor that cut sharply into the premium rental space on the lower floors. Even if space were sacrificed, the danger remained that higher and thus heavier buildings with their thicker walls would shift and sink into Chicago's sandy and treacherous subsoil.

Both problems were addressed in the ten-story stone and brick Montauk Building, erected for Peter Brooks in 1882. It was hailed as the world's first skyscraper. The solution, devised by Brooks's Chicago property manager Owen F. Aldis and architect John W. Root, was the floating raft foundation—a concrete slab reinforced with layers of steel rails that effectively spread the weight of the building over a greater area. The new foundation was so space-effective and cost-efficient that it soon became a standard for Chicago skyscraper construction. Even so, masonry buildings still went up stone resting on stone. The height to which they could go was limited by the weight the structure could support. William Le Baron Jenney used his experience as a bridge builder for the U.S. Army Corps of Engineers in designing the Home Insurance Building, completed in 1885. The building was the first to be built and braced on an iron and steel frame. The brick and stone exterior was needed only to support the window frames and to serve as the decorative facade. The true steel skeleton building was just a footstep away.

Tenant demand for space in higher floors remained subject to public skepticism over both the future of tall buildings and the safety of the elevator as a means of transportation. But the limited land area of the central business district and the growing market for new office space were compelling incentives to build higher. The office skyscraper as a new development concept flourished in the 1880s, particularly in the area around the Chicago Board of Trade Building at the foot of La Salle Street. The Rookery, Rialto, Temple Court, and Chicago Opera House buildings were among the early skyscrapers built in this district.

While Chicago was leading the nation in skyscraper construction, it was also learning the financing techniques that made ever larger development projects possible. Healthy doses of capital were being channeled into the real estate and devel-

Chicago Loop at the turn of the century. [opposite page] In the period 1880-95, block after block of downtown land yielded to Chicago's golden age of development. The elevator building and then the skyscraper rose to dominate a dense and geographically contained center for commerce and trade. The configuration of today's downtown, and many of its landmarks, can be seen in this 1909 map of the central business district. [George F. Cram, engraver and publisher—Chicago Historical Society]

opment fields from both resident and nonresident sources. Eastern capitalists invested millions of dollars in Chicago real estate both before and immediately after the Great Fire, and reinvested in the Chicago market in 1880 and beyond. The Yankees brought a particularly useful financing mechanism to Chicago. This was the Massachusetts Trust, created to circumvent a state law common at the time prohibiting a corporation from owning any real estate or building not used in its own business operations. The trust allowed a group of investors to pool their resources while retaining most of the advantages given to a corporation. Created to help a few wealthy investors reduce their exposure to risk, the Massachusetts Trust within a short time became the vehicle used by many small investors to form investment groups. It was the forerunner to today's real estate investment trusts (REITs).

The safety deposit company offered investors another inventive way of pooling their resources while skirting the spirit of the law. By this device, a "safety deposit" company was incorporated under state law with the sole rights of building, maintaining, and operating safety deposit vaults. The company was not required to specify where the vaults were to be located, nor did state law expressly prohibit the vaults from being built into new structures. It was no coincidence that many companies chose to erect new buildings to secure the vaults. The fact that safety deposit companies were not at all interested in the safekeeping business was well known to state and local officials. Their real business, that of developing new buildings, was endorsed by growth-oriented local governments. In the last two decades of the nineteenth century, some thirty downtown buildings were erected with funds pooled by this method.

Another source of capital came from within the city itself. Chicago capitalists and entrepreneurs channeled money into new office, warehouse, and manufacturing space, at the same time investing personal fortunes in Chicago real estate and development. Like their mentors Potter Palmer and Ernst Lehmann, dry goods tycoons Marshall Field, Levi Z. Leiter, and Otto Young were to become the city's wealthiest real estate entrepreneurs.

The expanding industrial base of the city rapidly filled any new rental space coming onto the market. The number of printing and publishing firms tripled in the 1880s, gravitating to office and loft space on South Dearborn Street. Garment houses moved to Franklin, Wells, and Market streets. The stockyards on the South Side and new industry around the Calumet area, including the Pullman Works, spun off new neighborhoods.

Board of Trade Building. The Board of Trade Building, built in 1886 at the foot of La Salle Street, established lower La Salle as the financial center of the city, fanning battles over scarce land and heightening demand for ever higher office towers in this district. The Rookery and the Royal Insurance Company buildings are at left in this photograph from the late 1890s.
[J. W. Taylor, from *Chicago and Its Makers*]

Although the decade of the 1880s was the age of the skyscraper, this period was also the era of large-scale movement to the dozens of new suburbs growing up around the central city. There were many reasons. The inner city had become a harsh place to live. Lake View Township, just north of the city, and Hyde Park, to the south, were attractive meccas as summer residences for the wealthy. The planned community of Riverside, laid out by landscape architect Frederick Law Olmsted on the Des Plaines River west of the city, was considered Chicago's most elegant suburb. For the working and middle class, the little-money-down, wood-framed cottages developed by such entrepreneurs as Samuel E. Gross and built along commuter rail lines—and just outside the fire code prohibiting them that had been imposed by the city following the fire of 1871—fulfilled dreams of home ownership.

But not all was well in Eden. Chicago's population more than doubled in the 1880s, with well over half the populace of recent immigrant origin. By 1890 the census numbered almost 1.1 million, and the city had expanded its limits, by annexation, to 168 square miles. Meanwhile, Chicago's captains of industry were rapidly becoming richer and the laboring classes becoming poorer. The May 4, 1886, Haymarket Square riot touched off a long period of labor unrest in Chicago. More than five hundred strikes were called in the years from 1887 to 1894, including the infamous Pullman Strike that rallied the nation's railway workers around Eugene V. Debs's American Railway Union. Many of these work stoppages severely affected the building industry. To minimize the time lost, developers extended the building calendar with sheds erected over construction sites so that work could continue through the winter.

Buoyed by unremittent civic pride and a bold business community, Chicago dared in 1890 to challenge New York's hegemony as a world-class city. The news that Chicago had been named over New York, Philadelphia, and Washington D.C., to host the World's Columbian Exposition spurred another building boom. The results were particularly evident on the South Side, in the area around the 686-acre Jackson Park fair site. The exposition drew more than twenty-one million visitors. It was the city's finest hour. But the triumph was clouded in the fair's closing days, first by the assassination of Carter Harrison, Chicago's popular five-term mayor, and then by the advent of the financial panic of 1893, the worst business depression in the nation's history to that date. Although new construction was all but halted during the long depression, the downtown area flourished in the years just before and during the Columbian Exposition. Office buildings built within the period included the Monadnock, Manhattan, Old Colony, Marquette, and Reliance—all still standing.

Considering the times, the flowering of the central city in the 1880s was a remarkable accomplishment. Many forces threatened the development industry. The 1880s and '90s were years of unprecedented graft and corruption in city hall, and labor problems had become increasingly critical by the end of the period. A major recession lay just over the horizon. These problems were not diminished by the threat to the future of the skyscraper in Chicago that came from within the real estate community itself. The surge in tall building construction had, by 1890, alarmed the antiskyscraper camp, which renewed its periodic agitation for a city ordinance limiting building heights. Many of those lobbying for height limitations were owners of land close to the downtown area who would benefit from a horizontal expansion of the city. Others were owners of low buildings downtown who saw their tax assessments rising to match the valuations of land under taller buildings. For a time they prevailed. The ordinance adopted by the city council in 1893 limited the height of buildings to 130 feet (well below the scale of buildings of this period, such as the Manhattan, which stood at 210 feet). The battle over height limitations was not clearly resolved in favor of the skyscraper until after the turn of the century. The outcome was inevitable. The war had been won the moment the skyscraper was conceived. As stated by the Chicago *Tribune* in 1885: "Men of advanced ideas, if they want more space, take it out of the sky."

FIRST SKYSCRAPER

Peter C. Brooks
(1831-1920)

Peter C. Brooks.
[From *Annals of the Harvard Class of 1852*—Harvard University Archives]

On February 5, 1881, a Massachusetts investor named Peter Chardon Brooks III wrote a letter to Owen F. Aldis, his property manager in Chicago, outlining ideas for construction of an office building on a lot that had become available on the north side of Monroe Street between Dearborn and Clark streets. The letter itself seems so prosaic that it might have gone unremembered among the hundreds of letters exchanged over the years by Brooks and Aldis—were it not for the significance of the project envisioned.

Brooks wrote that a building of eight stories in addition to the main floor and basement "may be large enough to warrant an elevator," provided that "the earth can support it." The reference was to the unstable clay substratum at the lake level that over the years had caused buildings of far lesser size to shift, list, and even sink into the fabled Chicago mud. "If you can get this lot for $100,000 cash I am rather inclined to purchase it," Brooks concluded. He suggested that the building he described be called the Montauk. Thus Brooks had, in a seemingly routine and ordinary letter to his Chicago agent, proposed both the construction of the world's first office skyscraper and the means—the elevator—by which higher spaces with better light could ever after command the highest rents. Brooks's direction to buy the lot was followed by a letter to Aldis dated March 22 in which he observed with characteristic understatement that "tall buildings will pay well in Chicago hereafter, and sooner or later a way will be found to erect them."

Aldis took the plan to two young architects, Daniel H. Burnham and John W. Root. Root's engineering problem was to develop a foundation that would spread the weight of a tall building evenly over Chicago's treacherous subsoil. Aldis's problem was to assure that the foundation, by virtue of the sheer size of the building's footings, would not wholly consume valuable basement and lower floor space. Their solution was a "floating raft" constructed of iron beams embedded in a flat concrete slab, or envelope, which when laid into the ground became the foundation for the building, distributing the weight of ten stories of brick and stone as evenly as a set of snowshoes.

The steel skeleton, yet to be invented, would eventually become "the way" by which the tall buildings foreseen by Brooks could be pushed to ever higher reaches, releasing the builder and the architect from the bondage of the heavy masonry construction employed in the Montauk. The Montauk itself was a transitional building, using fireproofed iron beams for structural reinforcement but dependent still on load-bearing masonry walls for support. The building caused a commotion. The very idea that a structure could rise, brick upon brick, to a height of more than one hundred feet was a phenomenon that drew people in droves to the construction site (now occupied by the plaza of the One First National Plaza Building). A witness to the building's construction recalled that "the very idea of such a building set the building and architectural world agog."

Art historian Thomas Tallmadge, later commenting on the Montauk's significance in the history of building, said that "what Chartres was to the Gothic cathedral the Montauk Block was to the high commercial building." Although Chicagoans of the day would in no way have compared the Montauk to a cathedral—anything but—they were aware that the structure defied common wisdom as to what a building should be in two very visible respects. It was dangerously tall. And it was notably plain, utterly without any pretension to the elaborate stone trimmings and quasi-Parisian grandeur that were the fashion of the time. What Brooks demanded for the Montauk was an unadorned brick structure that claimed to be no more than what it was: a highly functional office building providing the best services to its tenants while yielding the best return that could be had on the developer's investment. He wrote Aldis in March 1881 that "the building throughout is to be for use and not for ornament. Its beauty will be in its all-adaptation to its use." It would be another four decades before Peter Brooks's concept found memorable expression in Louis Sullivan's pronouncement that "form follows function."

Brooks was explicit in his requirements and attentive to

Montauk Block. Located at 64-70 West Monroe, between Dearborn and Clark streets, Peter Brooks's ten-story, decidely utilitarian Montauk Block is considered to be the world's first office skyscraper. In hiring Daniel Burnham and John W. Root for the project, completed in 1882, Brooks and his Chicago agent Owen F. Aldis gave the young architectural team their first commercial commission.
[Woodcut from *Chicago Buildings*—Chicago Historical Society]

every detail of the building's construction. Architectural historian Carl Condit points out that ''Brooks knew precisely what he wanted and he laid down an exact prescription for his architects.'' In his letters to Aldis, Brooks reveals an extensive knowledge of construction techniques and materials and a clear vision about the use of the building. Above all else, he sought utility and was alert to future costs of maintenance; he suggested, for example, that ''the less plumbing the less trouble. It should be concentrated as much as possible, all pipes to show and be accessible, including gas pipes. It might also be advisable to put in wire for future electric lights.''

Plans for the building were completed within five months, but when they were submitted, Brooks grumbled that ''the building is much more extravagant than my original design.'' The age-old tension between the developer's budget and the architect's aesthetic impulse reared its head throughout the spare Montauk construction. In his authoritative study of the Chicago school of architecture, Condit gives the match to the developer. The character of Brooks's objections, Condit writes, ''shows with what extraordinary thoroughness Peter Brooks had grasped all the details of a large office building and how valuable such a grasp was for the subsequent development of commercial architecture.''

Monadnock Building, c. 1893. The northern half of the powerful Monadnock, designed by Burnham and Root, and completed in 1891, stands on Dearborn Street between Jackson and Van Buren streets. The southern section, then known as the Katahdin and designed by William Holabird and Martin Roche, was nearing completion when this photo was taken. At sixteen stories, Peter Brooks's Monadnock was the tallest load-bearing masonry building ever erected in Chicago and the world's largest office building.
[J. W. Taylor—Chicago Historical Society]

Windows were an issue. Brooks had sought the ultimate advantage for light in the offices (he had originally considered a U-shaped building for the site), but he objected to the extensive use of plate glass and the weight of the large windows envisioned by Burnham. Brooks proposed instead that the windows be divided horizontally, with "common glass" used in the upper half, "which is not to look through." The notion could not have been pleasing to Burnham, who in the rebuilding boom after the Great Chicago Fire had briefly made his living selling plate glass. Brooks later complained about another Burnham touch. He wrote, "Colored glass is mere nonsense —a passing fashion, inappropriate in a mercantile building and worse than all, it obstructs the light. Strike it all out."

Peter C. Brooks and his brother Shepherd, also a major investor in Chicago real estate, were born to a considerable fortune accumulated by a thrifty New England family that traced its ancestry to the arrival of the Puritans in Watertown, Massachusetts, in 1630. The family money was made in the shipping insurance business in the years just after the Revolutionary War. Peter C. Brooks's grandfather, for whom he was named, founded the immensely profitable New England Marine Insurance Company in 1789, and multiplied his wealth many times over through investments in mortgages and loans. At the time of his death in 1849, he was reputed to be the richest man in New England.

By 1850 the family interests were far-reaching, and it appears that from an early age, Peter Brooks took the leadership role in managing the Brooks investments. Shepherd was the more conservative investor. Peter possessed not only a penchant for practical detail and a shrewd eye for the bottom line but also a talent for innovative moves. He was a man of great authority, imagination, and self-confidence. It also seems that Peter Brooks led something of a double life. Architectural historians readily acknowledge the preeminence of Brooks's contribution to high-rise office tower development in Chicago, but acknowledgements of his acumen as a businessman and his role as a visionary builder are surprisingly barren of any information about Peter Brooks the man. This, perhaps, is as Brooks intended it. At home in Medford, Massachusetts, Peter and Shepherd Brooks were known as the "landed proprietors" of the three-thousand-acre Brooks estates. They were remembered as "practical farmers, understanding the raising of vegetables, the rotation of crops, the care of cows, the laying of stone walls and the grading of roadways." Brooks actively managed the daily operations of the farms, although, it appears, he denied even that.

On the occasion of his graduation from Harvard in 1852, he

wrote of himself that "previous to entering college, nothing of any vital importance had occurred to him, nor is he aware of any since." In fact, after leaving Harvard, Brooks went to New Orleans to work in the office of his maternal grandfather. The Brooks brothers eventually would make a considerable investment in New Orleans real estate. He traveled for two years in Europe before returning to Medford.

Although Brooks had a winter home in Boston, where he spent more time in his later years, he preferred life in Medford. There, in addition to his unpublicized business pursuits, he attended to his extensive art collection and his library. He did not marry until he was thirty-five. In his mid-eighties, Brooks reported to the historian of his Harvard class that he had no profession, insofar as "his delicate health [had] prevented his entering on any active career." His obituary notice, published in the *Medford Mercury,* similarly notes that Peter Brooks was "never actively engaged in business." The numbers and significance of Peter Brooks's Chicago office tower developments, and his voluminous personal correspondence with his Chicago agents and property managers, sustained over a period of four decades, tell quite another story, as do his meticulous and vigorous instructions visualizing every elevation, pipe, and plumbing fixture.

Peter Brooks's involvement in Chicago property development is usually traced from the date of the Montauk construction in 1881-82. In fact, Brooks had invested in Chicago real estate as early as 1863. In that year, he acquired from another Bostonian a four-story building and lot at the southeast corner of Dearborn and Washington streets. This was the original Portland Block. When the building was destroyed in the 1871 fire, Brooks rebuilt, anticipating his own historic Montauk development by a full ten years. He commissioned William Le Baron Jenney to design an eight-story building for the site, to be equipped with a passenger elevator. Both the proposed height and an elevator that would carry not freight, but people, were departures unheard of in Chicago at the time.

It was perhaps auspicious that for his first Chicago project Brooks turned to Jenney, whose office would become the incubator for the young architects who forged the first Chicago school of architecture: Daniel Burnham, William Holabird, Martin Roche, and Louis Sullivan. With the exception of Sullivan, Brooks placed all his bets with Jenney's young men. Brooks and Aldis gave Burnham and his brilliant partner John Wellborn Root their first major commercial job with the Montauk commission in 1881 and turned to them again as architects for the Rookery and then the Monadnock buildings.

William Holabird and Martin Roche similarly secured some

of their earliest commissions from the Brooks brothers. These included the Pontiac Building (1891); the Monadnock south addition (1893); the Champlain (1894); the elegant Marquette Building (1894); Shepherd Brooks's Cable Building (1889); the Venetian (1894); and ultimately the twentieth-century Monroe and Brooks buildings. It can be said that Holabird and Roche, like Burnham and Root, got their start as designers of office skyscrapers under the tutelage and patronage of Peter Brooks. The two firms and their successors eventually became Chicago's—and the nation's—most prolific designers of tall buildings.

The new Portland, designed by Burnham, Holabird, and Roche's mentor, William Le Baron Jenney, actually was built as a five-story building, but the elevator remained in the designs. The Portland thus was very probably the first Chicago building to introduce a passenger elevator. The building was unique in another respect; it used brick for the exterior walls instead of stone, which in Chicago was thought to be the only material suitable for a major office building. Typical of Brooks's projects, the Portland was a building of decidedly

Portland Block. Boston investor Peter C. Brooks acquired the original Portland Block, on the southeast corner of Washington and Dearborn streets, in 1863. After the 1871 fire, Brooks commissioned William Le Baron Jenney to design this eight-story elevator building for the site.
[Lithograph from a painting by Richard Richard—Chicago Historical Society]

utilitarian nature. What was saved on external embellishments was spent on features that would make the building convenient and desirable to tenants. John W. Root later commented that the Portland was "in its day the sensation of the town." In 1879 Peter Brooks dispatched a letter to another native New Englander, Owen Aldis, then a young Chicago lawyer, asking him to act as agent and attorney in the management of the Portland Block. A year later two more stories were added to the Portland, and the elevators—now there were two—were converted from steam to William E. Hale's new hydraulic system. Although Brooks was pragmatic, he was not parsimonious, as was evident in future developments such as the historic Monadnock Building.

With Aldis as their agent, the Brooks brothers began to step up their investments in Chicago, recognizing the strategic location of the city as a center for trade and speculating that land values would rise in the geographically contained central business district. Favoring corners, between 1881 and 1884 they acquired a number of corner properties in the downtown area. Many were on Dearborn Street, where they would later build the Pontiac, the Monadnock, and the Marquette buildings. The Brookses' dollars and Aldis's instincts seemed an unbeatable combination, with one fateful exception—and even that may have had its silver lining in that it broke through the Brooks brothers' propensity for investment in existing properties and unlocked a flurry of Brooks development activity that was without equal in the 1880s and '90s. The event was the Grannis Block fire.

On Aldis's advice, Shepherd Brooks had purchased the vacant lot on Dearborn immediately south of Peter Brooks's Portland Block. In 1880 he leased the property to carpenter Amos Grannis, who put up a seven-story building. Four years later, Shepherd Brooks purchased the building, content with Aldis's assurance that it was a safe investment—a factor of considerable importance to the cautious Shepherd Brooks. In the early evening of February 19, 1885, just months after Brooks had acquired it, the Grannis Block went up in flames. The event put quite a strain on relations among Daniel Burnham and John Root, who had designed the building and had offices there; William E. Hale, who installed the elevators, which at first were thought to be the cause of the fire; Aldis, the trusted agent for the purchasers; and the Brooks brothers, who discovered too late that the building Shepherd had bought was poorly constructed and grossly underinsured.

The fire, which occurred in subfreezing weather, ravaged the interior of the building and turned the exterior into an ice palace. The catastrophe was a source of some fascination in a city with a morbid fear of fire and a lingering distrust of the tall building as a place safe for conducting business. Thousands of sightseers thronged to the corner to view the icy remains and trade tales of how the fire might have begun. The *Tribune* described the Grannis as "a veritable fire-trap," suggesting that "the purchaser got a poor bargain when he bought the Grannis Block," a statement that could not have warmed the heart of Owen Aldis. Only $65,000 was recovered from insurance, against the estimated $175,000 Shepherd Brooks had paid for the building. On April 30 the newspapers announced that Brooks had leased the lot to a vault company organized by W. K. Nixon, who would put up a new building on the property. At the time of the fire, the *Tribune* observed editorially that "the destruction of the Grannis Block strikes terror to the Brooks estate." Terror may have been too strong a word, but the fact remains that from that date forward the Brookses bought no more buildings for income purposes. They built their own and made sure they controlled what they were getting.

When an investors' group pooled resources in late 1885 to build Chicago's famous Rookery, the Brooks brothers acquired the majority interest, with Aldis himself also becoming an investor. Brooks projects soon came to include some of the most significant buildings characterizing the Chicago school of architecture. In all, the Brooks brothers would either build or be major investors in well over a dozen major downtown buildings, including some that are still in use—notably, the landmark Rookery, Marquette, Monadnock, and Pontiac buildings, and the Brooks Building at 223 West Jackson, diagonally across Jackson from the Sears Tower.

Peter Brooks did not lose interest in the smallest detail of construction and management of these buildings and the many others the Brooks estate built, often through Aldis-directed investment syndicates, over the next two decades. Correspondence between Aldis and Brooks in the summer of 1885 about the Pontiac Building, for example, deals with such matters as the cost of material for window sills, the selection of lights for a basement, and the virtues—or lack thereof—of brass chains for window sash weights.

Without question, Peter Brooks's most enduring monument— and probably his own favorite project—was the powerful Monadnock Building at Jackson and Dearborn streets. Brooks began planning the Monadnock in 1884. Construction of the northern section, designed by Burnham and Root, began in 1889 and was completed in 1891. The southern section of the building, built by Shepherd Brooks and designed by William Holabird and Martin Roche, was completed in

1893. Characteristically, as with the Montauk, the Brooks brothers chose geographical names of American Indian origin for the building, in this case the names of New England mountains. The two northern sections were originally called the Monadnock and the Kearsarge. The later sections were the Katahdin and the Wachusett. At sixteen stories, the Monadnock was the tallest load-bearing masonry building ever erected in Chicago and the world's largest office building. It was also the greatest elevator building in the world, a fitting tribute to Peter Brooks, the developer who introduced the passenger elevator to Chicago.

By 1900 Peter Brooks's interest in Chicago real estate had peaked, and he began investing more of his money in railroad and electric stocks. His own last project in Chicago was the Brooks Building, built in 1909-10. The sixteen-story Monroe Building, at 104 South Michigan, completed in 1912, was Shepherd Brooks's last Chicago development and one of the last of the tall office towers to be built by a single investor. By 1905 the Brookses were disposing of outlying properties and were beginning a process of converting assets into family trusts. Owen Aldis's career and the impact of the Brooks family investments on the building of Chicago had been closely intertwined over the thirty-year span of their association. By the time the Brooks Building was completed, Peter Brooks, then nearly eighty years of age, had transferred the management of his property to his son-in-law, U. S. senator and former Massachusetts governor Richard M. Saltonstall. Shepherd Brooks's son Gorham was assuming management of Shepherd's interests, and Aldis was planning his own retirement from business. Aldis took up residence in Washington, D.C., in 1910, and after 1912 moved to Paris.

Peter C. Brooks portrayed the developer's role at its best. He brought capital, creativity, imagination, attention to detail in every aspect, and a clear vision of what he wanted and why to every project. Although Brooks himself seldom visited the city, he could not be classed among the ranks of Chicago's out-of-town investors and absentee landlords. His influence on the development of Chicago's central city in the late nineteenth century and his definition of a new architectural style was as immediate, persuasive, and challenging as the mind of Peter Brooks himself.

OFFICE TOWERS

Owen F. Aldis
(1853-1925)

Owen F. Aldis.
From *National Cyclopedia of American Biography*—The Newberry Library]

It was the right place: Chicago. It was the right time: four years after the Great Fire. It was the right man: Owen F. Aldis. Aldis was twenty-four years old when he arrived in Chicago in 1875, equipped with a new law degree and an old New England ancestry. On the surface, it is hard to imagine that a young lawyer from Vermont would become known as the man responsible for the modern office building. But such was the judgment of architect Louis H. Sullivan—a judgment substantiated by the facts of Aldis's long and innovative career as a Chicago developer.

The Aldis name does not appear over the door of any of the world-famous office towers that he created on behalf of investor-clients. It doesn't need to. The signature of Aldis's work is written across the face of the city. The buildings he developed gave rise to Chicago's permanent business district and created in America a new definition of office space. The success of his projects may be expressed in numbers. Aldis's first building, the historic Montauk Block, went up in 1882. By 1902, almost one-fifth of Chicago office space was Aldis-produced and -managed.

Owen Franklin Aldis was born in St. Albans, Vermont, in 1853, into a family of distinguished New England jurists. His grandfather and father between them held the seat of chief justice of the Supreme Court of Vermont for some forty years. As would be expected for a young man of his background, his education included travel and study in Europe before his enrollment at Yale University in 1871. At Yale, Aldis was chairman of the *Yale Literary Magazine,* an early sign of the dedication to literature and the arts that ran through the Aldis families in Chicago, leaving a significant mark on the cultural life of the city. When Aldis graduated from Yale in 1874, his father, Judge Asa O. Aldis, was serving on the U.S. Court of Claims in Washington, D.C., and would later be appointed to the French-American Claims Commission. Aldis began his study of law at the Columbian Law School in Washington.

Aldis's decision to leave the East Coast for Chicago within the year was no doubt influenced by the friendship formed in this period with Bryan Lathrop, a Virginia native who married Aldis's sister Helen in Washington in 1875. The couple soon left for Chicago, where Lathrop was in the real estate business. Owen Aldis went West also, to pursue real estate and title law. He was admitted to the Chicago Bar in 1876 and set up a law practice that came to include property management activities on behalf of clients in the East who had invested in Chicago real estate in the postfire period, including Judge Asa Aldis.

From the time of his arrival in Chicago, Aldis was an accepted member of the town's growing community of business elite. In December of 1878, he married Leila Russell Houghteling, a daughter of William De Zeng Houghteling, an early settler of Chicago and prominent lumber merchant. Leila, the eldest of the three Houghteling daughters, was remembered as "the lovely Mrs. Owen Aldis, an exquisite blonde." She died in 1885, just seven years after the marriage and six years after the birth of a son, named Owen Jr., in 1879. Aldis remained a widower until 1912, living for much of that time at the Lathrop home (now the Fortnightly of Chicago) on Bellevue Place. Aside from business activities, his primary pursuit after his wife's death was the development over a twenty-year period of one of the nation's finest collections of American literary first editions.

In 1879 Massachusetts investor Peter C. Brooks commissioned Aldis to serve as his agent in the management of the Portland Block, a Chicago office building developed and owned by Brooks. No partnership could have been better designed by fate or destiny than the pairing at this moment of Owen F. Aldis with Peter Brooks and his brother Shepherd.

The Brooks-Aldis relationship, which coincided with a period of unprecedented investment in the Chicago business district, introduced to the world the tall office building as an economically viable enterprise. At the time of their meeting, Chicago was poised for a radical transformation, brought about in part by the opportunities left in the wake of the Great Fire, in part by the surging investment climate that followed the westward expansion of the railroad, and in part by the coming of age of new technologies and the introduction of new building materials. That technology included the use of steel in construction and the advent of central heating, electric lights, and the telephone. A factor of greatest importance was the refinement of the elevator, then becoming an increasingly common means of hoisting freight and machinery, if not people. The portent of these innovations for redesign of the office environment was not lost on Aldis. From the beginning of his prolific work with the Brooks brothers, Aldis showed a talent for applying the products of a rapidly changed technology to profitable ventures.

The first building that Owen Aldis erected as agent for Peter Brooks was the ten-story Montauk Block, built between 1881 and 1882 on an undeveloped lot on the north side of Monroe Street between Dearborn and Clark streets. The extraordinary fact about the Montauk was not that it was Aldis's first office block, nor that it was also the first office building designed by Chicago's master office builders, Daniel H. Burnham and John Wellborn Root, but rather that at the time the building was planned, no commercial structure of such a height had ever before been attempted. With the Montauk Block, Owen Aldis and Peter Brooks—and their architect, John Root—opened the door to a new era in the history of architecture. They gave birth to the skyscraper.

Public acceptance of the office tower did not come easily. Many proclaimed that they would never go up in such a tall building. Interestingly, it was an embryonic architectural firm, one that Aldis would turn to frequently after Root's death, that first saw the light. William Holabird, with his partner Martin Roche, were glad to lease top-floor office space in the Montauk when no one else would have it, and were even more pleased, Holabird recalled, to get the rooms "at very favorable terms." It took time but, one by one, Aldis was able to convince tenants of the value of the new office space he offered. Within very few years, Owen Aldis succeeded in turning what had been secondary space on the higher floors of office buildings into primary space, changing forever the economics and feasibility of high-rise buildings.

As property manager and agent for building owners, Aldis's first concern was to make the buildings he developed on behalf of his clients profitable. Nowhere is this more evident than in the massive Monadnock Building, whose northern section, like the Montauk Building and the Rookery that followed it, was designed by Root. Here the value that Aldis placed on enhancement of natural light as a rental feature prevailed over both the desire of Peter Brooks that the building present a

Pontiac Building, northwest corner of Dearborn and Harrison streets. The Pontiac, planned as early as 1884 but not completed by the Brooks estate until 1891, reflected Owen Aldis's belief in the future of South Dearborn Street. The building was constructed to accommodate storage and light manufacturing [specifically the printing trade] but designed by architects Holabird and Roche for ready adaptation to office use when the market emerged. The building is now listed on the National Register of Historic Places.
[Barnes and Crosby—Chicago Historical Society]

simple facade and the original designs prepared by Root. Aldis argued, successfully, for the introduction of the bay windows that are today a significant architectural feature of the building, reasoning that the window bays would not only gain more light but—of even greater importance—would add income-producing space.

An Aldis idea that would serve today's downtown districts well had it been followed was his recommendation that high buildings should be separated by low buildings. At the time of the construction of the Commercial Bank Building, located on Adams Street just west of the Marquette Building, for example, Aldis urged that a low building be placed between the two tall buildings and that white enamel brick be applied to the facing sides of the taller buildings to capture and reflect good light.

The magnitude of his real estate operations in the decade of the 1880s notwithstanding, Aldis continued to maintain his law practice. His decision in 1889 to turn his full energies to real estate coincided with the arrival in Chicago of his younger brother, Arthur T. Aldis. In that year Owen Aldis established the property management firm that would later become Aldis and Company, taking his brother and Anayas Stafford Northcote as partners.

Owen Aldis was the first Chicago developer to make extensive use the Massachusetts Trust, the forerunner of today's real estate investment trust, as the means of assembling capital for building projects. Aldis favored the trust as a financing vehicle over the more commonly used safety deposit company, believing that the trust could successfully withstand a challenge based on a law, common to many states, prohibiting a corporation from owning real estate other than that needed for its everyday operations.

Although Aldis served as president (on behalf of the Brookses) of the Central Safety Deposit Company, which built the Rookery on South La Salle Street in 1885, Aldis was never comfortable with the fiction of the vault company as a cover for development activities. Nevertheless, he was a subscriber to the Central Safety Deposit Company, as was Daniel Burnham.

Aldis's views on the matter of the vault companies surfaced at the time of the construction of the Marquette Building, which replaced the old Honoré Block at the northwest corner of Adams and Dearborn streets. Aldis was unsuccessful in advocating that Brooks and other investors in the Marquette Building Company, which had been formed in 1888 to purchase the Honoré, should reorganize as a trust on the Massachusetts model. Aldis ultimately was proven right. In 1911, the Marquette company did reorganize as a trust, and ten years later safety deposit companies were ruled illegal, as Aldis had predicted they would be.

Aldis was a man accustomed to getting his way. From the time of the Marquette construction forward, he maintained firm control over the financing vehicles through which his buildings were developed. In 1890 he formed the Chicago Real Estate Trust with a total capital investment of $2.5 million. This organization, which closely paralleled the Massachusetts model, appears to have been the first of the general real estate investment trusts in Chicago. The Brooks brothers were subscribers along with other Boston and Chicago investors. Trustees named to manage the fund were Owen Aldis, his brother-in-law Bryan Lathrop, Lathrop's brother-in-law Henry Field, and Chicago banker Byron L. Smith. The announced purpose of the trust was to purchase, hold, and manage Chicago real estate "for the benefit of the children of subscribers." This trust remained active until 1979.

In succeeding years, a number of other trusts were formed by Aldis and Company. The City Real Estate Trust was created in 1891 after the capital of the Chicago Real Estate Trust was fully subscribed. This trust built the Venetian Building on Washington Street, just east of State Street. Other trusts were created to carry out specific purchases. The Chicago Leasehold Declaration and Agreement Trust bought the leasehold of the northwest corner of State and Madison from Otto Young in 1892 and built the first Champlain Building. Aldis, Lathrop, and Northcote were subscribers, as were William Holabird and Martin Roche, the architects. The Caxton Trust was organized to acquire the South Dearborn Street Caxton Building, built by Lathrop and Arthur Aldis's father-in-law, William T. Reynolds. Many considered a building like the Caxton to be an unattractive investment because of its location, beyond the boundaries of the central business district and surrounded as it was by run-down buildings, rooming houses, bars, and brothels. Aldis thought otherwise. He saw the potential for the development of the south sector of the business district as a viable office center, and acted upon that vision.

Between 1881 and 1885, Aldis made many important land purchases in the area for the Brooks brothers, often at bargain prices. These included corners on Dearborn Street at Adams, Jackson, and Harrison. During this period, he also purchased the southeast and southwest corners of Van Buren and Clark streets. Soon Aldis and the Brooks brothers began allocating development dollars to the lots.

Peter Brooks and Aldis began planning the Monadnock Building, at Jackson and Dearborn streets, as early as 1884. In 1885 they announced plans for the Pontiac Building at Harrison and Dearborn. Each represented an even deeper plunge southward from the accepted central business district. When Aldis and Brooks launched the first phase of the Monadnock construction in 1888, members of the Chicago business community were as dismayed by the project as they had been by the construction of the improbable Montauk building. Some believed that Aldis had gone mad. E. A. Renwick, an architect in the office of Burnham and Root, later summed up the prevailing opinion of the time: "When he put up the Monadnock on Jackson Boulevard, there was nothing on the south side of the street between State Street and the river but cheap one-story shacks, mere hovels. Everyone thought Mr. Aldis was insane to build way out there on the ragged edge of the city. Later, when he carried the building on through to Van Buren Street, they were sure he was."

The Monadnock Building, extending south along Dearborn from Jackson to Van Buren, was built by the Brookses as two buildings, each with two units, and all named for New England mountain peaks. The northernmost building, whose two sections were called the Monadnock and the Kearsarge, was completed in 1891. The southern additions, the Katahdin and the Wachusett, developed by Shepherd Brooks, were completed in 1893. The real estate community was forced to recognize Aldis's foresight with respect to this "ragged edge of the city" when Chicago's real estate journal, the *Economist,* noted on July 2, 1892:

> The rapidity with which the Monadnock and Kearsarge buildings, managed by Aldis, Aldis & Northcote, have been rented is one of the phenomenal features in the real estate market of this city. The erection and successful renting of these structures has simply established, in an incredibly short period of time, an important business center at the southwest corner of Jackson and Dearborn streets, a point which was but a short time ago considered altogether too far south for a prosperous business center.

In moving the Brooks operations southward, Owen Aldis evidenced an insight based not upon traditional investment attitudes but rather on a vision of the city as it could and should be. In these decisions, he demonstrated the creative development mentality that looks beyond an income and expense statement in determining the value of a property and sees in land and in location possibilities for change. By identifying an early trend or emerging area, as Aldis did, opportunity was appropriately exploited, and the economics fell into place.

In the late 1880s, Chicago was a rising star among America's cities—a locus of titanic energy and ingenuity. The Chicago business establishment was eager that the city claim its place as a center not only of commerce but also of culture. They planned nothing less than to bring the World's Fair to Chicago. It was the most ambitious of the undertakings of the city's leaders in these years when faith in the power of the city —and in their own power to make the impossible happen—was virtually without limit.

Owen Aldis was recognized as an oracle of the real estate industry and a man who controlled a great deal of the investment capital in the city. It is therefore not surprising that his name would appear when the forty-five-member board of directors of the World's Columbian Exposition was announced in April of 1890. Site selection, of critical importance to the success of the exposition, became a matter with power to make or break land values and careers for many concerned. The thankless task of mediating among contentious factions fell on the shoulders of the Buildings and Grounds Committee. Aldis's role as head of that committee proved to be critical to the ultimate success of the exposition.

Like most of the directors, Aldis favored the downtown area now occupied by Grant Park as the fair site, a choice that had much to recommend it but one that was complicated by the legal position taken by the Illinois Central Railroad, whose tracks ran through the site. Aldis's confidential negotiations with Stuyvesant Fish, the railroad's president, reached a paralyzing deadlock. With time running out, and the future of the event at stake, Aldis forced the issue to a decision. In a unilateral move engineered by Aldis, the Buildings and Grounds Committee presented the directorate with John Root's plans for a Jackson Park site—and no other. The directors were offered no option. The year-long wrangle over a fair site was settled.

Aldis is said to have met John Root at a reception, probably in 1879, and found in Root the traits that Aldis—never one to mingle with the common man—admired. Root, like Aldis, had a classical education, had studied in Europe, and moved gracefully in the circles of eastern-bred society. Daniel Burnham was a more rugged type, rougher around the edges in the early days of the partnership. Aldis's communications with the Burnham and Root firm seemed to go mainly through Root. After Root's sudden death, shortly after the fair site plans were approved, Aldis redirected most of his business from D. H. Burnham and Company to Holabird and Roche, his early tenants in the Montauk.

Aldis remained the Brooks brothers' sole agent in Chicago, but after the turn of the century, Aldis and Company became more diversified, handling more mortgage business and other investment activities. Simultaneously, the Brookses began consolidating their investments and putting properties into family trusts. Owen Aldis shifted more of the firm's responsibilities to Arthur Aldis, Russell Tyson, and other partners after 1905. By 1911, he had curtailed most of his business activities, largely because of increasing problems with his eyesight. At this time, Aldis established a second home in Washington, D.C., and made a gift to Yale University of his remarkable collection of American first editions, which then numbered six thousand volumes.

In May 1912, an automobile trip through Europe marked the beginning of a new episode in Aldis's life. That summer, Chicago social columns were abuzz with news of the prospective marriage of the wealthy widower who had so long eluded society's grasp to Marie Madeleine du Mas, the twenty-two-year-old daughter of a titled but impoverished French family. Aldis was fifty-nine. Romance, it seemed, blossomed when Mlle. du Mas was invited by friends to join the Aldis party, which included Arthur Aldis's wife, playwright Mary Reynolds Aldis, as they motored through Germany. The precipitating event was quite literally an accident. At a crossing near

**Marquette Building,
northwest corner of Adams
and Dearborn streets, 1897.**
Owen Aldis argued against the
organization of Marquette
investors as a safety deposit
company, a legal fiction
commonly used in the 1880s
to skirt a state law prohibiting
corporations from engaging in
development activities. Aldis
was later among those
responsible for introducing the
concept of the real estate
investment trust in Chicago.
The Marquette, completed in
1894, was designed by
Holabird and Roche.
[Chicago Historical Society]

Metz, Aldis had alighted from the car to read a road sign when
his chauffeur, brought by Aldis from Washington, backed up,
knocking Aldis to the ground. In breaking his fall, Aldis also
broke his arm. The Chicago *Tribune* later gave more details of
the incident:

> There was of course great excitement in his party and Mlle. du
> Mas, being very high strung, was about to faint. Whereupon
> Mr. Aldis, his right arm hanging limp and helpless, reached in
> for his traveling bag with his left hand, opened it, took out his
> flask of brandy, and insisted on her taking some—a very heroic
> act, under the circumstances, as eight breaks in a right arm
> mean pretty intolerable suffering.

During his convalescence in Metz and a subsequent motor
trip in France, the report continues, Aldis "poured into the
young French girl's attentive ear a really extraordinary flood of
information about her own land and people. The world for
her grew more wonderful every day." Aldis and Mlle. du Mas
were married in Paris in October 1912, and subsequently made
their permanent home in France. Aldis died in Paris in August
1925 from the effects of a stroke suffered some weeks earlier.
He was seventy-two. His brother Arthur, who became execu-
tor of the estate, was at his bedside.

Marie Madeleine lived into her nineties. A relative commented that Owen Aldis had "made her life quite delightful,"

recalling also that when friends warned her not to marry an American, she had replied, "But the Aldises know what to talk about, what to eat, and how to dress. It is like marrying into my own family." After Aldis's death, she maintained an apartment and a country estate in New York, but preferred to live in France in the gracious style her income as Aldis's widow afforded.

Arthur T. Aldis remained an active force in the Aldis firm throughout his life. The Aldis home at 1258 North Lake Shore Drive, in an unusual departure for architects Holabird and Roche, was modeled after a Venetian palace. Known in its time as the Desdemona House, the Aldis home is now a Chicago landmark. Arthur and Mary's son, Graham Aldis, joined Aldis and Company in 1918, becoming president, partner, and later director of the firm. Aldis and Company remained one of the city's leading property management firms until it was dissolved and its assets sold in the 1960s.

MAN OF PRINCIPLE

William E. Hale
(1836-98)

William E. Hale.
[From *National Cyclopedia of American Biography*—The Newberry Library]

The name William Ellery Hale is irrevocably linked to the passenger elevator and to the Hale Elevator Company, which grew up with Chicago's tall buildings in the 1880s and '90s. But the elevator was by no means Hale's first, last, or only pursuit. Hale was also a developer of skyscrapers, including one of State Street's greatest, the landmark Reliance Building. He was a devoted worker for the Congregational Church, a thorn in the side of graft-ridden public officials, and the father of the internationally renowned American astronomer George E. Hale. But Hale began his career in Chicago as none of the above. He started out in the paper business, dealing with items as diverse as flour sacks and men's paper collars, which were the rage among fashionable Chicagoans in the 1860s.

William Hale was born in 1836 in Bradford, Massachusetts, one of three sons of a New England Congregational minister. In 1857 the Hale family moved to Beloit, Wisconsin, where the father, Benjamin E. Hale, had taken a ministry. William joined the Beloit-based Rock River Paper Company and in 1862 became the company's Chicago agent. By 1865 he was head of the Chicago office and an officer in the company. Two years later, his brother and lifelong partner George W. Hale joined him in Chicago and went to work for the Congress Paper Collar Company, a subsidiary operation of the Rock River company.

Hale Building, southeast corner of State and Washington streets. William E. Hale acquired this choice State Street corner in 1867 when he built the first Hale building, but interrupted his real estate career to perfect and market the hydraulic elevator. Hale passenger elevators would become a key factor in the development of the office tower in Chicago in the 1880s and '90s. [Chicago Historical Society]

Hale put up his first Chicago building, a six-story retail and office structure at the southeast corner of State and Washington streets, in 1867. It was a choice location, just south of Potter Palmer's imposing "marble palace," occupied by the Field, Leiter and Company store, and opposite the site where some twenty-five years later Hale would build the Reliance Building. His partner in the venture was the building's architect, E. S. Jenison. When the first Hale Building was demolished in the Great Chicago Fire, Hale and Jenison rebuilt, this time in partnership with Lucuis G. Fisher, Hale's friend from Beloit and colleague in the paper business. As the second Hale Building was going up, Hale joined Fisher briefly in the firm that would later become the giant Union Bag and Paper Company.

As Chicago rebuilt in the months after the fire, Hale began giving more thought to the potential of the elevator than to the future of the flour sack. Soon the Hale brothers were out of the paper business and into the business of supplying freight-bearing Otis hoists to the developers of the new Chicago buildings. Two years later, W. E. Hale and Company, "Manufacturers of Water Balance Elevators," was established. By 1875 the brothers had added a New York branch. Hale bought out Otis Brothers in 1883, and soon after expanded the business to London, Paris, and Berlin. When William and George's younger brother Stedman joined the firm in 1888, the company was renamed the Hale Elevator Company.

By the mid-1880s, the Hale elevator had taken its place in the history of the commercially successful tall building. Early Chicago architect and historian Thomas E. Tallmadge observed in his 1939 comments on the origin of the skyscraper that "the high building is not owing to the invention of the steel skeleton but rather to the passenger elevator." Louis H. Sullivan had made a similar point when he wrote in 1916 that "the men who are responsible for the modern office building were William E. Hale and Owen F. Aldis." The *Inland Architect and News Record* stated more specifically in 1887 that the quality of the elevator installed in a new building could make the difference between success or failure for a development: "The elevator system of our modern large buildings has become of such an importance to the structure that owners and architects have to exercise great judgment in selecting the best, realizing that the renting of the upper floors depends on a safe and rapid transit."

And Hale elevators were the best. The name became synonymous with speed, comfort, and quality. The *Inland Architect* described the Hale products as "models of the cabinetmakers' art." A trip on them, the journal observed, "will convince the most skeptic that they combine the qualities of swiftness and smoothness of running, and that all the modern devices for safety have been provided."

The elevator business was not without its down side, and Hale over the years was sorely troubled by a cutthroat business climate. A major pursuit of the Hale Elevator Company and its competitors was protection of their patents, which for Hale and Otis numbered several hundred. In 1890 it was estimated that the country's five major elevator companies were spending half a million dollars a year suing one another. It was widely believed that the two Chicago companies, Hale and Crane, had interlocking directorates, or at least handshake agreements, which amounted to a "combine," or monopolistic trust. The Hales denied the accusations, but the rumors persisted. In 1891 a third Chicago company was formed, bringing with it brutal charges of patent infringement, countercharges of patent theft, and injunctions that the newspapers came to characterize as the "War in Elevators."

Perhaps wearied by the battle, but engaged also in his struggle to build the Reliance Building (see next page), Hale announced his retirement as president of the Hale Elevator Company in 1893 and his intention to pursue his development interests instead. In his comments to the press, Hale reiterated the company's motto: "Do the best work at a fair price and let the other man get the poor jobs at ruinous prices."

Like many developers, William E. Hale had a consuming interest in his life that had nothing to do with building skyscrapers or making money, except perhaps to the extent that he shared his financial and business success in furthering another cause: Hale was a committed, practicing Christian who was resolute in his support of education and the home mission work of his church. He served the church in many capacities, primarily as a trustee of the South Side Congregational Church of Chicago and a director of the Chicago (Congregational) Theological Seminary. Beyond his local interests, he was a lifelong supporter of the American Board of Missions of the Congregational Church and served as president of the New West Educational Commission, a group dedicated to establishing Christian schools in Utah, Arizona, and New Mexico. Hale was also a trustee of Beloit College and a generous patron of that institution.

Throughout the 1880s, Hale was active in the development of Chicago's central business district, both on his own and as a participant in syndicates formed to finance the construction of the new office towers. His investments included holdings in the safety deposit company organized by Edward C. Waller to build the Rookery and in the Insurance Exchange, Rialto, and

Reliance Building under construction. William Hale's sixteen-story Reliance Building symbolized Chicago's mastery of steel construction. "Incredible as it may appear, it is a fact that less than two days were required to run up the steelwork of each of the upper stories," the *Chicago Tribune* reported. [From *Architectural Record*, Aug. 1, 1894, courtesy Art Institute of Chicago]

Illinois Vault Company (Illinois National Bank) investment groups organized by Wilson K. Nixon. In the mid-1880s, he bought the Calumet Building on South La Salle Street, renaming it the Hale Building. All of the buildings in which Hale was an investor were designed by Burnham and Root.

Hale and Daniel Burnham had a falling-out in the winter of 1885 when the Grannis Block, designed by Burnham and Root, burned. Burnham—whose offices were in the building—quickly publicized his opinion that the fire had originated with the mechanism of the building's Hale elevator. Hale proved otherwise, leaving the conclusion that the rapid spread of the fatal fire had been the result of shoddy construction and substandard materials. There would have been no point for either Hale or Burnham to perpetuate the feud. Over the next decade, Burnham-designed office towers equipped with Hale-designed elevators would take the town by storm. Indeed, after the Grannis fire, Hale remained a steadfast client of the Burnham firm, commissioning it to design his own home at 4545 Drexel Avenue and later the Kenwood Physical Observatory, built on the grounds of the Hale home, where the young George E. Hale (for whom the Hale telescope is named) made the world's first photographs of solar flares. Hale also enlisted Burnham and Root as architects for the Reliance Building; for the Midland Hotel in Kansas City, codeveloped with Norman Ream; and the D. K. Pearsons Hall of Science at Beloit College.

The 1880s in Chicago were not only a golden age for building; they were also a golden age for graft and kickbacks. Hale, a man of uncompromising standards, had more than his share of problems with the "boodlers" who managed the lucrative city and county construction contracts. His personal run-ins with the county commission began as early as 1882. The conflict reached a peak two years later when county commissioner John E. Van Pelt and Chicago alderman E. J. Cullerton mounted an audacious challenge to the investment syndicates and trusts through which much of the major downtown building was being financed. Van Pelt and fellow commissioners proposed that a personal property tax be levied on construction bonds, liens, and mortgages—a tax, in short, on borrowed money. The Chicago *Tribune* predicted that, if enacted, the "Van Pelt Double-Taxation Scheme" would bring downtown construction to a halt.

Fortunately for the developers, Van Pelt, in the arms of hubris, went on to propose that a tax also be levied on the contents of grain elevators and warehouses. This ordinance, Van Pelt suggested, was to be considered retroactive for an unspecified number of years, with inspectors (the newspapers' term was "tax ferrets" and "back-tax spies") hired to seek out any undisclosed or underassessed property. With this, Van Pelt had gone too far. Chicagoans, goaded on by *Tribune* editorials, were outraged by the county board's attempt to "foist irresponsible spies upon the public." The tax ferret scheme was abandoned, and the development tax went down with it.

Hale's own outrage over the Van Pelt scheme no doubt was compounded by another problem he faced in 1884 involving this same group of county commissioners. In 1880 the county had awarded Hale the contract to install four hydraulic elevators in the new County Building then under construction at Clark and Washington streets. The commission later withheld a portion of the payment due Hale, claiming that the Hale elevators failed to meet specifications for both load and speed. Hale's request to inspect the equipment was denied, as was his second request, made in 1883, for payment. That same year, Hale bid in good faith on the job of installing elevators in the administration building of the Cook County Hospital. The hospital at that time was being run by the infamous William "Mac" McGarigle—at considerable profit to himself and others. McGarigle's principal line of work was managing the enormously lucrative bribes and kickbacks paid by contractors and vendors who did business, real or fictitious, with the county. It can be safely assumed that Hale had no intention of doing business on McGarigle's terms. When Hale's bid was the only one received, the commission extended the date for submission of bids, no doubt to allow McGarigle time to develop a more "suitable" source. Six months later, at the precise time the Van Pelt taxation plan was gathering steam, Hale presented a letter to the county commission claiming infringement of patent with respect to the elevators installed in the county hospital. Hale's letter was buried in committee, as his invoices had been. But the point was made. W. E. Hale could not be intimidated.

To be appreciated, Hale's position with regard to the county commission should be seen in the context of his development activities and other business relationships in 1883-84. In this period, he was entering into investment partnerships with the core group of capitalists, property managers, and developers who in the 1880s were virtually creating a new skyline for Chicago. The group included Wilson K. Nixon, Edward C. Waller, Owen F. Aldis, Arthur T. Aldis, Bryan Lathrop, and, through the Central Safety Deposit Company, the Brooks brothers of Boston. All, especially Waller, were adept at working behind the scenes to circumvent—in Mayor Carter Harrison's words—the "plug-uglies" in public office. Hale had little to gain by a confrontation with the corrupt commission, and

Reliance Building, southwest corner of State and Washington streets, 1900. [opposite page] Developer William E. Hale created a prime retail space for the Carson Pirie Scott Store in 1890 by raising the upper stories of an existing office building and building a new foundation, street-level floor, and mezzanine beneath them. When the leases on the upper stories expired four years later, Hale demolished the old structure and completed the landmark glass and steel tower. [Chicago Historical Society]

much to lose by angering a vindictive Van Pelt and possibly placing at risk personal and business relationships he valued highly. But for Hale, protest was necessary. It was a matter of principle.

By 1886 the county commissioners had become too open in the reach and extent of the corruption. In mid-January of 1887, the Chicago *Tribune* closed in on the board in a devastating series of articles exposing the kickbacks and "commissions" being taken by the boodlers on county contracts. Much of this activity centered on the dealings of the county hospital. Van Pelt had retired from the county commission in 1886, which was not soon enough. In early 1887, Van Pelt and twelve of his fellow commissioners were indicted on charges related to the boodling schemes. All were convicted. Hale settled the matter of the County Building elevators, dealing now with an entirely new county board.

A decade later, Hale took a stand against another notoriously corrupt city official, South Town assessor Richard C. Gunning, and succeeded where all others had failed in bringing Gunning to a trial that resulted in his conviction. Arthur Aldis acknowledged the toll this cause took on Hale's energy and failing health. Hale's pursuit of Gunning, Aldis said, was "one of the best things he did." High praise indeed for a man whose life and every action were governed by personal morality and broad philanthropic motives.

Hale had investments outside Chicago, in addition to those related to the elevator business. His principal partner in these other enterprises was Norman B. Ream, who made his fortune in the livestock commission market and as a trader in railroad and transportation company stocks. In 1886 Hale and Ream built the seven-story Midland Hotel in Kansas City. Three years later they bought up abandoned rail lines in Toledo, Ohio, and reorganized them into a cable and electric street car system. Hale and Ream must have had an interesting partnership, given the dramatic differences in the two men's lifestyles. Hale stayed close to home and church, his only extravagance being the generosity of his gifts to schools, Congregational missionary work, and other charities. Ream, on the other hand, was a conspicuous capitalist who invested millions in the creation of a Connecticut estate described by the *Tribune* as "truly royal in its size and beauty."

By far the best known of Hale's development projects was the fourteen-story Reliance Building (now known as 32 North State Street). Hale had purchased the valuable but narrow site (which came to be known as "Mr. Hale's Famous Corner") in 1882. The principal tenant of the five-story building that stood on the lot was the First National Bank of Chicago. When the bank moved to new quarters in 1890, Hale announced plans to develop the corner with a retail and professional building "constructed and equipped in the most elegant manner." The plans, drawn by John Wellborn Root, envisioned a steel and glass structure that would go as high as sixteen stories. Such a building would be the tallest yet on State Street.

The prospects for the project were promising. Hale's ground floor and mezzanine level tenant was to be the Carson Pirie Scott department store, which even then was vying with other emporiums for control of choice State Street corners. There was just one small obstacle. Although the bank had moved on, tenants of the upper three floors of the old building had not. Leases for these tenants would not expire for another four years. Hale was under some pressure to begin construction immediately, not only to hold the valuable retail tenant but also to get the project under way before the city imposed a rumored limit on building heights.

The solution found was unusual but not without precedent in Chicago, a town accustomed to the "lifting" of buildings. The builders of the Reliance raised the upper stories of the old building on jacks and proceeded to slip underneath them a new foundation capable of supporting a sixteen-story building. The elegant street level and mezzanine floors to be occupied by Carson's were then constructed, leaving the upper floors of the old building—and its tenants—in place. The plan was that when existing leases expired, the upper floors of the old building would be demolished and construction of the remaining stories of the new building would proceed.

As the work progressed, it appears that Hale, who was financing the building himself, had second thoughts about allocating such a large amount of capital to a project that would not see a full return on rentals for some time to come. Rumors that Hale might sell or lease the property began to circulate. And he did. In 1893 the newspapers announced "A Big Transaction." Hale had sold the State and Washington corner for the sum of $480,000 to Otto Young, a major holder in the Fair department store and owner of a number of other State Street properties. As part of the deal, Young leased the lot back to Hale at very favorable terms for a period of 198 years. Thus Young got the property, a matter of some importance to him. Hale retained ownership of the building and acquired the capital needed to complete it. It was a financing strategy that Young would use again in gaining control of the land and buildings that Carson's later occupied at State and Madison streets.

That transaction completed, work to complete the building proceeded rapidly. The lifting of the old bank building to construct the first stories of the Reliance Building had been considered a remarkable feat, even for Chicago. The speed at which the next twelve stories went up after the old leases expired was even more amazing to observers. "Incredible as it may appear, it is a fact that less than two days were required to run up the steelwork of each of the upper stories," the Chicago *Tribune* exclaimed in 1894.

The light and airy Reliance Building, now listed in the National Registry of Historic Places, was described some seventy years after its construction as "a remarkably advanced structure for its time." Hale's building, however, symbolized much more than Chicago's mastery of skeleton construction. Built on a mere sliver of land, the Reliance was a glass tower soaring skyward from the heart of Chicago's world-famous State Street. It pierced the central city skyline like a needle, visible from the railway yards and industrial centers on the south, the financial district on the west, and the mansions of Chicago's Gold Coast on the north. The Reliance Building, much like New York's twentieth-century Empire State Building, was, in its time, a symbol of the spirit and aspirations of the city.

Hale in the 1890s had suffered recurrent bouts with nephritis, or Bright's Disease, as it was then known. In early October 1898, while returning from a business trip to New York, he suffered a relapse. Hale died at home on the morning of November 16, 1898. He was sixty-two years old.

It seems fitting that the Reliance Building, William E. Hale's last downtown project, would become almost a prototype for twentieth-century steel and glass high-rise construction that would make the elevator, even in Hale's lifetime, the universal denominator of the modern city.

THE INSIDE TRACK

Edward C. Waller
(1845-1931)

Edward C. Waller.
[From *National Cyclopedia of American Biography*—The Newberry Library]

One of the most significant buildings in the history of high-rise architecture was the work of one of the most creative but least known of Chicago's late nineteenth-century developers. The structure was the 1885 Home Insurance Building, the first skyscraper anywhere to use iron and steel skeleton construction. The architect and engineer was William Le Baron Jenney, whose name is still celebrated for the achievement. The developer was Edward Carson Waller, who at a critical time in the evolution of the new technology backed the project not only financially but also with the full force of his personal charisma and his network of friends.

Waller, a real estate broker and property manager, was also the guiding force behind the construction of the equally interesting building known as the Rookery, built a year later through the same Waller-managed syndicate that directed the development of the Home Insurance Building. No less significant than his role in the development of the tall building was Waller's lifelong belief that high-quality, affordable rental housing could be brought within the reach of Chicago's lower-income families. In pursuit of this vision, Waller became one of the earliest and most faithful clients of Frank Lloyd Wright. A confidant of Chicago mayors and a comrade of Daniel Burnham, Edward Waller has been classed with Owen Aldis as one of the great creative patrons of the Chicago school of architecture. He was also one of the founders and leading developers of the village of River Forest. Waller was a man with persuasive ways and imposing presence, described by Wright after their first meeting as "the handsomest and most aristocratic individual I had ever seen."

Edward Waller was born in Maysville, Kentucky, in 1845, one of the ten sons and daughters of Henry Waller, a West Point graduate, Kentucky legislator, and well-known lawyer who was politically active on behalf of the state's favorite son, Henry Clay. Shortly before the Civil War, Henry Waller and his three brothers relocated their families from their homes in Kentucky to Chicago. Edward, James, and William Waller settled on Chicago's North Side, but the Henry Wallers chose the West Side, the heart of Chicago's vigorous and affluent Kentucky colony.

Neighbors of the Wallers across the way on the corner of Jackson Boulevard and Ashland Avenue were the Carter H. Harrisons. Harrison and his son, Carter Harrison II, between them eventually would serve ten terms as mayor of Chicago. Old Kentucky ties were not forgotten in later years when Edward Waller established himself in the business world and the Harrisons garnered political power and great popularity in the city.

Ed Waller had no inclination for law and apparently little interest in formal education. Within the West Side Kentucky enclave, which maintained large land holdings and small farms along with their highly sociable family life-styles, Waller enjoyed the easygoing ways of a popular and prosperous country gentleman. His circle of friends included Daniel H. Burnham, with whom he shared a youthful adventure. In 1868 Burnham, who was a year younger than Waller, failed the entrance examinations at both Yale and Harvard and returned to his father's home in Chicago to contemplate his future. After a year of tutelage in William Le Baron Jenney's firm, Burnham, restless for fame and fortune, joined his school friend Waller in an ambitious, but somewhat misguided, expedition heading west to Nevada mining country.

Burnham and Waller staked claims in White Pine County, Nevada, a slice of terrain near the Utah border that dramatically failed to match the promise of Virginia City's fabled Comstock Lode in the western part of the state. Waller lost a great deal of money in the enterprise, according to a Burnham biographer, and Burnham lost an election. Failing to find fortune, Burnham sought fame. In Nevada he ran, unsuccessfully, for the state senate as the representative from White Pine County. The story goes that the two came home broke, on a cattle train. But the experience solidified a lifelong friendship between Waller and Burnham that influenced many of the in-

Home Insurance Building, northeast corner of La Salle and Adams streets, completed in 1885. Developer Edward Waller backed architect William Le Baron Jenney through storms of controversy over the design of the first building to use iron and steel skeleton construction.
[J. W. Taylor—Chicago Historical Society]

formal relationships and interactions between Chicago's investor-developers and architect-engineers in the boom years of the late nineteenth century.

As a youth, Waller had worked briefly as a grocery clerk on South Water Street, but at the age of twenty-one had gone into the real estate brokerage business. He returned to real estate after the Nevada adventure and established the firm that eventually became the Edward C. Waller Company. Burnham, inspired by the rush of business that followed the 1871 Chicago fire, decided to try his hand again at architecture. The years after the Great Fire were a time of opportunity for both. Waller quickly gained a reputation as a specialist in downtown Chicago real estate, and Burnham similarly cultivated the connections that would later build his practice.

In 1878 Waller moved his family to rustic River Forest, then a community of only twenty homes. The Waller estate, which he named Au Vergne, was a fifteen-acre wooded property nestled in a deep bend of the Des Plaines River. The site today is still prime residential property, a stretch of privately owned riverfront surrounded by Forest Preserve parkland. There Waller built the Queen Anne mansion that was the family home for half a century. By 1882 Waller and his wife Rebecca had four daughters and two sons. Rebecca died in 1883 after giving birth to a third son, who also died three weeks later. Edward Waller, with five children under the age of twelve to raise (the youngest was sent to Virginia to live with an aunt), did not remain a widower for long. In 1884, when he was nearly forty, he married Mary Kirk, the daughter of a River Forest pioneer family. Their daughter, Mary Kirk Waller, was born a year later.

While Waller was establishing his home and family in River Forest, he was also launching two office development projects in Chicago's central business district that would make architectural history: the Home Insurance Building and the Rookery.

Waller organized the Central Safety Deposit Company in 1883 as a vehicle for the construction in 1884-85 of the Chicago headquarters of the New York Home Fire Insurance Company, unleashing a chain of events that were no doubt rooted in the close relationship between Waller and Dan Burnham forged during the Nevada prospecting expedition, if not earlier. Waller's building site, at the corner of La Salle and Adams streets, was just a block north of the new Board of Trade Building. It was a "hot property." Competition for the commission to design the building was keen. The Home Insurance Company announced that the architect for its headquarters building would be chosen in a national contest, to be judged by the building committee of the company.

Burnham's mentor, William Le Baron Jenney, won the competition, but under circumstances that strongly suggest that Jenney, in the words of his biographer, Theodore Turak, had an "inside track" with the judges. The "inside track" very probably was Ed Waller, who could have been expected to communicate a Burnham appeal on behalf of Jenney to the committee. Certainly, the Burnham connection surfaced again in the controversies that continued to swirl around the Home Insurance Building construction. The project was imperiled from the beginning. As the iron frame for the building —so different from anything seen before—began to take shape in 1894, sidewalk superintendents crowded around to scoff at the unthinkable structure. Jenney's rivals, some embittered by the outcome of the competition, were among the critics. By August, the gossip had become dangerous. Rumors that the structure could collapse at any moment, probably with great loss of life, struck fear in the hearts of Home Insurance Company executives.

Construction was suspended while the company dispatched an outside expert to reevaluate Jenney's design. In the resulting standoff, a new consultant was called in. This second "expert" was none other than Dan Burnham. In a secret conference with the committee, Burnham pronounced the plans sound. William B. Mundie, then a draftsman in Jenney's office, recalled that "after Mr. Burnham had spoken, the investigation ended." It is not difficult to imagine the role that Ed Waller played behind the scenes in managing the conflict and saving the project.

Waller played a similar role in the acquisition of the southeast corner of La Salle and Adams streets, opposite the Home Insurance Building, as the site for the famed Rookery, designed by Burnham's partner John Root. The property, known colloquially as "the rookery" and "the old barrack and rat den," was the site of the old city reservoir, which was converted to a library after the fire, and the temporary city hall that had been put up around it. Pigeons and rats notwithstanding, it was a highly desirable corner. But it was not for sale. It was public land, dedicated to school use. Nonetheless, the property was far too valuable to escape the attention of a group the Chicago *Tribune* later described as an "aldermanic gang." In a series of actions in January and February 1885, and amid rumors of intrigue and crooked deals, the council engineered a ninety-nine-year lease of the land, without benefit of competitive bid and at very favorable terms, to a syndicate represented by one Henry S. Everhart. Everhart's bid was not the only one submitted. It was merely the only one considered.

Waller, hearing of the upcoming Everhart transaction, had submitted an offer—which was ignored by the council—as had

"The Old Barrack and Rat Den" (library and temporary city hall). The old city reservoir built on public lands at La Salle and Adams streets was converted to a library after the Great Fire of 1871, and a temporary city hall was put up around it. The property, a favorite roosting place for pigeons, was known colloquially as "the Rookery." The name stayed with it, even after the corner was acquired in 1885 by Edward C. Waller for a group of investors who would have preferred to name their building "The Central." [From *Chicago and Its Makers*]

two other interested parties. The prevailing interpretation of events, as set forth by the *Tribune*, was that the Everhart group was paying off aldermen (to the tune of $40,000), that the cash for those who cooperated with their vote was being held by "a leading Democratic gambling boss," and that these funds were themselves the proceeds of an earlier stock swindle. Speculation was that the group would build a space-holder structure and then sell the leasehold at a huge profit. Everhart, who had acquired three other leases in the area in the months preceding, was paid a flat-rate bonus of $25,000 for each transaction.

In a February 16 veto message, Mayor Carter Harrison I, the Waller family's old friend and neighbor, spelled out in generous detail the improprieties and loopholes in the Everhart deal, including the assertion that the council had no power to make a lease. The aldermen and the mayor were at impasse for several months, time enough for the parties to marshal their forces. In May, when Waller presented his offer for the third time, it was stalled by the so-called aldermanic gang, but in a sudden reversal was approved by unanimous vote the following day. Although the terms did not differ significantly from the Everhart lease, the mayor offered no objection, and the *Tribune*, which had followed the matter very closely up to this point, offered no explanation other than to note that Waller and Harrison had conferred after the vote about the schedule for removing the old building.

The Rookery, 209 South La Salle Street, 1886. Although Owen F. Aldis spoke for the majority shareholders' decisions regarding the Rookery, designed by Burnham and Root, Edward C. Waller is remembered as the man "who conceived the Rookery and remained its guiding genius during its long life." [Barnes-Crosby—Chicago Historical Society]

Chicago builder Henry Ericsson, not a party to the transaction, was never satisfied that all concerned had the public good at heart. He commented in his memoirs that "there was some looking askance" at the Waller lease deal, noting that had the property been held for sale for the schools, it eventually would have been worth "hundreds of millions of dollars." And there were other objectors. Work on removal of the "old barracks" began in June, but was halted when a rival bidder group filed suit seeking to annul the Waller lease, charging Mayor Harrison, City Comptroller Theodore Gurney, and Waller with "conspiracy."

The legal cloud was not lifted until December, at which time the lease, transferred through Waller to the Central Safety Deposit Company, was finally signed. In addition to Waller, stockholders included the Brooks brothers; their property manager Owen F. Aldis; Norman B. Ream, a Waller associate in other investments; elevator magnate William E. Hale; and Daniel Burnham. Together they invested $1.5 million to build the Rookery. (Peter Brooks, in a letter written in October, had suggested that Burnham and Root be selected as the architects. Waller, very likely, had the same intent.)

When the trust announced its officers, it was clear that the Brooks estate had taken the lion's share of the stock in the Rookery building syndicate. Aldis assumed Waller's former role as president of the Central Safety Deposit Company, and Waller became secretary. Waller chafed under the constraints of the relationship, as also did Aldis, who kept a close eye on matters relating to building management and leasing, which by contract were Waller's domain. Aldis, as his correspondence with Peter Brooks reveals, saw his duty as Brooks's agent with punctilious clarity. Waller could not have been pleased when, in 1889, Aldis asked Hale and Ream act with him as an auditing committee to straighten out Waller's books. It may not have helped. Five years later, Aldis complained that Waller was closemouthed and "a little too secretive" in sharing financial statements with Aldis. He was careful to add, "Now I think Mr. Waller a competent and careful man. He rents well and he manages well." But, Aldis concludes, "he is not a judge of bookkeeping."

Waller may well have felt that Aldis, backed by the Brooks brothers dollars, had in effect stolen the building from him. Resentments probably ran quite high. Thomas E. Tallmadge, who as a young architect shared offices with Burnham in the building, later wrote that it was Waller "who conceived the Rookery and remained its guiding genius during his long life." He records Waller's own belief that "here was developed the modern office building plan."

The Rookery Lobby, c. 1907.
Edward C. Waller was instrumental in securing for his friend Frank Lloyd Wright the commission to remodel the Rookery lobby in 1905, giving Wright's work a showcase in downtown Chicago. This center court is at the bottom of a large interior space that brought light and air to all the offices not facing on the street.
[Barnes-Crosby—Chicago Historical Society]

Edward Waller stood apart from his peers in the close-knit group of Chicago's financial and business leaders in the 1880s and '90s. While his position as a key player among the city's business elite was unquestioned, as a private citizen he spent more time in building Au Vergne, in the pursuit of light farming, and at golf and whist in River Forest and Oak Park than in the parlors and walnut-paneled chambers of the downtown businessmen's clubs. Life at Au Vergne was gracious and hospitable. Frank Lloyd Wright was a regular visitor, as were "Uncle Dan" Burnham and the Carter Harrison II family. In his memoirs, Harrison described Waller as "the feudal baron of River Forest." Mrs. Harrison wrote of the "white asparagus, mushrooms, strawberries and broiled chicken" served at Waller dinners, all raised on the eighty-acre Waller farm in northeast River Forest and "never surpassed anywhere." The Waller Sunday dinner table, she wrote, was always set for twenty to fifty guests.

The twenty-four-room Waller home, with its broad porches and twelve marble fireplaces, acquired a memorable addition with the ballroom-pavilion designed by Frank Lloyd Wright and connected to the main house by an all-glass arcade. The pavilion was the scene of the luminous family Christmas and dancing parties that always included Wright as a special guest. The Wallers also entertained at their Charlevoix, Michigan, summer home, which in spite of its distance was the site of a Chicago summer colony. Burnham, a frequent Waller guest at Charlevoix, bought his own lot in the Waller tract in 1910. In his diary entries for 1906, Burnham records something of the fabric of the Wallers' leisure pursuits at Charlevoix with entries such as "Went to Charlevoix, Mich to visit E. C. Waller. Played golf, sailed in afternoon, played cards at night. Stayed whole weekend."

In 1888 Frank Lloyd Wright moved to Oak Park, the sister community to River Forest. He was then a young draftsman working with Dankmar Adler and Louis Sullivan to complete Ferdinand Peck's Auditorium Building. Wright's move to Oak Park marked the beginning of his long friendship with Ed Waller—and produced his first independent commission: the William H. Winslow home, built in 1893 on Auvergne Place on a lot purchased from Waller.

Waller's admiration for Wright extended in many directions. In 1894 he organized a dinner party to introduce Wright to Daniel Burnham, who had been director of works for the World's Columbian Exposition. Waller had a purpose in mind. After dinner, Burnham made Wright an extraordinary offer. He would sponsor six years of study in Paris and Rome for Wright, including support for his wife and children, if Wright would return to work with Burnham's firm as a designing partner. Waller strongly urged Wright to accept the offer, advising him to "think of your future, think of your family." Wright declined, recognizing that Burnham's firm was by then strongly identified with the classical revival movement in architecture, an idiom that Wright did not wish to emulate.

If Waller was disappointed over Wright's rejection of Burnham's offer, the event did not diminish his admiration of Wright's potential as an architect, nor did it lessen his efforts on Wright's behalf. His personal patronage of Wright extended over three decades and included fifteen or more commissions, beginning with their work in 1895 on the prototype Waller Apartments building and its addition, the Francisco Terrace apartment house. The Wallers' own dining room, the ballroom, and other additions to Waller's property, including a copper-canopied chicken house, were done by Wright between 1898 and 1901. In 1902-03 Wright did two designs for Charlevoix residences for Waller. In 1909 a bathing pavilion at

**Francisco Terrace
Apartments entranceway.**
Edward C. Waller and Frank
Lloyd Wright collaborated at
the turn of the century to
provide quality, low-cost
housing for Chicago's rapidly
growing working class. Their
first West Side project, the
Waller Apartments, was
followed by the much more
expansive Francisco Terrace
courtyard complex at 253
Francisco Avenue.
[Grant Manson,—Oak Park [Ill.] Public
Library]

Charlevoix was added to the growing list of Waller commissions given to Wright. Waller also brought Wright other work, including the landmark Robert W. Roloson row houses on Calumet Avenue, built for the father of a Waller son-in-law; clubhouses for the River Forest Golf Club and the River Forest Tennis Club; and the famed Midway Gardens restaurant and entertainment complex, built in 1913-14 by Waller's son Ed Waller Jr. and considered to be one of Wright's most significant achievements.

Waller was instrumental in securing for Wright the commission to remodel the Rookery lobby in 1905, giving Wright's work a showcase in the downtown business center. He also worked with Wright on a number of major but ultimately unexecuted projects, including the long-planned, but ill-starred development of the South Side Cheltenham Beach property, the massive Lexington Terraces apartment complex, and designs for three prototype houses planned by Waller when he was contemplating development of Waller Farm as a residential subdivision. Waller's patronage of Wright reveals something about the mind of the man. As conventional as Waller's life as a prosperous businessman may seem, it can be assumed that, like many developers, he possessed a strong artistic and technological orientation. It was that combination of daring and vision that would predispose Waller to support such untried structural work as the innovative Home Insurance Building and the equally untried designs by Frank Lloyd Wright, even at a time when Wright's work was ridiculed by more traditional critics.

Waller began thinking about the need for decent low-cost rental housing for Chicago's rapidly growing working class around the time that he met Wright, and soon afterward (1895) the two began their collaboration on the Waller Apartments at 2840-58 West Walnut Street, on the city's rapidly growing West Side. The Waller Apartments, which are still in use, are considered to have been the first subsidized housing project in Chicago—in the sense that the developer held the anticipated return on his investment to three percent, half the yield common among real estate projects in this period (including that of George Pullman's company town built to house Pullman Palace Car workers).

The precedent, however, was set. In his prototype Waller Apartments and Francisco Terrace developments, Edward Waller had proven that construction of well-designed, low-cost housing was feasible. Other developers and architects followed Waller's example, although not in great numbers. Projects on Woodlawn Avenue and South Park Terrace (on South Parkway, now King Drive), designed by H. Waterman, followed the plan of the Waller developments. Later philanthropic projects for low-income families, such as the Michigan Boulevard Apartments (at Forty-seventh Street) built by Julius Rosenwald in 1929 and the Marshall Field Garden Apartments built in 1929-30 on Sedgwick Street on the North Side, adopted the model created by Waller in 1895. A 1987 Commission on Chicago Landmarks study recognized Waller's "pioneering quest to set standards for the development of low-cost housing" in Chicago.

Residential development was not unfamiliar terrain for Waller when he commissioned apartment houses. As early as 1890, he was improving large lots in River Forest with handsome Victorian mansions, many of which are still standing. In these years, Waller also served ex officio as director of public works for the village, involving himself in sewage and drainage projects, development of a municipal water system, road construction, and establishment of a modest business district. In later years, he built the River Forest State Bank, which he served as a founding director, and subdivided the verdant Waller Farm for development as the North Woods residential district.

Edward Waller remained active in his downtown real estate office and managed his affairs in River Forest until 1930, when he retired from business at the age of eighty-five. He died at Au Vergne in 1931 of complications of arteriosclerosis. The Waller home was demolished in 1939. Mary Kirk Waller, who moved to a Chicago lakefront highrise, which she shared with her daughter, lived to be ninety-nine. While Waller's name is remembered by very few, the contribution he made to the city of Chicago is as current as if he lived today. The magnificent restoration of the Rookery, completed in 1992, is an enduring monument to the landmark building's principal developer.

COMPANY TOWN

George M. Pullman
(1831-97)

George M. Pullman.
[Chicago Historical Society]

Whatever history's judgment may be of George Pullman the man, few would deny his accomplishment in creating on the shores of Chicago's Lake Calumet the nation's most perfectly planned industrial town. Although the town of Pullman failed, and failed dramatically, as an experiment in social planning, the plan for the town itself was an astonishing work of human ingenuity.

George Pullman, the founder of the Pullman Palace Car Company, built the Pullman works in 1881 to be a wholly self-contained industrial plant for the manufacture and maintenance of railroad sleeping cars and other rolling stock. To assure a reliable and, Pullman hoped, contented pool of laborers and skilled workers to run the massive Pullman works, Pullman built a model town around it. The town, like the industrial plant, provided—on the surface—everything that could be needed for the perfectly ordered proletarian life.

Early Chicago's prolific historian Arthur T. Andreas was rhapsodic in his judgment of Pullman's achievement and took pains to point out that the town had not sprung up by magic but was the work solely of its developer. "No Aladdin save George M. Pullman erected the city, and in the brain of its creator every detail had an existence ere its prototype was produced in material form," Andreas wrote. Pullman's lawyer, William G. Beale, made the same point in fewer words. Beale described Pullman as "the biggest brained businessman" he ever knew.

The railway sleeper car magnate's beginnings were hardly auspicious. George Mortimer Pullman was one of ten children born to John and Emily Pullman in Brocton, a town in Chautauqua County in western New York. In 1845, at the age of fourteen, George abandoned his studies to take a job as a clerk in a nearby village store. He soon joined an older brother in the cabinetmaking trade in Oneida, New York, a town that was itself the site of an experiment in communal living in the years between 1848 and 1881. When his father died in Albion, in western New York, in 1853, Pullman moved there to help support his mother and younger brothers and sisters. He found work raising and moving buildings along the route of the Erie Canal, which was then being widened and deepened. During this time, he heard stories from Great Lakes shippers about Chicago, a city whose star was rising, but which was literally sinking into the mud. Pullman heard opportunity knocking. He arrived in Chicago in 1859, offering his services as a house raiser. In short time, he earned a place in local legend for his role in raising Chicago's famed Tremont House, a five-story hotel that occupied a full city block. Five thousand jackscrews, manned by five hundred men, were used to lift the building six feet to the new grade. True to Pullman's oft-quoted promise, not a wall nor a teacup was cracked.

During the period that Pullman was raising and moving Chicago buildings, he was also formulating his ideas for a better railway sleeping car. The idea was to develop a jolt-free car to replace the bunkhouses on wheels (known as "rattlers") that in the 1850s were the only sleeping accommodation available to the long-distance rail traveler. The design for the convertible sleeping car that was to make Pullman his massive fortune was born in 1863. Working out of a Chicago and Alton line carbarn in downstate Bloomington, Pullman spent $18,000 of his own funds and a year of his time creating the prototype, which he named the Pioneer.

The Pioneer received national attention when Pullman dispatched it to Washington in April 1865 to bear the body of Abraham Lincoln back to Illinois. (It is an interesting footnote to history that thirty-two years later, Lincoln's son, Robert Todd Lincoln, succeeded Pullman as president of the Pullman Car Company.) George Pullman knew how to make news. Shortly after volunteering the Pioneer to carry Lincoln home, he invited a group of Chicago opinion leaders, including the editor of the Chicago *Tribune,* for a ride in the Pioneer. At the end of the journey (which included a nap), the *Tribune* reported, Pullman "explained his labors, and the hopes he entertained regarding the invention which was to make him famous and rich beyond the dreams of avarice." The reporter who recorded those words could hardly have known how apt his phrase, "rich beyond the dreams of avarice," may have been in reference to George M. Pullman, who in later times was described as "the nastiest man ever to rake in a dollar from the free enterprise system."

In 1867, the year that the Pullman Palace Car Company was incorporated, Pullman married Harriet (Hattie) Sanger, the daughter of an early Chicago settler family. The life-style of the Pullmans was lavish, and their mansion on Prairie Avenue became the scene of some of Chicago's grandest receptions. Pullman himself had few friends, but among those few was his Prairie Avenue neighbor Marshall Field, with whom he lunched daily at what became known as "the millionaires' table" of a downtown Chicago club.

By 1879 the Pullman Palace Car Company had become one of the most successful industrial enterprises in America. It operated out of four major locations, including shops in Atlanta and Detroit. Pullman, seeing the need to consolidate, quietly began buying up three thousand acres of prairie and marshlands on the shores of Lake Calumet, twelve miles south of the Chicago city limits. A second corporation known as the Pull-

Pullman houses, c. 1881.
George M. Pullman built a model town on the shores of Lake Calumet, south of Chicago, to house the workers of his Pullman Palace Car Company. Although the concept of a self-contained industrial town failed as a social experiment, the design represented a masterful effort in urban planning.
[Chicago Historical Society]

**Pullman Administration
Building and Water Tower.**
Pullman's 4,300-acre industrial
town included 1,400 housing
units, a library, a hospital, a
market hall, a church, a hotel,
sports facilities, and other
amenities—all designed to
return a profit to George
Pullman and stockholders in
the Pullman Land Association
and all eventually beyond the
means of Pullman workers.
[Chicago Historical Society]

man Land Association was established to develop the tract,
with Pullman as president and majority stockholder. The land
was drained, water lines were brought in, and a gas works was
established.

Pullman hired a young architect, Solon S. Beman, and landscape architect Nathan F. Barrett to begin the work of designing a town. Barrett had introduced Beman to Pullman in 1879
when Pullman was planning to build a summer house on his
property at Long Branch, New Jersey. Beman, who was born
in Brooklyn, had just opened a small architectural office in
New York City and had formed an informal association with
Barrett. Pullman was pleased with Beman's designs and asked
him to come to Chicago to supervise renovation of the Pullman home on Prairie Avenue. In December 1879 Pullman
asked Beman and Barrett to prepare preliminary designs for
the new town that he was planning to build. It was an incredible opportunity—and a huge undertaking, which was accomplished with remarkable speed.

Ground for the six-hundred-acre development was broken in April 1880. Work on the plants, community buildings, and 1,750 residential units moved rapidly. The first family moved into their new rental home in January 1881, and in the summer of that year, the factories of Pullman produced the first sleeping cars to be manufactured solely on this site. The industrial plant was itself the perfect machine, with everything needed for the manufacture of the Pullman Palace Car in place. In Pullman's mind, the acquisition and maintenance of a skilled labor force was a management matter to be treated in roughly the same manner as the acquisition and maintenance of the great Corliss Engine that powered the Pullman shops. Pullman was concerned, as well he should have been, about wildcat railroad strikes and the escalation of labor unrest in the city. The Lake Calumet site was sufficiently distant, Pullman reasoned, to insulate his plant and its workers from the social disorder and restive mobs he had seen in Chicago in 1877, as well from as the contaminating influence of the labor unions that were then being organized in the city. There is no doubt that Pullman saw his town on one level as a planning experiment—an attempt to create orderly development in a period in Chicago's history in which the urban landscape was growing rapidly and without control. But more important, he expected that he could also create a stable, sober (and captive) work force by providing a controlled environment, molded in every detail to enhance the physical welfare and moral well-being (as he defined it) of the several thousand Pullman Palace Car Company employees who lived in the compound (many other Pullman employees lived in Chicago and commuted to Pullman by train).

The town of Pullman, true to the founder's vision, was in every physical respect the ideal community. The village was laid out all in one sweep, with broad streets, parks and recreation areas, and community buildings set out in their proper (and "harmonious") place. Solon Beman, Pullman's architect, was responsible for the design of every structure, and so was able to create a uniformity of roof and lot line and a balance of mass and open space that is extraordinary even by the standards of today's planned developments. Pullman quickly became America's most famous planned industrial town. It attracted international attention during the 1893 World's Columbian Exposition, when special trains were run to Pullman carrying visitors from around the world to admire the picture-perfect development. But the picture concealed a stark truth: The town was a disaster waiting to happen.

Few workers were able to use the five-thousand-volume Pullman library because they could not afford the required an-

nual fee. The beautiful church on 111th Street went largely un-
used because no congregation could afford the $3,600 rent
Pullman charged for the building. The town's water was
bought from the Township of Hyde Park and resold to tenants
at a 10 percent markup. When the financial panic of 1893
swept the nation, orders for the several types of railroad cars
that Pullman manufactured diminished. George Pullman responded to the loss of orders for new cars by laying off Pullman Palace Car Company employees and then cutting wages
of those who remained by an average of 25 percent. At the
same time, he instructed the Pullman Land Association to
maintain rents at the previous inflated level.

History generally views the town of Pullman as the failed
experiment of a benevolent capitalist, but in truth the town
was conceived from the beginning as a profit-making venture.
Although George Pullman felt free to cut workers' wages, he
made no compromises when it came to the Pullman Land Association profits. Throughout the crisis, he continued to pay
eight-percent dividends to stockholders and maintained some
$25 million in undivided profits. He ignored Illinois Gover-
nor John Peter Altgeld's attempts to intervene on behalf of
the workers and refused to negotiate with their representatives
in Eugene V. Debs's new American Railway Union. Pullman
workers went out on strike on May 11, 1894. The strike became a national issue when union members across the country
were ordered to cut Pullman cars loose from trains. In July,
President Grover Cleveland sent four thousand federal troops
to Chicago to occupy the town and restore order.

The Pullman railroad strike was broken, but so was the nation's image of Pullman as the perfect industrial town. In the
late 1890s the Illinois Supreme Court decreed that ownership
of the town's land and buildings be transferred from the Pullman Land Association to private hands. On May 7, 1907, the
town property went on the market. Although the town passed
out of the company's control, the Pullman company itself remained one of America's great industrial forces for as long as
the railroad remained preeminent in America. The last Pullman Palace Car was manufactured in 1981, exactly a century
from the date the town was founded.

George M. Pullman was an industrialist, capitalist, and developer of far-ranging abilities. He built and equipped New
York's Metropolitan Elevated Railway, in defiance of New
York rail titan Commodore Cornelius Vanderbilt. He was the
first president of the New York Metro and personally held
one-third of the stock. He also built and provided cars for
rapid transit lines in a dozen other cities.

In 1885 he built the eight-story Pullman Building at Michi-

Pullman Building, Michigan Avenue at Adams Street.
The eight-story Pullman Building, built in 1885, housed the offices of the Pullman company, with the higher floors given over to luxury residences.
[From *Select Chicago, Illustrated in Albertype,*1889—Chicago Historical Society]

gan Avenue and Adams Street. The building, designed by Beman, was a mixed-use structure that was unique in its time. Three floors of the building housed the offices of the Pullman company, and the remainder was given over to apartments, including Beman's own and those of his assistants, Irving and Allen Pond. They were Chicago's first lakefront luxury apartments. Beman later designed Chicago's 1890 Grand Central Station, which was considered one of the finest of nineteenth-century American railroad stations. His Merchant Tailors' building at the 1893 World's Columbian Exposition became the prototype for many Christian Science churches. He was also the architect for the first and second Studebaker buildings (now the Fine Arts Building) on Michigan Avenue, completed in 1895.

George Pullman died of a massive heart attack on October 19, 1897. He was sixty-six. Norman B. Ream, a Prairie Avenue friend and neighbor, was summoned by terrified house guests at three o'clock in the morning to be with Pullman in what would be his last moments. Ream's comment to the newspapers the following day was intended to be laudatory: "Every effort in his business life was for the benefit of the stockholders and the company." The quoted remarks of another friend, General T. T. Eckert, president of the Western Union Telegraph Company of New York, were more ambiguous: "So George Pullman is dead. Well, well!" Chicago Mayor Carter

Harrison II's testimonial was creatively circumspect. Harrison recognized Pullman as "one of the most widely known Americans in the world" and stated that "those who knew him immediately loved him." Harrison was quick to add the caveat that he himself "had no personal acquaintance" with the man.

The Pullman interests could not assure that George Pullman's embittered enemies would not dance on his grave, but they did all that was humanly possible to make sure that his final resting place would not be desecrated. Pullman was buried at Chicago's Graceland Cemetery under cover of darkness and beneath tons of concrete reinforced with steel rails. His last will was executed just a month before his death. By its terms, Pullman was scarcely more generous to his family than he had been to his employees. His daughters, Florence and Harriet, received property and $1 million each, but Pullman's twin sons, George Jr. and Walter, were provided an annuity amounting to no more than $3,000 annually. Mrs. Pullman eventually was able to break the will by claiming her dower rights under Illinois law. She received a one-third life interest in Pullman's real estate holdings and one-third of his personal property. Hattie Pullman's action in this case was understood to be an effort to provide an adequate legacy for her sons.

The Pullman District of Chicago today encompasses a sixteen-block area in the vicinity of 111th Street and Cottage Grove Avenue that was designated a national landmark in 1970 and a Chicago landmark in 1972. To George Pullman's credit as a developer, the town is much more than a historical curiosity. It is a viable neighborhood, home to hundreds of families who now live comfortably in the harmonious surroundings that Pullman envisioned in his grand design.

LAND BARON

Marshall Field
(1834-1906)

Marshall Field.
[Chicago Historical Society]

When Chicago's great retailer Marshall Field died in 1906, he left one of the nation's largest fortunes and a last will and testament so extraordinary that the federal government rewrote inheritance laws to assure that no one could do again what Field had done. The offending feature of Field's will was the provision that the bulk of his $120 million estate be held in trust for his two grandsons, then aged ten and twelve, until the older of the two reached the age of fifty. The effect was to withhold from the government for some forty years what would have been considerable inheritance taxes on the Field fortune. The more interesting provision of the will was the requirement that one-half of the legacy should be continuously invested in real estate. Field even spelled out the conditions that would govern this investment, including the instruction that no land was to be leased unless the lessee agreed to put up "substantial modern buildings."

The will accurately reflected the personality and style of its maker. Its terms, as unusual as they may have been, were entirely consistent with the mind of a man who learned early in life that all things come to those who wait. He was right on that count. By September 1943, when Field's older grandson, Marshall Field III, turned fifty, the value of the Field holdings had appreciated through real estate and stock investments from $120 million to an estimated $300 million.

Marshall Field was first and always a merchant—the founding spirit of Chicago's world-famous Marshall Field department store and the undisputed king among Chicago's nineteenth-century merchant princes. It is for this he is remembered. In the second phase of his career, however, Field became also the largest single owner of Chicago business district property and was a major force in shaping the development of the city in the years after the Great Fire.

Field was born in 1834 on the family farm in the Berkshire Hills of Massachusetts, near the town of Conway (for which one of the office buildings developed by the Field Estate was named). He was the third of the seven children raised in the hardworking, God-fearing, Congregationalist family headed by John Field and his wife Fidelia. Young Marshall, who had a head for figures, left the farm at the age of sixteen to take a position as a clerk in a dry goods store in the little town of Pittsfield, some twenty-five miles from home (the namesake of another of the Field Estate buildings). Field had acquaintances in Chicago, including Charles B. Farwell, a young city official who had married a Pittsfield schoolteacher. In 1856, at the age of twenty-two, Field moved to Chicago and became a clerk with the dry goods business then known as Cooley, Wadsworth and Company, in which Farwell's younger brother, John V. Farwell, was a junior partner. In time the firm became Farwell and Field, with Levi Z. Leiter, the head bookkeeper and accountant, as a junior partner.

Field worked long hours, socialized little, and was able to accumulate a considerable amount of capital through wartime investments in real estate and in bank and railroad stocks. Late in 1864 Potter Palmer, Farwell and Field's greatest competitor, startled Chicagoans by announcing his decision to retire from the dry goods business. He offered his company to Field, who put up $260,000, and Leiter, who bought in for $130,000. Palmer left another $330,000 in the business and remained a silent partner until such time as Field and Leiter could buy him out. In 1867 the firm became Field, Leiter and Company.

Thus in a period of not quite ten years in Chicago, the frugal New Englander had risen from a position as a $400-a-year clerk in a dry goods business to become head of a large company destined for extraordinary success. In 1873, secure in his place as one of Chicago's most respected businessmen, Field established his wife Nannie, their six-year-old son Marshall Jr., and infant daughter Ethel in an elegant red brick home at 1905 Prairie Avenue. The Field mansion was austere on the outside, befitting Marshall Field's plainspoken New England style. But the interior of the house, designed by Richard Morris Hunt, architect to the Vanderbilts, was opulent to the extreme, reflecting Mrs. Field's artistic interests and social aspirations. Field's marriage to Nannie, like his other partnerships—

Levi Zeigler Leiter. Marshall Field and his early partner Levi Leiter had a contentious relationship, but by 1881 they had accumulated between them more real estate than anyone else in the city.
[Chicago Historical Society]

Marshall Field's Store [Singer Building], 1896. This was the third Field store at this State Street site. The first, Potter Palmer's "Marble Palace," was destroyed in the Great Fire of 1871. The second, built by the Singer company, burned in 1877. The Singer company rebuilt, and then sold the building to Field. The State Street portions of today's Marshall Field's were built between 1902 and 1907. [J. W. Taylor—Chicago Historical Society]

including those with Farwell and Leiter—did not run smoothly. Mrs. Field, who was said to be chronically ill, spent increasingly longer periods in Europe, where she traveled in search of cures. Sometimes Field and the children accompanied her, but they did so less and less frequently as time went on. She moved permanently to the South of France in 1892 and died there in 1896.

The year 1868 marked the beginning of a decade of the best of times and the worst of times for Field, Leiter and Company. The best of times followed the firm's rise to the status of the city's paramount mercantile house, the jewel of State Street. The worst of times were bracketed by the destruction of the beautiful State Street store in the 1871 Chicago fire and the loss of the store to fire again in 1877. Potter Palmer had done Field a favor by selecting him as heir to the prosperous Palmer dry goods business. Field returned the favor by leading the move of Chicago's great retail stores from Lake Street to Palmer's State Street development district. The 1868 reopening of the Field, Leiter and Company retail store in Palmer's six-story "marble palace" at the northeast corner of State and Washington streets was the social event of the season. Field begrudged Palmer the $50,000 annual rental, but welcomed the astonishing increase in trade that followed the move.

The ordeals of the 1870s began over the night of October 8, 1871, and continued through the next day as three hundred thousand Chicagoans helplessly watched the Great Fire level much of their city. In the early hours, Field fought the fire side by side with his employees in the vain hope of saving the building and its contents. At dawn on October 9, the wind-driven

State Street, looking north from Madison Street, 1889.
In the 1880s the street was the shopping capital of the Midwest, and the Marshall Field and Company store, at the center of this photo, was its grandest emporium.
[Inter-State Photo Service, from *Chicago and Its Makers*]

fire took a sudden turn, and Field was forced to abandon the building. The employees barely escaped, carrying as much of the remaining stock as could be loaded with them on the last wagons out. Leiter clutched a satchel filled with insurance policies he had rescued from the building vault.

Field and Leiter moved quickly to make their services available to a city whose populace would be in desperate need of goods of every kind. Such stock as they had been able to save from the fire had been carried to the barn at Leiter's home on Calumet Avenue near Twentieth Street. Merchandise ordered and already in transit from the East was intercepted and stored in an abandoned railroad roundhouse in La Porte, Indiana. Within two weeks Field and Leiter were back in business, operating out of an old Chicago City Railway barn at Twentieth and State streets.

As both a merchant and an investor in downtown property, Field was not above taking advantage of the chaos that followed the fire. With his keen sense for bargains in real estate, he snapped up properties that he judged would lie in the path of new growth. Sometimes he combined the roles of merchant, investor, and developer, as he did when he leased the northeast corner of Madison and Market streets within days after the fire and quickly put up a large new building to house the company's wholesale business. It was a shrewd move, characteristic of Field's strategy as a developer in this period. The sailors' boarding houses and taverns that dominated this stretch of Market Street (now South Wacker Drive) had been swept away in the first leap of the fire across the river from the West Side. The area's reputation was seedy, but the location was very favorable for Field's purposes, being readily accessible to buyers arriving by rail from the North and West sides of the city. Moving quickly, Field was able to lease the land at prefire prices. Following his lead, other dry goods firms, including Farwell, began moving their wholesale operations to the area. Within a matter of months, property values in the district had increased by 50 percent.

To finance reconstruction of the Palmer House hotel, Potter Palmer sold the Field store's choice State and Washington corner to the Singer Sewing Machine Company, which built a five-story glass-domed structure that was even grander than the marble palace that burned. On October 9, 1873, exactly two years from the day of the fire, Field, Leiter and Company reopened their retail division in the Singer Building at State and Washington—their joy in the occasion dampened only by the $75,000 a year in rent demanded by Singer.

Four years later, fire again struck the Field, Leiter store, and only the outer walls were left standing. The Singer Company

Marshall Field Wholesale Store [Adams, Quincy, Franklin and Wells streets]. Field chose the famed architect Henry Hobson Richardson to design his massive wholesale house. The seven-story building, completed in 1885, housed eighteen hundred employees. The building was destroyed in 1930 to make way for a parking lot. [Chicago Historical Society]

rebuilt on the State and Washington corner, but Field had decided he would no longer be at the mercy of a landlord. He would own the property. Leiter was entrusted by Field with concluding the negotiations for the purchase when Field found it necessary to be in New York. The deal very nearly fell through. Leiter, a man of imperious manner, refused to budge from his first offer of $500,000. The Singer group was equally firm in its asking price of $700,000. Wearied of Leiter, the Singer Company turned around and leased the building to a competing dry goods firm, Carson, Pirie and Company.

Field returned from New York in time to head off disaster, but it had been a close call. At risk was his hegemony over State Street and the claim he had staked for his store on the prime State and Washington corner. He eventually got the building, but at Singer's price, plus a $100,000 bonus he was forced to pay Sam Carson and John T. Pirie in return for their agreement to give up the lease. The experience must have been very painful to a man of Field's rigid and thrifty disposition.

Leiter's bungling of the Singer lease marked the beginning of the end of Field's long-running but always contentious partnership with Leiter. By 1880 the relationship had reached the end of its frayed rope. Field forced Leiter to sell his interest in the company, reportedly for a very low price. In early 1881 the firm became Marshall Field and Company. The split unleashed a flurry of speculation about the details of the deal. To Field's horror, an enterprising newspaper reporter searching out the terms of the dissolution of the partnership ended up exposing the full extent of Field's enormous real estate holdings, and of Leiter's, most of which were entirely unrelated to the dry goods business. The reporter concluded that "individually and collectively they are the largest real estate owners in the city."

Field's distress over the disclosure of the extent of his land investments was not great enough, however, to curtail his continuing acquisition of property. By 1885 he controlled the entire square block bounded by Adams, Quincy, Wells, and Franklin streets (just east of today's Sears Tower), where he proceeded to build a new wholesale store building to replace the one he built immediately after the 1871 fire. The architect of the Madison and Market wholesale building is unknown, but the architect that Field selected for his new wholesale store was one of the best-known and admired architects of his day: Henry Hobson Richardson.

The new seven-story Marshall Field Wholesale Store did for Field, the merchant, what Field, the developer, intended. It was a strong, functional, strategically located building that encompassed twelve acres of floor space and housed eighteen hundred employees. But the building did more than that for Chicago. It was a Richardson masterpiece, one that has been considered the finest expression of his spare Romanesque style. A powerful presence in the central business district, the store was one of the few buildings that Louis Sullivan openly admired, as can be seen in his own designs for the 1889 Auditorium Building and Theater. The building was demolished in 1930, but the Auditorium endures as a Chicago landmark.

Back on State Street, Field proceeded with all deliberate speed to realize his plan—and Palmer's—to make Chicago's State Street one of the world's great shopping districts. He reasoned that a concentration of quality emporiums around the Field store, and the increased traffic they would generate, would not only improve his store's sales volume but would enhance also the value of his personal real estate holdings in the area. First, he lured the Mandel Brothers to State Street by offering them a lease on the property on the northeast corner of State and Madison, which Field had owned since 1873. He then encouraged the Schlesinger and Mayer store to move to the valuable southeast State and Madison corner, which Leiter had acquired in the breakup of the partnership, and which would later become the site of Carson Pirie Scott and Company's famed Louis Sullivan-designed building.

Field then set out to acquire the remaining property in the block bounded by State, Washington, Wabash, and Randolph streets, where the Marshall Field and Company retail store stood. In 1887 he succeeded in buying Leiter's remaining interest in the State-and-Washington land and building. Six additional purchases on Washington Street and Wabash Avenue were recorded in July 1892. That year Field began the massive construction program that led ultimately to the expansion of the Field retail store buildings over the entire block and into the twenty-story Field annex building on Wabash and Washington. All of the five buildings in the Marshall Field's block and the annex building were designed by D. H. Burnham and Company. Only two were completed in Field's lifetime.

After the breakup with Leiter, Field stepped up his investment not only in downtown real estate but also in securities of flourishing corporations, especially railroads and banks. (He was, for example, one of the largest stockholders in his good friend George Pullman's railway car company.) But the departed Leiter remained an irritant. Leiter sued Field at least twice in the years immediately after the dissolution of their partnership—in one case requiring Field to physically partition into two halves a jointly owned building. Leiter's harassment did not change the course of history, but it did have a certain nuisance value that Field did not forget.

Nicknamed "Silent Marsh," Field was a man of few words, but it was his habit that those few words should be the last ones. This turned out to be the case in his dealings with the irascible Levi Leiter. He had only to wait for the opportunity. This came in the winter of 1897-98 when Leiter's son Joseph took a fling in the grain market, thinking that he had an airtight corner on winter wheat. His scheme collapsed, and he lost $20 million. To preserve the family name, Leiter was forced to put much of his property up for sale, including the prized southeast State and Madison corner occupied by the Schlesinger and Mayer department store. Field was ready to buy, and to pay cash. Leiter, who had not spoken to Field for fifteen years, was compelled to go his former partner, hat in hand, to close the deal.

The Leiter sale of the State and Madison property to Field generated as much interest in Field's real estate holdings as had the dissolution of the partnership in 1881. At the time of the Field-Leiter State-and-Madison transaction, the real estate press published a list of nineteen properties in the central business district alone owned outright by Field, with a total value, according to tax commission records, in excess of $23 million. In 1904 the Chicago *Record-Herald* announced that "Marshall Field pays taxes on a greater amount of property than any other man in the United States." Field was assessed taxes on an estimated $40 million worth of real estate and personal property in Cook County alone. New York's John Jacob Astor was second in the nation, with property valued at $35 million. At the time of his death in 1906, Field owned well over seventy Chicago corner lots and income-producing buildings.

Always known as tight with a dollar—except perhaps when it came to his choice of architects—in the last years of his life Field became a generous philanthropist. He was one of the top ten early benefactors of the University of Chicago. In 1893 he agreed to contribute $1 million to acquire artifacts from the World's Columbian Exposition as a core collection for a Chicago museum of natural history. Over the next ten years, Field donated another $1.5 million to the development of the museum. He completed his endowment of the institution, which would be named for him, with a bequest in his will of $8 million.

In September 1905, having been a widower for some nine years and separated for many years before that, Marshall Field married the girl next door. His bride was Mrs. Arthur Caton, a longtime friend and neighbor to the Fields on Prairie Avenue. Delia Caton, who ranked just behind Bertha Palmer as a queen of Chicago society, was one of the few among Field's acquaintances known to be able to thaw his frosty demeanor.

The city's gossips had for years hinted at a clandestine relation-ship—even to the point of speculating about the existence of a secret passageway between the Field and Caton mansions. The marriage, which took place in London, appropriately awaited Mrs. Caton's widowhood. But the event came as no surprise to Chicago's Four Hundred. Reflecting on the significance of Field's remarriage, New York's *Harper's Weekly* characterized Field as "the richest, and in many ways the most influential, man in Chicago." The new Mrs. Field was described as "the unquestioned 'vice-reine,'" of Chicago society. The writer speculated that "her name, her wealth, and her personality, it is generally admitted, may again shift the social capital from the 'North Side' back to the 'South Side.'" The question soon became moot. On New Year's Day of 1906, Field traveled to Wheaton to play golf (in the snow) with his nephew Stanley Field and his friend Robert Todd Lincoln. Field became ill on the return to Chicago, but he refused to curtail his activities. He died of pneumonia two weeks later in New York City, where he had gone on business. Delia Caton Field, his wife of just a few months, was with him.

Marshall Field's real estate and development activities in his lifetime had included his role in making State Street one of the world's great retail centers, his relocation of the city's whole-sale district to the West Loop, and, through gifts of land and endowments, the establishment of the University of Chicago in Hyde Park and the construction of the Field Museum of Natural History complex at the south boundary of Grant Park. But it did not end there. From beyond the grave, by vir-tue of the terms of his extraordinary will, Marshall Field, Chi-cago's master merchant, controlled the development of such Chicago landmarks as the Marshall Field Garden Apartments and the massive Chicago Merchandise Mart, built to provide new quarters for the Field wholesale division and exposition space for its customers. When the twenty-five-story Merchan-dise Mart, designed by Graham, Anderson, Probst and White, was completed in 1930, it was by far the world's largest office building. The forty-two-story Field Building at La Salle and Adams streets (1934) also earned a place in history. This build-ing, designed by the same firm and built on the site of the 1885 Home Insurance Building, dominated the skyline of Chi-cago's financial district for decades to come. It was the last sky-scraper built in Chicago until the late 1950s—long after the construction hiatus of the Depression and war years had ended.

VAULT COMPANIES

Wilson K. Nixon
(1826-1906)

Wilson K. Nixon.
[Chicago Historical Society]

Wilson K. Nixon was a music student and piano salesman, an ironworks and foundry executive, a builder of concert halls, and the developer who put up the only building in downtown Chicago to survive the Great Fire of 1871. Nixon, however, played a far greater role in the growth of the downtown business district than this footnote to history would indicate. Nixon, who pursued many careers, is remembered ultimately as the most prolific of the organizers of safety deposit vault companies in Chicago—those phantom corporations through which investors pooled their funds to back the development of Chicago's new office towers in the golden era of the 1880s and '90s. Although Nixon himself was not a major stockholder, by the turn of the century he was recognized nonetheless as the "promoter and builder" who "probably erected more important structures in Chicago than any other man."

Nixon was born in Geneva, New York, in 1826, but grew up in Cincinnati. As a young teenager, he traveled with his family for nearly two years in Europe, studying music. After his return to Cincinnati, Nixon—then just sixteen—went into the grocery business with a twenty-year-old friend, James R. Smith. The partners later expanded their interest into a successful tea trade and then sold out to establish a piano sales dealership. The piano business led to construction and development, beginning with the building of small concert halls where the company's musical instruments were displayed and promoted.

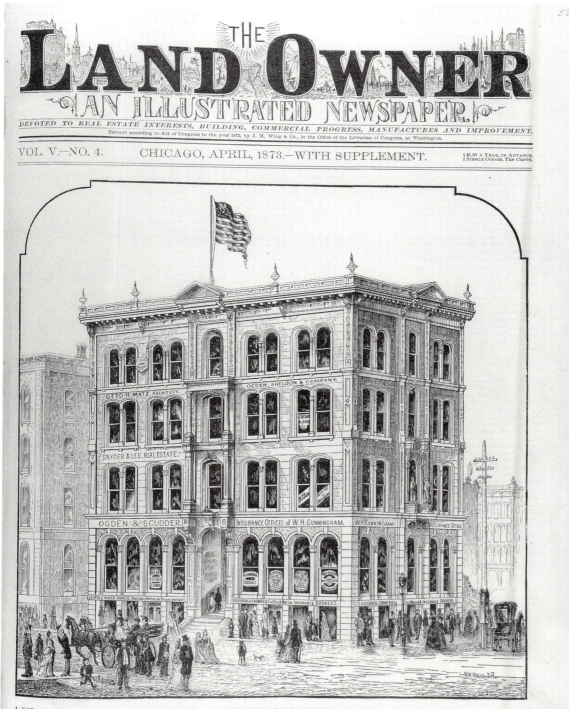

A NOTABLE BUILDING.—NIXON'S FIRE-PROOF BLOCK, THE ONLY STRUCTURE IN THE CHICAGO BURNT DISTRICT NOT DAMAGED BY THE FLAMES.

(See Description, page 59.)

Nixon Building, northeast corner of La Salle and Monroe streets. [opposite page] The five-story Nixon Building, which was under construction in 1871, came through the Great Fire almost intact. The *Land Owner* celebrated the extraordinary fact with this cover illustration, captioned "A Notable Building—Nixon's Fire-Proof Block, the Only Structure in the Chicago Burnt District Not Damaged by the Flames." [From the *Land Owner*, April 1873—Chicago Historical Society]

The iron business came about in another way. In 1854 Nixon married Martha Greenwood, a daughter of the owner of the Eagle Iron Works, one of the country's largest foundry and machine shop companies. At the outbreak of the Civil War, Nixon was serving as secretary of the Greenwood family firm, then a major manufacturer of muskets and other munitions. The Tippecanoe, an ironclad battleship, was built in the Greenwood foundry.

In 1863, on the advice, it was said, of his wife's doctors, Nixon moved his family to Chicago. He resumed his former occupation of piano dealer, at the same time looking for real estate investments. Nixon's first construction project in Chicago was the five-story Smith and Nixon Building at the southwest corner of Clark and Washington streets, built first as a concert and lecture hall and later converted to house the expanding piano and musical instrument business. Smith and Nixon's "Steinway Piano Depot" sold sheet music and organs and other instruments, but their premium line was the high-quality piano made by Henry Steinway and his sons in New York. Lyon and Healy's Music Store also had street level showrooms in the Smith and Nixon Building. (The Smith and Nixon Building was destroyed in the 1871 fire, but the melody lingered on. In 1884 the corner became the site of the ten-story Chicago Opera House Building.)

The fire that swept the city in October 1871 leveled the banks, the Board of Trade Building, and the office and mercantile buildings along La Salle Street. Everything in the path of the inferno fell, with the exception of W. K. Nixon's second major project in Chicago, a five-story office building then in the final stages of construction at the northeast corner of La Salle and Monroe. Many theories circulated at the time to account for the amazing survival of this building, alone among the hundreds of central business district structures destroyed by the Great Fire. These included the suggestion that newly installed wet plaster had repelled the flames. The fire, however, did not skip over the Nixon Building, as some suggested, but roared right through it. A quantity of raw lumber stored in the building was entirely consumed by the flames, but the walls, ceilings, and floors of the building itself remained remarkably undamaged.

The survival of the building may be less of a mystery than it seemed. The cause can be traced to the role that Nixon himself played in the unique design of the building and the use of the construction materials he favored. The roof was sheet iron, laid on iron beams; joists were rolled iron; and all the structural parts of stairways, including risers, were of iron. The building's infrastructure thus was as tough as an Eagle

Iron Works battleship. This web of iron was enclosed in an envelope of hollow walls of brick and stone. Concrete covered the tops of beams, and the floors were supported by brick arches. An 1873 study of the construction techniques employed in the Nixon Building published in the *Land Owner* noted that the design was the result of "much thoughtful and careful study on the part of both architect and owner." The architect was Otto H. Matz, who also built the first passenger terminal of the Illinois Central Railroad in Chicago. In a subsequent letter to the journal, Nixon gave credit also to "Mr. J. B. Corleis, an architect and builder of this city, who was the first person who presented to my notice the plan of fire-proofing carried out in my building, and to which it undoubtedly owed its preservation."

Work to complete the building resumed within days of the fire, and a week later tenants began to move in. The building was the first office structure to be occupied in the downtown district after the fire. Not surprisingly, the tenants included a number of architects—or would-be architects—and the Nixon Building became a nexus about which the work of rebuilding the city swirled.

The wave of bank failures that precipitated the national financial panic of 1873 came on the heels of a period of rampant speculation in Chicago real estate. The panic flattened the Chicago real estate market, sweeping away personal fortunes as surely and completely as the fire itself had swept away the business district. Nixon was among thousands of investors who lost their property when they were unable to meet mortgage payments and other heavy obligations incurred in the two-year boom that followed the fire. In the years between 1873 and 1877, Nixon endured at least eight foreclosures or other actions filed against him in circuit court by his creditors. He did not declare bankruptcy, as he might have, but again fell back on other occupations as he struggled to repay his debts.

By the end of the 1870s, the real estate market had begun to rally, and Nixon rallied with it. In 1879 he opened a real estate office on North Dearborn Street. Although he was never able to accumulate wealth, over time he was able to repay $300,000 of his indebtedness—apparently to the satisfaction of the courts and his creditors.

Even in the hard times, the Nixon family lived in fashionable circumstances. Before the fire, the Nixon home was at 111 Pine Street (now North Michigan Avenue). In the late 1870s and through the 1880s, the family lived in the same elite neighborhood, on Rush Street between Huron and Ontario, where they employed a "white butler" said to have been "the pride of the neighborhood."

Dearborn Street, looking south from Randolph, 1910.
Wilson K. Nixon focused his development activities in this two-block section of Dearborn Street between Randolph and Madison streets. Although Nixon could not necessarily have foreseen the traffic congestion of 1910, he did recognize in the 1880s the demand for office space in this district.
[Chicago Historical Society]

The years from 1880 to 1900, when Nixon was most active in building the downtown district, saw the birth of the sky-scraper and the development in Chicago of the distinctive form of commercial architecture known as the Chicago school. These years also saw the introduction of new mechanisms for financing development. These new approaches recognized the fact that few capitalists were willing—and even fewer were able—to finance the entire cost of construction of a very expensive, and often speculative, new office building. The catch was that while the costs of skyscraper construction exceeded the means of most single investors, state law prohibited investors from incorporating as a development syndicate.

W. K. Nixon saw an opportunity, and became a specialist at organizing a type of corporation known as a vault company, or safety deposit company. These investor associations were incorporated for the stated purpose of providing fireproof repositories, usually built into individual office walls, where business records and other valuables could be stored. Vault rental was the company's ostensible business, with the office towers being constructed out of necessity to house the vaults.

Nixon focused his activities on behalf of his investor-clients in two prime locations. Most of the Nixon developments were concentrated in the two-block area between Madison and Randolph on Dearborn Street, which was then, as it is now, the heartland of city and county government, and thus was an area in which office space was eagerly sought by lawyers and other professionals. For similar reasons, he also zeroed in on the new financial district on La Salle Street, close to the Board of Trade Building.

The architects for all of Nixon's major buildings in this decade were Burnham and Root. Most of these projects were office towers, with banks as principal tenants. The first of Nixon's Dearborn Street developments was the six-story Commercial Bank Building at the southeast corner of Dearborn and Monroe, completed in 1884. The Commercial Bank was followed in 1885 by the nine-story Insurance Exchange Building (later known as the Continental National Bank Building), at the southwest corner of LaSalle and Adams streets, financed by the Nixon-organized Northwestern Safety Deposit Company. The Insurance Exchange was the largest of Burnham and Root's early office building commissions.

Nixon benefited from the misfortune Shepherd Brooks suffered when the Grannis Block, located on a choice lot on the east side of Dearborn, south of Washington, was destroyed in a dramatic midwinter fire. Brooks had purchased the building only months before, and by the time the ice melted and the extent of his losses were known, he wished to have nothing further to do with the property. Nixon stepped in, moving swiftly to lease the lot and incorporate the Illinois Vault Company to rebuild on the burned-out site. The major tenant of the new nine-story Illinois Bank Building, completed in record time in 1885, was the National Bank of Illinois, which had previously leased space in the Grannis Block.

Owen F. Aldis, who was the management agent for Shepherd Brooks and his brother Peter, expressed a high opinion of Nixon's skill as a developer—rare praise indeed coming from the opinionated Mr. Aldis. Peter Brooks was the developer and owner of the Portland Block, which stood immediately north of the Grannis Block and which had shared a party wall with the Grannis. In a letter to Brooks dated July 7, 1885, Aldis wrote, "Mr. Nixon has executed and we have exchanged the agreement as to the party wall. He has made up his mind to use wooden beams with heavy terra cotta fireproofing in the construction of the new building, which will lighten the construction somewhat. He certainly has adopted a very good plan."

In the same letter, Aldis wrote approvingly of Nixon's arrangement with the bank tenant, which advanced $80,000 in construction bonds, and of the organization of what was apparently a closely held investors' syndicate. Prefacing these remarks, Aldis noted, "I do not much like the future prospects of two or three of the building corporations, which are constructing large buildings here now. From what I learn I think that some of the stockholders are considerably frightened at the number of office buildings constructed and in process of construction, and pay on their stock with great reluctance." He went on to assure Brooks that the building company being organized by Nixon would not have any deadbeat stockholders. He wrote, "In the new lease to Mr. Nixon or to the Illinois Vault Co. by Mr. Shepherd Brooks, I did not anticipate any trouble of that kind, as the principal stockholders are Mr. Nixon's own family. They will absolutely control the corporation."

In 1886 the nine-story Rialto Building, at Van Buren and La Salle streets just south of the Board of Trade Building, was completed. Nixon organized and served as president of the investment group, first known as the Chicago Deposit Vault Company and later as the Rialto Company. Nixon turned his attention back to Dearborn Street in 1889, organizing the group that built the Chemical Bank Building on the east side of Dearborn street, north of Washington (now part of the vacant "Block 37"). In the same year, Nixon's Abstract Safety Vault Company completed the new Williams Building, which was also on Dearborn between Washington and Randolph streets, and, like the others, designed by Burnham and Root. In 1891 Nixon formed the Columbian Vault Company to secure another coveted Dearborn Street property, the west side of Dearborn between Madison and Washington, across from the reconstructed Grannis Block. When plans for a sixteen-story building to be built on this site were announced, the *Economist* commented that "Mr. Nixon will naturally be president" of the company, adding that "Mr. Nixon's skill in such matters gives full assurance that the most will be made of the splendid opportunity for an office building at that point."

Although the volume of Nixon's building projects diminished after 1891, no doubt as a consequence of the 1893 financial panic, he remained an active manager of the several building companies he had formed and advocate in city and county government on behalf of downtown property owners.

Nixon died in 1903 at the age of seventy-six at the family home, which was then at 113 Cass Street (North Wabash Avenue) between Erie and Ontario streets. His body was returned to Cincinnati for burial. A death notice in the *Economist* described Nixon as "one of the most conspicuous figures in the business life of Chicago for many years," but added the poignant note that "an unkind fate left him in his later years with slender means of support." Although he is remembered for the building that withstood the fire, a historian writing in 1893 measured Nixon's contribution to the growth of the city in terms of the nearly full mile of street frontage he developed and millions of dollars in value his efforts had created.

It is perhaps ironic that the greatest danger posed to Nixon's fireproof office structures was not fire but progress. Nixon built well, but he also built on very desirable downtown sites. Economic demand for ever taller structures meant that Nixon buildings were razed young. By 1930 very few of his major commercial developments were still standing. By 1940, none were.

THE AUDITORIUM

Ferdinand W. Peck
(1848-1924)

Ferdinand W. Peck.
[Chicago Historical Society]

The man who built Chicago's landmark Auditorium Building and Theater was seated on the right of the President of the United States at the theater's dedication in December 1889, and was so well known to the thousands present that he needed no introduction. The featured speaker of the evening acknowledged him simply as "a citizen of large public spirit and broad philanthropy," adding, "I shall not name him, I need not name him, but if you ask for his monument look about you." The planner, builder, and philanthropist of whom he spoke was Ferdinand W. Peck, heir to a family real estate fortune amassed in the early years of the Chicago settlement. Peck was a cultured man—decisive, pragmatic, visionary—whose fondest dream was to bring grand opera to Chicago. He was the sole, single-minded force behind the creation of the Auditorium Theater. Ferd Peck was also the developer of the Chicago Stock Exchange Building and was among those civic leaders responsible for bringing the 1893 World's Columbian Exposition to Chicago.

Ferdinand Wyeth Peck was born in 1848, the youngest son among the eight children of Mary Kent and Philip F. W. Peck, a Chicago pioneer and the founder of one of the city's first mercantile businesses. The senior Peck was also a member of Chicago's first fire company, a voter in the first city election, and the holder of the first post office box assigned in the new town. He was the builder of Chicago's first brick house, which stood at the southwest corner of La Salle and Washington

Auditorium Building and Theater, north side of Congress Parkway, 1897.
Ferd Peck's single-minded dream was to bring grand opera to Chicago and make it available to the general populace. To support his concept, Peck created a mixed-use building not unlike a modern convention center. A seventeen-story office tower, a four-hundred-room hotel, and two banquet halls generated income to offset the cost of maintaining the four-thousand-seat opera house. Dankmar Adler, famed for his knowledge of acoustics, and his partner, Louis Sullivan, designed the complex, which was formally dedicated in 1889.
[Chicago Historical Society]

streets, where his sons would later build the Chicago Stock Exchange Building. Over a period of forty years, Peck laid the foundation of one of the city's first great real estate fortunes, largely by the technique of buying property as it was offered by the government and refusing to sell, at any price, in the boom and bust waves of land speculation that swept Chicago in the early years.

Peck's son Ferd was a native Chicagoan—a rarity at the time. He attended Chicago public schools and the first University of Chicago. He earned a law degree from the university's Union College of Law and in 1870 married eighteen-year-old Tilla Spaulding, also of Chicago. They would have four sons and two daughters. The senior Peck died just two weeks after the Great Chicago Fire of "congestion of the brain" caused by a head injury suffered in a fall, whereupon son Ferd, then just twenty-three and newly married, abandoned law to assume the full-time job of managing the family real estate interests and to pursue his own growing commitment to enriching the city's intellectual and cultural life.

Even in his early twenties, Peck was involved in promoting the cause of better education for all Chicagoans regardless of their economic status. Over the course of his career he would serve as president of the board of the Chicago Athenaeum, a so-called "people's college" offering general education and vocational training; as vice president of the Chicago Board of Education; and as one of the first trustees of the new University of Chicago. In the 1870s and early 1880s, Peck began formulating his personal plan to bring culture to Chicago at the popular level. He had discovered his love for grand opera when he first traveled in Europe. With each subsequent European visit, his dream of creating a home for opera in Chicago grew more vivid.

As a first step, Peck organized an ad hoc group that he called the Chicago Opera Festival Association and contracted with the Mapleson Italian Opera Company to bring the company and its famed diva Adelina Patti to the city for a two-week run in April 1885. The opera company was guaranteed $50,000, to be advanced by Peck and other directors of the Opera Festival Association against future proceeds from the event. Additional capital was put up by the directors to renovate the Inter-State Exposition Building, located in Grant Park where the Art Institute of Chicago stands today, to house the event.

Peck was confident that the backers would be fully reimbursed from revenues generated by ticket sales, but the other directors were not so sure of that—especially after Peck announced that the great majority of seats would be priced at one dollar. (The prevailing price for a seat for an opera was then eight to ten dollars, a figure greater than most workers' weekly earnings.) The Chicago *Tribune* applauded Peck's courage in tailoring the event not to the interests of the "wealthy and fashionable minority," but to needs of "the popular and unfashionable majority." The newspaper's characterization of the opera project as "courageous" seems an understatement. Peck's plan was nothing less than astonishing. To make expenses for the two-week run, at a one dollar per seat, Peck would have to attract an attendance of one hundred thousand! The idea of drawing this kind of crowd to grand opera, at any price, seems even more improbable in light of Chicago's reputation, even by the 1880s, as a brawling, bawdy frontier town —hell bent for commerce but with little concern for culture.

The barren Exposition Building where the spectacle would take place did not add much to any appeal the festival might have. The hall had been built in 1873 by Potter Palmer and others to house nineteenth-century Chicago's version of a state fair and trade show. It was later home to symphony orchestra conductor Theodore Thomas's first concerts in Chicago. On these occasions, the building's glass and steel dome proved to be an acoustic disaster. When Peck promised that this and other problems with the hall would be solved in the renovation planned for the festival, he had an ace up his sleeve. That was his long association with architect-engineer Dankmar Adler, who by the mid-1880s had become noted as a builder of theaters and for his skill in the science of acoustics. His theaters included the Central Music Hall, sponsored largely by the Peck brothers and other civic leaders as a new pulpit for the liberal preacher David O. Swing after his trial before the Chicago Presbytery on charges that he had committed heresy against the mother church.

Adler's partner Louis H. Sullivan later wrote, "Hence Peck, the dreamer for the populace, sought Adler, the man of common sense. Between them they concocted a scheme, a daring experiment." That scheme, which was accomplished in a matter of weeks, was to erect a huge temporary auditorium entirely within the Exposition Building. The acoustics were superb, and the festival was a triumph. The *Tribune* reported that over the course of the two-week run, between 110,000 and 115,000 people had attended the festival. Receipts totaled $170,000. Even after the directors had been reimbursed, a surplus remained.

The event might have ended quite differently. Three weeks after the festival closed, the city building inspector and the fire marshal inspected the makeshift auditorium at the request of the city council. Their finding, the *Tribune* reported, was that "the opera hall is a fire-trap" and that "large audiences should not be permitted to gather there in view of the chances for a great holocaust." The officials stated that the interior wooden shell was precariously built and highly combustible, a hall from which, "in case of fire, few people could make their escape." If, after the fact, Peck thought of how close he might have come to tragedy, he never spoke publicly of the matter.

Peck now focused all of his creative energy on the task of building a truly great auditorium for Chicago. He envisioned a multiuse center that would provide a home for opera, symphony, dance, music festivals, and large social events as well as facilities for political conventions. As Peck conceived it, the Auditorium Building and Theater would also house business offices and a great hotel that together would provide enough revenue to support the theater and its offerings. With the huge popular success of the opera festival still fresh in the minds of the backers, Peck approached members of the ad hoc festival association and other well-placed friends with his idea of forming a stockholder group to construct a permanent opera house and convention center for Chicago. The Grand Auditorium Association was informally organized even as the temporary festival hall was being demolished.

A year later, on May 29, 1886, Peck went public with his plans, choosing the influential Chicago Commercial Club as his forum. In a speech to its members, Peck touched all the right chords, appealing to the members' financial interests first, patriotism second, and their cultural sensibilities third. He said:

> Many of your members and other citizens as well as myself have thought for a long time that one of our greatest needs in Chicago was a large public auditorium where conventions of all kinds, political and otherwise, mass meetings, reunions of army organizations, and, of course, great musical occasions in the nature of festivals, operatic and otherwise, as well as other large gatherings, could be held.

Although Peck's own interest was cultural, in addressing this group he stressed the city's potential to become "the convention city of the continent," provided a permanent hall large enough to house national conventions were built. (Years later, Chicago's real estate journal, the *Economist,* observed that "Mr. Ferd Peck, who is entitled to the gratitude of the people of this city as the founder of [the Auditorium], used to say that the only grudge he ever had against the Auditorium was that it once paid a dividend." Peck's view of the role he saw for the Auditorium, the paper said, is that "it was and is an educational institution.")

With the Chicago Commercial Club's endorsement, subscriptions began to roll in. By November three-quarters of a million dollars had been pledged. On December 8, 1886, the Chicago Auditorium Association was formally incorporated, with Ferd Peck as its president. A quiet search for an appropriate site had been under way for more than a year prior to the incorporation. The location chosen was the north side of Congress Street between Michigan and Wabash avenues. Agreements were forged with the owners of the five parcels of land involved in the package. Peck succeeded in securing highly favorable ninety-nine-year leases on most of the properties. In 1891 he managed to extend those leases for an additional ninety-nine years—that is, until the year 2085—at fixed fees and without reappraisal clauses. The provisions of these leases were the factor that ultimately protected the Auditorium from almost certain demolition in the 1920s.

At the December 1886 meeting of the newly incorporated Auditorium Association, Peck announced that removal of the existing buildings on the site would begin immediately. The selection of an architect was now an important and pressing matter. The commission was being sought by every architectural firm in town. Peck favored Dankmar Adler, as did Nathaniel K. Fairbanks and Martin A. Ryerson, who, with Peck, had been stockholders in the 1880 Central Music Hall project. The choice was not so clear in the minds of the other directors, whose concern perhaps was cost. They were not enchanted with the gabled and turreted preliminary drawings for the building's exterior prepared by Adler's partner Louis H. Sullivan in the fall of 1885. They urged the consideration of other firms.

But there was no real contest. Frank Lloyd Wright worked as a young draftsman on the project. He later wrote, "Prompted by Ferdinand Peck, when the matter came up, Adler was naturally the man to be entrusted with a great civic enterprise like the Chicago Auditorium to seat five thousand people." The directors awarded the job to the firm of Adler and Sullivan. That Sullivan was merely part of the package was acknowledged by Sullivan when he wrote that "Adler was Peck's man. As to Louis, he was rather dubious, but gradually came around." But Peck did not come around on the matter of Sullivan's concepts for ornamentation of the building's exterior. His instructions were that the style should be simple, massive, and direct, along the lines of the 1885 Field Wholesale Building, designed by the much-admired Henry Hobson Richardson. Adler accepted Peck's direction, and the plans were redrawn to his requirements.

Peck was less precise in his directions regarding the interior of the building, very likely because cost had become a less critical factor but also because of his preoccupation with maintaining the flow of material and manpower needed to meet a stringent construction schedule. In considering the apparent incongruity in styles, Adler later lamented, in print, that the exterior of the building had been deprived "of those graces of plastic surface decoration which are so characteristic of the internal treatment." Costs for the project did mount, but so did the funds available. Of a capital stock of $1.5 million, $1.2 million had been sold to 160 subscribers by March 1888, and more money was coming in almost daily. The Auditorium was by far the largest development project attempted in Chicago up to that time, eventually costing $3.2 million.

By the winter of 1887-88, the rush was on to complete the building by June, in time for the Republican National Convention. Construction work continued around the clock. The schedule was merciless, allowing no pause even for the deepest days of winter. The hall was roofed over in advance of other construction priorities so that work on the inside could continue, warmed by open fires. Anxieties about shortages of materials and completion dates ran high. Peck, who was present on the construction site every day, took extraordinary measures to keep the project moving. When delivery of the granite being used for the first four floors of the exterior of the building fell behind schedule in early 1888, Peck and the Auditorium Association bought the Minnesota quarries where the rock was mined and reorganized their work forces in an effort to get the stone out faster. He made his June deadline, but masonry work on the exterior walls continued, even as the convention was in progress.

On the eve of the opening session, Peck said, "I never despaired of being ready in time, but I confess that at times the work seemed to drag along most tantalizingly, and I was worried. I think I was rather more worried than I ever was before." If so, the fact was not evident to others. A reporter wrote that amidst the clamor of the last hours before the con-

Auditorium banquet hall, c. 1895. When it opened in 1889 the Auditorium was the world's first fully wired building, providing an opportunity that was not lost on architect Louis Sullivan. Sullivan used electric lighting skillfully to heighten the effect of the soaring arches that were a hallmark of Adler and Sullivan's work on the Auditorium Building.
[Chicago Historical Society]

vention, Peck, in his top hat and frock coat, maintained the cool appearance of "a gentleman of leisure with no heavier burden oppressing him than that which concerns the cut of his trousers."

The formal dedication of the Auditorium Theater on the night of December 9, 1889, was the event of the decade. A crowd estimated at twenty thousand gathered on the streets to watch a stream of carriages arrive at the Congress Street entrance and discharge Chicago's Four Hundred families and distinguished guests arrayed in all their finery. No one was disappointed. The theater, with its magnificent lobbies and lavish ornamentation, was dazzling. Hundreds of carbon-filament lamps illuminated the suspended arches of the great gold and ivory ceiling. Harriet Monroe had written an ode for the occasion. Adelina Patti sang "Home Sweet Home" without accompaniment. It was said that she sang directly to Peck, never taking her eyes off him. President Benjamin Harrison, seated in Peck's box, whispered to Vice President Levi Morton, "New York surrenders, eh?"

The newspaper report of the occasion noted that "almost invisible is the dark, modest face of the man who planned and carried out the Auditorium—Ferd Peck. Perhaps you would not have believed it if told who he was—he looked so young." The paper reported the crowd's insistence that Peck rise and make a speech. The evening had already been overwrought with oratory, and Peck modestly limited his own remarks to "a quiet, simple little response of thanks."

When the complex was completed in February 1890, the

Auditorium Building encompassed the theater, with four thousand permanent seats; a four-hundred-room hotel, with a banquet hall on the sixth floor and a grand dining room on the tenth floor; and a seventeen-story office tower, capped by a weather station and observation deck. Before the World's Columbian Exposition of 1893, a four-hundred-room annex to the Auditorium Hotel (the present Congress Hotel) was built on the south side of Congress Street and connected to the parent building by an underground marble-walled corridor. The Auditorium Building was placed on the National Register of Historic Places in 1970. It was declared a national landmark in 1975 and a Chicago landmark in 1976.

The completion of the Auditorium project and the national attention that the building attracted helped Peck and other Chicagoans convince Congress that the city had the capacity to organize and host a world's fair. Peck became vice president of the World's Columbian Exposition directorate and chairman of the committee on finance—a harrowing job that only a man of unbounded optimism would have accepted. Peck was recognized for his efforts on behalf of the exposition when President William McKinley named him United States' commissioner general to the Paris Exposition of 1900. The French government later awarded him the Legion of Honor.

In 1892 talk of a proposed relocation of the Chicago Stock Exchange captivated the business community, property owners in particular. "It is believed that wherever that body locates, an important financial center will be permanently established," the *Economist* commented, speculating that frontage around a new stock exchange building might well become the most valuable real estate in the world.

The Peck brothers—Clarence, Walter, and Ferd—had a property in mind. It was the southwest corner of Washington and La Salle streets, where the family home had once stood and property that was now leased by the Pecks to the owners of the Western Union Telegraph Building. In order to free up the corner for a new skyscraper, they bought—at a premium price—the five-story building that occupied the property and then demolished it. Again, Peck selected Adler and Sullivan as his architects. His instructions to them were to design the lower floors of the thirteen-story 30 North La Salle building specifically to meet the needs of the stock exchange. To seal the deal, the space used by the exchange was provided at a nominal rent for a period of fifteen years. Thirty North La Salle was the largest of Adler and Sullivan's steel-framed skyscrapers and the most modern building of its day. It remained one of the most significant structures in Chicago until it was razed amid great protest in 1972 (see author's commentary at the end of this chapter).

Chicago Stock Exchange Building, c. 1905. Shortly after the completion of the Auditorium, Ferdinand Peck chose Adler and Sullivan as architects for the famed 30 North La Salle Building, built by the Peck brothers to house the Chicago Stock Exchange. Completed in 1894, the building was demolished in 1972—amid public protest—to make way for a new office building. The entrance and trading room were preserved and are now at the Art Institute of Chicago. [Barnes-Crosby—Chicago Historical Society]

By the time of the World's Fair, Peck was known about town as "the Commodore," a nickname earned by virtue of his rank in the Oconomowoc, Wisconsin, yacht club. He was easily recognized in a crowd because of his habit of wearing a white silk top hat. This was a modest enough challenge to the dress code of the day for a someone known to be a rugged individualist, a founder, not a joiner, and very much his own man. When it came to matters of principle, he was a burr under the saddle—be the issue great or small. For example, when a fellow businessman sought an injunction to stop construction of a toboggan slide on the lakefront because it might attract "undesirable" elements to the neighborhood, Peck intervened on behalf of the tobogganists. He pursued the toboggan issue with the same indignation with which he tracked a man who had welshed on a million-dollar deal and had him returned to Chicago to pay damages.

Although Peck always maintained that there was no place in Chicago for a privileged class, it appears that Mrs. Peck did not share that view, but rather aspired to a position as a leader in Chicago society. It was Tilla Peck's misfortune, however, to have been born a contemporary of Bertha Honoré Palmer. Mrs. Palmer cast a long shadow indeed. The night of the dedication of the Auditorium should have belonged to Mrs. Peck. But Tilla, who wore a pink brocade dress and carried a bouquet of pink roses and violets, was—even at her moment of glory—upstaged by Mrs. Palmer, who arrived wearing a sleeveless Parisian gown of deepest burgundy and a dramatic opera cape, and carrying a white lace fan.

Mrs. Peck did have the honor of entertaining President and Mrs. Harrison as her house guests, and, to her credit, in the 1890s the Peck home at 1826 South Michigan Avenue became famous for its hospitality, particularly during the World's Fair. But the matter of Mrs. Palmer was not forgotten. When Peck became head of the American Commission to the Paris Exposition, Tilla looked forward to her role as the preeminent hostess of the American colony. Alas, Mrs. Palmer was also in Paris that summer, having been named by President McKinley as the only woman member of the American Commission. Mrs. Peck was outraged by the attention lavished on Bertha Palmer by the European royals and celebrities who gathered around her. She launched an open campaign to trim Mrs. Palmer's plumage, announcing publicly that she would not let Bertha precede her at social events connected with the exposition. The contretemps was covered with great interest by the European press.

One can imagine what Ferd Peck himself made of all this. His own tastes and aspirations were considerably simpler, and he was a man of highly independent views. Although the Pecks had a fashionable summer home on Lake Oconomowoc and maintained a constant presence in the social columns, it was also a well-known fact that Ferd preferred his own rough lodge on Lake Koshkonong. Friends recalled him as a hunter and a fisherman who enjoyed being up before dawn and roughing it in the woods. By 1920 Peck and his wife were no longer living together at the South Michigan Avenue mansion. He had moved into lodgings at the Union League Club, where he was a founding member. The Commodore, however, soon managed to tease, tweak, and irritate the stuffy members of the house committee to the point that, in exasperation, the committee "demanded his room." Peck promptly, and probably quite happily, moved on over to the Chicago Athletic Association. In July 1923 the *Tribune* reported that Peck had celebrated his seventy-fifth birthday, in the company of three hundred guests, at his summer home in Deal Beach, New Jersey. No mention was made of Mrs. Peck.

Ferdinand Peck died at Henrotin Hospital on November 4, 1924. A new opera opened at the Auditorium Theater on the night of November 5, and a moment of silence was observed in honor of the theater's founding spirit. He was buried at Rosehill Cemetery following a simple service attended by only a few family members and friends. The Peck family plot is marked by a spire of granite, but Peck's own grave—no doubt as he intended—stands in contrast to the grand mausoleums, fountains, statuary, and temples customarily erected for other Chicagoans of Peck's wealth and stature. The grave is marked with a simple stone on which are carved these words: "This Man Had Courage."

AUTHOR'S COMMENTARY

Thirty North La Salle immediately became the stock trading center of the Midwest and remained so until 1903 when the Chicago Stock Exchange moved to larger quarters. In late 1971 Mayor Richard J. Daley called me to his office, in my role as real estate consultant to the city, to discuss the pending demolition of the historic building. An investment group that included two Chicago lawyers—William Friedman, senior partner of Friedman and Koven, and Philip Corboy, one of the nation's preeminent tort trial lawyers and a past president of the Chicago Bar Association—had acquired the property and announced plans to demolish it and replace it with a modern forty-five-story office building.

Preservation groups had been seeking ways to save the Stock Exchange Building and were applying pressure to the city administration to respond to and assist their efforts. In reviewing the alternatives, it was clear that although the administration was sympathetic to preservation (not dedicated, but sympathetic), it did not feel that there was a legal basis to prevent demolition and redevelopment short of comdemnation. No appropriate public use had materialized, and there was no justification for the allocation of city funds to finance a condemnation.

During the course of the conversation, I told the mayor that I had a feeling that the project would run into economic difficulties, coming as it did in the wake of the building boom of the 1960s. Mayor Daley suggested that we attempt to convince the new owners to preserve the existing building rather than redevelop the site. He asked me to carry out an economic analysis of the proposed structure.

Our firm went to work on the project and found that the economic benefits to the developers of a new building on the site were very questionable. There was a significant oversupply of office space at the time, and a number of other new buildings were already in place or ready to enter the market at the same time as the proposed development. In fact, we were unable to economically justify the project. It was, in our opinion, destined to be an economic failure.

I reported our findings back to Mayor Daley, who asked me to share my report with the developers in the hope that they would reevaluate their plans. I subsequently met with Corboy and Friedman to share our report and explain our conclusions and the basis upon which they were made. Although they recognized the concerns and the potential difficulties in the market, they felt that they were too far along in the redevelopment effort to reverse the process, our analysis notwithstanding. They also believed that they had far too much invested in the property to bring about an economically successful restoration and rehabilitation. Consequently, the Stock Exchange Building was demolished and the new 30 North La Salle building erected in its place. Our predictions were, in fact, borne out by the market. It was only a few years before the building was in default and foreclosed upon by the Prudential Insurance Company of America, the mortgage lender. The developers lost a substantial amount of money and the city lost the building given to it by the Peck brothers and Adler and Sullivan.

SOUTH DEARBORN

Charles C. Heisen
(1854-1945)

Charles C. Heisen.
[From *Men of Illinois*—The Newberry Library]

German-born Charles Constantine Heisen was tall, handsome, and smartly dressed. A man of Old World manners and aristocratic bearing, he was also a highly entrepreneurial late-nineteenth-century Chicago developer who chose to operate as a loner and sole proprietor—outside the bounds of the close-knit circles of the business and social elite who built Chicago's central business district in the 1880s and '90s. Disdaining the scramble that was under way by the mid-1880s for centrally located development sites, Heisen laid claim to a neglected stretch of Dearborn Street south of Jackson and, in the words of Chicago's real estate journal, the *Economist,* proceeded with "extraordinary foresight and nerve" to create a new commercial center there. He later became one of the founders of Chicago's western suburb of Villa Park.

Heisen was born in the Hessian city of Kassel in 1854 and emigrated to America while still in his teens. He settled in Aberdeen, Mississippi, near the Alabama border, where he worked as a cotton merchant. In 1875, at the age of twenty-one, Heisen applied for and was granted United States citizenship. In 1881 he married Ida Wadill, a native of Vicksburg. Heisen prospered in the cotton trade and in the early 1880s began traveling with some regularity to the Chicago commodity exchanges. In 1886 Heisen left Mississippi behind to establish himself in the real estate and property investment business in Chicago.

In the early 1880s the area south of Jackson Street, between Wabash and Clark streets, was tough territory, untouched by the respectable influence of the new office buildings that were rising in the central business district to the north. Dearborn Street south of Van Buren—where Heisen would make his largest investments—was dangerously close to a section of the city known as Little Cheyenne, a colorful but unsavory area seething with saloons, gambling dens, and brothels. The district's reputation did not seem to bother Heisen. On his first trip to Chicago, in 1884, he purchased a lot on South Dearborn between Van Buren and Congress. Over the next several years he led a resurrection on South Dearborn that builder Henry Ericsson described as "one of the most phenomenal transformations of any area in the city's history."

Heisen's first development project was the seven-story Temple Court Building, built in 1887 at the corner of Dearborn and Quincy streets, an intersection that was nowhere near as far south on Dearborn as Heisen would eventually go, but which even then was considered beyond the boundaries of the established business district. In 1887 he built the Como Block at 443 South Dearborn (between Van Buren and Congress streets)—a lot he had purchased on one of his early trips to Chicago.

Experienced investors were amused, if not aghast, at Heisen's considerable investment in this district. Even as late as 1889, the *Economist* reported that the situation in that part of the city was considered to be at the very least "forbidding to ordinary observers." Although recognition for opening up the South Loop generally goes to the developers of the Monadnock Building, the fact is that Heisen's Como Building was built two blocks below the Monadnock and a full four years earlier. The nine-story Como, rising as it did in splendid isolation above the taverns and dime hotels of South Dearborn, was truly the first tall building erected south of Jackson.

Heisen followed the Como Block with the Monon Building in 1890 and the Manhattan Building in 1891. These also predated the Monadnock. The Monon and the Manhattan were the twin towers of the day, built facing one another at 436 and 431 South Dearborn. Heisen had a reputation for being tight-fisted (his tendency to overlook his tax bills brought him into court on more than one occasion), but he was not a pinch-penny builder and he cut no corners when it came to choosing an architect. He hired John M. Van Osdel, Chicago's first—and very likely oldest—architect to design the Temple Court, the Como, and the Monon buildings. The Monon, as it turned out, was Van Osdel's last project. For the Manhattan, Heisen turned to another old-timer, William Le Baron Jenney. Jenney perfected in the Manhattan what he had begun in the

Home Insurance Building six years earlier: The Manhattan was the first tall building to use skeleton construction throughout and the first to employ a wind-bracing system.

Heisen built well. He also built tall. The Monon and the Manhattan were the first buildings in the city to reach the respective heights of thirteen and sixteen stories. His buildings rented well, too. Within a year of the completion of the Monon, the *Economist* tipped its hat to Heisen, noting that "the investment in an office building of that size in that location was regarded by many of the more conservative investors as a venturesome step, but results have justified Mr. Heisen's courage." Commenting on the South Dearborn phenomenon, the paper characterized Heisen as both the "leading pioneer and the heaviest operator" in the area.

The leading developers and heavy operators of the day were quick to follow in Heisen's footsteps. Owen Aldis and the Brooks brothers completed the southern addition to the massive Monadnock Building on Dearborn between Jackson and Van Buren in 1893. Aldis's brother-in-law, Bryan Lathrop, built the Old Colony Building for Boston investor Francis Bartlett at the southeast corner of Dearborn and Van Buren in 1894. The Fisher Building, built by paper mogul Lucius G. Fisher II, went up on the northeast corner of that intersection in 1896 (a lot that Fisher had purchased from Heisen). By the mid-1890s, a new business district dominated by the publishing and insurance trades had taken over the badlands of Little Cheyenne.

Heisen stayed ahead of the pack. As early as 1890 he had begun to assemble the land at southwest Dearborn and Harrison where in 1911 he would build his largest, southernmost, and most troublesome office structure, the twenty-two-story Transportation Building. In 1896, as the Fisher Building was going up on Dearborn at Van Buren, Heisen was building another, the Star Insurance Building (later named the Morton Building), designed by Jenney and Mundie, in the block between Congress and Harrison.

As was the case with many other successful developers of this period, Heisen's investment strategy was systematic. He focused his attention on an undeveloped area and bought land cheaply as it became available, often in small parcels. The Manhattan property, for example, was pieced together from four separate purchases. Heisen then improved the property with buildings that could not be ignored. Unlike developers such as Potter Palmer, who followed the same strategy for land acquisition, Heisen turned his developments over fairly quickly. The Como was sold in 1889; the Monon in 1891; and the Manhattan and the Star Insurance buildings in 1907.

Almost immediately upon his arrival in Chicago, Heisen

Heisen mansion, 1250 North Lake Shore Drive. In 1891 Charles Heisen built a Romanesque mansion for his own residence (at left in photo). He later moved on to open farmlands west of the city, where he established the town of Villa Park. The Heisen mansion was among seven historic lakefront homes given Chicago landmark status in 1989. In 1991 it was converted to luxury condominiums.
[Illustration by Harold Portnoy, Brian Keith Advertising and Design; Art Frigo, Artgo Development Corporation]

made a name for himself as a daring investor. Although he remained a loner in business, he seems to have joined the ranks of Chicago society soon enough. He was a member of the city's gilt-edged Union League Club and in 1890 purchased a lakefront lot in Potter Palmer's new Gold Coast district that was flanked by the prestigious residences of Robert Todd Lincoln and society preacher David O. Swing. There, at 1250 Lake Shore Drive, Heisen built a three-story turreted mansion that resembled the Palmer residence a few doors north at 1350 Lake Shore Drive. The Heisens and their two sons and two daughters lived only a few years in this foreboding, Romanesque brownstone. But the house itself, designed by Ohio-born residential architect Frank B. Abbott, survived twentieth-century high-rise development to become notable as one of only seven Gold Coast lakefront mansions still standing in the 1990s. In 1989 these few surviving old homes were designated a Chicago landmark district. In 1991 the Heisen home was converted into luxury condominiums.

By 1907 Heisen had tired of city life. The damp and often windy lakefront weather aggravated his rheumatism, he said. Heisen considered making a permanent move to Florida, a climate he favored, or even to the South of France, but settled instead on the western suburbs of Chicago. He purchased fifty-five acres of open prairie located along the Chicago, Aurora and Elgin Railroad tracks west of Elmhurst in an area sparsely populated by German farmers. He built an imposing twenty-one-room mansion (modeled after George Pullman's Florence Hotel) on twelve acres and subdivided the remaining property. The neighborhood at the time consisted of Heisen's new home, two other houses, and a real estate office. Mrs. Heisen reportedly took one look at this not-so-little house on

Dearborn Street, looking north from Congress Street, c. 1905. Charles Heisen was a pioneer in the development of South Dearborn Street, as can be seen in the progression from the south back toward the central business district of the buildings in this photograph. The earliest of these structures, on the right, is the 1887 Como Building, designed by John Van Osdel. Heisen's 1891 Manhattan Building, designed by William Le Baron Jenney, is the next building to the north.
(Barnes-Crosby—Chicago Historical Society)

the prairie and beat a hasty retreat back to the city. Heisen sold the Lake Shore Drive House in 1910, and Mrs. Heisen moved permanently to New York, where the theater beckoned. (Although his wife's stage career may have been unremarkable, Heisen's eldest son, Carl, made a name for himself in vaudeville in the 1920s as a member of the Heisen and Dixenson dancing team.)

Otto Stephani, a home builder who grew up in Villa Park and who knew Heisen well, says that Heisen had originally planned to call the subdivision ''The Park of Villas,'' a reference to the tile-roofed Mediterranean-style homes that Heisen had admired in the South of France and which he planned to reproduce on the Du Page County prairie. The name of Villa Park, however, was adopted as a shorter form by the community's pragmatic midwestern inhabitants. In 1914 the three hundred residents of Villa Park and Ardmore, the companion subdivision to the north, incorporated as the Village of Ardmore. In 1917, when a post office was established, the name was registered as Villa Park.

In 1910, when he was establishing his base in Villa Park, Heisen was also engaged in building the Transportation Building (originally called the Heisen Building) at Harrison and Dearborn streets. His architect was Fred V. Prather. The project was a difficult one, made more difficult in 1911 by widespread general strikes precipitated by warring trade unions. The Transportation Building was the largest construction project in the city at the time, employing more than a thousand workers. When the conflict between rival union groups broke

into the open, the Heisen job site became a hotbed of sabotage and thuggery. A Heisen night watchman was shot, and a policeman was hit by subsequent random gunfire. Heisen himself was charged with contempt of a court order when, in an effort to stop the spread of sympathy strikes, he fired striking steamfitters and replaced them with tradesmen from a rival union affiliated with the American Federation of Labor. His action had little impact. The Chicago labor war ultimately ignited a wave of strikes nationwide.

After the strike, Heisen decided it was time to close out his Chicago development activities. In May 1912 he took steps to convey the two-year-old Heisen Building to his son-in-law, Malcolm G. Bruce of Richmond, Virginia. Later the same year, Heisen's daughter, Myrtle Heisen Bruce, turned over Heisen's first building, the Temple Court, to the Chicago Title and Trust to sell. In 1914 Heisen was able to complete the sale of the Transportation Building to a bona fide buyer: Louis W. Hill, a director of the Great Northern Railway Company, who gave the building its current name. In part payment Heisen took 265,000 acres of land in Oregon and a large number of workers' houses in Flint, Michigan. He then established the Central Oregon Land Company, with himself as president, but despite frequent motor trips to the Northwest, he was not able to turn the Oregon project into a profitable venture. He did, however, manage to retain at least a portion of the Michigan properties, which included a hotel.

With the Transportation Building behind him, Heisen devoted most of his time and energy to the development of Villa Park. He is remembered there as a "fine gentleman" and a gracious host who also "liked the ladies." In 1910 he installed the village's first water system. In 1912 he built a community church and meeting place. He then turned his attention to the construction of homes. During this period, Heisen gained a local reputation as a parsimonious and somewhat eccentric builder. Many a house in Villa Park, it is said, was framed with lumber that had started life as scaffolding in the construction of the Transportation Building. When the old homes of the Gold Coast began to give way to high-rise apartment construction, Heisen bought windows, built-ins, and other architectural artifacts by the truckload. He built some unique houses in Villa Park that were designed specifically to accommodate the odd lots of windows and other salvaged inventory he accumulated.

He did attempt to bring the Mediterranean to Villa Park, but somehow the gently pitched tiled roofs never quite worked out in the Illinois winters. He also built houses copied after one or more homes that he built in Florida, in one case

Transportation Building, Dearborn Street south of Harrison Street. [opposite page] The monolithic Transportation Building, which originally housed railroad offices, was Charles Heisen's southernmost development on Dearborn Street, and his last development within Chicago. Disheartened by a wave of general strikes in the construction industry, Heisen sold the building three years after it was completed in 1911. [Kaufmann, Weimer, and Fabry Co., from *Chicago and Its Makers.*]

substituting a photograph of a Florida look-alike in an advertisement for a Villa Park house. The picture was fine—except for the palm trees. Otto Stephani's own home is one of Heisen's Florida models. Typical of Heisen's modus operandi when it came to materials, the Stephani home has shower stalls lined with the same light marble that can still be found in the lobby of the Transportation Building.

Even as a builder of office towers, Heisen had a stubborn and independent streak, especially when it came to taxes and utilities. When he was planning the Monon and Manhattan buildings, he conceived the idea of sinking artesian wells on the site to save the costs of buying water from the city system. He later set up his own electric generator at the Villa Park waterworks in protest of electric rates. In later years Heisen divided his time between Florida and Villa Park. His sons and daughters were frequent visitors in both places. Heisen sold the large home on Villa Avenue in 1919 and settled for a time in a smaller Heisen-built house on Villa and Highland avenues. Thereafter he enjoyed a rather itinerant life, even within Villa Park, moving from one newly completed Heisen home to another, and moving again when the house was sold. In the 1930s, when no houses were being built, Heisen bunked at the waterworks, Stephani recalls.

The years of the Great Depression were not kind to Charles Heisen, who by the mid-1930s had reached the age of eighty and had lost the status that wealth and power once afforded him. He continued to visit Villa Park and collect the water bills, but he maintained his principal residence in Florida, in a climate he always said was kinder to his rheumatic knees.

Heisen died at his home in Daytona Beach in 1945 at the age of ninety-one. In 1913 the *Economist* had described Heisen as a "pioneer on Dearborn Street"—the man who had "erected more buildings on that thoroughfare south of Adams street than any other person." In his independent way, Heisen once again had bested the Chicago capitalists with whom he had competed in the 1880s and '90s. He outlived them all.

WORKINGMEN'S HOMES

Samuel E. Gross
(1843-1913)

Samuel E. Gross.
[Brands Studios—Chicago Historical Society]

Samuel Eberly Gross was known in his lifetime as "the world's greatest real estate promoter." He may well have been. Without question, Gross was the most prolific home builder in Chicago history. In 1896 he claimed to have subdivided and sold 44,000 lots, built 7,500 houses, and established more than eighteen suburban towns or villages, most of which have now been absorbed into the City of Chicago. His talent was marketing, and his niche was the workingman. Gross built two-story brick or frame houses, row upon row of them, and sold them at reasonable prices to the wage-earning families that were doubling and redoubling the population of the city in the late nineteenth century. He made individual home ownership possible for the common man by introducing the concepts of little money down and easy monthly payments to Chicago and carrying the mortgages himself.

Gross subdivisions include large areas of Humboldt Park, Brookfield, Calumet Heights, and the street of row houses on Alta Vista Terrace, in the North Side neighborhood known as Wrigleyville. Entire city blocks of Gross-built houses and cottages are still very much a part of Chicago's residential landscape. Many neighborhoods at and beyond the western boundary of Lake View bear the characteristic stamp of Gross's early housing design and subdivision development. The name of S. E. Gross became a household word in Chicago in the 1880s. He was so well known to the workingman that union leaders tried to persuade him to run for mayor in 1889. In the 1890s Gross's personal net worth was estimated to be in the range of $5 million. And yet when he died in 1913 in a Michigan sanatorium, he was bankrupt, living in self-imposed exile from the city he helped build.

Samuel Gross was born in 1843 in Dauphin County, Pennsylvania, twelve miles northwest of Harrisburg, on the Susquehanna River. His parents left family roots behind in 1845 and settled in Carroll County in northern Illinois. With the coming of the Civil War, Gross, although under age, enlisted and eventually became one of the youngest men to achieve the rank of captain in the Union Army. After the war, he returned to Illinois, enrolled in law school, and was admitted to the bar in 1867. Having had an early interest in real estate, Gross bought property and built a number of houses in the years between 1867 and the financial panic of 1873. He also played a part in the planning of the Chicago park and boulevard system. In 1874, Gross married English-born Emily Brown and later built an imposing home on Lake Shore Drive at Division Street, in Potter Palmer's Gold Coast district.

Even though S. E. Gross built housing for the multitudes, he himself was never a common or ordinary man. In the economically stagnant period of the mid- to late 1870s, Gross retired for a time from real estate, retreating to his extensive library. There he turned his attention to more unusual pursuits—as a scientist, scholar, inventor of mathematical instruments, and playwright. In this period Gross wrote *The Merchant Prince of Cornville*, a serious drama in verse featuring a poet with a heart of gold who stood beneath a balcony wooing a lady on behalf of another, less eloquent suitor. The story line is not unlike that of French author Edmond Rostand's later work, *Cyrano de Bergerac*. In 1902, much to Rostand's surprise, a Chicago judge ruled that Gross, not Rostand, was the creator of the character of Cyrano. The French theater company named as defendant in Gross's plagiarism suit was enjoined from producing Cyrano in America. Gross was awarded nominal damages of one dollar, which he graciously waived. He had, as will be seen, more grandiose plans for what he considered to be his literary property.

By 1879 the real estate market had begun its recovery from the effects of the 1873 financial panic, and Gross left his study to begin the serious business of building new suburbs. He started modestly, laying out several subdivisions southwest of the city. Although he was by no means the first of the Chicago subdividers, Gross was by any reckoning the most energetic. By the turn of the century he had established, by his count, more than one hundred and fifty subdivisions. Gross Park, his

Advertisement for S. E. Gross houses. Calling them "the handsomest brick cottages in chicago," Gross advertised his modestly priced homes extensively and creatively. This 1883 broadside announcing the sale of sturdy brick cottages in a Gross subdivision at Division Street and Western Avenue made a special appeal to the stable and rapidly growing German population of the city. [Chicago Historical Society]

first major planned community, was built in 1883-84 on open land along the Chicago and North Western Railroad line, at what was then the northern edge of the city. Other major developments followed, including Brookhaven, Dauphin Park, and Under Linden (Unterdenlinden). The most enterprising and comprehensive of Gross's developments was the town of Grossdale, founded in 1889 on five hundred acres of prairie traversed by the Chicago, Burlington and Quincy Railroad. The site was just west of the already well-established suburb of Riverside. Grossdale now lies within the incorporated city of Brookfield.

Like Riverside, Grossdale—along with the later extension West Grossdale—was planned as an upscale community with many amenities provided by the developer, including a brick and stone railway depot, a grand boulevard, a landscaped park, and a theater and general store in addition to paved streets and brick sewers. Gross reported that eight hundred lots were sold within the first thirty days that the property was on the market. In 1893 Gross developed the sister community of Hollywood (now part of Riverside), reporting that in less than a year three fourths of the properties had been sold.

At the same time, Gross built hundreds of homes in the Lake View area along the proposed extension of the Lincoln Avenue street car line. The advertisements were enticing, offering convenient transportation to the city, but "No City Taxes!" Gross flyers candidly proclaimed: "Outside Fire Limits! You Can Build Wooden Houses!" The implication, of course, was that Gross-built frame homes, lying as they did beyond the reach of the city fire code, could be built more cheaply than the brick or masonry structures required by the stringent Chicago fireproofing ordinance.

Gross's development strategy did not differ markedly from that of other late-nineteenth-century subdividers. The method was to purchase large tracts of land along railway lines, build a commuter station as an inducement to the railroad to stop there, subdivide the land into residential lots, and install utilities. The railroads profited from a growing commuter business; some also owned land company stock. In the case of the Calumet Heights and Dauphin Park developments, Gross and other land investors built their own transportation line and later established the Calumet Electric Railroad. In common with some other developers, Gross frequently created the framework for a town by putting up a commercial building, providing land for a school, dedicating a park or town square, and giving land to congregations to establish churches. After platting a subdivision, Gross typically improved it also, building his standard-plan houses. He then sold lot and house as a package, further easing the burden on the buyer, who otherwise would have to pay off the lot before building the house.

What set Gross apart from other subdivision developers was the ingenuity of his enterprises, his flair for sales promotion, and his emphasis on volume. His sales techniques were imitated but never surpassed. Gross advertised extensively in the newspapers and also distributed his handbills in factories and city workplaces. These sheets typically represented his newest suburban development as a popular choice, a haven of hearth and home, and within the financial reach of the workingman. A typical handbill, headlined "Where All Was Darkness, Now Is Light," depicts an angel floating before a weary construction worker and pointing to a radiant circle of light surrounding an S. E. Gross cottage. The caption reads "A Home—At $10 a Month." In an 1890 advertisement Gross depicted himself at the center of the pool of light wearing a prizefighter's championship belt whose links were made up of the names of sixteen Gross subdivisions. The belt was secured by a star-studded buckle proclaiming "S. E. Gross, Owner of the 'Champion Real Estate Belt of the World.'" Gross also wrote his own ad copy, which in one case took the form of a short story extolling a clever housewife's role in securing a home for her family. The published story, copyrighted by Gross in 1886 under the title *The House That Lucy Built*, or *A Model Landlord*, was distributed as a booklet which, not coincidentally, contained advertisements for S. E. Gross cottages.

Gross frequently printed his advertisements in German, astutely targeting the city's largest and fastest-growing ethnic group. The Germans represented a solid and stable market for homes, a fact that other developers either failed to recognize or chose to ignore. The concentration of German middle-class settlements at the northern edge of the city, particularly in the west Lake View and Under Linden areas, was due in large part to the availability there of S. E. Gross housing.

Gross accommodated prospective buyers in every conceivable way, even chartering railway cars to transport would-be homeowners and their families to the subdivision site for entertainments and free meals under a circus tent, accompanied by a sales pitch. The first public transit on West Division Street was a horse car hired by Gross in the mid-1880s to carry buyers to a Gross subdivision in the Humboldt Park area. He made it as easy as possible for the wage earner to purchase a lot and a home. His subdivisions were promoted under the banner "Low Down Payment, Low Monthly Installments." A typical S. E. Gross cottage built in the period before the 1870 had a sitting room, dining room, kitchen, and bedroom on the first floor and three bedrooms on the second floor and was priced at $2,000. A $5,000 frame house built in the same period had a parlor, sitting room, dining room, and kitchen on the first floor and four bedrooms on the second floor. By the 1880s, when Gross did the greatest volume building, prices had gone up somewhat, but payments remained low. In 1884, for example, Gross advertised a subdivision of seven-room houses priced at $7,500 with monthly payments of $15.

Novelist Upton Sinclair in *The Jungle* wrote of the Chicago land sales companies that sold flimsy houses to workers in the packinghouse district with the expectation that sooner or later the purchaser would not be able to make a payment. "When they failed, if it were only by a single month, they would lose the house and all that they had paid on it. And then the company would sell it over again," Sinclair explained. In marked contrast, Gross rarely foreclosed on a mortgage. In fact, rather than recycling houses, Gross recycled owners, making it easy for families to "trade up" from one S. E. Gross home or subdivision to a larger home or better location as their station in life improved.

Gross's whirlwind of subdivision activity had peaked by 1893. By the turn of the century, signs of Gross's deteriorating financial situation—and perhaps deteriorating mental condition—were becoming apparent. The labor problems of the late

Alta Vista Terrace, looking south from Byron Street. Between 1900 and 1904 Samuel Gross created Alta Vista Terrace, a picturesque block of row houses built facing the interior of the block that lies between Byron and Grace streets west of Kenmore Avenue. This undated photograph was taken before landscaping was added. In 1971 the block became the first residential district to be designated a Chicago landmark.
[From a postcard, photo by Charles R. Childs—Chicago Historical Society]

1880s and the severe effects of the 1893 financial crisis no doubt were contributing factors, together with probable over-extension by Gross and the loss of sales revenues as his early projects matured. In 1897 Gross unleashed a burst of publicity announcing the speed with which S. E. Gross lots were selling, many "even before the train reached the suburb," he declared. The sales reported, however, were in older subdivisions, specifically Dauphin Park, Grossdale, and West Grossdale. Gross

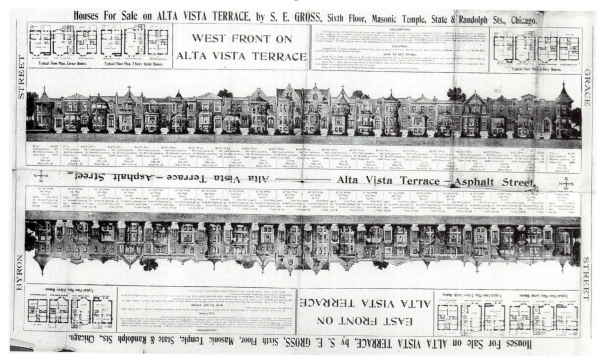

"Street of Forty Doors" [Alta Vista Terrace]. In this broadside, Samuel Gross advertised the Alta Vista Terrace row houses, sometimes called the "Street of Forty Doors," with an illustration showing that the facades of the east and west sides of the street are reversed mirror images. [Chicago Historical Society]

no doubt hoped that reports of great activity in his subdivisions would revive interest in still-unsold properties and generate needed cash.

In 1900 Gross resumed building, but his target now was the more affluent buyer, with the accompanying greater profit margins found in the higher-cost housing arena. His projects between 1900 and 1903 included the University Park development in the 5200 block of Greenwood Avenue in Hyde Park, undertaken in partnership with the estate of Charles Counselman, which owned the land. The Counselman arrangement itself suggests that Gross was in trouble financially. Other signs of trouble were repeated disputes with partners after 1900. In 1904, for example, Gross was sued by L. G. Fisher, who charged that Gross had not reported or distributed profits on an Indiana property that Gross and Fisher purchased in 1890. A more serious complaint was filed by the Counselman group in an effort to settle a claim over the use made of a building loan secured for the University Park projects.

In spite of his precarious financial position in this period, Gross managed to build Alta Vista Terrace, the S. E. Gross development that is perhaps best known to Chicagoans today. Alta Vista, the "Street of Forty Doors," is a short block of picturesque and now carefully maintained town houses suspended between Graceland Cemetery on the north and Wrigley Field on the south. The architect is presumed to have been Gross's staff architect at the time, J. C. Brompton. But the concept undoubtedly sprang from the romantic imagination of Samuel Gross. In 1971 the block became the first residential district to be designated a Chicago landmark. Gross created Alta Vista Terrace with the intention of making one of the four centerpiece three-story town houses his own home. The dream didn't hold together.

In a final effort to recover his financial footing, in 1903 Gross undertook another group of volume projects that involved the construction of three hundred houses in Chicago and in Milwaukee. The foundations had been laid when the Midwest was struck by a storm so severe that all building operations ceased for the remainder of the winter. Gross could not meet his notes. Unsettled debts ultimately included not only the major liens and mortgages, but unpaid office rent, bills for advertising, and salesmen's commissions.

Gross left Chicago—and his many creditors—in 1904. His wife's subsequent statement was that her husband, who "considered himself to be in poor health," was "traveling." By 1907 Gross had settled in Battle Creek, Michigan, perhaps to take advantage of Michigan bankruptcy laws. The bankruptcy petition he filed in 1908 listed liabilities of $500,000 against assets of $100,000, mostly in Chicago real estate. The Chicago *Tribune* reported that Gross had been an "inmate" in a Battle Creek sanatorium for the seven months prior to the declaration of bankruptcy. On April 20, 1909, Emily Gross filed for divorce, charging desertion. She testified that she and her husband had "lived apart" under one roof for a number of years. The decree was granted the day after the suit was filed. At this point, Mrs. Gross joined the ranks of Gross's creditors, seeking to recover $25,000 that she claimed Gross had invested for her and lost.

On April 23, Gross, who had been in Chicago during the divorce hearing but had not attended the proceedings, announced his plans for recovery of his decimated fortunes. Through his attorney, Gross informed the *Tribune* that he was negotiating with theatrical producers in the East to revive *Cyrano de Bergerac*, which he now described as "his play." His spokesman noted that Gross had returned to Battle Creek that day to attend to "some important business that is coming up in connection with his plans to embark in theatrical production." On May 2, 1909, less than two weeks after the divorce hearing, Gross, who was sixty-six, married Ruby Lois Houghey, who was eighteen years of age. The bride was the daughter of a Battle Creek building contractor. The account of the wedding noted that Gross had presented her with "diamonds, rubies and pearls valued at several thousands of dollars," and that after a wedding trip to New York and Atlantic City, it was the bridegroom's plan to take the new Mrs. Gross abroad where she would cultivate her singing voice in preparation for a career on the stage.

During the time that Gross lived and worked in Chicago, he was not known as an eccentric man, the grandiloquence of his later years notwithstanding. A historian of his time wrote of Gross: "In physique, he is robust; in character, positive yet not dogmatic; in intellect, intuitive and far-sighted; in disposition, genial; in tastes, cultivated and refined; and in his relations to his fellow man at once upright and liberal." Gross belonged to the best clubs, but acknowledged in an article written in 1904 for a Chicago journal that "I do not see much of what is popularly called society—that is, the dining and dancing set." He claimed more affinity to "the literary society, the rarest, the purest, and fairest society that has ever existed in the history of America or any other nation."

Gross died in Battle Creek four years after his May-December marriage. He had left Chicago behind him, but he left behind in Chicago a stock of thousands of sturdy frame houses that enhanced the lives of tens of thousands of Chicago families.

A MODEL SUBURB

J. Lewis Cochran.
[Engraving, Chicago Historical Society]

J. Lewis Cochran
(1857-1923)

Not all late-nineteenth-century developers were drawn to the central city and its potential to develop the "tall building." Some, after weighing the high costs and uncertain rate of return of downtown development projects, decided to turn their sights and their investment dollars instead to the city's outskirts. There opportunity awaited developers willing to build single-family housing and low-rise business blocks for the multitudes eager to flee the growing congestion of the inner city.

J. Lewis Cochran was one of these developers, as was Samuel E. Gross. But unlike Gross, whose specialty was working-class housing built on standard floor plans along the established routes of the railroads, Cochran looked to the inviting and underdeveloped lakefront to the north of the city limits, where he envisioned a first-class residential subdivision that would attract Chicago's elite families. The result was the community of Edgewater, a name coined by Cochran that came to evoke images of gracious homes and the leisurely recreational pursuits of the upper middle class. Cochran is remembered as the developer of Edgewater, but he was also a powerful force in the establishment of the commuter rail system that opened up Chicago's Sheridan Road and the North Shore to intensive residential development in the years between 1900 and 1930.

Cochran's father was a civil engineer from Pennsylvania who trekked westward in 1849 to join the California gold rush. He spent just ten months in the gold fields before turning his energies and resources to other pursuits, principally investment in Sacramento real estate. John Lewis Cochran was born in Sacramento but educated in Philadelphia. In 1877, at the age of twenty, he left school to become a sales representative for the Blackwell Durham Tobacco Company. In 1881 he was transferred by the company to Chicago.

Cochran's first venture into Chicago real estate was the purchase of a tract of land on Oak Street in the area that Potter Palmer was then reclaiming along the lakefront. As Chicago society migrated to Palmer's Gold Coast, Cochran was able to sell his Oak Street land at enough profit to enable him to search for larger undeveloped properties. Following Palmer's example (and the example of Hyde Park developer Paul Cornell a generation earlier), Cochran looked for lakefront land. His first major purchase was a seventy-six-acre tract in Lake View Township, bought with coinvestors in the fall of 1885. Lake View was then largely a farming community, but the area had become a favored locale for the summer homes of wealthier Chicago families. From Belmont Avenue, where these summer homes clustered, to as far north as Evanston the lakefront itself was largely undeveloped. Cochran subdivided this first tract, bounded by Lake Michigan, Evanston Avenue (now Broadway), and Foster and Bryn Mawr avenues, and Edgewater was born. The plan from the beginning was to create an idyllic suburb, a site that would be inviting to buyers who lacked true pioneering spirit but who sought a gracious country life-style just beyond the city limits.

In the first months of his development activity, Cochran laid out curbed streets and sidewalks, installed sewers, and

Edgewater stable building.
Cochran provided many amenities for affluent Edgewater residents, including a stable and livery, a gun club, boat club, and bathing house. [Edgewater Community Council—Edgewater Historical Society]

North Edgewater train station. J. L. Cochran persuaded the Chicago, Milwaukee and St. Paul Railroad to stop at Bryn Mawr and later at North Edgewater (now Granville) to accommodate buyers in his Edgewater subdivision. The North Edgewater Station shown here was built in the style of the romantic Edgewater homes designed by J. L. Silsbee.
(Edgewater Community Council—Edgewater Historical Society)

planted elm and ash trees. He built ten homes and a community building. A major attraction to prospective buyers, Cochran believed, would be the "Edison Incandescent Electric Light." Accordingly, he installed a generator, incorporated the Edgewater Light Company, and advertised that the streets of Edgewater were lighted and that all the homes were wired for electricity. The first sale in the new suburb was made in 1887, and Cochran celebrated the event by throwing the switch on the generator. A contemporary account relates that "no sooner had the first resident entered into occupancy of his new home than the electric plant was put in operation and the streets were lighted and the solitary inhabitant was able to read his evening paper by the clear, steady light of an incandescent burner in any room in his house." Within a year Cochran had built thirty homes along the lakeshore and more were under construction.

Cochran accepted a risky trade-off in planning his community on the shore. He had the lake to offer. But there were at the time no transportation services linking Edgewater with the city—a resource needed if Edgewater was to be competitive with other upscale suburbs such as Hyde Park and Riverside. However, the Chicago, Milwaukee and St. Paul railroad had trains running through the area. Cochran persuaded the railroad, whose route ran along the route now used by the Chicago Transit Authority elevated train, to stop at the street he had named Bryn Mawr Avenue. There he built the first Edgewater depot. A stop at North Edgewater (Granville) was added later.

In 1892 Cochran organized an electric trolley firm known as the Chicago North Shore Street Railway Company, which between 1892 and 1894 laid track connecting Evanston Avenue to Diversey. There riders changed to other cars that would take them downtown. The streetcar line, however, was only a stopgap in Cochran's transportation planning. By far the most important development for Edgewater—and ultimately the entire North Shore—was the organization in 1892 of the Northwestern Elevated Railroad Company, now known as the Howard El. Cochran was a leader among those who established the North Side line and served as a director of the company. A city ordinance passed in 1894 authorized construction of the elevated track from downtown to North Avenue. In 1900 the elevated line was extended to Wilson Avenue, stopping just short of Edgewater. In 1908 Cochran's long-sought connection was realized when the link from Wilson running through Edgewater to the southern boundary of Evanston at Howard Street was completed.

**"Fresh Every Morning"
Edgewater advertisement.**
Cochran promised buyers of
his Edgewater homes the good
life. This newspaper ad advises
readers to "Watch the people
who get on the cars at
Edgewater," noting that
"they're feeling better for
having passed another night
there—and they'll keep on
feeling better every day." A
move to Edgewater, the copy
promises, "means clear heads
for Chicago business men and
healthy bodies for the family at
home."
[Edgewater Community
Council—Edgewater Historical Society]

Cochran had a clear idea of the style and tone he wished to set for Edgewater, and he was fortunate in finding an architect capable of capturing—on paper at least—his vision of a suburban mansion. The architect was Joseph L. Silsbee, who himself was fortunate in employing during the period of the Edgewater work two assistants who would be heard from again. They were George W. Maher, who became one of the most popular and prolific architects of the residential Prairie school, and a young draftsman named Frank Lloyd Wright. Wright's work with Silsbee in 1887 was his first job in Chicago. Wright found Silsbee to be a bold and imaginative artist, describing his work as having a "charming picturesque effect." But not all buyers were enchanted with the Silsbee style of home design, which some likened to a "large farmhouse." Urban graystone mansions, in the mode of Palmer's Gold Coast development, were more in vogue among the well-to-do. Cochran was not averse to meeting the demand by employing other architects. Maher became a favorite of the buyers seeking stone houses as well as those preferring frame construction.

Cochran may have had another, equally practical, reason for employing architects other than Silsbee. Frank Lloyd Wright agreed that Silsbee was "a kind of genius," but suggested in his autobiography that Silsbee's talent was in designing a charming exterior without much concern for how the interior plan would be executed. Wright wrote, "I saw Silsbee was just making pictures. And not very close to what was real in the building." A Silsbee sketch, Wright recalled, would be brought from the master to the drafting room "to be fixed up into a building, keeping the floor-plan near the sketch if possible." When Wright wrote, "I learned a good deal about a house from Silsbee," he may well have meant that he learned the hard way.

Cochran was a community planner from the outset. He designed Edgewater to suit an upper-income clientele and embellished it with social amenities that reinforced the exclusive image of the community. He was one of the founders of the Saddle and Cycle Club, located first at Bryn Mawr and Kenmore Avenues and later relocated to the lakefront clubhouse designed by the colorful architect Jarvis Hunt. He built a stable and livery and saw to it that a gun club, boat club, and bathing house were built and maintained for residents.

Although Cochran understood the value of snob appeal, his advertisements also stressed convenience and individuality. His first large advertisements featured a Frank Lloyd Wright drawing of a spacious and charming Silsbee country home. His pitch was that improvements such as paved streets, sewers, and electric lights were not merely promised ("The Usual

Edgewater home. This J. L. Silsbee design for an Edgewater home is signed by Silsbee's young draftsman, Frank Lloyd Wright. [From *Inland Architect and News Record*, March 1888—Chicago Historical Society]

Way''), but in fact were already in place (''The Edgewater Way''). His ad copy described houses that were ''Modern, Artistic, With All Conveniences''; with ''No Two Alike''; and available ''On Terms That Will Suit You.'' Cochran pointed out that building loans would be arranged at no commission.

Cochran was a good businessman as well as a good salesman. He continued to build north as far as Elmdale Avenue, using the Edgewater aura he had created to promote sales of lots and houses in two subdivisions west of Evanston Avenue developed for the less affluent. Thus, after 1890, with the first phase of the Edgewater development firmly established, Cochran began to employ an even wider variety of architects and builders to produce more moderately priced homes for the smaller lots. In 1895, for example, three different architectural firms were used for eight houses Cochran built along Kenmore and Winthrop avenues. For eleven houses built in the first half of 1903, Cochran used five different builders. But for all his skill in promoting Edgewater, Cochran himself did not live there, except for very brief periods. During the first years of his subdivision activity, he lived on the Near North Side, at 65 East Division Street. When he married in 1892, he moved into an Edgewater home, but soon returned to the Gold Coast, where the family lived on North State Parkway and later moved to a luxury apartment at 1415 North Astor Street.

Cochran maintained his real estate business as the Edgewater development matured, but over the years his emphasis shifted from development to the mortgage loan field. In 1904 William B. McCluer joined Cochran as a partner. The Cochran and McCluer firm remained in business in Chicago well into the 1940s. Cochran also pursued investments outside of Chicago. In 1920 it was reported that he held title to thousands of acres of Texas Gulf Coast land where he was planning to sink oil wells. In civic life he was a vestryman of the St. James Episcopal Church, a director of the Chicago Title and Trust Company, and a consultant to Mayor Carter Harrison II in the 1898 revision of the city's building ordinance.

Cochran's success with the first Edgewater subdivision inspired imitation, and even before the turn of the century, similar subdivisions had sprung up around it, riding wherever possible on the prestige of the Edgewater name. These included Edgewater Heights, Edgewater Park, and the area that became known as North Edgewater. By 1900 the Edgewater community had taken on a life of its own, growing rapidly in the years before and just after World War I. Although Cochran intended Edgewater to remain a community of single-family homes—and in fact wrote restrictions to that effect into land deeds—the character of the neighborhood changed as it grew. After the arrival of rapid transit in 1908, many apartment buildings and residential hotels went up in the area, particularly on Kenmore and Winthrop avenues. Cochran was powerless to stop the persistent flat builders. It is ironic that he himself had opened the door to change by helping to build the elevated line, providing people of modest means ready access to the neighborhood. The face and residential character of Edgewater changed again in the 1950s, '60s, and '70s, when a wall of towering apartment buildings rose up along Sheridan Road, replacing the turn-of-the-century lakefront mansions. In the same period, progressive waves of ethnic groups settled along the tree-lined streets where flats had proliferated in the 1920s and where the old homes that did remain had been converted to other uses.

As they did most summers, the Cochran family spent the summer of 1923 at their vacation home at Mackinac Island. But instead of returning to their home on Astor Street in the fall, the family leased an apartment in the new Lake Shore Drive Hotel (now the Mayfair Regent Hotel), at 181 East Lake Shore Drive. Cochran, reportedly despondent over a lingering illness that curtailed his activity, jumped from the seventh-floor window of that apartment on the morning of September 25. He was sixty-five years old and left an estate valued at $400,000.

WALLER'S LOTS

Robert A. Waller
(1850-99)

Robert A. Waller.
[Moffett—Chicago Historical Society]

The developers of residential subdivisions have been known to wax poetic over the attributes of their properties. It is much less common for a celebrated poet to choose a developer's property as the subject of verse. But such was the case when Chicago poet Eugene Field perpetuated the name of his landlord and neighbor, Robert A. Waller, in a popular rhyme called "The Delectable Ballad of the Waller Lot":

> Up yonder in Buena Park
>   There is a famous spot,
> In legend and in history
>   [Known as] the Waller lot.

Robert Alexander "Bob" Waller, the developer of Buena Park, was a successful insurance executive, a controversial president of the Lincoln Park Commission, and an upstanding city comptroller. He also built downtown office towers and was a leading force in the development of North Lake Shore Drive and its Sheridan Road extension.

Born in Lexington, Kentucky, in 1850, the oldest of the two sons of James B. Waller and Lucy Alexander Waller, Robert Waller grew up among the colony of transplanted Kentucky families who took root and flourished in Chicago in the years prior to the Civil War. The family had made the move to Chicago in the late 1850s, together with James Waller's three brothers, William, Henry, and Edward.

Buena Park home. Robert A. Waller's Buena Park subdivision featured substantial brick and stone homes in the area bounded roughly by Graceland Cemetery, Irving Park Road, Montrose Avenue, and Broadway. Other landowners in the area followed Waller's example, employing such well-known architects as William Le Baron Jenney and George W. Maher. [From *Inland Architect and News Record*, February 1890—Chicago Historical Society]

James Waller settled his family in Lake View, north of Chicago, where he bought sixty acres of land near the lake and built a brick mansion that he named "Buena House." The Waller home, according to press reports of the time, was "constructed as nearly after the ideal Kentucky homestead as it was possible to erect it at that time" and was considered large enough for half a dozen families. Buena House stood in a heavily wooded tract in the triangle now bounded by Broadway, Sheridan Road, and Buena Avenue. The area around the original Waller homestead soon came to be known as "Buena Park." The family property in time included most of the land between Graceland Avenue on the south (now Irving Park Road) and Montrose Avenue on the north, extending from the Chicago, Milwaukee and St. Paul Railroad tracks to the lakeshore.

Robert's Buena Park boyhood was spent in the company of the numerous Waller cousins and the children of other transplanted Southern families who, like the Wallers, built country homes in areas just beyond the Chicago city limits. His mother was a first cousin of Carter H. Harrison I, and the Waller families frequently gathered at the Carter Harrison and Henry Waller homes on Ashland Avenue for the Kentuckians' weekly picnics and dances. Numbered among Waller's child-hood friends were Edward C. Waller, who later built the Rookery; Carter Harrison II, who, like his father, would become mayor of Chicago; and the children of another Louisville family, the Henry H. Honorés, whose daughter Bertha, who would marry Potter Palmer, became Chicago's reigning society queen in the 1880s and '90s.

Robert Waller attended Chicago public schools but, in the family tradition, completed his education at Washington and Lee University in Virginia. After graduating with high honors, he returned to Chicago and entered the insurance business. By 1875 he had become a partner in the D. L. Bowmar Insurance Company. When Bowmar retired in 1879, the firm was reorganized as R. A. Waller and Company. Waller's specialty was fire insurance, a difficult and unstable field in this period, but one in which he achieved considerable success. Between 1874 and 1893 he served as agent and underwriter for a total of seventeen major insurance carriers.

In 1876 Waller married Lina Swigart Watson, another of Chicago's Kentucky-born ladies known for their wit and festive family entertainments. The couple had one son, Robert A. Waller Jr. Like her sister-in-law, Mrs. James B. Waller Jr., and other educated women in her North Side social set, Lina Walker was active in the Friday Club, an 1890s literary group whose center of gravity was playwright Mary Aldis, the wife of Arthur Aldis and sister-in-law of Owen Aldis.

Waller began his career as a real estate developer in 1887 when he expanded and subdivided the family land holdings, which in all probability had been planned for development from the time of James B. Waller's Lake View land purchase in the 1850s. The first Buena Park subdivision included the "Waller Lot" commemorated by Eugene Field, but also extended west to the boundary of Graceland Cemetery, south to Irving Park Road, and north to Montrose (then called Sulzer Avenue). Broadway (then Evanston Avenue) was the eastern boundary. An 1889 addition extended the development eastward along Buena Avenue to the lake.

On the eve of Waller's platting of the district, the real estate journal *Economist* announced that Waller had already built twenty houses in the area, in addition to his own, and that Buena Park was being developed with paved streets, wide sidewalks, and access to water, sewer, and gas lines. In 1892 it was reported that James Gamble Rogers had drawn plans for another group of the brick and brick-and-stone houses that characterized Waller's subdivisions.

Waller's residence was at 4210 North Sheridan Road (until 1899 that section of Sheridan was known as Sheffield Avenue). This was the northwest corner of Sheridan and Buena

Avenue, just a stone's throw from the original family home. Waller eventually built about one hundred and fifty houses in Buena Park, many of them on the street named Alexander Avenue after his mother's family. (The segment of Kenmore Avenue that parallels the eastern boundary of Graceland Cemetery was formerly Alexander.) Other early landowners in the area followed the Wallers' example, developing the lakefront properties along streets they named Hazel, Kenesaw Terrace (now Hutchinson Street), Gordon Terrace, and Buena Terrace, and employing such well-known architectural firms and residential architects as William Le Baron Jenney and George W. Maher. But the name taken from the Waller homestead prevailed. The district, then and now, is Buena Park. St. Mary of the Lake Church, built in 1917, stands on the site of Waller's home. The Waller family themselves were among the founders of the Buena Memorial Presbyterian Church, which stands a block north of St. Mary of the Lake on the site of the original homestead. The land and a fund for construction of the 1922 sanctuary were bequeathed to the church by Lucy Alexander Waller.

By 1886 Waller had become active with the group of property owners and park commissioners who were working to extend Lake Shore Drive through Lincoln Park, on through Lake View Township, and eventually to the Evanston boundary. He became the first president of the Sheridan Drive Association. By 1889 this group had succeeded in having Sheffield Avenue, where it passed through Buena Park, declared the first link in the new north-south thoroughfare. The importance of this to future development of the Waller subdivision was not overlooked: The *Economist* noted that "Buena Park is the first suburban point that Sheridan Drive directly influences." In 1893 and 1894 Waller served as president of the board of Lincoln Park Commissioners, in the period when the board succeeded in extending North Lake Shore Drive from Fullerton through Lincoln Park.

Waller had received his appointment as park board president from Governor John Peter Altgeld, and it was Altgeld who summarily removed him from the board when Waller refused to pad the park commission's payroll with party appointments. The ensuing struggle between Waller and Altgeld, a *cause célèbre* in 1894, included an exchange of letters, published in the newspapers, that was long remembered. Following his public falling-out with Altgeld over patronage, Waller was appointed by Mayor Carter Harrison II to serve as one of the three members of the city's first civil service commission.

Robert Waller turned his attention in the 1890s from Buena Park to downtown office building development. In 1891 he

Ashland Block, northeast corner of Clark and Randolph streets, 1890s.
The sixteen-story Ashland Block, designed by Burnham and Root and completed in 1892, was a popular office location for lawyers and judges who did business at the adjacent City and County Building. In this view the old Garrick Building and Theatre can be seen just east of Epstean's New Dime Museum and the Bijou.
[W. T. Barnum, from *Chicago and Its Makers*]

formed the Ashland Block Association to buy (from the Alexander family) the land at the northeast corner of Clark and Randolph streets and finance construction of a new, sixteen-story Ashland Building. The first Ashland Block, a six-story postfire office building, had been built on that site by another Kentuckian, General Simon B. Buckner, and named for the Kentucky home of statesman Henry Clay. Waller was happy to perpetuate the name in his new office tower. Daniel H. Burnham was an old family friend, and the commission to design the new Ashland quite predictably went to Burnham and Root. The Ashland Building's North Loop location, then just east of the Sherman House Hotel and diagonally across the street from the City and County Building, made it a popular choice for the city's lawyers and judges. The Ashland was demolished in 1949 to make way for the downtown bus terminal, which, in turn, was replaced by the 1992 Chicago Title and Trust Building. Much of Chicago's government business remains centered at this site, just as it was when Waller developed it in 1892. The Ashland Block corner is embraced by the Daley Center to the southeast, the City and County Building to the southwest, and the State of Illinois Center to the northwest.

In 1896 R. A. Waller, D. H. Burnham and Company, the George A. Fuller Construction Company, and others formed the Merrimac Building Corporation to build the twelve-story Stewart Building at the northwest corner of State and Washington streets, with D. H. Burnham and Company as the architects. Whereas Edward C. Waller focused his development activities in the 1880s in the southern section of downtown, Robert Waller in the 1890s clearly preferred to develop in the central area, close to the City and County Building.

Waller was active in Chicago civic affairs even before his appointment as city comptroller in 1897. He was one of the original directors of the 1893 World's Columbian Exposition and was among the group of business leaders who went to Washington in 1891 to lobby for the legislation that brought the fair to Chicago. In 1897 Mayor Harrison found himself wedged between a rock and a hard place in his need to satisfy both the spirit of civil service reform and the demands of the political spoils system. His solution was to fire two of the three incumbent members of the civil service commission and appoint members more compliant with his own somewhat flexible interpretation of the civil service code. The third member of that independent-minded civil service commission, the mayor's friend and kinsman Bob Waller, posed more of a problem. Aware of Waller's defiance of Altgeld in the matter of party patronage, Harrison could not risk keeping him on the civil service commission—nor could he fire him. The solution was serendipity. Harrison removed Waller from the civil service commission by promoting him to the more powerful post of city comptroller.

As it turned out, the appointment was a critical one for Harrison, who needed the support of the business community and who even then was engaged in battle with Charles Yerkes and other forces seeking to control the city utilities and traction franchises. Harrison wrote in his memoirs:

> Where was I to find a man for comptroller commanding my confidence, so favorably known his very naming would establish beyond peradventure the financial stability of the new administration? If ever I had an inspiration it was then. . . . I deputed my brother to ask Robert A. Waller as a proof of personal friendship to accept the comptrollership for a while, long enough not only to give me a breathing spell but to assure the public of my determination to give Chicago the best in the way of financial direction.

The *Economist* reported in 1897 that "businessmen are very happy with Mayor Harrison for his selecting R. A. Waller as controller." Waller did not disappoint Harrison. As comptroller, he took on the utilities contractors and exposed gross overbilling in the street repair work done after installation of water mains and electrical conduits. A triumphant Harrison wrote of the subsequent confrontation: "It was the first time a great utility had been pounded to its knees by a public official, the first time the might of boodle had more than met its match." The mayor looked forward to another two years with Waller at his side. But this was not to be. In early February 1899, three months before the election, Waller caught a cold that became pneumonia. He died at his home in Buena Park on the afternoon of February 17, of pneumonia complicated by heart failure. He was not yet fifty years old. Waller was buried at Graceland Cemetery, near his beloved Buena Park neighborhood. In 1901 the city's new north division high school at Orchard Street and Armitage Avenue was named the Robert A. Waller High School, a name the school retained until 1980, when it was renamed Lincoln Park High School.

CITY FOR THE TWENTIETH CENTURY

1900-29

Chicago's status as an American city beyond compare was assured by the turn of the century. Home to 1.7 million people, Chicago churned with energy. It boasted lakefront parks, an advanced transit system, major industrial complexes, and an expanding service economy. The city was renowned as the birthplace of the modern skyscraper and the distinctive style of commercial architecture known as the Chicago school. The nineteenth-century capitalists had brought not only commerce but culture to Chicago. Their philanthropies supported opera, theater, and a symphony orchestra. The University of Chicago was well endowed. The Art Institute of Chicago was stocked with treasures. A matchless museum of natural history was in the making. The city had an active progressive element, exemplified by Jane Addams and her Hull House settlement. Men such as banker Lyman J. Gage backed reform campaigns designed to purge the city of corrupt politicians and their appointees. Aaron Montgomery Ward repeatedly sued to preserve the downtown lakefront for public use. Business leaders such as Martin Ryerson lavished money and talent on civic improvement initiatives such as the 1909 Plan of Chicago.

Chicago also had become the center of the American labor movement, but gains made by the unions in the late 1890s gave way to severe setbacks in 1900 and again just after World War I. Labor problems in the first two decades of the twentieth century included long lockouts and violent union-busting

Chicago Skyline, 1927. The years from 1918 to 1928 produced more building in Chicago than in all the preceding years of the city's history. [Kaufman and Fabry, from *Chicago and Its Makers*]

activities that took a terrible toll on the workers. The building industry lurched from crisis to crisis. In 1900 some sixty thousand workers were idled by a lockout that would last for fourteen months. Most new construction in the downtown area came to a halt. Building activity rebounded in 1901, and in 1906 reached an all-time high, only to be stalled again by a national financial panic in 1907.

Chicago's merchant princes were particularly active builders at the turn of the century. Their State Street dry goods stores had become the emporiums of the Midwest. Local trade was swelled by the swarms of passengers dropped off near their entrances by the elevated Loop railway that opened in late 1897. No wonder that to keep their competitive edge the great Marshall Field and Carson Pirie Scott stores pursued new building programs from 1900 through 1906, as did the Rothschild, Boston, and Mandel companies.

In the same period, Chicago created America's first industrial park, known as the Central Manufacturing District, around a spur railroad that served the Union Stock Yards. By 1920 this forerunner to today's industrial and business parks had developed more than 300 acres of land in the area centered at Pershing Road and Ashland Avenue specifically for the use of its more than two hundred industrial tenants. The 1900 opening of the Chicago Sanitary and Ship Canal, billed as the

Eighth Wonder of the World, reversed the flow of the Chicago River, sending the city's sewage south—away from the Lake Michigan water supply. The typhoid outbreaks that periodically had swept the city all but ceased. Celebrating this phenomenal engineering triumph, Chicagoans directed their attention to no less an undertaking than a transformation, by virtue of enlightened urban planning, of the entire city. A committee of business leaders turned to Daniel Burnham, the impresario of the 1893 Columbian Exposition, to create a plan for the city of the twentieth century.

In 1909 Burnham's far-reaching Plan of Chicago was received with rave reviews by the Commercial Club, sponsor of the three-year project. It was formally adopted in 1910, and the first Chicago Plan Commission was established to oversee its implementation. The Burnham Plan was a heroic achievement. It was not just a pretty picture to be saved for ''someday,'' nor was it an impossibly grandiose vision. It was treated as a working document to be acted upon without delay. Among other things, the plan called for construction of a Michigan Avenue bridge, creating the ''boulevard link'' that would connect Lake Shore Drive and the North Side with the central business district. Work to widen what was Pine Street into the broad new boulevard that became Upper Michigan Avenue began, with the support of a referendum, soon after

Streeterville, 1924. Some of Chicago's most desirable real estate today is concentrated in the area known as "Streeterville," bounded by the Chicago River, Lake Michigan, and East Lake Shore Drive [lower left] and North Michigan Avenue [extending on a diagonal from the Drake Hotel at Oak Street Beach at lower left to the Tribune Tower and Wrigley Building at the Michigan Avenue Bridge at upper right].
[Chicago Historical Society]

the plan was adopted. Burnham proposed a two-level bridge, with the upper level reserved for pedestrian and passenger traffic and the lower level designed for heavy commercial traffic. The upper level of the new Michigan Avenue Bridge was opened before a cheering crowd on May 14, 1920. The festivities were almost spoiled when the bridge tender began raising the south span of the bridge to let a steamer pass, unaware that autos were on it. Policemen alerted the bridge tender by firing shots into the air. A related plan for redevelopment of the south bank of the river was endorsed by the Chicago Plan Commission in 1917. The new Wacker Drive bilevel roadway opened on October 20, 1926, named for Charles H. Wacker, who as head of the Chicago Plan Commission since its inception, had led the campaign for public support for the plan.

While a new downtown was rising up off the drawing boards, suburban expansion, always a feature of Chicago development, continued. From 1900 to 1920, Cook County beyond the city limits grew faster in population than the city itself. Those who were able built grand new homes north, west, and south of the city in Evanston, Wilmette, Lake Forest, Oak Park, Hinsdale, Homewood, and Flossmoor. Residential patterns within the city limits also changed in this period. The North and Northwest sides of Chicago developed rapidly as many of the city's middle management and service workers relocated to the more comfortable neighborhoods that were growing up along the lines of the elevated railway and the reliable (but slower moving) streetcars.

The arrival of the automobile accelerated the movement of residents from the city to the suburbs, but worsened the chronic problem of traffic congestion in the central business district. In 1910 close to 14,000 motor vehicles were registered in the city, compared to 58,000 horse-drawn vehicles. By 1926 almost 375,000 motor vehicles were registered. Developers responded to off-street parking ordinances by erecting multistory parking garages and garages built into office buildings, including the innovative 35 West Wacker Building.

The building industry started the second decade of the twentieth century with a burst of activity as developers hastened to meet a growing demand for downtown office space. But projects proceeded by fits and starts. Many were stalled by the renewal after 1910 of labor union disputes and lockouts. The ratification of the income tax amendment in 1913 forced many investors or potential investors to withdraw their funds from real estate and development activities in favor of safer, tax-exempt vehicles such as state and municipal bonds.

America's entry into World War I in 1917 further stalled development as the federal government ordered all work on nonessential projects stopped to conserve materials and labor for the war effort. Controls were lifted after the armistice that ended the war in 1918, but costs soared. Chicago labor problems were carried to the U.S. District Court, with the result that unions that refused to accept the terms of the wage settlement decreed by Judge Kenesaw Mountain Landis were outlawed and their trades placed on an open shop list. With a subdued labor force and stabilization of the cost of materials, entrepreneurs dreamed again of tall buildings. A climate of renewed prosperity, capital available from new sources, and changes in state laws governing development fueled a building boom of unprecedented proportions in the 1920s. Building height limitations were raised after 1923 to match the soaring spirit of the city.

The ten years from 1918 to 1928 produced more building in Chicago than in all the preceding years of the city's history. Over 14 million square feet of office space was added to the central business district between 1923 and 1930. Skyscrapers of stone, brick, steel, and terra cotta shot up on the newly completed Wacker Drive, replacing the riverside jumble of the old South Water Market. By 1928 more than 750 feet of frontage on Wacker Drive had been improved, with investment totaling almost $60 million. Upper Michigan Avenue was another hotbed of activity. The founders of the North Central

Merchandise Mart, c. 1929-32. [opposite page] The Merchandise Mart, built by Marshall Field and Company between 1923 and 1931, epitomized the expansive spirit of the 1920s. Sited over the Chicago and North Western Railway tracks on the north bank of the river, it was one of Chicago's first air-rights developments. With a floor area of nearly four million square feet, it was the world's largest building until the Pentagon was constructed in Washington, D.C., during World War II.
[Raymond Trowbridge—Chicago Historical Society.]

Business District Association promoted the redevelopment of sleepy old Pine Street as a grand boulevard studded with smart shops, hotels, apartments, and office buildings. The twin sentinels of the Wrigley and Tribune buildings stood watch at the south end of the avenue at the river. The elegant Drake Hotel and, by the end of the decade, the towering Palmolive Building defined the north end of the boulevard.

A tiara of luxurious high-rise apartment buildings grew up along the arc of the lake at East Lake Shore Drive, extending northward. By the late 1920s, high-rise apartment buildings, for both the affluent and the middle class, were scattered across the city. They could be seen along the lakeshore north as far as Evanston and south as far as 79th Street. Between 1919 and 1929, nearly a quarter of a million apartment units were constructed, compared to no more than sixty-five thousand houses built during the same period.

The Illinois General Incorporation Act of 1919 for the first time allowed investors to form a corporation for the explicit purpose of erecting a building. A wave of inexperienced, part-time developers leaped into the business. The rush to build was further fanned by the ready availability of capital raised through the sale of real estate bond issues secured by the mortgage on a projected building. Known as "gold bonds" because an investment in real estate in the 1920s was considered to be "as good as gold," these popularly priced securities promised even the most modest investor a high rate of return on the contribution of as little as $100. Fired with a boom mentality, would-be developers discovered that it was possible to lease land, obtain a bond issue using the leasehold as security, and make a building start without the investment of any appreciable amount of equity. More than one unscrupulous operator kited from one project to another funds received from the sale of cooperative shares in apartment buildings still under construction.

Warnings of an overbuilt market and the fragility of largely unregulated financing mechanisms were evident to some, but went largely unheeded. As early as 1927, a full two years before the crash of the stock market in 1929, many developers were in default on the interest payments due on second mortgages. Others were already in foreclosure. The worst was yet to come. The crash of 1929 and the sharp drop in economic activity on all fronts dealt the legitimate Chicago real estate industry a mortal blow. Property after property passed into the hands of mortgage holders. In 1932 well over fifteen thousand mortgages were foreclosed. Banks that were heavily invested in nonliquid real estate were forced to close when they were unable to pay out the huge amounts of cash demanded during runs on their deposits. Two thirds of Chicago's 225 banks closed in the period between the end of 1929 and summer of 1932. Gold bonds became all but worthless. Chicago waited with the rest of the nation for prosperity to return. Periodically, reports were issued predicting an upturn just around the corner. But time passed, and when no sustained revival occurred, the forecasts were quietly put aside.

In 1933 and 1934 the city bravely staged its second world's fair, A Century of Progress. More than thirty-nine million people visited the fairgrounds to view such wonders as a 200-foot thermometer, an automobile assembly line, and the two 600-foot towers built to facilitate the Sky Ride. The fair was a boon for Chicago in a very dark era. But unlike the World's Columbian Exposition of 1893, the event generated no more than a fraction of the development activity expected.

Most of Chicago's leading developers saw their careers abruptly ended by the Great Depression. Many lost their buildings to foreclosure and their energy to days that passed without the abundance of business and civic activities that had filled their lives. Even in the worst of times, no one could have foreseen that more than a generation would pass before another skyscraper would be built in Chicago.

TITAN OF STATE STREET

Otto Young
(1844-1906)

Otto Young.
[From *Men of Illinois*—The Newberry Library]

At the turn of the century, Otto Young—co-owner with E. J. Lehmann of Chicago's fabulous Fair department store—controlled more land in the downtown commercial area than any individual before or since. His holdings on State Street alone included the massive Fair building and the land under it at State and Adams, the Carson Pirie Scott buildings and leaseholds at State and Madison streets, and the coveted southwest corner of State and Washington streets where the Reliance Building stood. His properties on Michigan Avenue were described in a 1903 newspaper account as "appalling in extent."

Although Young was both merchant prince and land baron, neither term accurately defines his role in the growth of Chicago in the expansive years of the 1890s. Young was a financier. His most public activity was the decisive role he played as the lead fund-raiser for the 1893 Columbian Exposition. More typically, he operated very much behind the scenes as a prime backer—sometimes white knight—in State Street retail development and the development of the Wabash Avenue wholesale jewelers district. It is of more than passing interest that Young, as the developer of the 1906 addition to the world-famous Carson Pirie Scott Store, was also the perpetrator of one of the most notable snubs in the history of Chicago architecture—the selection of Daniel Burnham as architect for the addition over Louis H. Sullivan, who designed the original building (now a Chicago landmark) at the corner of State and Madison.

E. J. Lehmann's Fair Store [under construction, 1891]. The building, developed by Otto Young between 1891 and 1897, occupied the entire block along the north side of Adams Street between Dearborn and State streets. The first section [at left] was completed in 1891 as the steel-frame structure for the second section, at the corner of Dearborn and Adams, was

Otto Young had the mind of a chess master, moving with subtle but deliberate strokes. He was patient, tenacious, and unassuming—and he always got his way. But Young was also a man of contrasts. His office space at the Fair Store was spare, even spartan, furnished only with a table and a straight wooden chair. His residential surroundings, however, were quite different. Young built a fifty-room summer home on Lake Geneva, in southern Wisconsin, and furnished it with oriental carpets, tapestries, and fine antiques. The house was finished with exquisite woodwork ornamented with gold leaf and decorated with gold-plated electrical switches. Young named the mansion Younglands. Others called it "the Italian Palace."

Chicagoans in the late nineteenth century were proud of the city's self-made men, and Otto Young typified the kind of success story they loved to tell. The story most widely circulated was that he had been born into an impoverished German family and that after the death of his father, he had been sent to live with relatives in New York, in the hope that in America the boy would find a better life. But the truth about Otto Young's early life is somewhat different and is much more interesting for what it reveals about his personality and his single-mindedness in pursuit of an objective. The family was by no means impoverished. Otto was born in 1844 at the family home, a comfortable manor house in Elberfeld, Germany. His father and grandfather were successful architects. It was expected that Otto would follow in the family profession. It is true that his father died when Otto was ten years old, but the real consequence of this event was that his mother remarried and moved to New York City. Otto was left behind in Dusseldorf.

The "relatives" in America referred to in accounts of Otto Young's early life were, in fact, his own mother and her second husband. Otto was not sent to America. He came on his own, as a runaway, and with the intention of joining his mother. Although he was hardly more than a child and spoke very little English, he made his way first to London, where he worked at odd jobs to earn his passage across the Atlantic. He arrived at

The Fair Store decorated for the 1899 Fall Festival. In 1906 two additional stories were added to the original building, designed by William Le Baron Jenney and William B. Mundie.
[Chicago Historical Society]

his mother's doorstep in New York in 1859, unexpected, uninvited, and apparently much to her astonishment. She immediately enrolled him at a military academy on the Hudson River that was appropriate for boys of his age and families of her standing. Otto ran away from school eight months later and returned to New York City—not to his mother's house, but to begin a new life.

He found a job as a clerk in a cigar store and eventually established a small business as a vendor of jewelry and "fancy goods." In 1867 he took a job as a traveling salesman for a larger jewelry and luxury goods company and began scouting for more promising opportunities. By chance, Young was in Chicago in October 1871 when the city was destroyed by the Great Fire. He liked the spirit of new beginnings that swept the city in the wake of the disaster. A year later he returned to Chicago and with his savings was able to buy an interest in a Chicago wholesale jewelry house. By 1881 Young had bought out the remaining partner, and the firm's name had been changed to Otto Young and Company. This business remained in existence until the 1960s.

In 1886 Young purchased a half interest the State Street department store established by E. J. Lehmann, a fellow German with a background as an itinerant peddler and jewelry salesman. Lehmann's emporium, which he called the Fair, was a cross between today's giant discount store and an army surplus outlet. It carried goods of every description—whatever became available—and specialized in volume sales at low prices with quick turnover. One of Lehmann's expansion strategies was to buy out both the inventory and the leases of failing businesses and then take over the premises. Through this means, by the mid-1880s the Fair operation sprawled through most of the former storefronts and upstairs flats on the north side of Adams Street between State and Dearborn.

The growth of the business after Young joined Lehmann was phenomenal, with capital value increasing fivefold in the first four years of the partnership. Young managed the company's business affairs, while Lehmann, an old-time carnival barker, continued to handle promotions and merchandising. Young's role in the business changed—literally overnight—in April 1890, when Augusta Lehmann secured a court order committing her forty-year-old husband to an "eastern asylum for the insane." A second order issued the following day made her conservator of his $2.5 million estate. From that day until Lehmann's death at the sanatorium in 1900, the burden for managing the Fair operations rested on Young's shoulders. These ten years would prove to be the decade of the Fair's greatest growth.

From the beginning of the partnership, Young had set his hand to acquiring the land under the south half of the block bounded by State, Dearborn, Adams, and Monroe, as the site for a substantial new retail building. In mid-1890 Young closed on the last of the ten parcels involved. The value of the real estate was placed at $3 million, making the Fair property acquisition the largest consolidation of downtown property in the city's history.

Young and Lehmann had planned a substantial building designed specifically for retail. They selected William Le Baron Jenney and his new partner William B. Mundie to execute the plans. When the first of the four sections of the new building was completed in 1891, and the last, carrying the store through from State Street to Dearborn, was completed in 1897, real estate writers calculated that Chicago's famous Fair Store had more than six miles of counter space. Two additional stories were added in 1906, bringing the building's height to twelve stories. (In 1965 the Fair Store was remodeled for use as a Montgomery Ward store and was finally demolished in 1985.)

When Ernst Lehmann died, Augusta became half-owner of the Fair . She immediately named her companion and personal business manager as secretary-treasurer of the company. In 1905, when she wanted to bring her sons into the business, Young was more than willing to accommodate by selling her his half-interest in the store. The popular press headlined the news that Mrs. Augusta Lehmann had acquired full control of the Fair Store. Less notice was taken of the more important fact that the half-block of extremely valuable Loop real estate on which the store stood was transferred to Young. Mrs. Lehmann may have become sole proprietor of the Fair, but Otto Young structured the deal in such a way that he became her landlord.

The transaction with Augusta Lehmann in which she took the business and the building and he got the land was entirely consistent with Young's long-range land acquisition strategy. In 1893, for example, Young acquired the southwest corner of State and Washington streets from William E. Hale, in a way that was advantageous to both parties. Hale needed capital to complete the Reliance Building, which he had begun on that site. Young bought the land under the building from Hale for $480,000, leased it back to Hale for 198 years, and construction went forward.

In 1904 Young masterminded a similar, but altogether more complex, series of transactions that in the end left him in control of not only the land but also the buildings in the block now principally occupied by the Carson Pirie Scott Store. In the process, Young dealt architect Louis H. Sullivan a painful blow. The Sullivan-designed Carson Pirie Scott corner building, which with its renowned iron facade and second-story entresol is now a Chicago landmark, was built by retailer David Mayer to house the Schlesinger and Mayer department store. Mayer and his partner Leopold Schlesinger had occupied the choice State and Madison corner since 1881 when they moved their dry goods business from West Madison street to the Bowen Building, which then occupied the site. The store thrived in the State Street retail environment, and Schlesinger and Mayer soon began a series of renovations and expansions that continued through 1897.

Adler and Sullivan were their architects of choice from the beginning. Schlesinger was an active member of the Chicago Sinai Congregation. The Sinai synagogue, completed in 1875, marked the first collaboration of Dankmar Adler and Louis H. Sullivan. In 1884 Schlesinger commissioned Adler and Sullivan, by then partners, to build his home on South Michigan Avenue. Other projects for the Sinai Congregation followed. With his passion for opera, Mayer would have known Adler and Sullivan also for their work on the 1879 Central Music Hall. The firm's work on the Schlesinger and Mayer store renovations and expansions began in 1885.

In 1898, under pressure to remain competitive with other, more modern State Street establishments, Schlesinger and Mayer announced plans to replace the old Bowen Building with a completely new structure. Adler and Sullivan had dissolved their partnership, but Mayer remained loyal to both. Sullivan, who at that time had no other clients, was commissioned to design the new building. Adler was commissioned separately to design the store's power plant. The nine-story Madison Street section of the new building was completed in 1899. But the centerpiece corner building—Sullivan's masterwork and one of the landmarks of the Chicago school of architecture—was not completed until 1903-04, and then only at tremendous cost to the Schlesinger and Mayer partnership, both personally and financially. The high rents that they were paying to Marshall Field for the lease on the State and Madison corner, compounded by escalating construction costs and loss of revenues during construction periods, created critical cash flow problems for Schlesinger and Mayer.

Schlesinger had wearied of the struggle by 1902 and sold his interest in the business to a third party. But even an infusion of new capital was not enough to stem the tide of red ink. Mayer had a beautiful building going up, but he was in serious trouble. He saw further expansion as the only means available to him to generate enough revenue to save the business. At this point, Mayer turned to Otto Young, who owned parcels on State street toward Monroe that Mayer needed to complete the store's expansion along State. Young agreed to give Mayer a ninety-nine-year lease on the properties at a fee based on a valuation of $18,000 per front foot. This was an astonishingly high figure—six times the leasing rate Mayer paid Marshall Field for the State and Madison corner parcel.

Then a curious thing happened. According to the Chicago *Tribune,* "insurmountable differences arose involving the building to be erected and the deal fell through." Mayer's need for additional State Street property was so great that he had been willing to pay an exorbitant rental for it. But he drew the line over some condition imposed by Young regarding the building to be constructed on the property. The problem, one may surmise from later events, was Louis Sullivan.

The debacle engendered bitter feelings. Young and Mayer, in the wreckage of the State Street property deal, entered into a high-stakes game in which each party attempted to block the other from acquiring additional frontage in any part of the city block bounded by State, Madison, Wabash, and Monroe. By 1904 resources of the Schlesinger and Mayer company had been strained to the breaking point. Mayer reluctantly realized he had to sell. He might even have been willing to sell to Otto Young, but Young would not have been in the market for a department store. He was in the process of getting rid of one himself.

And then another seemingly curious thing happened. Suddenly, Gordon Selfridge, who had been a partner in Marshall Field and Company for fifteen years, approached Mayer—as an individual—with an offer to buy the Schlesinger and Mayer business and buildings. Within a week the transaction was complete. Selfridge took possession of the property on Saturday, June 11, 1904. On the following Monday morning, Selfridge sold the Schlesinger and Mayer buildings and leaseholds to Otto Young. Young leased the buildings back to Selfridge. Within a period of just a few weeks, Selfridge sold the business to the Carson Pirie Scott department store group. John G. Shedd, who was then chairman of the board of Marshall Field and Company, negotiated the transaction. Shedd's subsequent memorandums reveal that Otto Young was a major, though silent, player in the transfer of the Schlesinger and Mayer business through Selfridge to the Carson group.

In the entire complex transaction, it seems that everyone—except Louis Sullivan—prospered. Young got the State and Madison leaseholds and buildings. Mayer got out of the retail business without losing face to Young and went on to become a successful property developer in his own right. Selfridge took the money he made on the Carson transaction and moved to London, where he established the successful Selfridge's store on Oxford Street. The Carson group, which moved from the Reliance Building into the Sullivan-designed building in the fall of 1904, got the highly desirable State and Madison location, the busiest intersection in the city and therefore a prime retailing location.

Young immediately signed an agreement with Carson Pirie Scott to build the addition that Mayer had planned before his falling-out with Young. The terms of the lease were straightforward—the only interesting provision being that the tenant could not sell or serve "spirituous liquors" on the premises. This clause may yield a clue to Young's problem with Sullivan, who was known as a heavy drinker, but would not seem in itself to have constituted any "insurmountable difficulty." The agreement provided that Young would erect for his tenant, Carson Pirie Scott, a twelve-story building to the south along State Street to be consistent in style with the 1903-04 Sullivan building that occupied the State-Madison corner. The difference being that the architect of Young's choice was not Sullivan but D. H. Burnham and Company.

Young's decision to use the Burnham company to complete a building that Sullivan considered his own deeply offended him. Two years after the event, Carson Pirie Scott gave Sullivan a luke-warm letter of recommendation that acknowledged Sullivan's demand for recognition as the original architect but provided little consolation. The letter praised the "high taste and skill of Louis H. Sullivan," noting particularly the beauty of the corner entrance of the building. The conclusion was cool: "We learn from Messrs. Schlesinger and Mayer that their transactions with Mr. Sullivan were perfectly satisfactory, and gladly add our words of approval to his skill and success as an architect."

It should be noted that Young had a prior relationship with Daniel Burnham. Young had been pleased with the Burnham company's work on the 1897 Silversmith Building, a develop-

Carson Pirie Scott Store, 1912. [opposite page] The nine-story Madison Street section [1899] at left, and the landmark centerpiece building [1903-04]—with three bays on Madison Street, a curved bay at the corner, and seven on State Street—were designed and built under the supervision of Louis H. Sullivan for the Schlesinger and Mayer department store. After Otto Young bought the property in 1904 and leased it to Carson Pirie Scott, he extended the State Street frontage [1906] with a five-bay addition. [Chicago Historical Society]

ment he supported as a means of keeping the Wabash and Monroe area attractive to wholesale jewelers. Some years later, Young and a son-in-law, Lawrence Heyworth, developed the eighteen-story Heyworth Building—located at the southwest corner of Madison Street and Wabash Avenue adjacent to the Silversmith—for the same reason. Young's own jewelry business, Otto Young and Company, occupied the sixth floor.

In the case of the Heyworth Building, Burnham was the one who was not so pleased with Young. Burnham's diaries in the early weeks of 1904 attest to his careful cultivation of the client, leading to a letter advising Young on March 3 that he had decided upon white glazed terra cotta for the exterior of the building. Young summarily overruled Burnham, sending word through Heyworth, that, on the contrary, the finish would be brown brick. "This means an entire change of our plans and very much delay," Burnham wrote irritably to a colleague on March 7. The Heyworth was completed, presumably on schedule, in 1905, but the exterior was a compromise: It was brick, but with terra cotta on the lower four and top three stories.

Young's next project—for which he had planned long and carefully—was to have been a luxury hotel on Michigan Avenue, at the same site on which Tracy and John Drake later built the Blackstone Hotel. Young did not live to see the fulfillment of his Michigan Avenue plans. He had been in poor health for some years, but became acutely ill and died at his Lake Geneva home late in November 1906. The cause of death was tuberculosis complicated by diabetes. He was sixty-two. The Chicago *Tribune* reported his death in a front page story that described Young as a man "who cared little for society" and added, "He was noted for his hatred of sham, for his unassuming manner and for his habit of keeping to himself." The Chicago news magazine *Inter Ocean* said simply: "He was one of the men who built Chicago."

Young's fortune was estimated at $25 million, about $17 million of it in real estate. He left a will that was similar to that of Marshall Field in its intention to conserve assets for a future generation. He provided generously for his wife and four daughters, but instructed that the major part of the estate be held in trust for his grandchildren. Final distribution was to be made after the deaths of Young's four daughters, and then only when the youngest grandchild had reached the age of twenty-one. This did not occur until 1956, when Young's last surviving daughter, Daisy, died.

Otto Young's will and the trust he established had, in the intervening half-century, been buffeted by a barrage of claims and lawsuits brought against the estate by heirs, heirs-to-be, in-laws, ex-in-laws, the son by another marriage of a former Young son-in-law, and even the second wife of a deceased former son-in-law. The wait was worthwhile for some of those who lived long enough. But not for all of them. Several of the heirs, including Daisy's own son, spent their inheritance long before its distribution. They did this by borrowing, through speculators' assignments, against the anticipated value of the estate. Otto Young himself was a man who never took out a loan and never held a bill longer than twenty-four hours. He always paid in cash. He planned long and well. It is sad and ironic that his last act, provision for a responsible transition of his wealth to heirs, should have gone so badly awry.

Tracy C. Drake.
[Lewis-Smith Studio—Chicago
Historical Society]

John B. Drake.
[From *Chicago and Its Makers*]

CHICAGO'S INNKEEPERS

Tracy C. Drake
(1864-1939)
John B. Drake
(1872-1964)

In 1885 John Burroughs Drake threw a party at the Grand Pacific Hotel for some five hundred of his closest friends. The occasion was Drake's thirtieth annual Thanksgiving Game Dinner, a robust tradition in the city since 1855, when he first set up shop as a steward and part-owner of the Tremont House hotel. On hand was an elaborate spread of gourmet offerings gathered from throughout the continent and prepared by the most talented chefs Drake could assemble. And a good thing that was, because a Drake game dinner menu featured such items as boiled buffalo tongue, roast opossum, saddle of black tail deer, broiled jack snipe, and ragout of squirrel—more than fifty similarly enticing dishes in all.

Forty-five years later, the sons of John B. Drake were still employing the nation's best cooks and confectioners, but at their own hotels, the Blackstone and the Drake. Restaurant critic and Chicago historian John B. Drury advised in 1931 that "if you are an epicure—and more so if you are not—you will receive the culinary thrill of your life in gazing over the Blackstone's catalogued à la carte menu, an impressive folio containing almost every dish eaten by civilized man." Except, we can be sure, ragout of squirrel.

Tracy C. Drake and John B. Drake II, who were the developers as well as the proprietors of the Blackstone and Drake hotels, were born to the innkeeper's trade. The senior John B. Drake, who arrived in Chicago in 1855, eventually became sole owner of the Tremont House. He remained associated with this famous hotel until 1873. In 1874 Drake purchased the lease and furnishings of the newly rebuilt Grand Pacific Hotel on the west side of Clark Street between Quincy Street and Jackson Boulevard. The Grand Pacific, whose guests over the years included Thomas A. Edison, Oscar Wilde, and Lily Langtry, flourished during Drake's management. Chicago was then, as it is now, a popular convention city, and the Grand Pacific, the favored hotel for the Republican Party kingmakers, rapidly became known as the "Republican Headquarters of the West," to the discomfort of the Chicago old timers who complained that at convention time "the slouch-hatted henchmen of Grant, Blaine, Logan, or Garfield usurped our

Blackstone Hotel. This view is looking north on Michigan Avenue at Balbo Drive. The Drake brothers' twenty-two-story hostelry was completed in 1910. Designed by society architect Benjamin Marshall and his partner Charles Fox, the elegant hotel enjoyed an international reputation and over the years became a center of national political activity.
[Barnes and Crosby—Chicago Historical Society]

easy chairs and sullied our favorite corners with their tobacco juice.''

In 1863 Drake married Josephine C. Corey, of Chicago, and they raised three sons and two daughters. Tracy Corey Drake, the eldest son, was born in 1864. John Burroughs Drake II was born in 1872. Tracy's education was begun in Chicago schools, but at the age of thirteen he was sent to the Vermont Episcopal Institute and from there to the Trinity Military Institute in Tivoli, New York. He was graduated from Rensselaer Polytechnic Institute in 1886 and returned to Chicago to learn the hotel business, at the feet of a master. He started as a clerk in the commissary department at the Grand Pacific, soon becoming the head steward and eventually a partner and part-owner. John attended the Harvard School in Chicago, and then, like Tracy, went East to school, first attending St John's Military Academy in Ossining, New York, and later Phillips Academy in Andover, Massachusetts. Before returning to Chicago and a position at the Grand Pacific, John traveled around the world.

Although the events that closed the Grand Pacific could not have been foreseen, even by 1890 the great hotel's days were numbered. It would fall victim to a stubborn confrontation between two obdurate old Chicagoans—John B. Drake and Levi Z. Leiter. As a result, the sons of John B. Drake, who had planned careers at the Grand Pacific, were forced to become instead the builders and developers of their own hotels. In 1886 Leiter, the former partner of Marshall Field and one of the city's most insatiable landholders, bought the land under the eastern half of the Grand Pacific Hotel from the estate of P. F. W. Peck. The building itself had been built by and had once been fully owned by the Pacific Hotel Company, a subsidiary of the Lake Shore and Rock Island railroads. That company in turn leased the premises to the hotel proprietors, the senior John Drake and his partner Samuel Parker. The western parcel of the land on which the hotel stood, and the western half of the building, were owned by Northwestern University at the time that Leiter came into the picture.

Leiter did not wait long to invoke a reappraisal clause in the lease for the purpose of raising the rent on his half of the land. The Pacific Hotel Company replied that under those circumstances, it was no longer interested in leasing the property and urged Leiter to buy the building and let the Grand Pacific transfer the Drake-Parker lease to him. Leiter was more than willing to become Drake's landlord, but refused to pay anything for the building, claiming that half a building was worthless and assuming that when the Pacific Hotel Company lease expired in 1890, the building would become his by default. It didn't work out that way. The railroads succeeded in having the matter referred to a three-man arbitration panel, whose members included Leiter's nemesis, Marshall Field. The panel ruled in favor of the Pacific Hotel Company. Leiter was forced to pay $40,000 for the company's half of the hotel building.

As half owner of the Grand Pacific Hotel building, Leiter was now in a position to put the screws on Drake, whose lease would come up for renewal in May 1895. Drake did not intend to take a rent increase peaceably. In 1894 he informed his landlords that they would have to undertake $500,000 in building improvements if they expected to retain Drake and Parker as tenants. Leiter responded with the wisdom of Solomon, stating that he would rather tear down his half of the building and replace it with an office tower. Drake was not impressed by Leiter's threat. It was well known that the city's newly imposed building height limitations had made construction of a tall building a poor investment. Furthermore, there was little demand for office space in 1894, as the country grappled with a deepening recession.

The *Economist,* Chicago's real estate journal, predicted that a compromise would be reached, based on the assumption that because Northwestern University owned half of the land and half of the building, it would be a party to the negotiations and a moderating influence. But Drake and Leiter were playing hardball. In the month before the lease was to expire, Drake put the hotel furniture up for sale. Leiter made no concessions. In May 1895 Drake refused to meet Leiter's demands and closed the doors of the Grand Pacific forever. The old timers did not forgive Leiter for this assault on a cherished Chicago tradition. Six months later, John B. Drake I, Chicago's master innkeeper, died.

It appeared the Drake hotel dynasty was over before it began. In 1896 Tracy and his wife Annie left Chicago to travel for two years throughout Europe and Asia. For a time, John had a position with the Illinois Trust and Savings Bank. (The institution occupied familiar ground. Shortly after the hotel closed, Northwestern University's half of the building was razed to make way for the bank's new headquarters.) Tracy Drake became a bond salesman on his return from his world tour. In the years between 1900 and 1907, however, the Drake brothers' primary business was management of their father's estate, which was valued at $2 million at the time of his death.

In 1898 Tracy Drake purchased a large tract of land on the south shore of Lake Geneva, in Wisconsin, and began construction of a white, colonnaded family home, designed by society architect Howard Van Doren Shaw. The setting bore no resemblance to the Hawaiian Islands, which the Drakes had come to love. Nonetheless, when the antebellum-style mansion was completed in 1901, they christened it Aloha Lodge. They named their steam yacht Kaiulani. While Annie Drake decorated the house to suit the needs of a family with young boys, Tracy replanted the grounds of the estate with one hundred sugar maples carried by bobsled across the frozen lake from a grove near Williams Bay. Over the years, the trees presented an annual mystery to Drake, who had brought them to Aloha Lodge because he admired the brilliant red foliage they displayed when he discovered them at Williams Bay. The maples thrived on the Drake estate and produced marvelous golden leaves, season after season. Gold, but never red. A modern botanist would explain that to achieve their red pigmentation, maples require full sun and other specific climatic conditions that no doubt existed at Williams Bay—but not at Aloha Lodge.

Since 1895 the Drakes had hoped to return to the hotel business. In 1908 the opportunity presented itself in the form of a lot at the northwest corner of South Michigan Avenue and Hubbard Place (now Balbo Drive). The location had sentimental as well as commercial value. The home of Timothy Blackstone had once stood on the site. Blackstone, a president of the Chicago and Alton Railroad, was of the same generation as J. B. Drake I, who had been a director of Blackstone's company. In 1906 the Drakes' friend and Lake Geneva neighbor Otto Young purchased the property from the Blackstone estate. It was the key piece needed by Young to begin development of a hotel on South Michigan Avenue, a goal to which he devoted the last several years of his life. Young himself died within months of acquiring the property. In 1908 Tracy Drake leased the Michigan Avenue corner from the Young estate and announced plans to build a fine hotel there. The *Economist* proclaimed the revival by the Drake brothers of the spirit of the Grand Pacific. The new hotel would be called the Blackstone, with proprietorship held by the brothers' newly incorporated Drake Hotel Company. Construction was capitalized at $1.5 million. A bond issue of $600,000 to $750,000 was anticipated. The architects were theater- and luxury-apartment builder Benjamin Marshall and his partner Charles Fox.

The twenty-two-story French Renaissance building went up quickly over the spring and early summer of 1909. Even as the hotel was being constructed, the brothers, in partnership with Marshall and others, began executing plans for a theater, also to be called the Blackstone, to occupy the site just west of the hotel. The Blackstone Hotel opened with characteristic flair in April 1910. Enrico Caruso, the toast of the western world, was the Drakes' honored guest at a post-theater supper on the evening the hotel opened. Within a year, the Blackstone had gained an international reputation. A European hotelier studying the world's great hostelries told the New York *World* in 1911 that "the Blackstone in Chicago is fitted out finer than any hotel I have ever seen."

Over the years the Blackstone, like the Grand Pacific before it, became a center of political activity. It was in a "smoke-filled room" at the Blackstone that the 1920 compromise nomination of the little-known Warren G. Harding was forged. Franklin Delano Roosevelt's third-term Democratic nomination was signed and sealed at the Blackstone in 1940. Harry S Truman was staying at the Blackstone when he received the vice presidential nomination in 1944. When Dwight D. Eisenhower won the Republican nomination on the first ballot in 1952, he heard the news first in his suite at the Blackstone.

The Blackstone became a barometer of social change in other ways as well. In July 1913 the Chicago City Council, not previously known as a bastion for the protection of public morality, enacted an ordinance that banned dancing in restaurants. The Drake brothers, in the spirit of their father, refused to comply. The city, like Leiter, pressed the issue and lost when a municipal court judge threw dance-ban prosecutions out of court and declared the ordinance invalid. The dance-ban brouhaha was not unusual. The Drake brothers were often challenged by would-be regulators. They stood their ground in every case but one. In 1915, seeing the writing on the wall, the Blackstone yielded to a state blue law, becoming the first Loop establishment to close its bar on Sunday. "Prohibition is on its way in the United States," Tracy Drake said to a Chicago *Tribune* reporter. "The Blackstone is prepared to meet it gracefully and not combatively."

In 1914 the Drake brothers announced plans to build a seventeen-story hotel on East Lake Shore Drive at North Michigan Avenue, at an estimated cost of $2 million. The land was owned by Blackstone architects Ben Marshall and Charles Fox and Marshall's mother Cecelia. The Drakes had a six-month option on the property. Tracy Drake said that the owners of the land would be given second mortgage bonds in the venture, and that the Drake Hotel Company would issue first mortgage bonds "to the limit of the building's value." John Drake had already sold $200,000 worth of stock in New York for the project, according to a *Tribune* report.

The new hotel would be called the Esplanade. The location was right, and the financing seemed to be in order, but the timing was wrong. The income tax had arrived in 1913. Europe was on the brink of World War I, which the United States would enter in April 1917. Restrictions on building materials

Drake Hotel. This view is looking north toward Oak Street Beach at North Michigan Avenue and Walton Street. Opened on New Years Eve, 1920, the Drake became one of Chicago's and the nation's great hotels—a reputation it retains today. The fame of the 700-room hotel was not enough, however, to save developers John and Tracy Drake from foreclosure during the Great Depression. [Kaufmann and Fabry—Chicago Historical Society]

followed, and until the war ended in November 1918, private construction was at a standstill in Chicago. In 1919 plans for the Esplanade, now to be called the Drake, were revived. A new company, the Whitestone Hotel Company, was formed to build it. In addition to the Drakes, stockholders included Marshall and Fox, J. Ogden Armour, James A. Patten, Honoré Palmer, and Potter Palmer Jr. The hotel was completed in December 1920. Total investment, including the land, had reached $8.5 million. Furnishings were said to have cost another $1.5 million. The fourteen-story Italian Renaissance building had eight hundred guest rooms and an array of fine restaurants. The *Tribune* commented on the impact that the Drake brothers' project would have on the future development of Upper Michigan Avenue. "The Drake hotel went north," the newspaper commented, accurately predicting that "hotels, theaters, fine shops, and stores will follow."

Drake Hotel dining room, 1931. The main dining room at the Drake was considered by restaurant critic John Drury to be "first and foremost of the Avenue eating establishments catering to Chicago's social world." The huge hall, with its marble columns and glittering glass chandeliers, was also a rendezvous for celebrities stopping at the Drake. [Chicago Architectural Photographing Co.—Chicago Historical Society]

The Drake was formally opened to the public on New Year's Eve, 1920, with a supper dance and "appropriate festivities." The occasion was dampened only slightly by the fact that this was Chicago's first New Year's Eve since the enactment of Prohibition. The Drake became Chicago society's own hotel in the 1920s, and over the years would entertain as many kings and queens, foreign heads of state, American presidents, and international celebrities as the Drake brothers' flagship hotel, the Blackstone. The decor, the decorum, and the Drakes' personal style elevated the hotel to world-class status, a reputation that has been preserved to the present day.

Tracy Drake brought a passion for detail into the business. A reporter who covered the city in the 1920s recalled an item he had written in which he noted the incorrect placement of the American and British flags at the La Salle Hotel when British Prime Minister David Lloyd George visited. The writer was awakened at seven-thirty on the day the story was published by a call from Tracy Drake. Drake wanted it known that the prime minister had only lunched at the La Salle, that he was staying at the Drake. "And please add that *we* have *our* flags placed correctly," Drake said.

The 1920s were a boom time again for the Chicago economy, and the city rose, literally, to the opportunities. The new Drake was the pacesetter, but other great hotels were also built in this decade. The new Palmer House was completed in 1925. The 3,000-room Stevens Hotel (now the Hilton Hotel and Towers) was completed in 1927, and the exuberant forty-five story Medinah Athletic Club (now the Inter-Continental Hotel) was finished in 1929. The Medinah would be the last large hotel to be built in the city for another three decades.

While the Drake Hotel gained fame, it also labored under a heavy debt. Investors in the Whitestone Company subscribed to $3.5 million in stock, and the company in 1919 took out a $2.5 million bond issue payable in ten years to five Illinois banks. In 1920, as the hotel's construction neared completion, the company negotiated a $5 million first mortgage bond with the Chicago-based branch of New York's S. W. Straus, payable in two to twenty years. In 1926 Tracy Drake went to New York to arrange a $4 million loan from the Metropolitan Life Insurance Company to pay off the Straus mortgage. In 1927 the Drake Hotel Company, which had built the Blackstone, purchased the Blackstone land for $1 million, and then took out an additional $1.7 million loan from Metropolitan Life, secured by the Blackstone building and lot. In hindsight, it was the wrong time for the brothers to be increasing their debt burden. By 1928 the hotel industry in Chicago was overbuilt and occupancy rates were declining. Price wars cut deeply into already diminished net profits. A tide of hotel foreclosures swept the country after the stock market crash in 1929. The Chicago Title and Trust Company alone was left with some thirty Chicago hotels and apartment hotels in receivership.

In 1932 the Drakes defaulted on the $1.7 million loan from Metropolitan Life, and the Blackstone went into receivership. The hotel was closed briefly but was refurbished and reopened in time for the 1933 Century of Progress Exhibition. The momentary boost came too late for the Drakes to recover. In that year Metropolitan Life foreclosed on the $4 million mortgage. Prior to foreclosure, the Drake had been reorganized under the control of a management company that had agreed to provide the Drakes with living quarters, meals, and a $15,000 yearly salary each. This arrangement was ended with the foreclosure. The Drakes carried the issue, without success, through the courts for a number of years. Both the Drake and the Blackstone survived the 1930s depression, but the memorable careers of Tracy and John Drake as Chicago's preeminent hotel men were over.

In 1935 John B. Drake joined the Hughes Oil Company. He and his wife Jessie lived to celebrate their sixty-third wedding anniversary together. After her death, he moved to the Tampa, Florida, area, where his daughter Elizabeth lived. He died in Florida in 1964, at the age of ninety-one.

Tracy Drake, who was nearly seventy when the hotel business collapsed, retired to Laguna Beach, California, where he died at the age of seventy-four. Annie lived until 1951. She was survived by her sons, Carlos and Francis, and four grandchildren, including movie star Betsy Drake, who was then Mrs. Cary Grant.

In 1958 Carlos Drake paid a visit to Lake Geneva and his childhood home, Aloha Lodge (the Drakes had maintained the estate until 1936). The visit was in many ways bittersweet. Carlos, a journalist and editor then living in Portugal, found much that was unchanged from his childhood, but much more was gone. He stopped at the abandoned railroad depot that had been the summer families' link to the city in the days near the turn of the century. He told an interviewer:

> Now the depot seems to typify the dusty end of something bright and gay and exciting. All I could think of, standing there, looking at the crumbling building, the once shining tracks rusted and overgrown with weeds, was a melancholy refrain from a poem by Edwin Arlington Robinson. It goes: ''There is ruin and decay/ In the House on the Hill:/ They are all gone away./ There is nothing more to say.''

MANSIONS IN THE SKY

Benjamin H. Marshall
(1874-1944)

Benjamin H. Marshall.
[From *Chicago and Its Makers.*]

Chicago architect, builder, and developer Ben Marshall was a prodigiously talented man who left a distinctive imprint on the landscape of Chicago in the first three decades of the twentieth century. He is remembered for his flamboyant tastes, swashbuckling style, and for the dazzling entertainments he hosted at his Wilmette mansion in the 1920s. But his legacy to the city of Chicago is far more substantial and visible than that. Marshall was a builder of palatial theaters, the designer of the famed Blackstone Hotel, and the architect-developer of the Edgewater Beach and Drake hotels. He was also the first of a progression of Chicago high-rise apartment developers who have created along Chicago's magnificent lakefront some of the most beautiful and functional multifamily buildings to be found anywhere.

Benjamin Howard Marshall was born in Chicago in 1874, the only child of Caleb Marshall, a prosperous bakery executive, and his southern-born wife, Cecelia. Ben attended the Harvard School in Kenwood, on Chicago's South Side, where he was a schoolmate of John B. Drake II. Marshall's career and that of John and Tracy Drake would later become closely linked. While the Drake brothers and other boys of Marshall's social and economic background went East to prep schools and colleges, Marshall chose at the age of seventeen to go to work as a clerk for a wholesale clothier. There he learned the art of clothing construction and, on his own, began designing men's suits.

Iroquois Theatre, c. 1905.
The Iroquois Theater on West Randolph Street was the third theater in Chicago designed by young Ben Marshall. On December 30, 1903, the Iroquois was the scene of the worst theater fire in United States history. More than six hundred people, most of them women and children, died in the disaster.
[Barnes and Crosby—Chicago Historical Society]

Work as a clothing cutter may seem an odd beginning for an artistic young man of privilege who would soon be making his own first million. But Marshall pursued a multitude of artistic interests throughout his life, most of them self-taught. He was a musician, a celebrated golfer and fisherman, a gentleman chef, and a *bon vivant extraordinaire.* Marshall created his own distinctive wardrobe, which he wore with great style. White suits, white shoes, and a white hat with a black band were a Ben Marshall trademark long before author Tom Wolfe was born.

After two years with the clothing company, Marshall discovered his interest in architecture and found a position as a clerk for architect H. R. Wilson. In 1895, at the age of twenty-one, he was made a full partner in Wilson's firm. In 1902 Marshall went on his own. From the beginning, Marshall mingled his roles as architect and developer. His first projects were residences, and his commissions prestigious ones. In all, he designed at least sixty homes in Chicago, including the Chicago landmark mansion at 1530 North Lake Shore Drive, built in 1916 for Bernard Albert Eckhart, director of the Chicago Board of Trade. Many of the early Marshall homes, however, were built as speculative ventures—a decidedly risky proposition for an innovative young architect without formal training.

Marshall had a lifelong love for theater and theater people. Florenz "Flo" Ziegfeld was among his closest friends. (So, too, it was said, were many of the Ziegfeld Girls, who often appeared about town on the arm of the dashing Ben Marshall.) Marshall soon gained a reputation as a designer of theaters. While still in his early twenties, he designed and supervised construction of the Illinois Theater at 65 East Jackson, the home of the Chicago Ziegfeld Follies. He then did the Powers' Theater on West Randolph Street and in 1903 built the tragically ill-starred Iroquois Theater, a block west on Randolph.

In 1904 Marshall entered into a twenty-year partnership with Charles E. Fox. Fox, a native of Reading, Pennsylvania, studied architecture at the Massachusetts Institute of Technology and came to Chicago in 1891 to work with the architectural firm Holabird and Roche. Marshall was an idea man, an artist, and an inventor who was startlingly innovative in his thinking. Fox had a more conventional orientation to the profession. He was a president of the Illinois Society of Architects and an organizer of the Architects Club of Chicago. But Fox was no stick-in-the-mud. He was a renowned yachtsman, a veteran of many Mackinac Island races, and a commodore of the Chicago Yacht Club.

In 1905 Marshall's father purchased a deep, undeveloped lot at the northwest corner of North Lake Shore Drive and

Cedar Street. There Marshall and Fox built their first apartment building. This eight-story structure, at 1100 Lake Shore Drive, was the first of Chicago's stately Lake Shore Drive luxury apartments, and the prototype for many to follow. Marshall, one of his associates commented, "had a sense of how wealthy people wanted to live." And that was what he provided. He built apartments in a manner calculated to allow their occupants to simulate the life-style of the Gold Coast's great mansions and maximize the aura of prestige that he sought to generate around all of his projects. Like most of Marshall's apartment buildings, 1100 Lake Shore Drive was built with high ceilings, spacious rooms, and one apartment per floor. It was designed for elegant living and arranged to accommodate entertaining on a large scale. All of the rooms were described by French names on the floor plans, a Ben Marshall touch that lent his designs the cachet of the grand Parisian apartments. Although apartment living was still uncommon in Chicago and, in fact, largely unknown among the city's upper-class families, the units in Marshall's 1100 building (now demolished) all were rented long before the building was completed in October 1906. The rent was $5,000 a year, a large sum for that time, but no matter. The list of tenants was decidedly gilt-edged.

In 1908 Marshall constructed an apartment house on East Cedar Street on a "joint-ownership" plan—an early forerunner to the cooperative apartment movement of the 1920s. This project attracted considerable attention when it was built, both for its design and for the unique financing concept that Marshall was pioneering. The $89,000 building was owned by five investors, each of whom then became the independent owner of one of the twelve-room apartments in the building. Marshall himself was among the investors, and for many years the house remained the principal residence for Marshall, his wife Elizabeth, and their son and two daughters.

By the time Cedar Place was completed, Marshall was already launched on another phase of his multifaceted career: the creation of luxury hotels. When Tracy and John Drake announced their long-awaited plans to erect the Blackstone Hotel on South Michigan Avenue, Marshall and Fox were named as architects for the project. The twenty-two story hotel was completed in 1909. In 1910 Marshall and Fox designed the Blackstone Theater, built adjacent to the hotel on Hubbard Court (now Balbo Drive). Again, Marshall was an investor in the project, as he would be in so many of the buildings he designed.

The combination of the Drakes' high standards as keepers of the flame of the grand hotel tradition with Marshall's taste for luxury in every detail of style and appointments was an inspired match. As construction of the Blackstone proceeded, Marshall turned his talents to the lavish interior designs of the hotel, which quickly became the Chicago home to visiting royalty, presidents, politicians, and stars of the entertainment world. The Blackstone's reputation as the place to be and be seen in Chicago was equaled only by that of its sister hotel, the Drake, which was built ten years later.

In 1911 Marshall returned to apartment building on a scale and in a style that set the stage for the boom years of the 1920s. He soon became the foremost architect and developer of Chicago luxury apartments—each, it seemed, with more space, more fireplaces, more silver vaults, more amenities than the one before. In 1912 he built the Stewart Apartments at 1200 North Lake shore Drive, followed in the same year by the ten-story 999 East Lake Shore Drive building. The 999 building, built for Ogden T. McClurg, was the first of the apartment buildings lining East Lake Shore Drive, now a Chicago landmark district. It was also one of the few buildings designed by Marshall in which he was not a principal and one of the few built with more than one apartment to a floor. When McClurg chose his site, the deep westward curve of the Drive that it occupies was just a sandy stretch of windswept beach. Chicago newsman and historian Emmett Dedmon noted that McClurg exercised a pioneer's prerogative by naming his building 999, in deference to his belief that nine was his lucky number. Five of the six buildings that followed continued the theme, taking the numbers 219, 209, 199, 189, and 179.

Marshall was a shrewd judge of the times and of the market. The 1920s were destined to become golden years for the construction of Gold Coast luxury apartments, and Ben Marshall was a decade ahead of other developers in his vision both of "how the rich liked to live" and how the new developments could be financed. In the decade of the 1920s, according to one historian, 80 percent of construction permits issued were for apartments. On the Gold Coast, the figure was nearly 100 percent. Many factors contributed to this phenomenon. After the opening of the Michigan Avenue Bridge in 1920, lakefront and Near North land values escalated rapidly, making the construction of single-family homes on lakefront lots uneconomic. Indeed, as the patriarchs of Chicago's great families of the 1880s and '90s passed from the scene, so did many of the old homes. Many widows established new residences in Florida, and one by one the old Victorian mansions were sold to the new generation of developers for the value that was in the land.

New types of financing also emerged, contributing to the construction boom. The ready availability of mortgage bonds in the 1920s and the recognition of the cooperative concept in Illinois law in 1923 fueled the growth of apartment house building. After 1924 the move to cooperative ownership of apartment buildings was in full swing. In 1925 McClurg's 999 East Lake Shore Drive building was converted to cooperative apartments. In 1926 McClurg and Marshall built the 209 East Lake Shore Drive building as a co-op. In 1929 Marshall sold 1100 North Lake Shore Drive to its tenants. The resident purchasers, who then set up a cooperative, included three of the tenants who had lived in the building since 1907—among them the soon-to-be-infamous public utilities magnate Samuel Insull.

East Lake Shore Drive by 1930 had become—and remains—one of the city's most desirable residential addresses. It was Ben Marshall's block from the beginning. Five of the eight East Lake Shore Drive buildings were built by Marshall: the 999 building (1912); "The Breakers" at 199 (1915) and its annexes (1916 and 1927); the Drake Hotel (1920); the 209 co-op (1926); and the twenty-nine-story Drake Tower Apartments at 179 East Lake Shore Drive (1929).

In 1911 Marshall purchased the land at the southwest corner of North State Parkway and North Avenue as the site for his elegant 1550 North State Parkway building, completed in 1913 at an estimated cost of $400,000. Again, Marshall was both architect and owner, and again he had outdone even his own most extravagant efforts. The 1550 building was built

1550 North State Parkway. In the 1550 building, at the corner of North State Parkway and North Avenue overlooking Lincoln Park, developer-architect Benjamin H. Marshall created the acknowledged leader among Chicago's luxury apartment buildings. The building, completed in 1913, was constructed with one twenty-room apartment per floor, except for the top floor, which was a twenty-four-room unit.
[Chicago Architectural Photographing Co.—Chicago Historical Society]

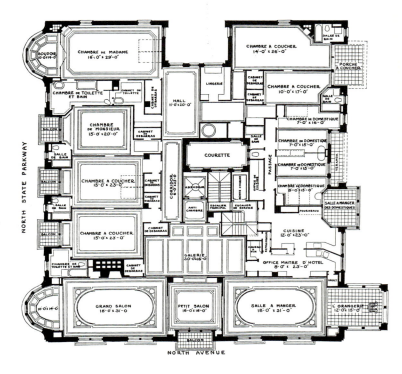

Floor plan, 1550 North State Parkway. Labeled with French names to suggest the grand apartment houses of Paris, the 1550 North State Parkway apartments were divided into three distinct zones. The entry hall and public rooms ran across the front of the building, facing Lincoln Park. Six family bedrooms, each with its own bath and three with large dressing rooms, were on the east and south sides of the building. The service area and servants' quarters were on the west side, with access and entranceways separate from the family quarters. [From *A Portfolio of Fine Apartment Homes*]

with ten apartments, one to a floor above the entrance level. Each apartment had twenty rooms. The top floor had twenty-four. The building was acclaimed as the finest apartment building yet seen in Chicago—perhaps even in the country. The *Economist* real estate journal reported, quite accurately, that "the structure is in a class by itself." In 1920 Marshall sold 1550 North State Parkway to the building's tenants. Again he was ahead of the times. Cooperative ownership, as a concept in Illinois law, was still three years away. The price, at $675,000, was thought to be remarkably low.

By 1915 Marshall had turned his time, his talents, and his financial resources to the development of his own hotel—a "Blackstone on the Sea," as Marshall described it. This was the Edgewater Beach, a glittering and glamorous resort on the lake that was to become not only a Chicago institution for fifty years but an event in the lives of generations of Chicagoans. The Edgewater Beach, located at 5349 Sheridan Road, between Balmoral and Bryn Mawr avenues, opened its doors in June 1916, with Marshall as a principal owner. As grand as the Edgewater Beach was, Marshall had even grander plans. In 1920 it was announced that the Edgewater Beach would become "the world's largest hotel," with 4,000 rooms planned at an estimated cost of $15 million. According to the *Economist*, Marshall disposed of a number of his properties, including 1550 North State Parkway, to pursue these plans.

In many ways, Marshall's Greater Edgewater Beach project anticipated, by half a century, the massive multiuse developments that emerged in many cities in the 1960s and 1970s, including Chicago's pacesetting Illinois Center. Marshall envisioned a complex of five buildings strung like pink pearls along the lakefront for three full blocks. These buildings would include the original resort hotel, light housekeeping apartments, a luxury hotel, and luxury apartment units. The centerpiece sixteen-story tower was to be a first-class men's hotel, to be called Bachelors Hall. The five units were conceived as one interrelated structure linked by a three-block-long corridor of shops.

Marshall was not able to complete his grandiose plan, but he did build an eighteen-story tower south of the resort hotel building in 1924, adding six hundred rooms to the four-hundred-room capacity of the original ten-story hotel. The Edgewater Beach Apartments building, located a long block north at 5555 Sheridan Road, was completed in 1929.

The Drake Hotel, at the curve of Lake Shore Drive where North Michigan Avenue intersects Walton and Oak streets, opened in December 1920. Stockholders in the $10 million project, organized by Tracy and John Drake, included Palmers, Armours, and Swifts—and the architects, Ben Marshall and

Edgewater Beach Hotel, 1916. Visiting Benjamin Marshall's palatial hotel on Sheridan Road was a memorable event for generations of Chicagoans. When sixty acres of lakefront were filled in the early 1950s to extend Lake Shore Drive northward past the hotel, the namesake beach disappeared. [Chicago Historical Society]

Charles Fox. Although the Drake Hotel was then, and will always be, associated with the personal management style of the Drake brothers, Ben Marshall's role in the creation of this masterpiece was far more than that of an architect and stockholder. When it came to the Drake, the hand of Ben Marshall was everywhere. After he had designed and erected the building, Marshall gave his full attention to creating the interiors, just as he had at the Blackstone. He supervised the furnishings and decoration down to the last detail of such memorable spaces as the restaurants, the Club International and Cape Cod Room (where Marshall's own recipes were included in the menu). His interest in theatrical production also found a home at the Drake. Encouraged by Ziegfeld, Marshall personally directed the shows featured at the Gold Coast Room, one of the country's finest nightclubs.

When the Drake brothers lost the hotel during the Depression, Marshall formed a real estate management company and on behalf of the receivers took over the Drake operations, sharing the responsibilities with Edwin L. Brashears, who had

been an engineer on the project. The Marshall and Brashears families managed the hotel in a closely held corporation until it was purchased in 1979 by Jupiter Industries. The Drake was not the last of the Marshall hotel enterprises. In 1927 he built the Edgewater Gulf Hotel, on the Mississippi Gulf Coast, halfway between Biloxi and Gulfport. For a time in the early 1930s, Marshall held the controlling interest in the Orrington Hotel, Evanston, Illinois. Marshall and Fox also built hotels in Dubuque, Iowa; Milwaukee; and La Salle, Illinois.

Marshall created luxury apartments on Lake Shore Drive of subdued elegance, but for his own home, he created an exotic palace on Wilmette Harbor. The Marshall Villa, as he called it, was a fabulous structure, a combination Disneyland and Playboy Mansion. It also housed the offices of the Marshall and Fox architectural firm. Even in the 1990s, there are those who remember at least hearing about the showpiece among showpieces at the Marshall Villa: the roof-top "Portico of Isis"—the Egyptian Room—with a billowing red-and-gold fabric ceiling, twenty-foot divan, and the famed disappearing table that rose out of the floor when dinner was served and then sank into a kitchen below to be replenished with the next course.

The legendary Ben Marshall and the Roaring Twenties were made for one another. It was his era. Marshall's star never faded nor did his talent dim, but as the Depression set in, much of the music died. The Marshall and Fox partnership, which had been so productive, ended acrimoniously in 1924. In the early 1930s, Marshall witnessed the financial ruin of the Drake brothers. In 1936 Marshall's beloved Villa—with all its treasures—was sold to Nathan Goldblatt, cofounder of the Goldblatt Brothers Department Stores, for a tenth of what Marshall had spent to build it. After Goldblatt's death, the house was again offered for sale but never found a buyer. In 1948 the furnishings were sold at auction, and in 1949-50 the house was demolished.

The Edgewater Beach Hotel survived the Depression, thanks to the 1933-34 Century of Progress fair, and remained popular through the 1940s. The hotel was sold in 1948, and a succession of management, maintenance, and labor problems followed. In the early 1950s, the lakefront Edgewater Beach lost much of its *raison d'être* when sixty acres of Lake Michigan were filled for the extension of Lake Shore Drive northward to Hollywood Avenue. The surrounding neighborhood was deteriorating, and the Edgewater's beloved boardwalk had disappeared along with much of its old clientele. The hotel closed in December 1967 and the buildings were demolished in 1970.

One cannot go far in Chicago without seeing evidence of

East Lake Shore Drive, 1925. [opposite page] Developer-architect Benjamin Marshall has been called the patron saint of the Gold Coast's East Lake Shore Drive, now a Chicago landmark district. Between 1905 and 1929 Marshall designed and built the 999 [far left], 209, 199, and 179 East Lake Shore Drive buildings, and the Drake Hotel [far right].
[Kaufmann and Fabry, from *Chicago and Its Makers*]

Marshall's work as an architect. In addition to their hotels and apartment buildings, Marshall and Fox projects included the South Shore Country Club, Lake Shore National Bank on North Michigan Avenue, and the former Lytton's Store on South State Street. Work outside Chicago included the Northwestern Mutual Life Insurance Building in Milwaukee, the Forest Theater in Philadelphia, and the Maxine Elliott Theater in New York City. In 1928 Marshall designed the Victory Memorial at Thirty-fifth Street and King Drive, honoring black soldiers in World War I.

Ben Marshall died of heart failure in 1944 at the age of seventy. His motto had always been, "I can build a better one." During his last illness, as the story goes, Marshall remarked on the structure of the hospital's oxygen tent, commenting that he could have designed it better. He probably could have.

BATTLING BUBBLY CREEK

Wallace G. Clark
(1863-1935)

Wallace G. Clark.
[From *Chicago and Its Makers*]

Wallace G. Clark began his career in the 1880s as a building contractor, putting up small homes in the Hyde Park area, and ended it in the 1920s with the development of the monumental 35 East Wacker Drive Building, a structure that formed the backdrop of an altogether new skyline on Chicago's riverfront. But there was another side to Clark's activities that left an even larger imprint on Chicago than the homes, apartment buildings, and office towers that he constructed over the span of his forty years as a real estate developer. Wallace Clark was a fearless political activist, an environmentalist long before the word had been coined, and a far-sighted advocate of planned development for Chicago.

Wallace Clark was born in 1863 in Watseka, Illinois, but his family moved to Chicago when he was a child. Wallace and his older brother Arthur began their own business careers while still in their teens when they opened a haberdashery, but they soon switched to homebuilding and construction—a far more promising field in the early 1880s. By the mid-1890s the Clarks had found their niche as developers. Wallace headed the real estate side of the team, with a partner, J. Milton Trainer. Arthur, who bought out a former partner in the contracting business, was the builder. The two firms, Clark and Trainer and A. R. Clark and Company, shared offices. In the early years, Arthur and Wallace also shared a home—even after both were married.

The Clark brothers' business plan was straightforward. The

Clark and Trainer company bought relatively small tracts of vacant land in residential areas and subdivided or resubdivided them. A. R. Clark and Company built houses that were then sold through the realty branch. The Clarks' specialty was well-built, middle- to upper-middle-class brick homes; their territory was the Kenwood—Hyde Park area, where they themselves lived. The growth of the business was methodical and steady. In 1897 the two companies began adding three- and four-story brick apartment buildings to their inventory; by 1905 they had shifted their major effort from home building to development of apartment buildings. In the 1910s and '20s, Clark and Trainer's activities expanded to include commercial real estate development and property management in the downtown business district.

Wallace Clark was successful from the outset in his work as a property developer, but he was equally active in another area of pursuit. His activities as a spokesman for neighborhood reform groups in Hyde Park's Sixth Ward brought Clark to the attention of the Republican Central Committee. In 1905 he was slated, along with young Robert R. McCormick and seven likeminded men, to run against the nine powerful machine Democrats who were then trustees of the Chicago Sanitary District. The work of the sanitary district—forerunner of today's Metropolitan Water Reclamation District—was of incalculable importance to Chicago in the early years of the twentieth century. At stake was a pure water supply, a comprehensive sanitary sewer system, and control of hydroelectric power produced in connection with the organization's primary activities.

The Chicago Sanitary District (also called the Chicago Drainage District in the early years) was created in 1889 by an act of the Illinois legislature. The district's first major act was construction of the Chicago Sanitary and Ship Canal, the massive public works project built between 1894 and 1899 that successfully reversed the flow of the Chicago River. The result was that Chicago sewage was flushed downstream toward the Mississippi Basin instead of into Lake Michigan, where for decades it had contaminated the city's water supply. Sanitary district trustees had independent taxing authority and also controlled large and lucrative construction contracts. It was a situation made to order for the favoritism and spoils system that were the norm for Chicago politics in the first decades of the twentieth century.

Clark and McCormick ran for office on a pledge to break up sanitary district contractors' rings, give projects to the lowest bidder, and require that contractors live up to their performance contracts. The party regulars who were the beneficiaries

Reversing the Chicago River.
The opening of Needle Dam on January 2, 1900, marked completion of the massive Chicago Sanitary and Ship Canal project—an engineering feat that succeeded at last in reversing the flow of the Chicago River and diverting sewage away from Lake Michigan. Wallace Clark and Robert McCormick were elected in 1905 to the Metropolitan Sanitary District Board on a pledge to end widespread corruption among board members.
[Chicago Historical Society]

of the drainage district largess responded to the Republican challenge by pressuring the Illinois legislature to cancel the 1905 election, thus retaining the Democratic incumbents in office until 1908. That effort came too late to escape public notice, and the elections went forward.

The McCormick-Clark ticket made a clean sweep, and Clark became chairman of the powerful engineering committee of the sanitary district board. He was reelected for four successive terms, although each year the Republican majority dwindled. In 1910 the Democrats won back the presidency of the board, which was the seat McCormick had held since 1905. Clark assumed McCormick's role as leader and spokesman for the reform element. McCormick went on to become president and publisher of the Chicago *Tribune*.

Outnumbered seven to two on the board after 1912 and stymied in his persistent efforts to keep the board honest through regular channels, Wallace Clark decided to go public with his complaints. It was a dangerous course of action for a man who, by virtue of his career in downtown Chicago property development, was highly vulnerable to harassment from the party henchmen who ran city hall. On October 21, 1914, a month before election day, Clark made an impassioned speech before the Illinois Women's Republican League. He had selected his audience carefully. The Chicago *Tribune*, with McCormick in charge, covered the event closely, quoting Clark word for word as he described the "spoils, greed, and mismanagement'' rampant in sanitary district board activities and charged that ''a constant stream of wealth is poured from the public treasury to help the present majority build a political machine.'' Clark spoke of ''blind, blanket vouchers for huge sums'' drawn from payroll accounts and of extravagant contracts that, he said, ''are let as freely as the passing out of tracts by a religious society.''

The board laughed at Clark's resort to a forum of women, but decided to take no chances. For the next three weeks, the president of the sanitary district board called the mandatory weekly meeting to order, declared that no quorum existed, and adjourned the session. Clark kept up the pressure, but ultimately did not prevail. Through the pages of the *Tribune* he charged: ''This board is afraid to meet. It fears the spotlight of public attention that will become focused on the rottenness that exists within it. The majority has boasted that no meeting will be held until after the election.'' That is just what happened.

In 1916, another election year, Clark renewed his campaign to clean up the mess on the sanitary district board, exposing rampant nepotism and kickback schemes at the highest level. Charges surfaced in early summer that district operatives had diverted electrical power from the pumping station that served Hyde Park, permitting sewage to run back into the water supply. Rumors linked a 1916 typhoid outbreak in the Hyde Park area to the incident at the pumping station. Women, who were permitted to vote in the sanitary district elections, crossed party lines by the thousands. The Republicans recovered a narrow five-to-four majority on the board. The machine-backed board president lost his seat to a reform candidate who had run on a promise of ending the corrupt practices detailed by Clark. Wallace Clark had proven himself to be a shrewd political strategist. He identified the one force in the city with the power to defeat the machine and run the spoilsmen out of office: the women's vote.

Righting the wrongs of the sanitary district board, however, was not the only cause that Wallace Clark championed in his years as a sanitary district trustee. Clark also took upon himself the task of ending forever the blight of the Chicago Union Stock Yards' infamous Bubbly Creek. Contrary to what its name may suggest, Bubbly Creek was no babbling brook. It was an open sewer, a stagnant dead-end slip on the South Fork of the South Branch of the Chicago River, near the corner where Thirty-ninth Street (now Pershing Road) intersected Ashland Avenue. For decades the slip had been used by the packinghouses as a dumping ground for animal blood, entrails, and other organic debris, which slowly settled to decompose in the river's putrid depths. The name came from the roiling pockets of gases generated by the decaying matter that rose and broke continuously over the surface of the slip.

By the turn of the century, Chicago had grappled with engineering projects of enormous magnitude—including raising the level of the city's streets, erecting buildings of remarkable heights, and reversing the flow of a river. And yet Bubbly Creek was allowed to live on for nearly fifty years—from 1870 until 1920—secure in its reputation as the "most pestilent spot in the city" and securely protected by powerful interests in the stockyards and their cronies in city government. Wallace Clark made the closing of Bubbly Creek a personal crusade.

Clark demanded that the packinghouses dredge the slip at their expense and build a large settling basin to capture slaughterhouse wastes, which, he said, were being carried into the city's sewage system. He offered sanitary district matching funds for the project. He threatened prosecutions in the state

Bubbly Creek at Morgan Street, 1911. Wallace Clark waged a lonely battle against packinghouse interests and a corrupt Chicago Sanitary District Board to end the blight of the infamous Bubbly Creek—an open sewer that for decades had been the dumping ground for slaughterhouse wastes and a perpetual threat to downstream water supplies. [Chicago Historical Society]

and federal courts. He surfaced the health and safety factor. He was supported by the city's commissioner of health, who announced in 1915 that disease-bearing effluent from Bubbly Creek, washed south through the canal, had taken an estimated eight thousand lives in Illinois in the preceding year. Clark pronounced Bubbly Creek a "disgrace to civilization," declaring that "it is absolutely unthinkable that the packing interests should continue this cesspool because it costs a few dollars to abate the nuisance."

Clark had begun his war on Bubbly Creek in 1906. It took another fifteen years before a coalition of social, political, and economic forces strong enough to overpower the packinghouse interests and bury Bubbly Creek emerged. The new coalition's plans, which included developing Thirty-ninth Street as a major east-west thoroughfare, were backed by the Chicago Plan Commission. The women's groups remained an articulate force in the battle. On September 8, 1920, the last days of Bubbly Creek were celebrated at a festive ceremony attended by representatives of the governor of Illinois and the mayor of Chicago, local congressmen, all of the trustees of the sanitary district, and Charles Wacker, chairman of the Chicago Plan Commission. A parade around the area was led by Armour and Company's own Fife and Drum Crops. Wallace G. Clark was accorded the honor of firing up one of the first steam shovels used in filling the stagnant slip.

Clark and Trainer began the downtown development phase of their firm's operations in 1913 when they formed the Michigan Avenue Trust Estate to purchase the southwest corner of Michigan Avenue and Washington Street, facing the Illinois Central Railroad tracks and the undeveloped lake fill that would become Grant Park. The property was part of the Aaron Montgomery Ward estate and had benefited greatly from Ward's insistent court battles to preserve the land opposite his Michigan Avenue properties for development as a public park. Their architect was Jarvis Hunt, a visionary who shared Clark's interest in urban planning. In 1912 Hunt had presented the plan to the Chicago Real Estate Board that resulted in the straightening of the Chicago River south of Van Buren Street. Straightening the river, Hunt believed, would ease congestion in the South Branch and facilitate drainage in the area. These were ideas that captured Clark's imagination and sparked his interest in Hunt.

The fifteen-story retail and office structure that Hunt designed for 30 North Michigan was completed in 1914, and Clark and Trainer Real Estate and A. R. Clark and Company, Builders, moved their offices from Dearborn Street into the new building. Originally called the People's Trust and Savings

35 East Wacker Drive, 1926. The Jewelers Building (as it was originally known), developed by Wallace Clark, was designed as an office building offering every amenity, including restaurants and a domed observation tower. The building also contained in its core a fully mechanized garage, extending from an entrance on Lower Wacker Drive to the twenty-eighth floor. [Ryerson and Burnham Libraries—Art Institute of Chicago]

Wacker Drive, looking east from Wells Street, 1927. The completion of the Michigan Avenue Bridge and the relocation of the old South Water wholesale market made way for the construction of a broad, bilevel Wacker Drive, named for Charles H. Wacker, first chairman of the Chicago Plan Commission. Wallace Clark and his partner Milton Trainer were at the forefront of the Michigan-Wacker development.
[Kaufman and Fabry, from *Chicago and Its Makers*]

Bank Building, the name was later changed to the Michigan Boulevard Building. Five more stories were added in 1923.

The completion of the Michigan Avenue Bridge and the relocation of the South Water wholesale market to make way for the construction of the broad, bilevel Wacker Drive was the beginning of a new era in the city's growth, one that by 1930 had brought about a complete transformation of North Michigan Avenue and the riverfront where the old city met the new. Traffic patterns were changed forever. Substantial private investment was drawn to the area. A new, decidedly less austere style of commercial architecture rose up on both riverbanks, typified by the Wrigley Building and Tribune Tower on the north and by 35 East Wacker and 333 North Michigan on the south.

The Clark and Trainer Company was at the forefront of the Michigan-Wacker development. Clark, for example, arranged the land purchases for the Tribune Tower, built by Colonel McCormick. The striking 35 East Wacker Building, known earlier as the Jewelers' Building and the Pure Oil Building, was Wallace Clark's own contribution to the new riverfront development. This building, completed in 1926 by the Wacker-Wabash Corporation, a syndicate organized by Wallace Clark, was the first office and commercial structure to go up on Wacker Drive. At forty stories, it was one of the tallest of its time and was the first downtown Chicago office tower built with indoor parking. Designed by the firm of Giaver and Dinkelberg with Thielbar and Fugard, the building was topped with a forty-foot-high glass dome that first served as a sightseeing observatory. The dome later became a restaurant called the Stratosphere and is now used as a studio by architect Helmut Jahn, who moved his offices to 35 East Wacker's twenty-fourth floor in the 1980s.

The building has undergone several renovations over its three-score-plus years and several changes of name, but it maintains a significant presence on the Wacker Drive riverfront. Hoping to attract Chicago's watch, clock, and diamond merchants as tenants, Clark named it the Jewelers' Building. But even with the security of an indoor parking system that delivered a tenant—and his automobile—from the street to his office door, the jewelry trade did not gravitate to the building as Clark had hoped. But the Pure Oil Company of Cleveland did. In 1926 Pure Oil entered into a long-term lease, heralded as "the second largest office lease ever negotiated in Chicago," for floors eighteen through twenty-three. The Jewelers' Building was speedily rechristened the Pure Oil Building. In 1962, when Pure Oil moved to northwest suburban Palatine, the building was renamed the 35 East Wacker Drive building.

In the late 1920s, with Bubbly Creek licked and Wacker Drive development booming, Clark focused his concerns on highways and transportation problems. He spoke and wrote of the accomplishments of the years since the Plan of Chicago was adopted in 1910, urging the business community to devote its energy now to the development of subways to ease downtown traffic congestion and to the creation of the rapid transit that "Chicago is entitled to enjoy." The Depression put a hold on Clark's work for a downtown subway system. The subway that he believed could be built by 1928 was not opened until 1943. It was an improvement Wallace Clark did not live to see. He died at his Hyde Park home in 1935 at the age of seventy-three.

UPPER MICHIGAN AVENUE

Murray Wolbach
(1876-1954)

Murray Wolbach.
[Wolbach family]

The years between 1918 and 1920 were a promising but precarious time in the history of Chicago's Upper Michigan Avenue. In this period, construction of the Michigan Avenue Bridge and the new bilevel Wacker Drive were nearing completion. Pine Street north of the river had been made an extension of Michigan Avenue and was being widened to handle the new bridge traffic. At the north end of the newly created thoroughfare, the elegant Drake Hotel was going up. At the south end, where the boulevard met the bridge, the Wrigley Building was under construction.

The path that development would take in the blocks between—the district that is today's Magnificent Mile—was, however, still unformed. The Chicago Plan Commission envisioned the boulevard of shops, hotels, galleries, and custom office spaces that is seen today. But without zoning or other means of enforcement of land use, there was no guarantee that this type of development would prevail over the warehouses, transient hotels, and small manufacturing operations that characterized the district just north of the river in the 1910s. Nor was there any guarantee that other, more insidious commercial uses, such as the "Automobile Row" showrooms that had spoiled South Michigan Avenue after the turn of the century, would not take over the boulevard.

At this point, the task of molding the future for Upper Michigan Avenue was taken firmly in hand by a small band of strong-minded men. Murray Wolbach, already a well-established builder of homes and apartment houses in the Kenwood-Hyde Park area, was among the prime movers in this group. Wolbach was one of the four sons of Samuel N. Wolbach, a Grand Island, Nebraska, dry goods merchant, and Rose Stein Wolbach, the daughter of a South Side Chicago family. Murray was born in Chicago in 1876, but spent his boyhood years in Grand Island, where his father was founder of the S. N. Wolbach and Sons department store, president of the First National Bank, and at one time, the mayor of Grand Island. Murray's brothers all pursued interesting, technically oriented professions. Burt became a professor of pathology at Harvard Medical School and a specialist in Rocky Mountain spotted fever; Edwin became a chemist; Emil, also a Chicago developer, became a flyer in the early days of aviation and died piloting his own plane. Murray custom-designed automobile bodies, which he had built by the Fisher Body Company.

While still in his teens, Murray Wolbach was sent to Frankfurt am Main, Germany, and later to Lausanne, Switzerland, to complete his education. In 1895 he returned to Chicago, where a position as a bookkeeper was waiting for him at the banking firm of Greenebaum Sons. Wolbach eventually headed the real estate department of the far-reaching Greenebaum business. In 1905 he married Edna Stern, a Chicago girl who had grown up on Prairie Avenue, and simultaneously launched his career as a builder of homes and apartment buildings.

In the years between 1905 and 1916, Wolbach focused his development activities on the Kenwood-Hyde Park area, where he built houses and hundreds of apartment units. These included developments on Calumet, Forrestville, and St. Lawrence avenues, and South Parkway and in the blocks between Sixty-seventh and Seventy-second streets south of Jackson Park. Wolbach was well known, well connected, and highly respected in real estate circles in these years, and indeed, throughout his life. He lived in Kenwood, in a rented house at 4823 Kenwood Avenue where the Wolbachs raised two daughters and a son. Murray Wolbach was a music lover and a golfer. He was a man with a passion for his business who nonetheless managed to travel widely with his family—often in pursuit of more congenial winter climates for Murray Jr., who as a child suffered from severe asthma.

In 1917-18 housing construction in Chicago was brought to a standstill by labor shortages and the diversion of materials to the war effort. At this point, Wolbach shifted his activities to Upper Michigan Avenue and later to Wacker Drive, where, with a new Michigan Avenue Bridge assured, he and others saw great development potential. In 1918 Wolbach and his close friends Frederick M. Bowes, William N. MacChesney, and Charles Rubens reorganized the North Central Business District Association, a forerunner of today's Greater North Michigan Avenue Association, and established a property owners association. Their mission was to assure development of the district as a first-class shopping boulevard, equivalent, they hoped, to New York City's Upper Fifth Avenue. The group commissioned a committee of architects to help draft a plan for the new boulevard. Members included such luminaries as Benjamin Marshall and Charles Fox, Howard Van Doren Shaw, Andrew Rebori, George W. Maher, and Jarvis Hunt, as well as representatives of the architectural firms of Holabird and Roche and Graham, Anderson, Probst and White. The charge to the committee inspired Rebori to declare that "no such an opportunity has presented itself in the history of the world, unless it was in that of the rebuilding of Paris."

While the architects worked, Murray Wolbach drafted the protective agreement by which the owners of Michigan Avenue frontage would pledge, for a period of twenty years, to observe self-imposed restrictions on the use of their property. The agreement specifically banned most manufacturing, warehouses, poolrooms, saloons, and public laundries. Rebori and the committee of architects prepared a plan, modeled on the example of Paris, that showed uniform cornice lines and ten-story building heights for the boulevard except at the river entrance to the boulevard where the design showed tall structures—such as the Graham, Anderson, Probst and White-designed Wrigley Building, which would be under construction within a year. As would be expected, Wolbach certainly did not oppose high-rise construction for the boulevard. His view was not inconsistent with the Plan of Chicago, which acknowledged that in the central area, as far north as Chicago Avenue, "buildings will rise to the height permitted by law" (which, with the adoption of the 1923 zoning ordinance, was virtually unrestricted). Wolbach's concern—and that of other early developers on Upper Michigan Avenue—was not height but usage. Even though he was a great lover of automobiles, Wolbach regarded garages and automobiles as a particularly insidious threat. "If we admit automobiles, we will see none but two-story buildings," he declared. "If we give them a finger they will soon take the whole hand."

The first signers of the agreement were easy to persuade. These were the plan's foremost backers, including Wolbach, Bowes, and MacChesney. Bringing the remainder of the property owners along was a far more difficult task. Nearly a year after the drive was launched, fully one-third of the property owners along the new boulevard were still holding out. As the North Michigan Avenue Bridge neared completion, Wolbach's committee turned up the heat. In December 1919 the signature drive went over the top. The real estate journal *Economist* announced that "owners and investors can now proceed with their plan to convert North Michigan avenue from the river to Chicago avenue into an 'Upper Fifth Avenue.'" The headline declared: "Only Fine Shops, Hotels and Office Buildings to Be Permitted."

Although Wolbach was not as heavily invested in Upper Michigan Avenue as Bowes, he had been able to buy several properties that he intended to hold for development. These included the northeast corner of Michigan and Erie, purchased from Bowes, and the northeast corner of Michigan and Grand. He was also watching the rapid growth taking place on the south side of the bridge on along the newly opened Wacker Drive. By 1921 Wolbach had acquired, through long-term leases, 269 feet of frontage on East Wacker Drive and old South Water Street and was thinking of plans for a skyscraper development.

Wolbach did not, however, launch any development projects on Michigan Avenue until the end of the decade. Instead, he turned his attention back to the Hyde Park area where, after 1924, developers were riding the cooperative apartment building wave. In late 1926 Wolbach became director of a $200 million apartment and hotel development project planned for the Chicago Beach area in Hyde Park. The property included the old Chicago Beach Hotel property and extended along East End Avenue between Forty-ninth Street and Hyde Park Boulevard. The developers' plans were to create a luxury apartment center to rival the Near North Side's Streeterville district. At least four of the planned cooperative apartment buildings were constructed in 1927-28, including the Powhatan, on South Chicago Beach Drive, and the Narragansett, at East End Avenue and East Fiftieth Street. Others were in the planning stages when the stock market crashed in 1929.

At this time, Wolbach was involved also in the development of a business and residential district planned for Cottage Grove Avenue and the area between Cottage Grove and Drexel at Sixty-fourth and Sixty-fifth streets. Wolbach's part of the project was development of sixty-six units of apartments to support developments being launched by MacChesney and Draper and Kramer.

By the late 1920s, Wolbach was ready to develop his Upper Michigan Avenue properties. In 1929, in association with his brother Emil, who owned the land, Wolbach built an elegant six-story building at 545 North Michigan Avenue. The sole

tenant was Jacques, a fashionable women's wear shop that had relocated from South Michigan Avenue. In 1930 he built 669 North Michigan Avenue as the new home for H. Stanley Korshak's exclusive clothing store, then known as the Blackstone Shop—another defector from South Michigan Avenue. The 669 building was later purchased by Saks Fifth Avenue and expanded. It remained the site of Saks retailing in Chicago until a new Saks store opened across the boulevard in 1990. The architect chosen by Wolbach for both the 545 and the 669 buildings was Philip B. Maher, son of George W. Maher, the noted designer North Lake Shore Drive luxury apartments and North Side residences.

Wolbach's last, but most memorable, Michigan Avenue project was the Michigan Square building (at 540 North Michigan), which occupied the entire block bounded by Michigan and Grand avenues and Ohio and Rush streets. It had taken Wolbach nearly ten years to acquire the entire property, which had been occupied by nearly thirty structures. The project, estimated to cost $3.6 million, was financed by a $3.2 million

Michigan Square, 1955.
Developer Murray Wolbach envisioned the 1930 Michigan Square building (later the Time-Life Building), at 540 North Michigan Avenue, as a forty-story, mixed-use structure that would include an eighteen-story tower rising from the west side of the building. The Depression and World War II intervened, and the original high-rise design by Holabird and Root was never executed. Michigan Square was demolished in 1973. [Hedrich-Blessing—Chicago Historical Society]

loan from the Northwestern Mutual Life Insurance Company. The development syndicate, headed by Wolbach, included Charles Rubens and Nathan W. MacChesney. The architects were Holabird and Root, a firm that had designed other Michigan Avenue buildings, notably the 333 North Michigan Avenue Building south of the bridge and the Palmolive Building at the north end of the boulevard.

The Michigan Square plans called for a structure to be built in stages. The first stage of the development was an eight-story courtyard building with shops on the first two floors and offices on the upper floors. Plans called for the eventual addition of a forty-story tower, for a total estimated cost of $22 million. The first stage was completed in 1930, but the tower was never built. Wolbach's concept for the building was finely tuned to support the type of development that he had long foreseen for Upper Michigan Avenue. The Michigan Square Building was built around a graceful rotunda, known as Diana Court, which itself featured a marble and bronze fountain topped by a delicate statue of the mythical huntress Diana. The fountain and sculpture, commissioned by Wolbach, was

Diana Court at Michigan Square. The famed Diana Court in the Michigan Square building was surrounded on two levels by small shops. The court became a symbol of the early developers' concept for a distinctly Upper Michigan Avenue style and character. Swedish sculptor Carl Milles was commissioned by Murray Wolbach to create the marble and bronze fountain that gave Diana Court its name.
[Hedrich-Blessing—Chicago Historical Society]

done by Swedish sculptor Carl Milles. The Michigan Square shops, at the street and balcony levels, were accessible from the street but faced also into the rotunda. The tranquil beauty of the Diana Court and the individuality that Wolbach encouraged for each shop's interior and exterior design were acclaimed by the Chicago *Tribune* in 1928 as "an important step in the development of Upper Michigan Avenue as the world's greatest shopping street."

In 1929 Wolbach was involved in promoting development of the lower level of Wacker Drive as a shopping and pedestrian mall. The plans were announced in July 1929. By October it was all over. The collapse of the stock market put an end to all of Wolbach's development plans and precipitated a relentless roll of foreclosures that hit Wolbach and other Chicagoans with brutal force.

Wolbach lost the Michigan Square Building in the early 1930s. The building was later purchased by Time, Inc., and renamed the Time-Life Building. In 1973 Michigan Square was demolished to make way for the Marriott Hotel, which now stands on the site.

Wolbach managed to maintain his real estate business through the 1930s and '40s and remained active in the leadership of the Chicago Real Estate Board. He was vice president of the North Central Business District Association in the 1920s and later became president and a director of the South Central Business Association. He remained involved in both organizations for many years afterward.

The Wolbachs moved from their Kenwood home to 2340 Lincoln Park West in 1924 and later lived at 220 East Walton Street. Murray Wolbach's daughters remember that he continued to walk daily from his home on Walton Street to his office on South Dearborn Street up until the time of his death in 1954 at the age of seventy-eight. His route would have extended the length of North Michigan Avenue. The walk must have been a pleasant one for Wolbach—one filled with more satisfaction than regret.

UNREPENTANT SWINDLER

William C. Bannerman
(1900-?)

William C. Bannerman's star soared briefly across the Chicago skies in the late 1920s, leaving in its trail a few good buildings and a lot of bad debts. The good buildings, all designed by architect Robert S. DeGolyer, included the 3000 Sheridan Road Apartments near Belmont Harbor, the Windsor Beach Apartments on South Shore Drive, and 1430 North Lake Shore Drive, which remains one of Chicago's most luxurious cooperative apartment buildings. The bad debts are another story—reflecting an explosive mix of boom-time investment, overextension, and inadequate regulation paired with an unscrupulous young builder who, had he been born fifty years later, might have made headlines instead in a trading floor scam. In a three-year period between 1925 and 1928, William Bannerman built a pyramid of twenty-three building and management corporations through which he kited a fortune in investors' dollars—and from which he extracted untold thousands more in kickbacks, hidden commissions, and unearned profits.

He also got caught. By 1930 a third of his corporations had collapsed or ceased to function, and the remainder were in foreclosure or court-ordered receiverships. Bannerman himself by that time was in court facing the wrath of investors he had defrauded in the syndication and financing of the elegant 1430 North Lake Shore Drive cooperative apartments. Were it not for the suit brought against him by the 1430 Lake Shore Drive shareholders, an accounting of Bannerman's business dealings might have been lost among the thousands of foreclosures that occurred after 1930. As it happens, the extensive records of these proceedings provide a fascinating insight into the operations of an unrepentant swindler—a man who no doubt rode on the coattails of the many good developers of the time.

William Campbell Bannerman Jr. was born in Chicago in 1900, served in the armed forces, and, for a time, studied law. But he made no name for himself to speak of until the early 1920s when, as young contractor, he caught the wave of the postwar building boom. His rise to the big time coincided with the cooperative apartment movement. The Illinois legislation permitting cooperative ownership opened the door for speculators such as Bannerman to launch new projects using shareholders' dollars, and then to supplement these funds through the sale of first mortgage bonds, which were readily transacted in the expansive and largely unregulated years after World War I.

In 1925 Bannerman incorporated himself as W. C. Bannerman and Company, took an attorney named Leo S. Samuels into his office as his counsel and general manager, and began a flurry of apartment and apartment-hotel projects in the Belmont Harbor and Edgewater areas of the North Side. Each project was incorporated as a separate entity, with Bannerman registered as director and principal stockholder. From the beginning, there was very little, if any, cash value in the Bannerman companies. The letters of incorporation represented that Bannerman's stock was purchased with equity he claimed in the real estate; in the value of the architects' plans; and in "contracts for construction and financing of the building." The contractor, of course, was Bannerman himself or, later, one of the dummy building companies that he established in conjunction with new projects.

In 1926 Bannerman organized another six corporations and building companies, two of them operating in the Belmont Harbor area, one set up to build the 2136-40 Lincoln Park West Apartments, and three more organized to construct two large-scale cooperative apartment complexes on South Shore Drive in the area of the South Shore Country Club.

Eight similar corporations and building companies, plus two management companies, were spun off in 1927 and 1928, including the shell companies that built and sold the 3000 Sheridan Road Apartments at Sheridan and Wellington Avenue. In one case, the Windsor Beach Apartments at 7321 South Shore Drive, four Bannerman corporations were layered onto the project: the South Shore Beach Building Corporation, the Windsor Beach Construction Company, the 7321 South Shore Drive Building Corporation, and W. C. Bannerman and Company, which was identified as the promoter-developer. The Windsor Beach project was typical of Bannerman operations in that all but one of the incorporators, directors, and stockholders of all four corporations were on the Bannerman payroll. These included the company switchboard operator; a file clerk; another low-level clerk; an individual later identified as a "personal assistant" to Bannerman; Bannerman's construction supervisor; and his two office managers.

Bannerman spawned these corporations almost as fast as the paper could be drawn up. The primary purpose was to distance himself from personal liability as his debt load mounted. He also used the multiplicity of corporate entities both as a means for moving funds among accounts to cover cash shortages and for concealing other dubious financial activities. Throughout 1927 and most of 1928, he distanced himself not only on paper but also in person from his increasingly complex machinations. Claiming chronic illness, Bannerman, who was still in his twenties, removed himself from his Chicago base of operations for months on end. He left attorney Samuels in charge of his band of dummy directors, but maintained tight control by mail, telephone, and telegraph over all operations and cash transfers.

In late 1926, declaring himself to be "in a very rundown physical condition," Bannerman left for California. He stayed in the Los Angeles area until March 1927, when he took up residence in Albuquerque, New Mexico. He later claimed that these moves were made on the advice of a physician who, Bannerman testified, "told me it would be impossible for me to return to active business, and that I should go to some health place, a sanatorium, for an indefinite period." The actual state of Bannerman's health is hard to assess. Samuels said he had been told that Bannerman had tuberculosis—a diagnosis that Bannerman declined to confirm under oath. Bannerman himself said that in 1929 he suffered from rheumatism and neuritis so debilitating that he was unable to walk. Bannerman maintained the home in Albuquerque (Samuels would testify that he was never a resident of a sanatorium) throughout 1927 and 1928, the most active period of his development career. Samuels visited him there several times, and Bannerman made strategically timed trips back to Chicago. He stayed on the move through 1929, but expanded his venue to include Arizona and Florida.

One thing is clear. Bannerman's capacity to do business was not impaired either by his disability, whatever that may have been, or by his long absences from the city. In 1927, the year that he first took to his bed, W. C. Bannerman and Company was very actively involved in the South Shore Drive, 3000 Sheridan Road, and 1430 Lake Shore Drive projects. Detailed correspondence produced as evidence in the 1430 Lake Shore trial proved beyond doubt that Bannerman was controlling every aspect of the business.

Bannerman's last big deal in Chicago involved the formation of Bannerman Hotels, Inc., early in 1928. He used this corporation to refinance four of the Belmont Harbor and Edgewater area buildings he had put up in 1925, plus the 2136-40 Lincoln Park West apartment hotel. The hotel deal amounted to reshuffling existing documents, a fact that did not deter Bannerman from claiming that his new hotel company was capitalized at $2.5 million. He later tried to squeeze cash out of hotel maids and clerks by demanding that they buy stock in the corporation or face losing their jobs.

W. C. Bannerman and Company was declared insolvent in April 1929, long before the Depression forced other developers into foreclosures, and in July the company was placed in a court-ordered receivership. Samuels, who had not been paid the salary promised him, jumped ship. In June 1930 he told what he knew to the stockholders in the 1430 Lake Shore Drive Corporation.

North Lake Shore Drive, looking north from the Drake Hotel, 1926. This stretch of the lakefront, known as Chicago's Gold Coast, is still the site of some of Chicago's most luxurious apartment buildings. William Bannerman was an organizer of the syndicate that built the 1430 Lake Shore Drive apartments, a block north of the Potter Palmer mansion, in the year that this photograph was taken.
[Kaufmann and Fabry, from *Chicago and Its Makers*]

According to Samuels's testimony, the 1430 Lake Shore Drive project began as a syndicate organized by Bannerman in April 1927 for the purpose of erecting a luxury apartment building on a narrow lakefront lot that had been the site of the old James Deering home. To his credit, Bannerman again chose Robert DeGolyer as architect. DeGolyer had worked for ten years with Ben Marshall and was himself the architect of the Italian Court Building on North Michigan Avenue, the Ambassador East Hotel, and numerous Gold Coast apartments. Samuels testified that Bannerman later whittled De-Golyer's fee from five percent to three percent of project costs. As the project progressed, the 1430 Lake Shore syndicate was incorporated, with shareholders entitled to convert their interest to apartment ownership under the cooperative plan. The seven original syndicate investors had put up $98,500, representing a one-third interest in the $300,000 declared par value of the shares. Bannerman subscribed for $161,000 and Samuels for $40,100. Three additional shares at $100 each were subscribed for the omnipresent Bannerman employee-directors.

The facts—as Samuels later disclosed and the judge affirmed—were that Bannerman had put up no money at all for the two-thirds interest he claimed to own nor for the shares he had subscribed for Samuels, reportedly in lieu of salary. The million-dollar building, the shareholders discovered, had been built on the backs of the minority stockholders and with blanket mortgage loans for which they as cooperative owners unexpectedly found themselves liable.

With Samuels's information in hand, the shareholders prepared their case with great care. They sprang it on Bannerman in a letter dated June 16, 1930, in which they demanded his payment for the 1,161 shares of stock to which he had subscribed and for the 401 shares assigned to Samuels. Bannerman ignored the letter. On June 23 the shareholders filed suit in the chancery division of the Circuit Court of Cook County. Bannerman did not take the news well. According to depositions and testimony taken in 1931 divorce proceedings, he went home and beat up his twenty-two-year-old wife.

There were three major areas of argument when the case came to trial: ownership of the land; Bannerman's claim that he had paid in one way or another for the stock issued to him and was therefore entitled to the equity and proceeds thereof; and the matter of inflated costs, kickbacks, and commissions. Of these, the primary issue was that of the ownership of the stock—and ultimately of many of the choice apartments—in the 1430 Lake Shore building.

The shareholders charged that Bannerman had willfully contrived to defraud bona fide investors by assigning two thirds of the stock in the corporation to himself under the pretense that he had paid for it in cash or in property. They also alleged that Bannerman paid himself commissions associated with the purchase of the lot and the sale of bonds and that he inflated construction estimates and appropriated the difference, which came out of the 1430 bond proceeds, to other Bannerman operations. They demanded restitution to the corporation of rents and other profits that had accrued to Bannerman from sales and rentals of the apartments he claimed to own as the majority stockholder in the corporation.

No one was surprised to find that the record books for the 1430 corporation were missing, and had been since 1928, when shareholders first asked Bannerman to produce them. But the plaintiffs were able to track the use of their money through other Bannerman accounts. They eventually documented claims that Bannerman had funneled more than a quarter of a million dollars out of the corporation, in addition to rentals and revenues accruing to him as the "majority owner" in the property. As the net drew tighter, Bannerman mounted an amnesia defense, declaring that he had no knowledge or recollection either of the state of his companies' books or the actions of his employees. "You can't hold me responsible for somebody else endorsing checks and manipulating my bank account when I was not in the city," he argued in court, adding at one point, "As a matter of fact, I don't see what I am wanted here for anyhow."

One year and some one thousand pages of testimony later, the judge in his final decree concurred with the essential findings of fact in all of the forty-three counts of the plaintiff's complaint. Bannerman was ordered to pay the 1430 Lake Shore Drive Corporation $205,055, with interest from the date of the decree. Bannerman's stock was sold at auction, at well below its face value, leaving a balance due to the corporation of $147,029.

Bannerman skipped town. And he left no friends behind. His lawyer had resigned from the case in the middle of the trial for the same reason that Samuels had defected from the company—his fee had not been paid—leaving Bannerman to conduct his own defense. Bannerman's wife Mary, who had long since returned to her father's home, filed for divorce a month after the trial ended, charging "extreme and repeated cruelty." Bannerman subsequently defaulted on the $40-a-month child support payments ordered on behalf of the couple's three-year-old daughter.

1430 North Lake Shore Drive. The 1430 building [the twenty-four-story vintage building on the right in this photo] brought to an end the unhappy dealings of developer William C. Bannerman in Chicago, but 1430—designed by famed residential architect Robert DeGolyer—remains one of the Gold Coast's finest cooperative apartment buildings.
[Doug Montgomery]

By the mid-1930s Bannerman had settled in Florida, where he appeared to have experienced a remarkable restoration of health and vigor. When Mary Newton Bannerman, who had remarried, sued for sole custody of her daughter in 1935, Bannerman responded with a countersuit. He declared himself to be ''of sound physical health . . . well able to have the custody and care of said infant child.'' This case, too, was settled in Mary's favor. William Bannerman, it seems, made no further appearances in Chicago.

AUTHOR'S COMMENTARY

Although I never met William Bannerman, and in fact have been unable to track his career after he left Chicago in the early 1930s, his story may not be altogether unique in real estate history. I am reminded of the more recent activies of Sam Banowit, who built the Borg-Warner Building. In itself, this was quite a successful project but Banowit's own concept of creative financing was not revealed until after his death when, as the story goes, investors who gathered in California for his funeral discovered in conversation with one another that the total of their respective interests in his properties far exceeded 100 percent.

CHICAGO RESURGENT

1945-92

Chicago after World War II continued to set the standard for creative development and design in urban architecture, readily adapting to the great social and economic changes that characterized the second half of the twentieth century in America. The first challenge of the post-war period was a critical shortage of available housing. As in other cities, the construction industry in Chicago slipped into a deep and troubled sleep after the collapse of the stock market in 1929. Wartime shortages of manpower and materials prolonged the hiatus in downtown building well into the 1940s. With the exception of public works projects constructed under the National Recovery Act, there were virtually no real estate starts in Chicago, in any category of property, for almost two decades.

In the same span of time, the city's population grew dramatically, swelled first by the arrival of families migrating to northern cities in search of work during the Depression. In the war years, population soared with the influx of people drawn to jobs in the defense industry. During this period, single-family homes and other buildings were converted from their original uses to accommodate more and more people. Increased density, overcrowding, and often severe economic hardship added to the cumulative deterioration of the city's housing stock. The housing problem reached crisis proportions after 1945, when hundreds of thousands of veterans surged back to Chicago. Many were returning to continue ca-

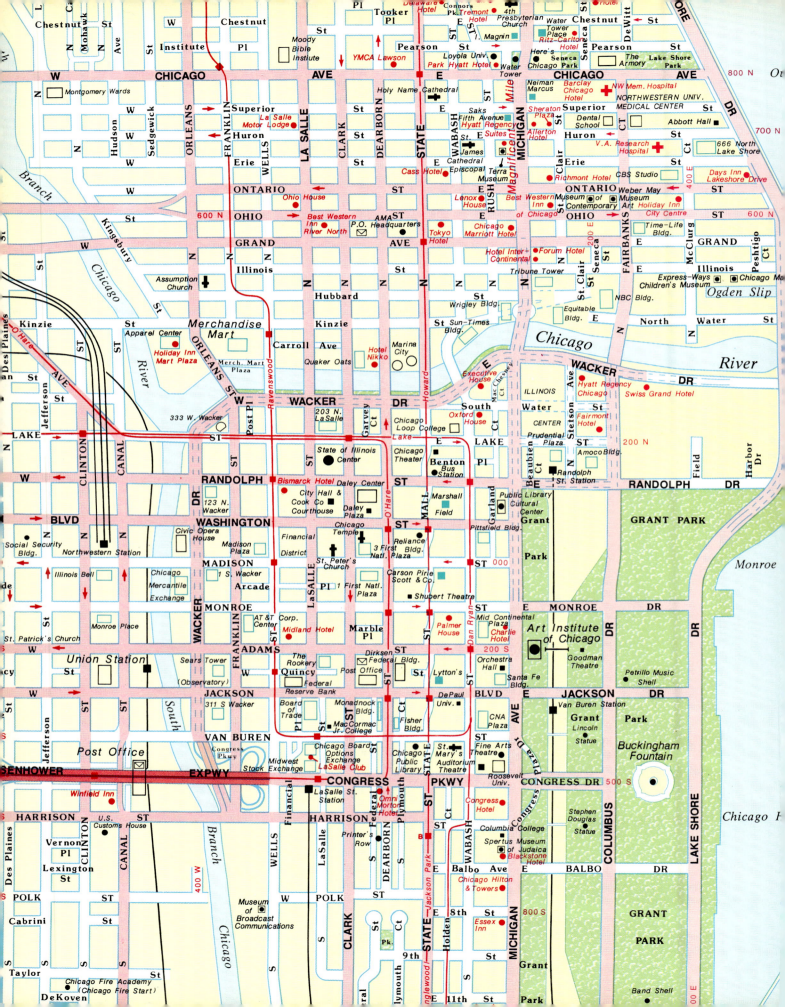

Central Chicago, Loop, and "Magnificent Mile." [opposite page]
[© 1988 Pierson Graphics Corp.]

reers or schooling interrupted by the war. Many more came in search of opportunities not available in rural America. Few were fortunate enough find apartments to rent. Fewer still found homes available for families now caught up in another form of population explosion: the postwar baby boom.

Chicago's response to its burgeoning population was, as historically it had always been, to create entirely new suburban communities—the modern counterparts of nineteenth-century suburban developments such as Hyde Park, Edgewater, and Brookfield. Suburban Park Forest, planned by Philip Klutznick and other Chicago developers in 1946, was the first privately developed new town in postwar America. It became a model for new communities springing up throughout the nation.

The suburban boom was augmented by a massive federal highway program that supported construction of a swift and efficient expressway system and by the availability of federally guaranteed home financing. These factors made the new communities both accessible to employment and affordable for young families. Developers built shopping malls, communities incorporated to provide schools, and a steady stream of middle-class families abandoned the city for the suburbs.

Although suburban development addressed the housing crisis at one level, at another level it compounded the problem. Much of the inner city remained severely blighted. Private capital to implement government-sponsored urban renewal projects was slow to materialize. Public housing programs proved inadequate to the need. The loss to the suburbs of tax revenues needed to support the increasingly heavy costs of education, public safety, and city services in overcrowded and economically depressed areas, particularly on the South Side, was keenly felt.

The response of some Chicago developers was to create a new residential market within the city. The luxury lakefront high-rise apartment house had been a phenomenon of the 1920s, the aerie of the very rich. Postwar developers such as Herbert Greenwald and John Mack and Ray Sher redefined and democratized the concept, bringing lakefront living within the range of young professionals and middle- to upper-income families. Tapping Federal Housing Administration financing programs, they built massive and much-imitated high-rise buildings along North Lake Shore Drive, replacing both the twelve-room luxury apartments and the mid-rises of the 1920s with the efficient and affordable one- and two-bedroom units of the 1950s and '60s.

Other developers, including Ferd Kramer, Arthur Rubloff, Albert Robin, and Daniel Levin, focused their attention on

the urban renewal and redevelopment programs to which the city had committed itself in the early 1940s. In the late 1950s Kramer led the effort to reclaim the severely blighted area around Michael Reese Hospital through land clearance and the construction of the Lake Meadows and Prairie Shores

Marina City. Built between 1964 and 1967 on the north bank of the Chicago River between State and Dearborn streets, architect-developer Bertrand Goldberg's twin-tower Marina City complex became a symbol of Chicago's new urban vitality. [Hedrich-Blessing—Chicago Historical Society]

Chicago and vicinity.
[opposite page]
[© 1986 Pierson Graphics Corp.]

John Hancock Center.
[opposite page] Opened in 1970, the 100-story John Hancock Center, 875 North Michigan Avenue, combined retail uses, office space, and high-rise condominium apartments, launching a new era in North Michigan Avenue development.
[Hedrich-Blessing—Chicago Historical Society]

apartment complexes. Rubloff and Robin used the city's urban renewal programs to build Carl Sandburg Village on the Near North Side in the 1960s. Levin undertook an initially successful experiment in integrated housing in the late 1960s when he developed the South Commons community on the Near South Side. Dearborn Park, developed in the 1970s through a broad-ranging partnership of business and civic interests led by Klutznick, Kramer, and John W. Baird, brought new vitality to the deteriorated South Loop district.

While inner cities elsewhere in America continued a long slide into urban decay, Chicago held its own, and in many ways prospered. The city's will to survive and drive to build was reinforced by the election in 1955 of Richard J. Daley to the office of mayor. Daley accumulated and consolidated great political power over the next two decades. His love for the city and his understanding of the political process from both the legislative and executive perspective, as well as his grasp of municipal finance, served Chicago well. His enthusiasm for huge projects and access to a rich vein of federal funds fueled the rapid redevelopment of the city in the 1950s and '60s.

Daley created the Department of Development and Planning in 1956, soon after the completion of the Prudential Building on North Michigan Avenue ended the paralysis in downtown construction that had persisted throughout the Depression. In the same year, he presided over the opening of O'Hare International Airport, an event that gave swift impetus to the development of northwest suburban industrial parks and the construction of more new residential communities. Daley's public building program was enormous, and he moved it swiftly forward. The Kennedy Expressway was fully opened in November 1960, the Dan Ryan in December 1962, and the final phase of the Stevenson was finished November 1966. The first McCormick Place went up in 1960. The new Chicago Civic Center and the University of Illinois at Chicago campus both opened in 1965. Significant public resources went into improvement of the city's infrastructure, and policies that encouraged development were initiated. Although building codes remained relatively restrictive, zoning codes were liberalized in 1957, opening the door to the torrent of downtown development that characterized the next three decades. By the early 1960s, a strong, bold city was on the brink of an urban renaissance.

Along with other American metropolitan centers, Chicago experienced a transition in the postwar period from an industrial to a service-based economy. In these years, Mayor Daley's ability to involve the corporate and business community in downtown development, together with the concurrent re-

sponse of business leadership, saved Chicago from the economic decline that plagued Detroit, Cleveland, and other Midwest cities in the late 1950s.

Responding to the influx of downtown office workers, apartment complexes such as Outer Drive East, Marina City, and McClurg Court Center sprang up within walking distance of the Loop, bringing a new wave of salaried young professionals into the city in the 1960s. Charles Shaw's innovative Lake Point Tower Apartments drew attention once again to the downtown lakefront.

Simultaneously, the city's urban renewal activity in Hyde Park, in partnership with the University of Chicago, set a high standard for the recapture of land occupied by slums as desirable residential areas. Similar private initiatives in the Old Town Triangle, on the Near North Side, stimulated public-private partnerships in the Lincoln Park district and supported the reclamation of entire neighborhoods. These in turn inspired the creation of new developments, including Sandburg Village.

The postwar building boom continued through the 1960s, surpassing in dollar value the pace of construction in any previous decade. Building emphasis moved from office to residential and back to office, creating a constantly changing Chicago skyline. The central business district was most significantly affected in this period as new, modern office towers such as the Brunswick Building, CNA Center, and the First National Bank Building and Plaza replaced older structures, many of them dating from the nineteenth century.

In the period from 1945 to 1990, Chicago, along with the nation, experienced some eight recessions, none of which approached the dimensions of the Great Depression or even the more severe of the nineteenth-century financial panics. Although these periods of economic crisis were serious and cyclically affected development, the general trend in this forty-five-year period remained up. And the direction that Chicago skyscrapers were taking was also up, peaking in the 1970s with the completion of the 100-story John Hancock Center in 1970 and the 110-story Sears Tower in 1974.

Enactment of a Chicago Planned Unit Development ordinance followed the 1957 liberalization of the zoning ordinance, giving the city the opportunity to grant greater densities and setting the stage for the often controversial mixed-use developments of the 1970s and '80s. These were the "cities within the city," such as Illinois Center, developed by Bernard Weissbourd; Water Tower Place, developed by Philip Klutznick; and Cityfront Center, developed under the leadership of Charles Gardner. Construction of Illinois Cen-

Sears Tower. [opposite page] Chicago's drive to build higher peaked in 1974 with the construction of the Sears Tower, which, at 110 stories, continues to hold the title as the world's tallest building. [Hedrich-Blessing]

State of Illinois Center. This building, completed in 1985, presents a thoroughly modern face to the corner of Clark and Randolph streets, the intersection that has been the traditional center of government in Chicago since the first courthouse was built there in 1853.
[Hedrich-Blessing]

ter, one of the world's largest mixed-use developments, began in 1970. This complex, with a planned buildout of twenty to thirty years, combined office towers, apartment buildings, hotels, and an underground shopping mall on a multilevel reuse of the much-litigated Illinois Central Railroad air rights space. The complex and ongoing negotiations between the city and the Illinois Center developers over issues such as infrastructure development, open space, and the ratio of residential to commercial uses broke new ground in urban planning concepts.

Water Tower Place, combining a "vertical shopping mall" with hotel, office, and residential uses, rose up next to the

State of Illinois Center atrium. The soaring atrium of the seventeen-story State of Illinois Center is oriented toward the Chicago Civic Center [Daley Center], diagonally across Randolph Street. This building, commissioned by Illinois governor James R. Thompson and designed by Helmut Jahn [Murphy/Jahn] is one of the most provocative and controversial ever constructed in Chicago. [Hedrich-Blessing]

towering Hancock building in 1975. Water Tower was followed by a succession of new multiuse buildings on North Michigan Avenue, surfacing the density issue in an area that was already perceived to be overcrowded, even at a time when the city as a whole was losing population. The issue was a difficult one, resolved in favor of both the impetus that these structures gave to the economic base and the continuation of Chicago's reputation as a center for innovative and creative architecture.

As the size of projects increased to megaproportions, so too did the capital demands needed to build them. The 1970s saw the transition in the development field from the individual entrepreneur, often backed in the postwar years by Federal Housing Administration loans, to the entrepreneurial-institutional partnership. The use of the real estate investment trust expanded rapidly in the 1970s, at the same time that pension funds and savings and loan investments were deregulated. Public corporations began to invest in real estate, and the insurance and mutual funds moved from their traditional position as mortgage lenders to equity participants in development projects.

With seemingly limitless capital available and tax incentives plentiful, the 1980s became the decade of the Big Boom, a new golden age in Chicago development. In this period, developers poured some $10 billion into Chicago's downtown area, financing well over three hundred individual building projects. Some seventy-eight major buildings were built during the decade of the 1980s, including the Chicago Mercantile Exchange; the NBC Tower; the Leo Burnett Building, developed by John Buck; One Financial Place, developed by a partnership headed by Robert Wislow; and Richard A. Stein's AT&T Corporate Center.

As the 1980s—probably the most significant period of real estate speculation since the 1920s—rolled over into the 1990s, another fifty projects were either under construction or in the predevelopment stages in Chicago. But the decade of the 1990s dawned with the realization that the boom was over. Office vacancy rates were up, a recession hovered, and Chicago developers began putting whatever projects they could on hold for the duration. The vacancy rate in the central business district of Chicago reached the 20 percent mark, and vacancy in the suburban markets was even higher, at close to 25 percent. The oversupply of office space was at the greatest level in the history of the city. The combination of excessive building, a decrease in the growth rate of service businesses, and the economic recession of 1991-92 suggested that the current supply would not be absorbed before the turn of the century.

The optimism of the 1980s had been expressed in the 1989 announcement by Chicago developers Lee Miglin and J. Paul Beitler of yet another world's tallest building, a 125-story spire facing the developers' triumphant 181 West Madison and 200 West Madison office towers. In 1992 Miglin and Beitler's world's tallest building still languished on the drawing boards, bereft of both financing and prospective tenants. It was a product of the excessive eighties and an inevitable casualty of the era.

But this is the stuff of Chicago's development history. The city rose again from the Great Fire of 1871. It recovered from the Great Depression and restored its downtown when other cities could not. It maintains its tradition of bold and great architecture. And it will, no doubt, in due time erect another world's tallest building.

URBAN RENEWAL

Ferd Kramer

Ferd Kramer.
[Draper and Kramer]

In 1989 Ferd Kramer was glad to see a new Mayor Daley moving into the fifth floor offices at city hall and bringing a new commissioner of planning with him. Kramer had had his fill of the previous administration, and he minced no words in expressing his opinion of the former mayor and his staff. But why should he? The issue was housing, a subject that Kramer knows a great deal about. When it comes to slum clearance and revitalization of inner-city neighborhoods, Ferd Kramer has more years of experience and more solid accomplishments behind him than anyone in Chicago—possibly more than anyone in America. Nonetheless, his idea for redevelopment of a public housing wasteland in Chicago's North Kenwood area on the South Side had been received, he said, with resounding indifference by the interim mayor, Eugene Sawyer, and Elizabeth Hollander, planning commissioner.

Kramer's proposal called for demolition of a group of forbidding and virtually uninhabited Chicago Housing Authority highrises located on the lakefront five miles south of the Loop. Razing of the CHA monoliths would be followed by redevelopment of the three-hundred-acre site with new low-rise housing. If accomplished, the Kenwood development would be the largest neighborhood renewal project in the city's history. It would also be the first instance in which a CHA project was torn down to make way for both public and private redevelopment. Anyone who has seen the war zone that Chicago "project" housing, built in the 1940s and '50s, has become would welcome change—any change. But Kramer's idea, linked as it was to middle-income lakefront development and construction of new scattered-site public housing, was a political powder keg.

No matter that Kramer was in his own eighty-eighth year when he launched his campaign to win city support for the Kenwood redevelopment and that he had no personal financial interest in the plan. He was no less formidable for that. At the time of his presentation to Sawyer, Kramer was working out daily with his tennis coach, training for the summer tournaments at which he would defend his title as a reigning national champion in his age group. He was in fighting trim.

Kramer's Kenwood proposal attracted national media attention in 1989, but the fate of the redevelopment plan remained in the balance. Kramer, who identified himself as the "catalyst" for the plan, not the developer, explained his passion to see it done in these words: "I want to make one last, significant contribution to this city that I love and that has been so good to me."

Ferd Kramer was born in Chicago and born to be in real estate. His maternal grandmother, Bertha Stein, was a daughter of one of Chicago's earliest settler families. The grandfather for whom he is named arrived in Chicago from Germany shortly after the Civil War and established himself in the wholesale dry goods business. In 1893 their son Adolph and a young friend, London-born Arthur W. Draper, formed Draper and Kramer, a small real estate brokerage and mortgage company. By 1901, when Adolph's son Ferd was born (in the house at 2912 Prairie Avenue where his father had been born), the business was doing well. The company would grow to become one of Chicago's great real estate management, brokerage, and mortgage businesses, expanding after World War II into residential and office building development and in more recent years into international joint ventures in property development. In 1988 Draper and Kramer, well into its third generation of family management, celebrated its ninety-fifth anniversary.

When Ferd Kramer graduated from the University of Chicago in 1922, he was assigned to the management of the Draper and Kramer South Shore Park office. He was then the same age that his father had been when he and Draper founded the business. In keeping with the dynastic character of the company, Ferd's partner in the South Shore office was Arthur W. Draper Jr.

Kramer's lifetime interest in housing and government-assisted housing programs emerged in the first years of the Great Depression. These were historic times, marking for the first time the entry of government into the housing field. Kramer put his shoulder behind President Franklin D. Roosevelt's New Deal promise to support demonstration programs for construction of low-rent housing. In 1934 he became chairman of the finance committee of Chicago's Metropolitan Housing Council, a quasi-official body concerned with targeting blighted areas for clearance and redevelopment. He would eventually serve nearly twenty years as president of the organization. The council (later called the Metropolitan Housing and Planning Council) became the link to federal public housing projects in Chicago. These were the planning experiments of the New Deal, and Kramer in these years found himself in turbulent territory. Landlords and builders, who he might have been expected to represent, opposed government condemnation of deteriorated buildings and the establishment of guidelines defining substandard housing. The New Deal recovery programs that Kramer supported demanded such actions.

Kramer's work in the housing field in Chicago did not go unnoticed. In 1940 he went to Washington as a program supervisor, and later became deputy coordinator for the federal government's Division of Defense Housing Coordination. His job was to set up the eleven regional offices across the country charged with developing housing for civilian defense workers and for the armed forces. These were exciting times, Kramer recalls. His office was responsible for building what amounted to entire new towns around strategic installations.

It is of more than passing interest that in this period Kramer formed a friendship with a young lawyer from Omaha with a similar background in New Deal housing programs. This was Philip Klutznick, who would go on to become commissioner of the Federal Public Housing Authority. Klutznick and Kramer renewed their association after the war in the creation of the town of Park Forest south of Chicago and more directly in the later development of regional shopping centers and residential communities. Later the two spearheaded the development of the Dearborn Park community, on Chicago's Near South Side.

Kramer returned to Draper and Kramer in 1942, and in 1944 became chairman of the board. When the war ended and housing emerged as America's most urgent national priority, Kramer moved the firm into the field of real estate development. Draper and Kramer's first postwar developments were faculty housing units built at Fifty-fifth Street and Dorchester Avenue for the University of Chicago. Kramer recalls that the University's president, Robert Maynard Hutchins, came to him and said, "Mr. Kramer, I have young professors from the

Lake Meadows Apartments.
The ten-building, 2,033-unit
Lake Meadows apartment
complex, completed in 1960,
was the first privately financed
urban renewel project in the
nation.
[Draper and Kramer]

Ivy League and California that I am about to sign up to become members of the faculty here. But I have no place for them to live. What do we do?'' Kramer replied, ''If you supply the land, we'll build the buildings for you.'' Kramer and his architects encountered uneasy times as they struggled with the challenge of designing high-quality apartments and row houses that could be built to rent at a price that university faculty and staff members could afford. Proud of the result, Kramer regards his second project for Hutchins, at Fifty-eighth Street and Dorchester, as a prototype for the federal urban renewal programs that followed in the 1950s.

In 1950 Draper and Kramer built the 1350 and 1360 North Lake Shore Drive apartments, on the site of the old Potter Palmer mansion. The 1350-60 complex was the first of the postwar apartment highrises to go up on the Drive and one of the first large buildings to go up in Chicago under the Federal Housing Administration 608 title insurance program. The development was a success, but it precipitated a period of personal distress to Kramer. At the time, Kramer was actively supporting Paul Douglas's campaign for reelection to the U.S. Senate, and a spurious connection was drawn between Kramer's political activities and the 1350-60 project. The press ran a story suggesting that Draper and Kramer had made a $1 million ''windfall'' on the FHA project. Forty years later, Kramer still fumes about the incident. ''It was headlines,'' he recalls. ''Paul Douglas raised hell about it, and the paper printed a retraction,'' he remembers. ''There was no windfall. It was absolutely untrue. It was an awful thing!'' Although developers as a group have a reputation for being thick-skinned, Kramer proves the exception to the rule. And he neither forgets nor forgives injustice.

Other commercially successful Draper and Kramer apartment developments followed, including the forty-three-story building at 1130 South Michigan, 4800 Chicago Beach Drive, and 2626 Lake View Avenue in the Lincoln Park area. But Kramer's abiding interest lay in the area of urban renewal, particularly as it might affect Chicago's South Side. The South Side had been hit hardest by the urban devastation that followed in the wake of the Depression, wartime neglect of domestic priorities, and the new social and demographic forces that bombarded the city in the postwar period.

When Michael Reese Hospital, centered at Thirty-first Street and Cottage Grove Avenue, began serious consideration of moving its facilities away from the urban blight that surrounded it, Kramer sprang into action. This was the neighborhood in which he had been born and raised. As a member of the hospital board, he strongly believed that a proposal to move the Michael Reese facilities to the North Side or to the West Side was an option too costly to consider. Slum clearance—as controversial as that idea was—and urban renewal were a better choice both for the hospital and the community, Kramer argued. Reginald Isaacs, Michael Reese planning department director and a veteran New Dealer who had been with the National Housing Agency in the 1930s and who was at the time head of the Harvard University Graduate School of Design, set to work on a plan to revitalize the neighborhood. This plan became the working document for the Central South Side Development Association (later the South Side Planning Board), a coalition of business and community interests, including Michael Reese and the Illinois Institute of Technology that was formed to coordinate South Side renewal programs.

The first residential project in the South Side renewal program was the 2,033-unit Lake Meadows complex built on a seventy-acre tract on Grand Boulevard (now King Drive) between Thirty-first and Thirty-fifth streets. Lake Meadows was also the first privately financed urban redevelopment project in the nation. The Chicago Housing Authority started the land acquisition and clearance process in 1947, but development capital was slow to follow. Kramer was instrumental in persuading the New York Life Insurance Company to take its real estate investment dollars to Chicago's inhospitable South Side and undertake redevelopment under a federal cost-sharing plan. Construction began in 1952 and was completed in 1960. In 1969 New York Life sold the project to a partnership formed by Draper and Kramer. With Lake Meadows well under way, the Prairie Shores Development Corporation was formed by Kramer, other members of the board, and friends of the hospital to build the Prairie Shores apartments adjacent to the hospital campus on Grand Boulevard between Twenty-eighth and Thirty-first streets. The five nineteen-story Prairie Shores buildings, completed in 1962, added another 1,677 apartment units to the area. Kramer moved his own family into the Prairie Shores development after living for twenty years in suburban Highland Park.

Lake Meadows and Prairie Shores are not without their critics. Both complexes, however, stand as monuments to the wisdom of an urban policy that Kramer had argued since the 1930s, namely, that the city must play an active and cooperative role in its own salvation. In 1952 Kramer warned the Metropolitan Housing and Planning Council that "we are making new slums faster than we can rebuild them." He urged city government to put an end to its own "bad housekeeping" and take the steps needed to attract private resources to rejuvenate

Dearborn Park. The question of whether the South Loop Dearborn Park residential complex would be constructed as an entirely town-house development was discussed during the planning stages. The developers, including Ferd Kramer, opted for a combination of high-rise, mid-rise, and town-house units. [Scott McDonald,—Hedrich-Blessing]

and develop the city wherever renewal was needed. Kramer is nothing if not perfectly consistent. These words were as true in 1988 when he presented his plan for the Kenwood CHA redevelopment as they were in 1952 when he fought for the planning and zoning support—and the private capital infusion—needed to rescue the Michael Reese community.

Over the years Ferd Kramer and Phil Klutznick, both old warriors in the housing campaigns, had maintained the friendship they forged in the years of defense housing and the working relationship that led them into the development of suburban shopping centers such as Old Orchard and Oakbrook. In the mid-1970s, at an age when other people are enjoying retirement in benign climates, Kramer and Klutznick took on yet another project. It was a design of monumental proportions, involving a larger and more complex cast of players than any of the foregoing Kramer or Klutznick achievements. The plan was to develop fifty-one acres of ragged South Loop railway lands just south of the abandoned Dearborn Street Station as an entirely new residential community.[1]

Residential development of the South Loop was recommended by the Chicago Central Area Committee in its *Chicago 21* planning document. No one doubted the potential vitality and economic benefit that South Loop development could provide for city. But it took a brave band—men and women with the vision of Chicago's premier planner Daniel Burnham, who urged "make no little plans"—to launch a $150 million development in this desolate location with no assurance that the properties could be sold or rented.[2] To the surprise of many, perhaps even the developers, within ten years of the 1977 groundbreaking, Dearborn Park had become a thriving community of 10,000 residents. By then the second phase of Dearborn Park, located south of Roosevelt Road, was under construction.[3]

The Dearborn Park phenomenon is about developers and their motivations. At a time when inner cities elsewhere in America were collapsing inward, Chicagoans like Ferd Kramer were turning the tide. They channeled their energy to the task of rallying corporate dollars, political clout, and all the savvy of their own decades of experience around a limited-dividend corporation committed to breathing new life into their city's downtown area.

When Kramer speaks of the city's seeming indifference to his proposal for redevelopment of the Kenwood CHA project site, he speaks with the voice of a man who is entitled to have his opinions heard. He is angered by critics who accuse him of scheming to drive poor families out of a lakefront housing project—the fact that the buildings are both vacant and uninhabitable notwithstanding. He doubts claims of city officials that people want to return to the project. "Who the hell would want to move back into those things, when you could have your own home and the safety of that situation?" Kramer asks. "Sure, you can have a beautiful view of Lake Shore Drive, and you can get raped in the elevator. I don't believe that this is what anybody wants," Kramer says. "I'm just trying to do better."

AUTHOR'S COMMENTARY

1. Kramer reminded me that the annual tax paid by the railroad for the twenty-four acres of vacant land occupied by the first phase of Dearborn Park was $40,000 a year. As of 1991 this parcel had been improved, with some twelve hundred housing units paying an estimated tax of $2 million. It is probable that the city's gain from the second phase built south of Roosevelt Road will equal or exceed this amount.

2. At the same time as the Dearborn Park project was initiated, Bertrand Goldberg was planning the River City complex, located immediately west of the site along the South Branch of the Chicago River. I consider Bertrand Goldberg to be an extremely creative and imaginative architect and designer who also possesses the vision, tenacity, and daring that is characteristic of the best developers. Certainly, Goldberg's 1963 Marina City multiuse complex, with its striking "corncob" towers, was one of the most innovative and influential concepts of its time. (The development has also been one of the most photographed and most widely recognized symbols of the new Chicago architecture and Chicago's urban residential style.)

   As vice chairman of the Chicago Plan Commission, I was less confident that Goldberg's original concept for the River City complex could succeed—a view shared by Planning Commissioner Lewis Hill. Ultimately, the plan commission refused to approve the plans. Goldberg had designed a very ambitious, extremely high-density development of three cylindrical towers of seventy-two stories each, to be financed under FHA programs. The concept reflected Goldberg's philosophy of the "city-within-a-city" in that it included within the three towers everything from shopping to schools to housing. It was conceived as a self-contained entity. And therein lay part of the problem, as we saw it. The Dearborn Park planners, while envisioning a total community, were motivated by a need to bring

33 West Monroe. The twenty-eight-story 33 West Monroe Street building where Ferd Kramer has his offices was developed in 1980 by the SDK Corporation, a partnership of Slough Estates, Slough, England, and Draper and Kramer.
[Hedrich-Blessing—Draper and Kramer, Inc.]

residential middle-class housing into the South Loop in the expectation of revitalizing the economy of a blighted area and providing a new anchor for South Loop business activity. We did not see the same potential for linkage to an existing, albeit deteriorating, neighborhood in Goldberg's River City plans. Similarly, we did not believe that the development could attract the numbers of residents required to support it. The concept was overly ambitious for the location and for the times. We were concerned that it would fail economically and revert to being another high-rise housing project, an approach that was by then already being discredited as a solution to urban housing problems.

With great persistence, Goldberg proceeded with a much smaller project: two low-rise, circular concrete apartment buildings at Harrison and Wells streets on the river's edge, completed in 1986. This project has subsequently failed. To this day, Goldberg believes that had the original project been completed as he envisioned it, it would have created an environment of its own and would have been a success. I am more convinced than ever that it would not have been. The project was too large, the location was uncertain, and the market was not proven. The experience of the massive Presidential Towers complex, a similar project whose developers defaulted on an FHA-guaranteed loan in 1990, would seem to bear out the judgment of the plan commission.

3. The South Loop Dearborn Park residential development has made money for its developers, has brought tax revenues into the city, has spurred new development in the area, and it has fulfilled a textbook planning dream of repopulating a downtown area with a middle-income, racially integrated community. But when Ferd Kramer and other business and civic leaders came to the Chicago Plan Commission with the Dearborn Park development plan, there was no guarantee that they would be able to make a go of it. Even after the first units were completed, it seemed that the area might have little to no market appeal. As a member of the plan commission, I remember our own early concern and the lengthy discussions of the direction this venture might take. The potential benefits to the city were great. We wanted the project to have every chance at success.

In 1972, when the Dearborn Park project was still in the talking stages, Lewis Hill, then commissioner of planning and development; Martin Murphy, then deputy commissioner; and I attended a seminar at Harvard University dealing with the connection between urban planning and development projects. During our free moments at the conference, we discussed a variety of projects that were in the planning stages in Chicago. The one that interested us most was Dearborn Park. At that time, Ferd Kramer was president of the Dearborn Park Corporation; his organization was involved from a marketing standpoint. Phil Klutznick was the principal force on the development side; Klutznick's staff were the troops in the trenches of planning. The several individuals and groups involved in the project were floating a variety of mixed-use development plans, and there was great uncertainty as to what the market would most readily absorb. This was a pioneering project and they were in a pioneering mode, in the sense that the Near South Side had not yet opened up as a marketable residential center. They were trying to get a variety of mixes and uses into the plan to see how the market would respond. To that end, and in order to run the least chance of monumental error, the planning incorporated town houses, mid-rise and high-rise buildings, and various apartment sizes and types.

In evaluating the plan, based on what we knew to be happening in Chicago and in the Chicago market area, Lew Hill, Martin Murphy, and I came to the conclusion that the project would have the best chance to move quickly if it were built as a total town-house project, eliminating the mid-rises and highrises. Town houses were going very well at that time, in both city and suburbs, and financing was available for them. It was a housing type whose time had come. We went back to Phil Klutznick's staff and suggested this plan, even furnishing some very rough drawings that Martin Murphy had done during the course of our two days in Cambridge. The developers saw and agreed, I believe, to a substantial extent, with our conclusions about the market. They continued to be concerned, however, about putting all their eggs in one basket. They chose to go with the mixed-development plan. For all its eventual success, the Dearborn Park project was slow to be accepted. As we anticipated, however, the town-house portion was extremely well received. In all probability, had the project been a totally town houses, the entire development would have sold out substantially faster than it did. However, as I view the Dearborn Park development today, I believe it is far better as a result of its mixed residential types, the slower start notwithstanding.

NEW TOWNS

Philip M. Klutznick

Philip M. Klutznick
[Dave Schuessler Photography]

When word of a new wave of National Industrial Recovery Act programs came over the wires in 1933, a young assistant city attorney from Omaha and a Nebraska senator hopped a train for Washington to see what they could see. It was a fishing expedition; they were looking for anything that might bring jobs to Omaha. And anything would do. What they uncovered on Capitol Hill was the germ of a New Deal plan to put federal dollars behind a few pilot programs in slum clearance and public housing. Nobody knew much about it. The concept of "public housing" was a revolutionary idea. The office that would administer the program was still in the process of being organized, and rules had yet to be written. There were no forms or guidelines available. But Philip M. Klutznick, that young city attorney, had no inclination to wait for the formalities. He grabbed the idea and jumped on the next train back to Omaha. "If we move fast, we can get it," he told the mayor.

Within seventy-two hours, the two had organized a citizens' committee on housing. Posthaste, the committee sent Klutznick back to Washington with applications—of his own design—not for one but two housing programs for Omaha. The committee knew where housing was needed, but had no idea what they would build. In the absence of architect's plans that the Washington agency said had to be submitted with the city's application for funds, Klutznick improvised. Designs for cottages that an architect on the hastily formed Omaha committee had sketched for another purpose were sent out to Klutznick on the morning train.

While the Washington offices pondered the new program, Klutznick hastened to advise the people back in Omaha that the government would probably expect the funds to be administered through a housing authority. It didn't matter that Omaha had no housing authority. Ten days later, when the Nebraska legislature adopted enabling legislation written by Klutznick, it did. This was Nebraska's first housing law. When the federal funds were allocated, Omaha found that it had been awarded both projects—a multimillion-dollar capital infusion for a city hit by both drought and economic depression.

Nearly sixty years later, from the vantage point of his office and library high over North Michigan Avenue, Phil Klutznick still gets a laugh out of the Omaha housing caper. "So that's how I became the great 'expert' in housing," he confides. The fact is, however quixotic his entry into the field, Klutznick quickly became a leading expert in Depression era and wartime housing programs. So much so that in 1944, President Franklin D. Roosevelt named him U.S. commissioner of public housing.

A career in government and diplomacy would not be improbable for an articulate and socially concerned lawyer with a talent for sizing up a situation and galvanizing energy and talent around him. A parallel career as a tough-minded businessman and industry leader in innovative real estate development would seem less likely. But Klutznick is a man of unusual talents. He does it all. As the founder of the massive Urban Investment and Development Corporation, Klutznick pioneered innovative development concepts that had the effect of recreating postwar America. These included the country's first comprehensively planned new town, regional shopping malls, the historic Water Tower Place development, and Chicago's South Loop Dearborn Park community. His concurrent career, as an ambassador to the United Nations Economic and Social Commission, U.S. secretary of commerce, adviser to seven American presidents, and activist in world Jewish affairs, has also been luminous.

Born in 1907 in Kansas City, Missouri, to eastern European, Orthodox Jewish parents, Phil Klutznick discovered both his innate internationalism and his flair for leadership as an undergraduate at the University of Kansas, where he became a national organizer of the B'nai B'rith youth movement. The organization's headquarters was in Omaha, so Klutznick transferred to the University of Nebraska in 1926, received his law degree from Creighton University in 1930, courted and married Ethel Riekes, and settled into what he hoped would be a comfortable private law practice in Omaha.

In the years that Klutznick worked as chief counsel to the Omaha Housing Authority and as an unpaid consultant to other government housing programs, Chicago real estate broker Ferdinand Kramer was pursuing a similar path as chairman of the housing committee of the Chicago Metropolitan Housing Council and an advocate for government-supported slum clearance and redevelopment projects. Klutznick came to Chicago frequently in his capacity as district president (and later international president) of B'nai B'rith, and he and Kramer met on a number of overlapping projects. When Kramer went to Washington in 1940 to serve as program supervisor for the federal Division of Defense Housing Coordination and Klutznick began to take ever more active roles in the National Housing Agency, the two found themselves working together on more projects—particularly the massive effort to establish wartime housing installations for defense workers. Klutznick and Kramer's collaboration, both in the public sector and later as partners in private development projects, has extended over more than fifty years.

In 1946 Klutznick resigned his post with the federal Public Housing Authority and accepted the invitation of a group of investors to return to Chicago to head their newly formed company, American Community Builders.[1] The goal they set for themselves was no less than the construction of an entirely new town, to be built on 2,400 acres of farmland thirty miles south of the Chicago Loop. The task was monumental, but the timing was right. By the end of 1945, more than a million men and women were being discharged every month from the armed services. In Chicago as in other American cities, the housing shortage had become increasingly acute throughout the Depression and war years. With demobilization it reached crisis proportions. Klutznick and his partners envisioned a total community, to be called Park Forest, designed specifically to meet the new needs of returning veterans and their young families.

Klutznick was not daunted by the scope of the Park Forest project. New towns were uncharted territory for private developers in 1946, but the idea was not new to Klutznick. "We'd built about a half a dozen of them during the war," he recalls. "And I learned one lesson in my work with the government: You don't develop land of any size with houses alone. You either build a community or it's a flop." As a housing program administrator, Klutznick paid attention to the fact that facilities were as important as lodging. "If we built a housing project, the first thing we took care of was a beauty parlor for Rosie the Riveter so she could get her hair done on the weekend."

The lesson was not forgotten in planning for Park Forest.

Water Tower Place. [opposite page] The 1975 Water Tower Place, flanked here by the Old Chicago Water Tower of 1869 and John Hancock Center, was America's first vertical shopping mall. But it is also a highly successful mixed-use building, with hotel and condominium apartments in the sixty-two-story tower. [Hedrich-Blessing]

The developers were, in effect, inventing a new American lifestyle. Clusters of garden apartment blocks, brick town houses, and eventually ranch-style homes rose up out of the cornfields—all built around a centerpiece shopping mall. Soon enough there were schools, churches, a firehouse, and a town hall. But it didn't happen overnight. In the beginning, there was no water system, no mail delivery, and no sidewalks. The streets, which wound among the newly landscaped residential units, were rutted with ice and snow in the winter and were rivers of mud in the spring. In the early years, the town was neither a park nor a forest.

When the community incorporated in 1949 as the Village of Park Forest, it was home to 8,000 people, including Phil and Ethel Klutznick, their daughter Bettylu, and sons Tom, James, Robert, and Sam. Klutznick, a visible target for tenant and homeowner complaints, says in retrospect that "it's easier to look back on those years than it was to live them." But the development was a success. By 1956 the population had swelled to 26,000, and by 1960 it had reached 30,000. Sociologist William H. Whyte turned Park Forest inside out in his book *The Organization Man,* dubbing the community America's "model suburb." The former commissioner of the federal Public Housing Authority had acquired a new, less formal title: Phil Klutznick, the builder of Park Forest.

As Park Forest put down its roots, Klutznick began to ease back into public life. In the early 1950s he became involved in the planning and construction of the industrial center and deep-water port at Ashdod in Israel. In 1957, in the Eisenhower administration, he served as a member of United States delegations to the United Nations, specializing in Third World development problems. When John F. Kennedy became president in 1961, he was appointed ambassador to the United Nations Economic and Social Council.

But Klutznick continued to mind the store back home. The world was changing fast in the 1950s, but so was the character of the American city and the surrounding metropolitan areas. As population marched forth to the new suburbs, Klutznick and his partners saw the future for shopping centers. They joined forces with two major retailers, Marshall Field and Company and Sears Roebuck, to ring Chicago with three of the largest and most innovative shopping malls in America: Old Orchard, which opened in 1956 in north suburban Skokie; Oakbrook Center, west of the city; and eventually, River Oaks, to the south, in Calumet City.

In the mid-1960s a Klutznick investment and development group organized community planning and home building companies to develop land around their regional shopping centers.[2] In 1968 the Klutznick core group and satellite companies reorganized as a new corporate entity—a development colossus they named Urban Investment and Development Company (UIDC). Two years later Urban was acquired by Aetna Life and Casualty Company, a development that significantly enhanced Urban's capital position. Urban's leadership remained the same, with Klutznick serving as chairman and CEO, Norman Cohn as president, and Tom Klutznick as executive vice president.

With four regional shopping center and community development projects (or "minitowns," as they were called) under its belt in 1970s,[3] UIDC turned its attention to the Chicago downtown area, anticipating a growing market for office development and a concurrent surge in urban residential construction. The first of these urban projects was North Michigan Avenue's precedent-setting Water Tower Place complex, completed in 1975. The strategy behind the regional shopping mall developments had been to create communities around the shopping center, thus providing a stable and reliable market for the retailers. With Water Tower Place, Klutznick reversed the formula, building an altogether new kind of shopping facility in the heart of an established—and affluent—market. Water Tower, however, was much more than a shopping center. It was one of the first, and remains one of the most successful, mixed-use developments in the country. Water Tower combined shopping, restaurants, theaters, banking, a luxury hotel, offices, and condominium apartments in one seventy-four-story complex. It set the stage for an era of high-rise development that would within a decade transform the geography of North Michigan Avenue.[4]

The project architects were Loebl, Schlossman, Bennett and Dart with C. F. Murphy and Associates, reflecting Klutznick's long association with Jerrold Loebl and Norman Schlossman, who were partners in the Park Forest development and the architects for the Old Orchard, River Oaks, and Oakbrook shopping centers. Water Tower Place, however, was a Phil Klutznick original all the way. (Klutznick quotes the line that "architects and lawyers are about as good as their clients".) The base structure, which he described as "the world's first vertical shopping mall," was a concept Klutznick had pondered for a number of years and had at one time considered building in Florida. When Gerald Sivage, president of Marshall Field and Company, approached Klutznick about opening a store on the Near North Side, Klutznick agreed that the time for a high-rise development was right.[5]

He had his eye on a site: the vacant property fronting on Michigan Avenue between Pearson and Chestnut streets. The catch was, the land wasn't for sale. Not then, at least. It was owned by the Joseph Seagram Company, whose principal stockholder was the Sam Bronfman family. Bronfman had considered using the site for a regional office building for Seagram, but so far had only erected a large billboard advertising Seagram's liquors.

Klutznick's strategy for acquiring the property was forthright: Go straight to the heart of the matter. He would deal only with Sam Bronfman himself, and he would do the deal himself, face to face, with no seconds in the wings. This was a match for the Titans. "I'll never forget that negotiation," Klutznick recalls. He tells the story well: Klutznick had determined his price—a generous one. It would be his only offer. "I said to the boys, we'll make one offer. If we start negotiating with the old gentleman, he'll never sell it. He thinks that land is like whiskey, that it ages in the bottle." Klutznick flew to New York and laid out the plan. The chairman said he'd think about it. Klutznick responded, "If you want this, let's make a deal. If you don't want it, let's be friends." Bronfman said "All right, you go home, we'll get our lawyers, and we'll send you the contract." Klutznick replied, "Hell, no. I'm here, and I'm a lawyer." Klutznick asked for a sheet of paper and sat down and wrote out the offer by hand, on behalf of his company and Marshall Field, payable in cash at closing. Bronfman signed it. Klutznick recalls, "So I came home with this piece of paper and our lawyers started laughing. They never saw such a piece of paper on this big a deal. I said, 'What's the difference what the size of the deal is?' So that's how Water Tower started."

The Water Tower Place development began with uncommon flair, and never lost it. As a retail structure, it established the standard for developments of its type not only in Chicago but throughout the country, and it remains unsurpassed as a successful retail property. Others may take the credit, but there is no doubt that Phil Klutznick is the developer whose ideas inspired the emergence of Chicago's North Michigan Avenue in the 1980s as the premier mixed-use development district in the world.[6]

No sooner was Water Tower Place completed in 1975 than Klutznick again joined forces with Ferd Kramer and other members of the Chicago 21 Corporation (later renamed the Dearborn Park Corporation), to plan a "South Loop New Town" that would involve the construction of three thousand town houses and apartment units in the vicinity of Chicago's abandoned South Loop railway yards. Klutznick, as chairman of the Dearborn Park Corporation's executive committee, led the negotiations that brought the city of Chicago into the project as a partner in planning, land acquisition, and development of the infrastructure.[7]

In the last half of the 1970s, under Tom Klutznick's leader-

Water Tower Place shopping mall. [opposite page] Developer Philip Klutznick sacrificed rentable space to provide the eight-story atrium and interior transportation system with glass elevators that lend visibility to the shops and vitality to the retail area. [Heitman Properties]

ship as president and then chairman, UIDC took on major development and management projects in cities from coast to coast: Seattle, Houston, Denver, Chicago, Cleveland, Hartford, Philadelphia, and Boston. Urban became a national force that by 1981 listed $760 million in assets, with $1.5 billion in projects under way. More than half of these projects had been put on the company's books by Tom Klutznick. In 1981 Tom Klutznick left UIDC to create his own company and shortly thereafter entered into a new partnership as the Chicago-based managing partner of Miller-Klutznick-Davis-Gray, a nationwide development firm with headquarters in Denver. In 1985 UIDC became a wholly owned subsidiary of JMB Realty.

Philip Klutznick, a man of enormous intellect and drive, never wavered from his beginnings as an advocate for Jewish causes nor did he cease to parlay his social concerns into a role as consultant to world governments. He headed foreign missions for President Lyndon B. Johnson and advised on national economic policy from 1970 to 1975 as a committee chairman for the Committee for Economic Development. In the late 1970s, Klutznick was recruited to help in resettlement planning as a member of President Gerald R. Ford's Advisory Committee on Indo-Chinese Refugees. In 1979 President Jimmy Carter named Klutznick to a cabinet post: U. S. secretary of commerce.

In the 1980s Klutznick turned the powerhouse of his personality to full-time involvement, as a private citizen, with Middle East affairs and the Chicago and international philanthropies he had supported throughout his business career. In his own eighth decade, Phil Klutznick lectures, writes, travels, and spreads his wisdom with the same energy with which he pursued his dual career as developer and diplomat.

Although Klutznick is known primarily for his very visible and oft-honored achievements, he is also known for his oratory—and for the length of his speeches. Reminded of his reputation for volubility, Klutznick responds laughingly, "Well, my speeches may have taken time, but people liked them," he says. "You can only make a speech about something you know something about. I like to think of myself as a student in all the areas in which I operate."

AUTHOR'S COMMENTARY

1. The principal partners in American Community Builders were Carroll Sweet Sr., a Chicago banker who, like Ferd Kramer, had served with the federal Division of Defense Housing Coordination during the war; Chicago builder Nathan Manilow, who had also worked on defense housing projects; and Philip Klutznick. The early management team, headed by Klutznick, included Carroll Sweet Jr. and architects Jerrold Loebl and Norman Schlossman. Klutznick's brother-in-law and law partner, Sam Beber, was involved in the operational aspects of the project from the beginning and eventually became a principal in the company.

2. As is typical in development ventures, the Klutznick partnerships formed and re-formed around specific projects or groups of projects, but with many of the same individuals involved. In 1963 Klutznick sold his interest in the Park Forest venture to Nathan Manilow and Sam Beber and formed Klutznick Enterprises, the association through which his sons Tom, Jim, and Sam came into the business. In 1964 Klutznick, Kramer, and Loebl, together with Norman Cohn, who headed Inland Construction, and investor Lester Crown formed KLC Ventures, a limited partnership, which then organized a subsidiary called United Development Company to build and market residential properties.

3. The four shopping and community development projects completed in the 1970s by Urban Investment and Development Company were: Hawthorn Center and New Century Town in Vernon Hills; Fox Valley Center and Fox Valley Villages in Aurora; Orland Square in Orland Park; and River Oaks West in Calumet City. Stratford Square opened in Bloomingdale in 1981.

4. High-rise bashing is a favorite pastime in Chicago—a diversion as popular and predictable as a game of darts in a British pub. And nowhere has it been more fervently practiced than over issues of North Michigan Avenue development. Public concern over high-rise development on North Michigan Avenue emerged in the late 1960s and early 1970s when the 100-story John Hancock Center was built near the north end of the boulevard, followed by Water Tower Place immediately south of it. The issue became focused in the late 1970s when it became clear that these two

buildings would be followed by other large-scale mixed-use developments. This prospect alarmed individuals and some community groups. Many wished to preserve North Michigan Avenue as it had been since the 1950s. Others objected to the higher density that high-rise development would bring to the area. Indeed, there were people in the city's planning department and on the Chicago Plan Commission who were very concerned about what was happening.

The issue we faced, as members of the plan commission, was whether to permit high-rise developments such as One Magnificent Mile, Olympia Center, and later, the 900 North Michigan Avenue building to replace what had been essentially a low- to mid-rise mix of commercial and retail buildings—or whether the plan commission should do something to try to stop it. On a personal basis, I was torn because, on the one hand, North Michigan Avenue was an extremely beautiful street with extraordinary charm—as close as Chicago would come to the architecture of Paris and the older European cities. On the other hand, we believed that legally we had no right to stop high-rise development under the existing zoning code. We had the tools to slow it down by denying increased density under planned unit developments, but we could not stop it.

Ultimately, the plan commission voted for approval at the planning level of these projects. Although we were distressed over the loss of the attractive older buildings that had given Michigan Avenue north of the river such a distinctive character, it became obvious to us that Chicago should not try to be something it wasn't. We were not Paris. We were not London. We were not Brussels. We were Chicago. And on North Michigan Avenue, Chicago was in the process of doing what it does best. If our city is known for any one thing besides Al Capone, it is for an innovative spirit that from the beginning has been conducive to creativity and versatility in high-rise architecture.

5. The original design for Water Tower Place was an eight-story retail center. The office space and the sixty-two-story hotel and residential tower were added later, after additional land purchases, in order to gain full site utilization. Klutznick believes that the immediate and continued success of the shopping center is attributable to the unique vertical transportation system. He recalls that the developers and architects spent weeks seeking engineers who could create the central elevator and escalator system envisioned. He explains, "This was the first high-rise shopping

Park Forest 1952. The new town of Park Forest, built primarily to meet the housing needs of returning veterans, was home to thousands of families by 1952, but trees and lawns took a little longer. The community was celebrated by the 1960s as "Americas Model Suburb."
[Owen Kent—Chicago Historical Society]

center. We had to make it easy for people to know where they were going and to see that there were shops everywhere." By insisting on the open atrium from the ground floor to the top, the developers gave up a significant amount of rentable space. "But we did it deliberately," Klutznick told me. "We wanted it to be wide open, and it proved itself."

6. By 1980, the year that I became chairman of the Chicago Plan Commission, I had come to see future mixed-use development of North Michigan Avenue not as a dangerous or destructive anomaly but rather as the most probable and historically consistent scenario for one of the city's finest streets. Mixed use was consistent with the 1909 Plan of Chicago, which saw Upper Michigan Avenue as a transitional bridge of office, retail, and residential uses linking

the Near North Side and the central business district. High-rise development was not precluded by the Burnham Plan, which acknowledged that buildings in this area "will rise to the height permitted by law." In fact, highrises built in the 1920s were among the first structures on the new North Michigan Avenue and did a great deal both to define the still-uncertain character of the district north of the river and to support the elegant retail center that was envisioned.

Consider the Wrigley Building, the Tribune Tower, the Allerton Hotel, the forty-four-story Medinah Athletic Club, and the thirty-eight-story Palmolive Building—all, like Water Tower Place, were bold ventures in their time. But they were in keeping with the early planners' dreams for the new North Michigan Avenue and entirely consistent with the high-rise development foreseen for the district in the 1923 zoning ordinance. Even the beautiful Michigan Square building—with its famed Diana Court—was planned as a forty-story retail and office structure. Had the Depression not intervened, it would in all likelihood have been so, and might still be standing.

In a market sense, the direction that development was taking in the 1970s was entirely logical. In weighing the options for North Michigan Avenue, plan commission members were aware of the sentiment evoked by some of the low- and mid-rise buildings, but came to the difficult conclusion that not every old building can or necessarily should be preserved. The planning dilemma always is to balance the interests of preservation, a free and clear lakefront, and open land with the continuing development so necessary to the economic life and existence of a large city. It cannot be done to the satisfaction of everyone.

In the case of North Michigan Avenue, as older buildings were replaced, we lost aspects of a unique and beautiful street, one that probably seemed broader when buildings were lower, and grander as it lives on in our memories. But arising in its place is a new and, I believe, better North Michigan Avenue. Water Tower Place has been a phenomenon in American cities by virtue of its sheer power to produce sales tax revenues that elsewhere have escaped to suburban shopping centers. It retains its attraction to out-of-towners who find significant interest there and whose impression of Chicago very often is created by their experience on the so-called Magnificent Mile.

7. The Dearborn Park development grew out of a collaboration among private development interests, the business community, and city government that exemplifies a devel-

opment climate existing in Chicago that is perhaps unique in the American urban experience. Dearborn Park was not regarded by any of the participants as a money-making enterprise. It was seen from the beginning as a means to vitalize a dead and dying sector of the city. The fact that it was also a commercial success was a by-product.

The number of business leaders involved was in the dozens, but it is possible to identify key players among them. The original development group, first known as Chicago 21, and later named the Dearborn Park Corporation, included Sears Roebuck and Company, the Continental Illinois National Bank and Trust Company, and the Commonwealth Edison Company as partners. Ultimately, more than thirty of Chicago's major corporations (including the Archdiocese of Chicago) became shareholders in the limited-dividend Dearborn Park Corporation. Tom Ayers, chairman and president of Commonwealth Edison, and John Perkins, president of Continental Bank, served respectively as chairman and vice chairman of the corporation. On the operational side, Klutznick, Ferd Kramer of Draper and Kramer, and John Baird of Baird and Warner formed an informal leadership triumvirate, with Klutznick heading the development and project management team and Kramer and Baird directing the marketing and property management aspects. Lewis W. Hill, as commissioner of development and planning, represented the city's interests and to a large extent acted as an informal consultant and adviser to the developers throughout the planning stages.

Even in a crowd with so many chiefs and so few Indians, Klutznick was perceived as the man in charge. At this time, he was serving on the federal Committee for Economic Development, dividing his time between Chicago and Washington. But, as Lew Hill put it, "while the others were here and inching along, they always waited for Phil to come back and bless what they were going to do." When movement on the project was slowed by the machinery of city government, Klutznick himself typically went directly to Mayor Richard J. Daley. He tells a good story about persuading the mayor that the city should install the utilities for the first (and later the second) phase of the development by showing Daley the kind of profit the city was realizing on the Dearborn Park water business. "That's one thing about Daley the First," Klutznick remarked many years later, recalling those meetings. "He was not interested in what you made. But he was interested in what the city got."

GLASS AND STEEL

Herbert Greenwald
(1915-59)

Herbert Greenwald.
[Lillian Greenwald and the University of
Illinois at Chicago]

On the morning of February 3, 1959, Chicago developer Herbert S. Greenwald boarded a plane for New York, bound for a business meeting at his offices in the Seagram Building. Hours later, associates in Chicago heard news that a Chicago–New York flight had crashed into Flushing Bay on its approach to La Guardia Airport. It was not until the following day that their worst fears were confirmed. It was Greenwald's plane that had gone down, and all aboard had been killed. Greenwald was young—forty-three at the time of his death—charismatic, and committed to building a better society by building a better urban environment. His mission was the city. His passion was the architecture of Ludwig Mies van der Rohe. His contribution to the Chicago skyline, even in the thirteen short years of his development career, was extraordinary. His 860-880 North Lake Shore Drive Apartments—"The Glass Houses"—became the most universally admired and imitated structural form in postwar America. At a memorial service a week after the accident, Mies summarized his insight into the character and commitment of his patron and friend: "Herb needed no hope to begin, and no success to persevere. He accepted defeat with the same balance and good sense with which he welcomed success. In this, he was a real philosopher."

Herbert S. Greenwald was born in St. Louis in 1915, the fifth of the seven children of an immigrant Russian Orthodox Jewish family, and the first to be born in America. With the

Promontory Apartments.
The concrete-framed, glass-and-brick Promontory Apartments at 5530 South Shore Drive, built in 1949, was developer Herbert Greenwald's first solo project and the first large commission outside the Illinois Institute of Technology campus for architect Ludwig Mies van der Rohe. At first the design was considered too innovative and too "ultra-modern" to suit the public taste, an opinion that Greenwald proved wrong.
[Bill Hedrich—Hedrich-Blessing]

hope that Herb would become a rabbi, his father sent him at the age of fourteen to New York's Yeshiva University. The family was disappointed when in 1933 Herb, then just seventeen, won a scholarship to the University of Chicago. There he would pursue his own dream of studying philosophy—becoming one of the first students involved in the Great Books program led by Mortimer Adler and Robert Maynard Hutchins.

While in the school, Greenwald moonlighted as an agent and later business manager for a Chicago real estate development company which, in the late 1930s and early '40s, built some of the first apartment complexes (including the 1938 River Forest Garden Apartments) to be constructed under the Federal Housing Authority mortgage guarantee program. Greenwald married his college sweetheart, Lillian Feldman, in 1940; volunteered for service in the U.S. Navy in 1942 (but was rejected); and began his intended career as a teacher and principal in Chicago Hebrew schools. With his first child on the way, he augmented his teaching salary with administrative and fund-raising work for agencies of the Jewish Federation, and soon found himself working full time in these causes.

Developers come into the profession from many directions, but teaching and social work is not often one of them. In Greenwald's case, the transition was probably more of a direct line than it would seem on the surface. Greenwald was a dynamic individual, brilliant, personable, and persuasive. He was thirty years old in 1945, with a wife and the first of the Greenwalds' two sons. He was ambitious and in a hurry. Through the Jewish Federation, Greenwald met Samuel N. Katzin, a Chicago real estate investor who also ran a prosperous automobile dealership. Katzin, who was active in several philanthropies, was a commissioner of the Chicago Housing Authority. This friendship, coinciding as it did with the post-World War II housing crisis, fused Herbert Greenwald's social concerns and his more worldly ambitions into a dramatic destiny. Once started, there was no stopping him.

With backing from Katzin, Greenwald established the Herbert Construction Company in 1945. Learning that a choice Hyde Park lakefront site was available, he decided that the property deserved no less than Chicago's finest postwar apartment development, designed by no less than an internationally known architect, and promoted by no less an idealist and entrepreneur than Herbert S. Greenwald. It was a bold beginning. Katzin and Greenwald acquired the property in 1946, and Greenwald, with becoming innocence, offered the project to three architects he had never met but whom he knew to be among the biggest names in the country: Walter Gropius, Eero Saarinen, and Frank Lloyd Wright. It was an eclectic choice, one that revealed both Greenwald's lack, at this point, of a personal philosophy of architecture and the importance he placed on having a world-famous architect on this project. Gropius and Saarinen were busy elsewhere, and Wright requested a $250,000 advance that Greenwald could not provide.

But Greenwald was riding a lucky streak. Gropius suggested

he try "the father of us," Ludwig Mies van der Rohe. It was a name that Greenwald had overlooked in his first round of solicitations. Mies had been director of Bauhaus, a school of design in Dessau, Germany, founded by Gropius in 1919 and closed by the Nazis in 1933. He came to Chicago in 1938 as the director of the department of architecture at Chicago's Armour Institute, which after a merger with Lewis Institute became the Illinois Institute of Technology. Greenwald made an appointment to see Mies, and, as Mrs. Greenwald recalls, "They began going steady right away." Mies had left Europe with a formidable reputation, but he was to become far more celebrated for his later work in America, partly as a result of his meeting at that moment with young Herb Greenwald.

Greenwald's project, the twenty-two-story, concrete-framed glass-and-brick Promontory Apartments at 5530 South Shore Drive, was Mies's first large-scale commission outside of the new IIT campus. But the project wasn't easy to sell. The design was considered too innovative, too "ultra-modern," with too much glass, to suit public taste. Lenders, still inexperienced in the postwar construction climate, feared that "highrise" meant high costs. Greenwald, who was himself an unknown quantity, made first mortgage applications to almost every source known at the time—with no takers. The Greenwald solution was to offer the apartments on the mutual-ownership plan, a cooperative investment concept that he had become familiar with during his university moonlighting years. To the astonishment of the real estate community, Greenwald sold more than half of the apartments from plans. The other half were sold before the reinforced concrete frame went up.

The cost of the building also came as surprise to the doomsayers. The project came in at a price below that of most of Chicago's public housing projects. By following the Miesian principle that "less is more," Greenwald had stumbled into every developer's dream: high quality projects, meeting the test of the market, and on the low side in terms of construction costs. *Architectural Forum* later acclaimed the Promontory Apartments, crediting the builder of such a "deceptively simple" structure with the kind of "all-around architectural thinking which amounts to genius."

In early 1949 Greenwald announced plans for the 860-880 North Lake Shore Drive Apartments. The 860-880 buildings, completed in 1952, were the first apartments to be constructed almost solely in glass and steel, ushering in a new era in high-rise construction and redefining the concept of urban living. The structures embodied the central idea of the modernist movement: beauty and function created in the form and material of twentieth-century technology. Moreover, the buildings were an economic success.

The Greenwald-Mies relationship quickly surmounted both the thirty-year difference in their ages and the traditional struggle between developer and architect. In Mies's designs and philosophy of rationalism, Greenwald sought the solution to the urban housing problem. He believed that mere men—developer and architect—held in their hands the capacity to create, in his words, "the perfect physical machine for living." Through Greenwald, Mies was able to translate design ideas he had nurtured since the 1920s into tangible features of the urban landscape.

The two met frequently and talked late into the night over cigars and brandy. The friendship was deep and exclusive. Their discussions probed social concepts, the role of architecture, and the nature of urban culture—as it was and as it should be. In Mies's eyes, Greenwald was a philosopher turned developer. For Greenwald, Mies's concepts became a compulsion. He declared his intention to build Mies buildings from coast to coast. "Greenwald began with an idea of the social consequences of his work; along the way he also discovered he was a very good businessman," Mies said after Greenwald's death.[1]

Both men were perfectionists, a trait frequently found among successful architects and developers. ("God is in the details," Mies often said.) Mrs. Greenwald recalls the attention that both gave to the placement of the 860-880 buildings on the trapezoidal site. Mies, she said, would drag a chair out to the seawall at the edge of the lake and study the site for days at a time. She recalls also that when Greenwald moved his family from the Promontory Apartments to a three-bedroom unit in the 860 building, their apartment became a laboratory for experiments Greenwald conducted when he was seeking just the right formula for tinted windows in curtain-wall buildings—all subtle shades of gray.

Greenwald and Mies occasionally differed, usually at the point where an interior detail was sacrificed to the economics of the project. But Mies, while an austere man of few words, was not rigid in his thinking or demands, Mrs. Greenwald recalls. A point on which Mies and Greenwald invariably agreed was the matter of draperies in their meticulously detailed structures. Tenants can "have any color they want," Greenwald once quipped, "so long as it's off-white."

Between 1949 and 1952, Herbert Construction Company and Metropolitan Corporation of America (the development partnership formed by Greenwald and Samuel Katzin) completed several more apartment complexes in the Chicago area,

Greenwald and Mies van der Rohe. [opposite page] The friendship between developer Herbert Greenwald and architect Ludwig Mies van der Rohe was deep and exclusive. Their discussions, which often went on long into the night, probed social concepts, the role of architecture, and the nature of urban culture—as it was and as it should be. [Bennet B. Greenwald]

including the Twin Towers Apartments at 5000 South Lake Shore Drive, built with federal funding as housing for Fifth Army headquarters military personnel. In 1954 Greenwald made his reputation as a man to be reckoned with in Chicago real estate when he and Katzin paid more than $1 million for the one-acre 900-910 North Lake Shore Drive property where Greenwald built the 900 Esplanade Apartments. It was the highest price paid for apartment land in Chicago since the boom days of the 1920s. At the same time, Greenwald and Katzin acquired the three-acre corner of Sheridan Road and Diversey Parkway as the site for the Mies-designed Commonwealth Promenade Apartments. An $11 million Equitable Life Assurance Society of America mortgage on these projects was publicized as the largest conventional loan financing ever arranged for new apartment construction in Chicago.

In 1954 Greenwald claimed to have $50 million in apartment construction completed or under way in Chicago. His work represented a remarkable output, even by the breakneck standards of the postwar construction boom. It is all the more notable for the fact that Greenwald was one of the last of the one-man developers. He was the sort, an observer has said, "who could juggle property transactions, loan negotiations, municipal codes, esthetics, market trends, and thousands of facts—all in his head." Greenwald, however, described himself quite differently. He said, "I would rather hang myself than think of myself as a financier." (He also said, Mrs. Greenwald recalls, "If I could write poetry or paint, I wouldn't be doing what I am doing.") Bernard Weissbourd, who was Greenwald's lawyer in this frenetic period, summarized the Greenwald style: "He had flair. He had imagination. And he did everything himself." Greenwald, Weissbourd adds, was also "in the Zeckendorf mode" in the mid-1950s, following the example of New York real estate tycoon William Zeckendorf. Greenwald was moving fast, but he had an appetite for more.

When Greenwald began his meteoric career in the late 1940s, America's inner cities were in a state of decay. In 1949 Congress recognized the problems with the enactment of the Title I Urban Redevelopment Act. Nothing could have been more suited to Herbert Greenwald's philosophy and personality.[2] He believed in the city. He had a relentless vision that demanded open spaces, the subordination of the automobile, and the nourishment of human values. "The city is damned but by no means doomed. Let's rebuild it," was his oft-repeated call to action.[3] The promise of vast canvases of central city land offered up by urban renewal programs, awaiting his touch and that of the master, Mies van der Rohe, was irresist-

ible to Herb Greenwald. Between 1956 and 1958 he took on huge Title I urban redevelopment projects in Detroit, Newark, Brooklyn, and Manhattan. He also assumed enormous risk and enormous debt—far more than most developers would have dared.[4] Greenwald's first central city redevelopment project, Lafayette Park in Detroit, was intended to transform the fifty-acre Gratiot slum clearance area into a middle-income high-rise and town-house community with housing for 1,700 families. It was a masterful effort, affording Mies and his colleague, city planner Ludwig Hilberseimer, the opportunity to create—on paper at least—an ideal urban environment. With the Detroit contract in hand, Greenwald moved faster and faster. In 1956 he entered the competition for the forty-seven-acre Chicago Hyde Park redevelopment, but lost it to Zeckendorf.[5] The Hyde Park renewal project had strong backing from the Chicago Land Clearance Commission and later from the University of Chicago, making it a model for similar redevelopment projects nationwide.[6]

In 1957 Greenwald took over a hopelessly stalled redevelopment project in Brooklyn, then being codeveloped with the Pratt Institute, and got the project moving. A year later he took over a thirty-acre redevelopment in Newark. At the same time, he snatched away from Zeckendorf, who he now described as his "archrival," a $25 million project in the Manhattan Battery District near Wall Street.

At the age of forty-one, Greenwald employed a staff of more than three hundred in his Chicago headquarters atop the Field Building and in his New York office. The *New York Times* reported in February 1958 that Greenwald had been responsible for $150 million worth of construction in the previous ten years and had $120 million in projects on his books. Greenwald was rapidly becoming a developer on a national scale.

In late 1958, the first of the Detroit Lafayette Park concrete and glass high-rise apartments was completed. That and the Brooklyn highrise were the only urban redevelopment buildings that Greenwald would live to see topped out. After his death in early 1959, Bernard Weissbourd created a successor company, Metropolitan Structures, Inc., to complete those of the Greenwald projects that he could and to hold together the Greenwald team. Daniel Levin, another of Greenwald's close associates, took over the Lafayette Park development. Weissbourd and Levin, both of whom started their careers as lawyers, went on to become notable Chicago developers themselves.

In retrospect, critics regarded Lafayette Park as among Greenwald's best works. Mies, who devoted himself to seeing

860-880 North Lake Shore Drive Apartments. [opposite page] The 1952 Greenwald-Mies steel and glass apartments at 860-880 North Lake Shore Drive presented a spare architectural form that was soon emulated throughout America. While planning the placement of the buildings on the trapezoidal property, Mies would take a chair to the seawall and sit for hours studying the site. [Hedrich-Blessing—Chicago Historical Society]

the project completed, agreed. The architecture critic for the *Nation* magazine concluded that the town houses completed by Levin in Lafayette Park "would have delighted [Greenwald] as much as anything that Mies van der Rohe ever designed for him."

In 1987 the Herbert S. Greenwald Distinguished Professorship in Architecture was established at the School of Architecture, University of Illinois at Chicago. The program for the dedication noted that

> Our Chicago skyline simply would not be what it is today were it not for the inspiration and nurturing that Herbert Greenwald provided for Mies van der Rohe. Nor indeed would twentieth-century world architecture be what it is today without the influence and enrichment of masterworks such as 860-880 Lake Shore Drive.

Lafayette Park, Detroit.
Greenwald tested his theories about how a central city should be in the Detroit slum clearance and redevelopment project known as Lafayette Park. Mies and Greenwald are flanked at the 1956 ground-breaking ceremonies by United Auto Workers leader Walter Reuther [left] and Michigan governor G. Mennen Williams [right].
[Bennet B. Greenwald]

AUTHOR'S COMMENTARY

1. The relationship between Greenwald the developer and Mies the architect was not unlike the friendship of Frank Lloyd Wright and his patron Edward C. Waller. I believe that what these two notable partnerships accomplished is not at all uncommon among developers and architects—opinion to the contrary notwithstanding. Developers I interviewed for this book frequently spoke of the creative dynamic that occurs between developer and architect when

each respects the ideas of the other. Greenwald himself suggested in a 1954 speech to the Chicago chapter of the American Institute of Architects that although some clients may be "barbarous" and some architects "pigheaded," the opportunities for successful collaboration are likely to outweigh these exceptions. "We've never overpaid an architect and we've paid some of the highest fees in the country," Greenwald said.

2. In principle, urban renewal had been endorsed by Chicago civic leaders and planners since the late 1930s. But through the years of the Great Depression and World War II, the city was able to do very little about it beyond watching central-city decay worsen. Population shifts from rural to urban areas in the years between 1930 and 1950 compounded the problems. Suburban flight in the postwar years further accelerated urban blight in Chicago as in other American cities. The goal of the Title I Urban Redevelopment Act was to bring new development into blighted areas by enabling cities to acquire slum land at fair prices by right of eminent domain. The city would then clear the land and offer it to private developers at a write-down—that is, at less than its cost to the city. The federal government would pick up two-thirds of the differential in the price of the land and the city would absorb the remaining one-third. On this low-cost land, developers were expected to build low- to-medium-income housing.

3. Although the measure of Greenwald's work is most often made in terms of his extraordinarily productive relationship with Mies van der Rohe, his greatest contribution could have been his vision for the redevelopment of American cities. It is regrettable that there was neither time nor opportunity for Greenwald to apply his intensely human concepts for the new central city—ideas that inspired Mies's plans for Lafayette Park in Detroit—to redevelopment projects in his own city of Chicago.

4. One of the difficulties with the urban renewal programs was finding developers willing to take the risk. The problems were manifold: Urban redevelopment planning was an enormous up-front commitment, one that could take years to show a return. Moreover, local government infighting could—and often did—hamstring a project for even more years while the developer's investment lay fallow. And, until 1954 when Federal Housing Administration mortgage insurance was added to the Title I pot, the financial institutions capable of lending the sums of money

needed for enormous projects showed little inclination to participate. One of the few developers who did see the possibilities offered by the Title I Urban Redevelopment Act was William Zeckendorf, whose company, Webb and Knapp, already had considerable experience in private redevelopment of urban areas. Title I fit the Zeckendorf philosophy—big projects offering maximum leverage with minimum equity investment. In the 1950s Zeckendorf was crisscrossing the country in his company plane pitching inner-city redevelopment to the nation's mayors. Title I was humorously dubbed the "Zeckendorf Relief Act" (a sobriquet that lost its punch in 1965 when Webb and Knapp collapsed in bankruptcy). But if Title I spelled relief to Bill Zeckendorf, it spelled opportunity to Herb Greenwald—opportunity to implement his ideas in an area he knew well and loved.

5. The now-historic Hyde Park—Kenwood conservation and redevelopment project was a natural for Greenwald, a University of Chicago graduate with strong feelings for the neighborhood and an appreciation of its social and racial integration. He was deeply disappointed when the Chicago Land Clearance Commission awarded the contract to Webb and Knapp.

6. The Hyde Park—Kenwood urban renewal program began with two small land clearance projects along Fifty-fifth Street. Greenwald supported a larger vision, calling the initial project "a patchwork." He proposed a complete restructuring of Hyde Park, one that would close streets to through traffic, and subsequently argued before the Chicago City Council's Planning and Housing Committee that the Zeckendorf plan selected by the Land Clearance Commission failed to spell out the future relationship of the development to the surrounding area. Mrs. Greenwald reminded me many years later that Herb believed that the conservation and renewal concept should encompass all of the area from Lake Michigan to Cottage Grove Avenue between Forty-seventh and Sixty-third streets.

In all of his redevelopment planning, Greenwald acted on the belief that the automobile must be subordinated to the residential environment, and he spoke articulately on this subject. He charged that the Webb and Knapp plan, which carried traffic around two eight-story high-rise apartment buildings, created what he called "a monoxide island." Greenwald's own plan proposed four high-rise apartments, mixed with several blocks of two-story houses, and set well back from Fifty-fifth Street in a park.

RENAISSANCE MAN

Bernard Weissbourd

Bernard Weissbourd.
[Metropolitan Structures]

In the summer of 1942, a young chemist assigned to the U.S. Army Signal Corps radar training school at Camp Murphy, Florida, received a most unusual set of orders. He was directed to change to civilian clothes and quietly return to Chicago, his hometown. His assignment, he was told, would be communicated to him through a downtown post office box. Bernard Weissbourd had just been recruited for the Chicago arm of the Manhattan Project, the ultrasecret wartime research program housed under the west stands of the University of Chicago's Stagg Field. There, over the night and the day of December 1 and 2, 1942, the world's first self-sustaining nuclear reaction was achieved. The material for an atomic bomb was at hand.

Weissbourd himself had been graduated from the University of Chicago a year before, undecided about whether to pursue a career as a chemist, a lawyer, or a professor of philosophy. With his assignment to the Manhattan Project, he found that for the duration of the war, at least, the decision had been made for him. As it turned out, he achieved success in all three fields: science, law, and teaching. As a scientist specializing in measurement of the energy of alpha particles, he worked side by side with Glenn Seaborg, the Nobel Prize–winning physicist who discovered plutonium. As a lawyer fresh out of the University of Chicago Law School, Weissbourd won a million-dollar settlement in an antitrust case tried in federal court. As a teacher, he now lectures in the urban studies program at the

University of Illinois and directs a research center committed to the study of a wide range of social issues. The most visible achievements of this modern Renaissance man, however, lie in another direction altogether. He is the founder and chairman of Metropolitan Structures, Inc., one of the oldest and most stable real estate development companies in the United States. Metropolitan projects include a score of pacesetting developments located throughout the United States and in Canada—among them Chicago's eighty-three-acre Illinois Center complex, at one time the largest mixed-use urban development in North America.

Weissbourd's office on the twelfth floor of Metropolitan's One Illinois Center is by no means the prime space that one might expect the chairman to occupy, but the office reflects its owner. The room fits Weissbourd like an old tweed jacket—comfortable, well-worn, unpretentious, more than a little professorial in aspect. But then Weissbourd himself does not fit very closely the image of a man who heads an international real estate development company. Soft-spoken and scholarly, Weissbourd has long been known as "the gentleman of the profession." Beneath the quiet demeanor, however, Weissbourd sizzles with the traits that characterize the most successful of developers: imagination, creativity, tenacity, and a willingness to take risks—albeit, in Weissbourd's case, risks that are as carefully calculated as the calibration of alpha particles.

When asked how he happened to become a developer, Weissbourd replies with characteristic understatement: "All the important things happened by accident." After the war, Weissbourd faced a choice between the practice of law and a promising career in science. When he discovered that the social issues emerging in postwar America interested him more than work in the laboratory, he returned to law school.

Shortly after going into partnership with attorney Joseph Antonow, Weissbourd tripped over the single important event that set him on his path as a developer. This was his meeting with Antonow's client Herbert S. Greenwald, a dynamic Chicago developer who had begun his own career as a teacher and principal in a Hebrew school. Greenwald and Weissbourd had much in common. They were young—Greenwald was in his early thirties and Weissbourd in his late twenties. Both had studied philosophy and Great Books with Robert Hutchins and Mortimer Adler at the University of Chicago. They shared deeply felt social concerns that focused on the condition of cities.

At the time the two met, Greenwald had already completed the Promontory Apartments at 5530 South Shore Drive, his first project with architect Mies van der Rohe. The famed

Mies-designed "glass houses" at 860-880 North Lake Shore Drive were under way. He was planning a twenty-two-story apartment building, which he had named "The Darien," to be built at the corner of Lake Shore Drive and Barry Street. "He took me to visit the site," Weissbourd recalls, "where I guessed correctly that his inspiration for the name of the building came from the 'peak in Darien' mentioned in a sonnet by John Keats. From then on I handled most of the work with Greenwald, and that was fine with Joe because he had lots of other clients." Greenwald's eldest son Bennet recalls his father saying of Weissbourd, "I think Bernie is the right hand I need. He has a conscience. He's brilliant. And he's the toughest negotiator I know." Greenwald was moving fast in the 1950s, and as his lawyer and business adviser, Weissbourd had his work cut out for him. Fueled by Federal Housing Administration Title I funds, Greenwald's projects by the end of the decade included urban renewal and community development projects in Detroit, Brooklyn, Manhattan, and Newark, as well as more Chicago apartment developments.

These were exciting times. Greenwald was totally engrossed in the revolutionary new architecture of Mies van der Rohe, while Weissbourd's activities were focused on the business aspects of the firm. "There was a side of things that I didn't know a lot about until later," Weissbourd recalled. "Greenwald and Mies would like to sit around at night and drink and talk about things. That's where the issues were decided. They didn't have formal meetings where others were present." Financing was always a problem. Greenwald was cre-

Illinois Central Railroad property, 1936. The Illinois Center megadevelopment was built on air rights over the Illinois Central Railroad yards, seen at the lower left of this aerial photo looking south over the central business district. [Chicago Historical Society]

Illinois Center, 1975. By 1975 construction had been completed on One Illinois Center, designed by Mies van der Rohe; its twin, Two Illinois Center; and the Hyatt Regency Chicago Hotel West Tower. These three buildings can be seen in the foreground of this photo, looking west over the Chicago River.
[Hedrich-Blessing]

ative, energetic, and excited about the social ramifications of large-scale urban redevelopment projects. He was overextended, but not so much so that he couldn't be rescued. "He was moving faster than the financial resources. Part of my job was trying to control that," Weissbourd says. He describes himself as the "brakes" of the Greenwald powerhouse.

When Herb Greenwald died in an airplane accident in early 1959, he was just forty-two years old and had left much undone. Greenwald's partners and employees came to Weissbourd and asked him to take over. The decision was not an easy one. As attorney for the Greenwald companies, Weissbourd was well aware that the assets of the estate would be tied up for a very long time in settling the debts to Greenwald's investment partners. Weissbourd concluded that he would not take over Greenwald's companies, Metropolitan Corporation of America and the Herbert Realty and Construction Company. He believed those should proceed to an orderly liquidation. But he did agree to start a new company.

And so in 1959 Metropolitan Structures was born, with Weissbourd as president. (In 1981 the firm became a joint venture with Metropolitan Life Insurance Company and the former Metropolitan Structures partnership.) Weissbourd did not regard the formation of Metropolitan Structures as a temporary measure. "I saw this as an opportunity. I had a very good law practice, and I could have stayed in that, but I had to make a decision. And I decided that I wanted to be a developer." The corporation's first major project was completion of work under way in Newark, followed by new projects launched by Metropolitan Structures itself, including the One

Charles Center office tower in Baltimore. By the mid-1960s Metropolitan had built two apartment buildings in Chicago: the 2400 Lakeview Apartments, a thirty-story building designed by Mies van der Rohe, and the DeWitt-Chestnut apartments at 260 East Chestnut Street. A host of residential and office buildings, built in several American cities, would follow, including the One South Wacker Drive Building, designed by Helmut Jahn and completed in 1983, and the twin-tower Chicago Mercantile Exchange (Fujikawa, Johnson and Associates), codeveloped with JMB Realty.

Weissbourd brought a new management philosophy to the company. Greenwald had been a one-man operator, but one who attracted talent that Weissbourd respected. Weissbourd kept the staff, but spread the responsibility and cut the risks, forging a low-profile management team accustomed to working with the numbers. "We're conservative compared to other developers you could name," Weissbourd says. "We don't take any risks that we can't control. We worry about every detail in a development. We did our own construction in the early days. We still do. Gives us control over costs." With these words, Weissbourd has covered the list of "do's" for successful developers. In 1989, thirty years after forming the company, he said, "We're a very lean organization, even now."

By the time Metropolitan Structures broke ground on its first Baltimore project, Weissbourd had formed his own strong relationship with Mies van der Rohe. Mies became the designer for many Weissbourd projects and master planner for Metropolitan's Nun's Island development in Montreal. Weissbourd, a man of quiet Old World manners himself, found European-born Mies van der Rohe a compatible companion. Architect and developer worked well together.

"His mission was to bring order into buildings," Weissbourd observes. "Now all the people in postmodernism have adopted Mies's central program entirely. The only thing they are doing differently is in how they decorate the buildings—interior and exterior. The fundamentals are the same." Weissbourd appreciated Mies's philosophy of functionalism in architectural design, and found, moreover, that Mies worked within the developer's budget. "If we were building a lobby, for instance, he would say, 'Tell me how much money you want to spend, and I'll tell you what you should have.' I wasn't going to tell him what kind of marble to use," Weissbourd explains.

In 1969 Metropolitan Structures began work on the Montreal community development that set in motion Weissbourd's extensive study and many publications in the field of American urban policy. The Nun's Island project, a 980-acre community on the St. Lawrence River, clustered garden apartments, town houses, and high-rise apartments around a commercial center. The 320-acre residential complex occupied a corner of the site; the balance of the land was committed to green space. Commuters from Nun's Island could reach downtown Montreal in five minutes by rapid transit.[1]

"I believe we can do a whole lot better with cities than we have," Weissbourd would say later—and say often. "Nun's Island was important for that reason," he believes. "I'm very proud of the land plan for Nun's Island." The development achieved a social goal that all but Weissbourd had thought impossible: the integration, in one community, of French- and English-speaking families. This pleased Weissbourd, as did the more whimsical fact that Nun's Island residents could fill up their cars at the only service station in the world designed by Mies van der Rohe. "It's a very nice gas station," Weissbourd comments.

With Nun's Island well under way in the early 1970s, Weissbourd escalated to the level of national policy a personal campaign for the revitalization of America's cities through the development of satellite towns. Weissbourd called his proposal for cities "an urban strategy." Urbanologists respectfully dubbed his vision "the Weissbourd solution." In this period, too, Weissbourd was deeply involved in the project that was described in 1971 as one of the most advanced developments in the world: Chicago's Illinois Center. It had been a long time coming. The eighty-three-acre site on the south bank of the Chicago River between Michigan Avenue and the lakefront was—and is, perhaps—the nation's most valuable landfill. Historically, the land had been the terminus and yards of the Illinois Central Railroad. It had also been a political battleground from the early 1850s, when the railroad gained control of the lakefront by building its tracks on a trestle paralleling the shoreline.[2]

The battle still raged a full century later. When the railroad decided to sell the air rights over the property, the city intervened, claiming ownership of the air rights. That issue was decided by the courts in 1966 in favor of the Illinois Central, but political debate over the development dragged on for a number of years, threatening the future of the project. Illinois Center began with three developers holding options on the air rights.[3] Weissbourd's company, Metropolitan Structures, was the only one of the three with the staying power to stick with the project throughout the prolonged period of litigation and negotiation.[4] The city approved the Randolph Terminal Planned Development Ordinance in 1969, and the project at last began to move forward.[5] In 1971 Metropolitan joined forces with the Illinois Central, forming a joint-venture devel-

Illinois Center Plaza.
[Ken Oaks—Metropolitan Structures]

opment partnership with the railroad's parent company, IC Industries. The association was a productive one. William B. Johnson, IC Industries chairman, said some fifteen years into the project that "as for the partnership" with Metropolitan, "we've never had a disagreement on any important matter. That's because I always give in to Bernie Weissbourd."

The initial master planning had been done by the Offices of Mies van der Rohe. Joseph Fujikawa, a Mies associate since 1945, and his firm, Fujikawa, Conterato, Lohan and Associates (later Fujikawa, Johnson and Associates), remained coordinating architects for Illinois Center development. By 1974 construction had been completed on One Illinois Center (designed by Mies), Two Illinois Center (a twin to One Illinois Center), the Hyatt Regency Chicago Hotel West Tower (A. Epstein and Sons), the Standard Oil Building (Perkins and Will), and Harbor Point Condominium (Solomon, Cordwell,

Boulevard Towers

Buenz and Associates). By 1982, the Hyatt Regency East Tower had been completed (A. Epstein and Sons), as had Three Illinois Center, Buckingham Plaza, Boulevard Towers North, and McHugh Levin Associates' Columbus Plaza (all by Fujikawa, Conterato, Lohan). Boulevard Towers South followed. In 1987 Metropolitan Structures added the Fairmont Hotel (Hellmuth, Obata and Kassabaum) on Columbus Drive to its list of Illinois Center developments. The Swiss Grand Hotel, designed by Harry Weese and Associates, was completed in 1988.

Over the first two decades of the Illinois Center buildout, the development, like Bernard Weissbourd himself, dramatically affected both the skyline and the life of the city of Chicago. By 1990 fifteen high-rise office, hotel, and residential buildings stood on the site, well over half built by Metropolitan Structures. More were in the planning stages. The complex, with its vast underground shopping mall, pedestrian-ways, and restaurants, has became a city within a city. True to its promise, the development created homes, jobs, and tax revenues. Moreover, it precipitated a new multi-level traffic system for the northeast quadrant of the downtown area, capped by the Columbus Drive Bridge, the eastward extension of Wacker Drive, and the broad new sweep of the reconstructed Lake Shore Drive.[6]

As a nineteen-year-old whiz-kid graduate of the University of Chicago, Weissbourd could not have foreseen his future as a developer, but he did foresee a future in science and social commitment. He never lost sight of those goals. In the immediate postwar period, Weissbourd helped form the peacetime Atomic Energy Commission. Over the years he has spoken and written widely on nuclear deterrence. In 1988, in recognition of a lifetime of humanitarian activities, Bernard Weissbourd was named Man of the Year by Israel's Weizmann Institute of Science.

AUTHOR'S COMMENTARY

1. The Nun's Island planning was one of the few occasions on which Weissbourd and Mies had significant differences. In the first instance, Weissbourd, the developer, wanted a curvilinear plan for the site, but the architect did not agree. "Mies gave in, but he didn't like it," Weissbourd told me. The second and more interesting issue was a classic example of the differences between the orientation of the developer, who must be sensitive to the market, and that of the architect, whose first concern is design. Weissbourd believed that the Nun's Island apartments should be built

Boulevard Towers [Illinois Center]. [opposite page] The first tower opened in 1982, the second in 1985.
[Hedrich-Blessing—Metropolitan Structures]

with balconies. "When the sun comes out in northern countries, like Norway and Sweden, people want to get out there and use it. From my point of view, it was unthinkable to build apartments in Canada without balconies," he explained. Mies had another opinion. "The balcony affects how the building looks, and the architect is very concerned about that," Weissbourd noted. "It took a long time for Mies to agree with me." The developer's judgment in a case like this can make all the difference. The reality is that apartment projects in Canada are, and have been, more successful when built with balconies.

2. Controversy over the Illinois Central Railroad land was nothing new to Chicagoans, including the leaders of the city's nineteenth-century business elite who coveted the site for the 1893 World's Columbian Exposition but who failed to get it. City planners revived plans for development of the IC property with the adoption of the Burnham Plan of Chicago in 1910. Concepts proposed in the 1920s were surprisingly similar to Illinois Center as we see it today, featuring a complex of office skyscrapers built on air rights over the Illinois Central tracks, with all the elements linked by a bilevel transportation system and pedestrian walkways. Had the Depression and World War II not intervened, this plan might well have been implemented.

3. The Illinois Center Corporation, then owned by Texas investors, held the central part of the property; Interstate Investments, Inc., a subsidiary of Jupiter Industries, held the lakefront portion, reflecting that company's interest in lakefront apartment construction (it built the Outer Drive East apartment building in 1963 on an extension of Randolph Street east of North Lake Shore Drive); and Metropolitan Structures held the Grant Park (Randolph Street west of North Lake Shore Drive) frontage. The Illinois Central Railroad bought back the Interstate Investment options in 1971, and Jupiter sold its interest to the new partners in 1972.

4. From the beginning, Illinois Center was plagued by conflicts among the several city departments with an interest in the development plan; among those departments and IC Industries, which owned the land; and among those parties and the three private development groups who held options on the air rights. The issues involved division of responsibility for the costs involved in new infrastructure; development densities and ratios; and the amount, type, and location of public open spaces. The tug-of-war be-

Fairmont Hotel [Illinois Center]. [opposite page] Designed by Hellmuth, Obata and Kassabaum, the hotel opened in 1987.
[Hedrich-Blessing—Metropolitan Structures]

tween city officials and the developers was further complicated by the activities of the several public interest groups with concerns over how the project would affect public use of the riverfront and access to the lakefront.

Emotions ran high on all sides, and for a time in 1966 it appeared that the project had become hopelessly bogged down in controversy. At this point, Mayor Richard J. Daley showed his hand, in a very quiet way. The position he took not only saved the Illinois Center development from further years of wrangling but set a precedent for city cooperation with development interests that has continued through succeeding administrations. At that time, I was serving as principal real estate consultant to the city. Mayor Daley called me to his office and said, "We've got a sensitive problem here. I want you to get involved in negotiations on the Illinois Central air-rights development. You're experienced on both the public and private sides." His instructions were clear. He said, "I want to be sure that this project gets developed. I want to be sure that the developers make a fair contribution to the infrastructure of the project. But I also want to make sure that the city doesn't stall this project because we're worried that we may be giving too much away or not getting enough."

My behind-the-scenes task was multifaceted. The city first had to negotiate the land development plan and infrastructure issues with IC Industries, headed by William B. Johnson. Ongoing negotiations with the developers regarding implementation of the plan would come later. Although Daley and Johnson were cordial to one another, the chemistry was not good. Mayor Daley was an emotional man who sometimes reacted emotionally to relationships. Don't ever think that those emotional responses overrode his intellect. They did not. But with Bill Johnson, there was no rapport, and Daley was aware of the problem.

I knew Bill Johnson well and had done consulting work for a number of his companies, including IC Industries. I was also friendly with Stanley Hillman, who was the number-two man at IC Industries and who eventually wound up handling the air-rights development for the IC at the highest policy level. In all likelihood, Lewis Hill, commissioner of the development and planning department, advised Daley of these relationships, and the mayor felt comfortable that I would be able to interface effectively with Johnson and Hillman. Once Mayor Daley made known his intention that Illinois Center was going to go forward, and that the division of costs would be equitable

10 and 30 South Wacker Drive. [opposite page] The home of the Chicago Mercantile Exchange, covering a block-long site on the banks of the Chicago River, was codeveloped in 1983 and 1988 by Metropolitan Structures and JMB Realty. This view shows the riverfront side of the building, with the 40,000-square-foot clear-span trading floor linking the two office towers. [Hedrich-Blessing]

both to the city and the developers, we were able to proceed quite smoothly to completion of the planned unit development for the project.

5. City planning officials had been concerned about carving in stone a plan for a project with a projected buildout of twenty or more years. There was no way to predict the market over such a long time. We came up with the idea of introducing exchange ratios into the planning document. I believe the Illinois Center plan was one of the first, if not the first, uses of this concept. In the late 1960s, residential markets in Chicago were very strong and the office market was overbuilt. As it turned out, the balance quickly shifted. By introducing a mechanism for exchanging a portion of residential units for a designated number of square feet of commercial use, or vice versa, we were able to provide a means by which the development could respond to a changing market over time. This, I think, has been a very significant planning advance—one that protects the planning integrity of an unfolding development without imposing rigid land-use standards that may be rendered obsolete by changing market conditions.

6. The dialogue between the city and the developers regarding the density and open space issues did continue over many years and through several amendments to the plan. The important point is that the door to that dialogue remained open. Whatever one's aesthetic judgment may be of the Illinois Center complex, the fact remains that at a time when many other American cities were falling into decay, this development recaptured that spirit of innovative growth and commitment to downtown development that from the beginning has made Chicago great. Illinois Center was a pioneer planning effort that became a laboratory for succeeding generations of similar megadevelopments. The key to making Illinois Center a reality was the position taken by Mayor Daley at a critical juncture. Daley foresaw the future for public/private partnerships and made sure that neither politics nor personalities would get in the way of getting done what needed to be done for the city.

John J. Mack.
[Barbara Mack]

Raymond Sher.
[Charlotte Sher Levine]

LAKEFRONT TOWERS

John J. Mack
(1904-77)
Raymond Sher

During the 1950s, '60s, and '70s, the character of Chicago's North Lake Shore Drive was dramatically transformed—from block after block of vintage apartment buildings, old homes, and open dunes, to a towering succession of postwar-modern high-rise apartments. Developers John J. Mack and Raymond Sher were pacesetters in the creation of both the new skyline in the postwar era and of a new urban life-style for tens of thousands of Chicagoans. In a period when Chicago was hungry for housing, Mack and Sher did better than build mere apartment blocks. They built soaring lakefront towers, beacons luring middle-class professionals back into the city and providing an alternative to suburban flight to others.[1]

Mack, a small but solidly built man, was voluble, affable, generous with family and friends, and aggressive in business. His early career as a hotelman suited him well. He was a visible presence in Chicago, a man who tipped his hat to whomever he passed on the street. Sher, tall and lean, with a more leisurely manner, had a mind for mechanical things, coupled with a shrewd sense for the bottom line. In spite of their differences, and perhaps because of them, the partnership between John Mack and Ray Sher worked and worked very well. In every relationship, Mack had to be the one in charge. He was the idea man, the deal maker. Sher was able to accept and work around Mack's forceful personality. From the beginning, they divided the responsibility. Mack found the properties, worked to arrange the financing, and met the public. Sher, along with his brothers and son-in-law, took care of the building management and construction sides of the enterprise. In business, as in their personal financial affairs, Mack and Sher were like the grasshopper and the ant, with Mack leaping from deal to deal and Sher steadily moving the operations forward.

John Mack was every inch a self-made man—a genuine American success story. He was born in Sevastopol in the Russian Ukraine in 1904, the third of eight children. The family was orphaned when Mack was thirteen. At fifteen he joined the Russian army, and at seventeen, he made his way to America. In New York, knowing very little English, he found a job painting apartments. It took him two years to save enough for his fare to Chicago. He was entirely self-educated and throughout his life was a voracious reader with an insatiable curiosity. In his early years in Chicago, Mack worked at any job he could get, gravitating in the late 1920s to real estate. In the mid-1930s he made his first big commission and began acquiring property through foreclosure sales.

His specialty was residential hotels. By the mid-1940s Mack had bought and sold interests in twenty-six hotels, including some of Chicago's favorites. Mack hotels included the Chicagoan, the Congress, the Croydon, and the Eastgate. He remodeled the old Congress Hotel in the early 1940s and then turned it over to the military for a wartime headquarters. In 1944 he bought the Medinah Athletic Club Building at 505 North Michigan at auction and remodeled it as the Hotel Continental. He had sold the Continental by 1947, and it became the Sheraton, later the Radisson, now the Inter-Continental.

Ray Sher was also born in Ukraine (in Odessa) but came to Chicago as a small child, in 1907. After graduating from Crane High School and Crane College, where he studied drafting, he went into the family furniture business. In 1927 Sher and his father bought a new one-hundred-room hotel. When his father was killed just six months later, Sher found himself responsible for taking care of the family.[2] A year later, Sher built another hotel, furnishing it at wholesale prices through his

201 East Walton. The 1951 Walton-Seneca apartment building was John Mack and Ray Sher's first development project as partners in the Lakeshore Management Company. With this building, Mack and Sher assembled a design and construction team that stayed with them throughout their prolific partnership.
[Bill Engdahl, Hedrich-Blessing]

connections in the furniture industry. The Depression was hard on the family, but the 1933 World's Fair, A Century of Progress, brought millions of visitors to Chicago and pumped fresh revenue into the hotel business.[3]

By 1935 Sher had been able to acquire half a dozen other buildings, some through receiverships. He had also taken over management of his uncle's lamp shade business. In a short time Sher turned the failing business around, largely by introducing a patented method for machine-stitching silk shades. When Sher sold the plant ten years later, it was producing more silk lamp shades than any other company in the country.

It could be said that the long friendship of John Mack and Ray Sher began with a poker game. Not just one poker game, but the regular Tuesday, Thursday, and Saturday games played by a group calling themselves the Lamplighters, who at the time met at the Hotel Chicagoan, at 63 West Madison Street, where Mack was a part-owner. "He'd come in and visit with us and play some cards with us, and that's how I became acquainted with John," Sher recalls.[4] The partnership came about quite out of the blue. In 1948 the two met unexpectedly at an auction sale of the apartment building at 40 East Oak Street. After exchanging greetings, Mack asked Sher as a favor not to make an offer on the property. "Ray," he said, "I want to bid and I want to show these guys up." Sher agreed not to challenge Mack's bid, and probably would have done the same for any other poker partner. Mack was one of eight potential buyers who had qualified by submitting the required certified check. Mack opened with the minimum bid. And that was it. There were no other bidders. "And so it was hammered down to John for, I think, $1.1 million," Sher remembers.[5]

Whether he intended it or not, John Mack had became the owner of 40 East Oak. Mack caught up with Sher after the auction and said "Ray, you can have any part of this deal, or you can have it all." Sher said, "At half, I'll be your partner. If you don't want to give me half, I'll take it all." This was the beginning of the partnership, setting a pattern for subsequent projects. Ray Sher and his brothers always maintained at least a one-half interest in their projects, but Mack frequently divided his interest with other investment partners. Shortly after the 40 East Oak transaction, Mack offered Sher a half interest in three properties in the Belmont Harbor area that Mack had acquired at a good price and intended to develop with Federal Housing Administration financing: 3121 Sheridan Road, 3101 Sheridan Road, and 350 Oakdale Avenue. Sher accepted, and the partners organized Lake Shore Management Company. In 1951 they began construction of the Walton-Seneca Apartments at 201 East Walton Street. The hotelman and the former lamp shade manufacturer had become developers.

The sheer volume of their work over the next decade was remarkable. Within ten years of the Walton-Seneca ground breaking, John Mack and Ray Sher added more than five thousand apartment units to the city's housing stock. Their buildings are a familiar part of the Chicago landscape. Starting on the north at Irving Park Road just off North Lake Shore Drive, the fifty-six-story, 901-unit Park Place (formerly Frontier Towers) still dominates its neighbors. Southward along the Drive, Mack and Sher apartment buildings loom up in remarkably close succession. The addresses are well known to anyone who has lived on Chicago's North Side. Approaching and rounding Belmont Harbor, one passes Mack and Sher's 3950, 3600, 3550, 3180, 3150, and 3130 North Lake Shore

Drive buildings, backed up by the 3121, 3101, and 2909 Sheridan Road apartments. Moving south, one goes by 1550, 1240, and 1150 North Lake Shore Drive. Farther south, on or just off North Michigan Avenue, are the former Continental Plaza Hotel (now the Westin), the 777 North Michigan apartments, and the Walton-Seneca building. Just off the Drive in the heart of the Gold Coast stand 1325 and 1445 North State Parkway. Scattered among all these buildings are a dozen others put up by Mack and Sher between 1950 and 1970 and at least that many more major buildings and properties that they at one time or another owned or managed, including the Sherman House (since demolished), Ambassador East and Ambassador West hotels, the Palmolive (later Playboy and now 919 North Michigan Avenue) Building, and the ground under the John Hancock Center.

It is not surprising that Mack and Sher buildings have a uniformity of appearance that makes them readily recognizable. The lakefront apartment towers have been criticized for being built to a formula, but if so, the formula was successful in doing what it was intended to do. With Walton-Seneca, Mack and Sher formed a team that stayed together through most of their subsequent projects. Alfred Shaw, in partnership with mechanical engineer Carl Metz and civil engineer John Dolio, was the architect they used most often.[6] Crane Construction Company was Mack and Sher's general contractor. Sher worked closely with Shaw, often introducing cost-saving ideas of his own into the layouts, such as the configuration of units around corridors in a way that maximized rental space.[7]

The luxury lakefront apartment buildings developed in the early years of the twentieth century were built to replicate the single-family mansion, with all the luxuries of space and appointment that the developer could provide. The need in the 1950s was to make comfortable apartment living available to a greater number of people at the lowest feasible development cost. Plans for Mack and Sher buildings were dictated by considerations of economy and efficiency, and by FHA mortgage financing formulas. But the structures were well built for their time.

In the second phase of their partnership, Mack and Sher revived their former interest in the hotel business. They had bought the Ambassador East, Ambassador West, and Sherman House hotels from New York developer William Zeckendorf. The Ambassadors were turned around and resold to Louis Silver even before Mack and Sher took possession. But they kept the Sherman House and operated it for two years before selling it too. They also established a strong foothold on North Michigan Avenue when they bought the leasehold on the

1150 North Lake Shore Drive. John Mack and Ray Sher's 1150 Lake Shore Drive building, built in 1959, had larger units than the typical FHA-financed Mack and Sher buildings of the 1950s. The semicircular face of the building is designed to maximize the number of units with lake views.
[Chicago Architectural Photographing Co.—Barbara Mack]

Palmolive Building. That property included the vacant lot to the south where, in August 1961, Mack and Sher announced they would build the Continental Plaza Hotel.

A month later, in September 1961, John Mack closed what could have been the biggest deal of his career. He and Sher bought the large, vacant property at 875 North Michigan Avenue just south of the Continental Plaza site, between Delaware and Chestnut streets. The rumored price was $3.5 million. Mack announced plans for a one-thousand-unit, sixty-five-story apartment building. It would be the largest and costliest project of the decade—a dream come true for John Mack. But, as sometimes happened, Mack's vision ran ahead of his resources. When Jerry Wolman, a land developer and entrepreneur who at that time was also the majority stockholder in the Philadelphia Eagles professional football team, made Mack an offer of $7 million on the property and gave him a check that day for $1 million, Mack took it. Wolman exceeded even Mack's vision when he put up the one-hundred-story John Hancock Center on the site.[8]

In 1966 Mack and Sher put together a complicated package giving them ninety-nine-year leases on the southeast corner of

Wabash and Monroe streets and the northeast corner of Wabash and Adams streets. Mack envisioned twin forty-story office towers for the corners. Shaw, his architect, convinced him to purchase the parking garage that stood between the two corners and create a unified project. In acquiring this property, Mack and Sher gained control of the entire frontage on the east side of Wabash in the block between Monroe and Adams. In planning the Mid-Continental Plaza building for that site, Mack and Sher entered a third phase of their partnership. At the time, they were beginning the huge Frontier Towers apartment building at Irving Park Road and close to completing a luxury apartment building at 1240 North Lake Shore Drive, the site of the former Robert Todd Lincoln home. With that work under way, the fifty-story Mid-Continental Plaza office building was a very big additional commitment, pushing the limits of the company's resources. With two million square feet of space, Mid-Continental Plaza would be the largest building to go up in Chicago in many years.

Although Alfred Shaw was widely known for the postwar high-rise apartment buildings he designed for Mack and Sher, he was by no means unfamiliar with large office building construction. As a junior partner in Graham, Anderson, Probst and White in the 1920s, Shaw designed both the Merchandise Mart, completed in 1931—then the world's largest office building—and the famed La Salle Street Field Building, completed in 1934—the largest office building in the Loop. Mack and Sher's Mid-Continental Plaza, which Shaw designed in partnership with his son Patrick Shaw, was his last work before his death in 1970.

Mack and Sher went public in 1969, incorporating as the Mid-Continental Realty Company. They raised $30 million— $12 million from the sale of shares and $18 million in debentures. The twelve residential buildings that Mack and Sher still owned and the parking garage at Randolph and Wabash were listed among the assets of the corporation. The two new apartment buildings under way and the Wabash-Adams-Monroe office building were listed as proposed assets. Mack and Sher controlled two-thirds of the stock.[9] Mid-Continental Plaza was close to completion by the end of 1972, but a heavy cloud hung over the project. With the exception of street-level rentals and a twelve-story parking garage, which would generate income, the building was virtually without tenants. The recession that hit in 1972 had severely affected the office rental market. Mack reluctantly faced the facts. In January 1973, he announced the sale of Mid-Continental Plaza to Tishman Realty and Construction Company "for an undisclosed amount of cash and assumption of certain related liabilities." Mack said

1445 North State Parkway.
Although John Mack and Ray Sher are best known for their lakefront high-rise buildings, they also built in the heart of the Gold Coast, including this 1959 building at the southeast corner of Burton Place and North State Parkway.
[Barbara Mack]

at the time that the transaction would recoup for the company its total cash investment and a profit. Sher confirms that statement.[10]

Ray Sher retired when the company was sold—he was nearly seventy. But John Mack, never a retiring type, had no intention of missing out on the action. Periodically the newspapers would announce that "Mack Is Back," but no major projects were completed after the sale of Mid-Continental Plaza. Mack, however, kept an office at the Playboy Building and continued to promote new deals. Even in the last year of his life, when he was unable to go into the office, his accountant came to his home to work with Mack on ideas for new projects. Mack died in 1977.

AUTHOR'S COMMENTARY

1. Mayor Richard J. Daley, who was committed to rebuilding Chicago with massive, federally sponsored projects, attended most of the ground breakings for Mack and Sher buildings in the 1950s and '60s. Sher recalls Daley telling the developers, "I want you fellows to know how much I appreciate you. You guys certainly have changed the skyline of the city of Chicago." This would be the kind of recognition that would have pleased John Mack at least as much as any financial reward from his developments.

2. Sher's responsibility as "father of the household," as he described himself, was a role he played throughout his career in real estate and development. As his brothers—William, Maurice, and Harry—entered the business world, Ray Sher brought them in as partners in his companies, called Sher Bros. and Sherbro Investment. Harry and Maurice shared a 50 percent participation with Ray in Mack and Sher's Lake Shore Management Company. Harry eventually became chief operating officer for the company, assisted by Maurice. Sher's son-in-law Morton J. Crane was general contractor for most of Sher's development projects.

3. The 1933 World's Fair, coming as it did in a time of deep economic depression, saved many Chicago families from disaster. I have long regretted the shortsightedness of the city's governmental and political leadership during the administration of Mayor Harold Washington when plans for a proposed 1992 Chicago world's fair were permitted to languish and die. Although we could not necessarily have foreseen the extended development downturn of 1991-92, the fact remains that a 1992 world's fair held enormous economic potential and promised long-term benefits for the city. I have no doubt that had the planning for the fair gone forward, some twenty thousand skilled and nonskilled jobs would have been created in a period that has turned out to be a time of significant unemployment. The problem in 1982-84, as I saw it from my perspective as a member of the Chicago 1992 World's Fair Executive Committee, grew from concern within the Washington administration that the fair would not advance the mayor's economic agenda for the black communities. This was coupled with a failure on the part of the business community to embrace the neighborhood organizations in the planning process. The political establishment had the power to bring these parties together in

a way that could have merged the mayor's interests with the interests of the fair's sponsors. Its failure to have done so is one of the great mistakes made by the city in this century.

4. The card club is the scene of my own first memory of meeting John Mack and Ray Sher. My father played with the group from time to time, and I remember as a youngster going to meet him after the games. Over the years they met at various hotels—the Chicagoan, the Ambassador East, the Continental, and later, perhaps, at the Sherman House. The tables would be set up in a large room or a series of rooms, with plenty of food laid out. Men of that generation liked to play cards together, and they would meet several nights a week.

5. Mack may have been surprised by this turn of events. Sher could not explain it, but did know first-hand that it was not a case of bid stifling. Bid stifling, a fairly common practice in those days, occurred when buyers or their representatives at an auction paid other prospective buyers not to bid, thus holding the price down. Some men made a fairly profitable business out of being "stifled." For all his bombastic and colorful ways, John Mack shared with Ray Sher a strong code of personal ethics and would not have engaged in this practice. Many years later, my family became owners of the 40 East Oak building. As Sher described the events of the 1948 auction, I clearly remembered the "little office" off the lobby where Sher told me Mack had gone to conclude the transaction.

6. The firm was Shaw, Metz and Dolio during the period of most of the apartment construction; the successor firms were Shaw, Metz and Associates and (when Patrick Shaw joined his father in the firm) Alfred Shaw and Associates.

7. In the Walton-Seneca building, Mack and Sher introduced the notion of providing an apartment building with a front desk and a concierge, a service-oriented concept that came out of their experience as hotelmen and builders of apartments. The idea soon became a standard in high-rise apartment construction.

8. The 1,105-foot John Hancock Center, then the world's tallest building, quickly became a symbol of Chicago. But it also brought financial disaster to the developer, Jerry Wolman. Wolman's undoing stemmed from a combination of problems that in sum became a developer's worst nightmare. The first sign of trouble came when the gen-

eral contractor, Tishman Realty and Construction Company, advised Wolman that the plans prepared by Skidmore, Owings and Merrill were not precise enough to enable Tishman to provide a firm estimate of construction costs. Relying on a 10 percent cushion in his short-term construction financing, Wolman decided to go ahead with construction without locking in an estimate. Wolman had confidence in his architects and faith in his

Mid-Continental Plaza. The fifty-story Mid-Continental Plaza building (now known as 55 East Monroe) was John Mack and Ray Sher's largest development—and their last. In this view, the aluminum-faced 1974 building is profiled against the historic roof lines of nineteenth-century Michigan Avenue structures. The 311 South Wacker Drive building, completed in 1990, is in the background.
[Tishman Speyer Properties]

own instincts and experience. He no doubt believed that the design details would be worked out as the project progressed, something that frequently happened.

The nightmare began when, at the point where the first steel columns were being set, an engineer discovered that one of the columns was settling. An investigation revealed faulty concrete work in the massive concrete caissons that were to anchor to structure to bedrock. Construction was halted for several months while core samples were taken of all the caissons, revealing in some places spaces as large as ten or fifteen feet. Ultimately, all the defective caissons were mined and reinforced with new concrete. A year was lost, but the clock never stopped running. The extraordinary overruns were coming out of Wolman's pocket. Eventually, costs doubled from the original back-of-an-envelope estimate of $50 million to a final cost of about $100 million. Although he had a promise of permanent financing—in the form of a first mortgage after the building was completed—from the John Hancock Insurance Company, Wolman was not able to secure the additional interim financing needed to complete construction. In December 1966, Wolman gave up on the project that was to have been his crowning achievement. He sold his interest to the John Hancock Company for $5 million—less than he had paid Mack and Sher for the land. He also sold his stock in the Philadelphia Eagles and declared bankruptcy.

9. The principal reason for the stock issue by the Mid-Continental Realty Company very likely was the usual one: to make a larger pool of money available, enabling the developers to act quickly in warehousing new deals. I also think that at this point in his life, John Mack placed significant personal value on being head of a publicly owned company. I believe it was important to him to be acknowledged among his peers as ''being on the big board.''

10. The stock in Mid-Continental Realty Corporation was sold to the Reynolds Development Company. In early 1974 Romanek-Golub and Company bought most of Mack and Sher's lakefront apartment towers from Mid-Continental Realty and did very well with the properties as condominium conversions. If John Mack had any regrets about pursuing his dream of developing a major office building—at the risk of losing, as he did, all his other properties—he didn't speak of it in those terms, even to friends and family.

MR. REAL ESTATE

Arthur Rubloff
(1902-86)

Arthur Rubloff.
[Oscar and Associates—Rubloff Inc.]

Arthur Rubloff emerged as one of the preeminent personalities in Chicago's postwar real estate community, the captain of an exuberant career that spanned six decades of the city's history. He was a maker of plans of grand proportions. America's first shopping centers, North Michigan Avenue's "Magnificent Mile," and the sprawling Carl Sandburg Village were all credited—in the public mind, at least—to the hand of Arthur Rubloff. As an individual, he was an Olympian figure. A towering and powerful presence— brilliant, decisive, manipulative, egocentric, demanding. Quick to anger and slow to forgive, strong-minded and opportunistic, Rubloff was, above all else, a man of great vision and great charm and had a great flair for self-promotion.

Arthur Rubloff was born in 1902 in Duluth, Minnesota, the eldest of three sons and two daughters of Russian immigrant parents. He was raised in a small mining town in the Mesabi Range, where his father owned a dry goods store. A self-confessed truant, by the age of seven Arthur was spending more time hustling a buck than he was in school. He distributed newspapers, set pins in the bowling alley, and sold shoe shines at the local hotel. His formal education ended with graduation from the eighth grade, which was when Arthur set off to seek his fortune. He worked as a galley boy on an ore freighter and in a furniture factory in Cincinnati—experiences that over the years stoked the "rags-to- riches" story that Arthur loved to tell. In 1918 he joined his family in Chicago, where his father had established a ladies' ready-to-wear manufacturing plant. Dispatched a year later to find new loft space for the family business, Arthur discovered his zest for making a deal and found his lifework.

In the 1920s Arthur Rubloff became the most persistent and one of the most successful commissioned brokers of space in the West Loop wholesale district. He made money during those years, and, he said, spent it as soon as he made it, indulging an appetite for a conspicuous display of affluence that stayed with him throughout his life. In 1930 Rubloff went on his own, naming himself chairman, president, and sole employee of Arthur Rubloff and Company. According to Rubloff, architect Ernest Graham helped him set up shop in a hallway in a West Loop office building. He bought $1,500 worth of signs on credit and posted the Rubloff name on every piece of property he represented. The company would in time become the largest property brokerage and management firm in Chicago and one of the largest in the world.

Rubloff often said, "If people think you're making deals, sooner or later you'll make them." The notion served him well in the lean years of the Great Depression, when there were precious few deals to be made. Rubloff took on the task of salvaging leases for the Marshall Field Company's stricken Merchandise Mart, designed by Ernest Graham's firm, Graham, Anderson, Probst and White. The Merchandise Mart was then the world's largest commercial building—and one of the world's emptiest. Rubloff wore out a lot of shoe leather pitching space to everyone he knew in the wholesale district, and he knew them all. He later claimed to have recovered 66 cents on the dollar value of Mart leases vacated by the first wave of Depression-era business collapses.

In the mid-1930s, at a time when Rubloff was building a business against great odds, he met and married Josephine Sheehan, a delicate Irish-Catholic lady who, until her death in 1974, was Arthur's greatest asset in his tireless quest for the recognition and approval of old-line Chicago society.

When World War II ended, the real estate industry—dormant for nearly two decades—took off, and so did Arthur Rubloff and Company. Through the 1930s and the war years, Rubloff had forged a reputation as a masterful broker and a decisive deal maker. Early tours de force included his roles in the cash sale of the 29 South La Salle Building to the Equitable Life Assurance Society of the United States and in brokering the $4.7 million Greyhound Bus Terminal project in the North Loop, which included destruction of Burnham and Root's 1892 Ashland Block office building. No hero to preservationists, Rubloff had also been responsible for the 1939 demolition of Burnham and Root's Masonic Temple Building, at the northeast corner of State and Randolph, to make way for an architecturally undistinguished low-rise building. When challenged on the point, Rubloff would respond that, in his opinion, the only old building in Illinois worth preserving was Abraham Lincoln's home in Springfield.

By the mid-1940s the Arthur Rubloff Company had grown large enough to move to new offices at 100 West Monroe Street, where it took over an entire floor. The Rubloff name became synonymous with the management and selling of big buildings. By this time Arthur Rubloff was also deeply immersed in the business of creating and living his own legend. He had become Chicago's "Mr. Real Estate," and he tenaciously promoted his image as a big operator, the man to see if you wanted something done.[1] Although the extent of Rubloff's personal wealth, at least until the real estate boom of the 1970s, was nowhere near what he would have had people believe, he nonetheless lived royally. He moved from one lavish apartment to the next on Chicago's Gold Coast and also maintained residences at New York's Sherry-Netherland Hotel and at the Breakers hotel in Palm Beach. His closets overflowed with wardrobes, purchased in triplicate, of custom-made suits, shirts, and shoes. He kept three Rolls Royce automobiles, tended by a trio of chauffeurs.

For all his eccentricities, Rubloff was nonetheless a shrewd, far-sighted, and hard-headed businessman, poised to pounce on any opportunity that came his way. His talent for seeing years into the future was evident as early as 1942, when he began buying up 176 parcels of land along a heavily traveled intersection on the Southwest Side of Chicago, where ten years later he would build Evergreen Plaza, a pioneer among the shopping malls that were to become an essential part of a new, suburban American way of life.

Rubloff had a talent for latching onto a good idea and claiming it as his own. The redevelopment of North Michigan Avenue is a well-known case in point. In the mid-1940s Rubloff became involved, as a broker, in a number of property transactions along Michigan Avenue, including sale of the block where Philip Klutznick would later build Water Tower Place and the lease of the corner at Chicago and Michigan avenues to the Walgreen Company.

Rubloff and his public relations counsel pulled off a great promotional stunt when they organized a press luncheon in April 1947 to announce Rubloff's plans for a new North Michigan Avenue that would be lined with "the last word" in stores, offices, and apartment buildings, and to display development and beautification plans prepared for him by the architectural firm of Holabird and Root. "Ladies and gentlemen," Rubloff declared on this occasion, "We give you the Magnificent Mile." The speech itself was vintage Rubloff, making no mention of the work of men such as Murray Wolbach and Frederick M. Bowes who thirty years before had organized the property owners' group that was the forerunner of the Greater North Michigan Avenue Association and who were the first to espouse development of Upper Michigan Avenue "as the most beautiful shopping thoroughfare in the world." Nor, apparently, had Rubloff consulted these gentlemen when he unilaterally dubbed the avenue "the Magnificent Mile." Arguments over the slogan went on for years and became something of a lightning rod for other business leaders' resentment of Rubloff's preemptive manner. Gordon Lang, North Michigan Avenue Association president, minced no words in telling Rubloff that "the words 'Magnificent Mile' make the Association look ridiculous." Although Rubloff cultivated his reputation as "the father of North Michigan Avenue" until the end of his life, the fact remains that he was neither a builder nor a developer of North Michigan. What he was, no less to his credit, was an energetic real estate broker and a latter-day promoter of a planning concept that had been set in motion in the 1910s and to a large extent accomplished in the boom years of the 1920s.

By the mid-1950s Rubloff had moved on to a far more spectacular scheme, a scheme that if it had it been realized would have lifted all of the city's centers of government—including the city and county courts, the board of education, and the Chicago Public Library—out of the Loop and dropped them down in the center of a 150-acre government, residential, and office complex on the north bank of the Chicago River. Rubloff's plan for the area even included a Chicago campus for the University of Illinois. Although the concept of a civic center out of the Loop was by no means a new one, Rubloff nonetheless claimed the plan, known as the Fort Dearborn Project, as his own "fabulous idea." And to a large extent, it was. Rubloff spent five years developing the plan, seeing it drafted by Skidmore, Owings and Merrill, and putting together a heavy-hitting team of sponsors, led by Marshall Field and Company's chairman, Hughston McBain.

Rubloff's timing in announcing the mammoth project in 1954 was unerringly good. Federal slum clearance funds were then available in abundance. The state legislature, urged on by newly elected mayor Richard J. Daley and Illinois governor William Stratton, cooperated by creating a Public Buildings Commission with power to sell revenue bonds earmarked for the project. The most remarkable thing about the Fort Dear-

Brunswick Building. [opposite page] The 1965 Brunswick Building, developed by Arthur Rubloff, heralded a wave of new office building in the Central Loop. Rubloff, the consummate real estate operator, made the Brunswick, located at the southwest corner of Dearborn and Washington streets, his headquarters.
[Hedrich-Blessing—Chicago Historical Society]

born Project is how close Arthur Rubloff came to actually pulling it off. The Public Buildings Commission established to facilitate the Fort Dearborn Project later became an extremely important vehicle for Mayor Daley in promoting the sale of revenue bonds for such public works projects as the addition to the City-County Building complex that is now known as Daley Center.

The Fort Dearborn Project eventually foundered in the face of diversions mounted by Loop property ownership and management interests, which could not afford to lose the lucrative office rentals that gravitated around the courts and public buildings. But Rubloff never relinquished credit for having had the "fabulous idea." In 1964 he described the new Richard J. Daley Civic Center as "an outgrowth of the Fort Dearborn Project," and implied the same claim for the Dirksen Federal Building. Illinois governor James Thompson would later say that it was Rubloff who opened his eyes to the possibilities for a new State of Illinois building opposite the Daley Center.[2]

Rubloff dropped back from the front lines of the Fort Dearborn Project in the late 1950s to pursue a far more pressing interest on Chicago's Near North Side. This was the North Clark–La Salle redevelopment project that eventually became the 2,600-unit Carl Sandburg Village residential complex, often cited as one of the best urban renewal developments in the nation. The North Clark–La Salle corridor, once a thriving German and Italian neighborhood, had become increasingly blighted in the war years. The area was targeted for redevelopment by the Chicago Land Clearance Commission in 1953 and approved for federal redevelopment funds in 1955. The project was a natural for Rubloff, who in 1955 was serving as president of the Greater North Michigan Avenue Association, an organization that had a very real interest in protecting nearby Gold Coast property values from any further encroachment of Clark Street blight.

In the process of promoting the Fort Dearborn plan, Rubloff had become savvy to the workings of the slum clearance and redevelopment agencies. His work on that project had, he implied, won him the ear of the mayor and the support of Alderman Tom Keane, chairman of the powerful Chicago City Council Finance Committee. When land clearance was completed in 1961, it came as no surprise that Arthur Rubloff emerged as spokesman for the development group that submitted the approved plan and highest bid for the property. He was so much of a spokesman that, after listening to Rubloff, people were often surprised to find that there were others involved, including Al Robin, George Dovenmuehle, Lou Solomon, and John Cordwell—all of whom made important contributions to the project. The $100 million Carl Sandburg Village development ultimately shattered relationships between Rubloff—always a one-man show—and his partners. And his persistent pressure on the city to deliver up valuable properties exempted from the original redevelopment plan strained his welcome at city hall. But Carl Sandburg Village was in every other respect a great success. It did what it was supposed to do. That included a $65 million dollar profit realized by the investors when Sandburg was resold.

In 1965 Arthur Rubloff and Company developed the Brunswick Building (designed by Skidmore, Owings and Merrill) at 69 West Washington Street, made the Brunswick its own headquarters, and triggered a wave of new office building development in the Central Loop. By the early 1970s Rubloff was ready to change the shape of the entire downtown. Chicago city planners had long envisioned a downtown urban renewal program that would revitalize the deteriorating North Loop area. When the city opened negotiations with the Hilton Hotel Corporation to clear North Loop land for a new Hilton, Rubloff jumped in with his own master plan for the area.[3]

Rubloff envisioned a seven-block redevelopment that called for the demolition of all but two of the fifty buildings in the designated urban renewal area—with himself as principal developer. "This will be the foremost development ever undertaken in any city in the nation," he said in 1978, when he revealed plans for a new state office building, city library, commercial office building, hotel, high-rise apartments, and a shopping mall to be constructed in the blocks between Wacker Drive and Washington Street. He touted his North Loop plan through the administrations of three mayors—Daley, Michael Bilandic, and Jane Byrne—watching it lose momentum with each change of government. "If Daley had lived, we would have gone forward with this project," Rubloff would later say, lavishing invective on advisers to Bilandic and Byrne who, he believed, had cheated him of the crowning achievement of his career. "They stole my plan and ran with it," he complained shortly before his death in 1986.[4]

In his lifetime Rubloff made his own rules and wrote his own script. He was one of a kind, and the last of his breed. Who would argue now with this statement, spoken by Rubloff in 1981, almost, it would seem, as his own valedictory:

So what can I tell ya? I am a creative developer. I did North Michigan Avenue's Magnificent Mile. Nobody helped me. I built Sandburg Village. Saved the Near North Side, that's what

"Magnificent Mile." [opposite page] In 1947 Arthur Rubloff announced redevelopment and beautification plans for North Michigan Avenue that included trees and planters such as those seen in this 1950 photo. Rubloff coined the term "Magnificent Mile" and considered himself to be the "Father of North Michigan Avenue." [Dr. Frank Rice—Chicago Historical Society]

I did. Everyone was against it. You don't think anyone would have ever come up with the North Loop Redevelopment Project if I hadn't started it or planned it—not in a hundred years! I have the kind of vision and knowledge and imagination to do these kinds of deals by myself, and I've done them many times.

In that interview, Rubloff did not boast of his personal philanthropies, which included bequests totaling $11 million to the Art Institute of Chicago; to Northwestern University, where a new building for the law school was named for him; and to the University of Chicago. He left another $60 million in trust to support a wide range of Chicago institutions. Late in life Rubloff said that he never made any fortune in Chicago. And to some extent that is true. Many of his biggest deals were done in other cities. But when Rubloff died, he gave back to the people of Chicago most of the money he had earned. It was a magnificent gesture.

AUTHOR'S COMMENTARY

1. Although I tried over the years of my relationship with Arthur Rubloff not to be surprised by anything he might do, I was in fact shocked and amazed when he appeared at a Chicago Plan Commission meeting that I was conducting in the mid-1970s to register his strenuous objection to the development of the 1100 North Lake Shore Drive apartment building. Arthur argued that an apartment building at that site, if approved by the plan commission, would create a serious traffic hazard at the corner of Lake Shore Drive and Cedar. (In truth, the development could have produced no more than a minuscule increment to the flow of North Lake Shore Drive traffic.) The point Rubloff did not mention was the more obvious fact that he, himself, lived at the Carlyle apartments, 1040 North Lake Shore Drive. The proposed building was not so likely to create a hazardous traffic condition as it was to affect to some extent Arthur's own scenic view of the lakefront and the Drive. Arthur Rubloff probably asked for more zoning variations and more special consideration from the City of Chicago than any other developer. His attempt to block this development—and for the spurious reason given—was, in my opinion, a singularly unattractive move on his part— and I told him so. My candor produced a rift in our relationship that lasted until the time Arthur decided that he might need something more from me. In all fairness, Ar-

thur was not so different from other people in objecting to the development of another apartment building in his neighborhood. Many people who buy an apartment, rent an apartment, or build a building are horrified when others want to do the same thing on the immediately adjacent site. I call this the last-building-on-the-block syndrome. What was appalling to me was that Arthur presented his objection in his role as a real estate person, but with a thinly veiled appeal for special consideration by the plan commission.

2. The block where the State of Illinois Center is located was the first block of the North Loop project to be redeveloped. In later years Rubloff criticized Governor James Thompson for not giving him the credit he thought was due him in North Loop redevelopment planning and for not supporting his further claims to the North Loop as his personal province. In the last years of Rubloff's life, he spoke to the governor but did not support him for reelection.

3. Arthur Rubloff always believed that Chicago's North Loop Redevelopment Project belonged to him—or should have. The fact that Mayor Richard J. Daley and subsequent mayors would not agree to turn the North Loop over to him was a bitter disappointment toward the end of his long and productive career in Chicago real estate development. Regardless of what he later claimed, redevelopment of the North Loop was not Arthur Rubloff's idea. The concept was born in the offices of the city's department of development and planning in the late 1960s. At that time, Chicago was one of the few major American cities that had not launched a downtown urban renewal project (although the Madison-Canal plan was then in the making). Planning Commissioner Lewis Hill and members of the plan commission, including myself, had been looking at the dilapidated North Loop area as a potential urban renewal area for some time. We were working on the numbers—analyzing the costs for acquisition, demolition, and relocation—when we learned that the Hilton Hotel Corporation was looking for a site to build a new hotel.

We believed that the Hilton project was a natural for the North Loop, and it became a stimulus to proceed with the renewal plan. (Typically, under the federal urban renewal program, a city would acquire and clear land in deteriorated areas and sell it back to private interests for redevelopment, in keeping with a city-approved plan. This was the procedure followed in the development of Sandburg Village.) Commissioner Hill discussed our plans for clearance of an eleven-block area with Mayor Daley, and Daley liked the idea. He liked it so much that—to the astonishment of Commissioner Hill—he announced at a businessmen's breakfast meeting the next day that the city was considering a project in the North Loop. Lew Hill recalls that even before Mayor Daley got back to city hall, Hill's phone was ringing with calls from the media asking for details of the North Loop plan.

I wouldn't be surprised if Arthur Rubloff also made a call that day, although his call would have been directly to the Fifth Floor (Daley's office). He was quick to scent a profitable project and seldom missed an opportunity to make his wishes known to the mayor. The fact remains, however, that it wasn't until some time after the mayor's announcement that Rubloff—amid great publicity—presented his master plan for the North Loop and asserted his personal claim on the property. Rubloff's idea was that the city acquire the land and sell it to him for redevelopment, at a write-down and without competitive bidding. This, of course, didn't happen, and in my judgment, was never even a possibility.

4. Although Mayor Daley tolerated Rubloff's frequent visits to city hall to update his "rights" to one property or another, including the Germania Club property that Rubloff coveted just north of Sandburg Village, Daley was uncomfortable with Rubloff, for many reasons. The mayor's tendency to play his hand close to the vest when dealing with Rubloff was attributable in part to Arthur's bombastic personality. But it might also have been attributable to the mayor's wariness of Tom Keane, the chairman of the city council finance committee. Keane's son Tom Jr. had worked for Rubloff for many years, and Daley very probably considered Keane to be Rubloff's man. Ever the astute politician, Mayor Daley was always concerned about a possible challenge to his authority and is likely to have felt that the Keane-Rubloff alliance was one to be concerned about. Rubloff, however, continued to assert his view that had Mayor Daley lived, the North Loop Redevelopment Project would have been his. He progressively blamed Commissioner Hill, Commissioner Martin Murphy (who succeeded Hill), and myself, after I was appointed to coordinate the development process, as the source of his problems. Rubloff's claim that he had a right to the project

notwithstanding, the city could not under any administration have named him both planner and developer, as he insisted, and certainly could not have given it to him without competitive bidding.

John W. Baird.
[Baird and Warner]

ALL IN THE FAMILY

John W. Baird

When the vintage Locklear Apartments at 3650 North Lake Shore Drive were torn down to make way for a new town-house development, Baird and Warner Chairman John Wyllys Baird made an interesting observation. He noted that the company had witnessed the entire life cycle of the building: The Locklear was built by Baird and Warner in the 1920s. It remained under Baird and Warner management for its allotted three score or more years. And, when the Locklear's days were done, the land and building were sold by Baird and Warner. The continuity in this building's story is unique, but perhaps not surprising, in the history of a company whose growth has paralleled that of the city itself. Baird and Warner is one of Chicago's oldest and largest independent real estate brokerage and service firms. Since 1862 leadership of the company has passed in an unbroken line, father to son, through five generations of the Baird family.

Lyman Baird came to Chicago from New Haven, Connecticut, in 1857 and joined his friend Lucius Olmsted's young real estate loan firm. The two quickly built a thriving business specializing in bringing eastern investment capital to Chicago. After Olmsted's death in 1862, another New Havener, Francis Bradley, became Baird's partner, and the firm was renamed Baird and Bradley. In 1883 Baird brought George L. Warner, his wife's younger brother, into the firm. In 1893 when Lyman Baird's son, Wyllys, and George Warner took over active management of the company, the firm assumed the name it carries today: Baird and Warner.

Although the story of the Bairds' place in Chicago real estate and development may appear on the surface to be a tale of lockstep dynastic succession, that is not necessarily the case. Baird and Warner's longevity—the very survival of the company, in fact—is due in far greater measure to adaptive management brought into the company at critical junctures by new generations of Baird leadership than it is to the circumstance that those leaders were born with the family name. The family itself does not assume that its sons will succeed their fathers. Ever since Wyllys Warner Baird took over the presidency in 1893, Baird and Warner presidents all have trained for other professions. Warner G. Baird, who became president in 1928, studied engineering at Cornell University and worked for an Illinois iron company before joining the family business. John Baird, who succeeded his father Warner as president in 1963, has a degree in history from Wesleyan University and a Harvard M.B.A. He was a captain in the U.S. Army during World War II and began his business career at General Motors Corporation. Stephen Baird, elected president in 1991, is a cum laude graduate of Harvard with a major in psychology and a minor in art history. His first business experience was as a store manager with an outdoor equipment company.[1]

John Baird is tall, cultivated, and soft-spoken in manner. A model of the reserve that seems to run in the Baird family's Scottish blood, Baird nonetheless defies any dour stereotype with the lively bow tie that has become a personal trademark. He explains the family's low-key approach to succession with characteristically few words: "Dad was always noncommittal about the business and didn't push us into it." John Baird's son Stephen makes a similar observation when he says "I wasn't raised in the family business. . . . For a long time I didn't exactly know what my father did for a living."

Nor have Baird and Warner's activities in Chicago real estate been as lockstep as many observers might imagine. Although it is true that Baird and Warner's principal business for nearly a century and a half has been mortgage loans, property management, and sales, the company has also been involved, to a surprising extent, in central city development activities—specifically the rebuilding of old and often severely blighted neighborhoods with new, integrated housing. The company's interest in central city redevelopment can be traced directly to the leadership of John Baird, who brought Baird and Warner into urban renewal projects in the 1950s, became an outspoken leader in the fight for open housing in the early 1960s, and pioneered the redevelopment and restoration of the Printers Row district in the South Loop in the 1970s and '80s.

1448 North Lake Shore Drive. [opposite page] During the building boom of the 1920s, the Baird and Warner company departed from their traditional business of providing mortgage loans to build several cooperative apartment buildings, including the eighteen-story 1448 North Lake Shore Drive building, at Burton Place, seen in this period photograph. [John W. Baird]

Development was by no means an unknown concept in the company. Traditionally, however, Baird and Warner has viewed development activity as a means of generating a market for the company's mortgage, management, and other real estate services rather than as an end in itself. In the rebuilding boom that followed the Great Chicago Fire, for example, the company became involved in suburban subdivision development, which in turn brought in mortgage loan business. The company revived its subdivision activities at intervals, such as after the annexations of 1889 and again after the completion of the North Side elevated railway.

During the building boom of the 1920s, the company carried its development activities a step further. In these years Baird and Warner built, marketed, and managed several North Side cooperative apartment buildings, including the Locklear and 1120 and 1448 North Lake Shore Drive. It renewed its subdivision activity in these years, too, developing the Deere Park properties and Skokie Ridge in north suburban Highland Park. But even in the high-rolling 1920s, when almost everyone hoped to ride either the stock market or the building boom to riches, "We never really thought of ourselves as developers," Baird states. "And we still think of ourselves primarily as purveyors of real estate services."

Baird traces the philosophy back not only to the company's origins as a small mortgage loan business founded in the 1850s but also to the tone set for Baird and Warner in the forty-four years that Warner G. Baird served as president. "Dad wasn't very much interested in development," Baird recalls. Understandably so. Warner Baird had brought the company through the dangerous years of the Depression and had made it profitable, even in a time when there were no mortgages to arrange and few buyers for property at any price. He did this by turning the company's energies to managing, on behalf of investors and bondholders, dozens of foreclosed buildings that Baird and Warner had financed in better days. Even as the economy showed signs of recovery during and after World War II, Warner Baird kept his eye on the company's traditional orientation. "We were in the mortgage loan business, and Dad's attitude was that if we got extensively into development, we would be, to an extent, competing with our customers," John Baird explains.

By 1950 the building industry had fully rebounded. The size and scale of development projects swelled to meet pent-up demand. There was an explosion of single-family home construction, and almost overnight, entire new suburban towns were created. These were followed by another postwar phenomenon, development of the regional shopping center. Baird and Warner kept pace with the times but remained true to its mission—expanding its mortgage financing activities to include suburban office complexes, shopping centers, and industrial parks. By 1980 the company had extended its residential sales division into thirty-four suburban offices.

But major social and economic changes were also occurring in the central city in the postwar period. Already grim conditions were exacerbated by the long construction hiatus and the flight of middle-class families to the suburbs. John Baird, trained as a historian, was particularly alert to the urban dilemma and to what was happening to the central city. When new funds for slum clearance and urban renewal projects became available through the National Housing Act of 1949, he was determined that Baird and Warner would be involved in the rebuilding process. Thus, even as Baird and Warner was becoming an increasingly visible presence in the suburban housing arena, it was also—more quietly—participating in the revitalization of the blighted central city. In the mid-1950s, for example, the company negotiated the land purchases for the Kenwood–Hyde Park urban redevelopment project, one of the largest urban renewal programs in the country. Baird and Warner then submitted a bid on Chicago's North Clark–La Salle urban renewal project (which became the 2,600-unit Carl Sandburg Village), and almost got it. In the 1960s John Baird joined Daniel Levin and James McHugh in the McHugh Levin Corporation's bold South Commons project, an integrated town-house and apartment community built on Chicago's Near South Side.[2] The company entered into the urban renewal arena on its own when it built Campus Green, a $12 million town-house and apartment development adjacent to the University of Illinois and Rush–Presbyterian–St. Luke's Medical Center.

Baird and Warner's participation in these inner-city projects was not inconsistent with its vision of itself as a purveyor of real estate services. But it was far more consistent with John Baird's personal commitment to providing good, integrated housing for the people of Chicago, whatever their income level. Baird's father, grandfather, and great-grandfather all had served as presidents of the Chicago Board of Real Estate. John Baird would take another path. In 1959 he was elected president of the Metropolitan Housing and Planning Council, where his outspoken stand in support of minimum housing standards, redevelopment of blighted areas, and open housing legislation led to an ideological confrontation Baird later referred to as "my split from organized real estate." The issue was joined in 1963 when Baird, as spokesman for the housing and planning council, appeared before the Chicago City

Council to advocate civil rights legislation that would ban racial discrimination in the rental or sale of housing. The very public position taken by John Baird on the open occupancy issue brought on a storm of controversy within the industry. But the controversy did nothing to moderate Baird's views on the matter.[3] Writing in a Chicago real estate journal, he warned that "social rehabilitation and the assimilation of the white and nonwhite immigrant population is a responsibility which cannot be postponed" and advised that "schools, churches, service organizations, and community leadership have the opportunity to show the way." Baird translated words to action by organizing and serving as president of Interaction, an interracial group of Chicago businessmen that in collaboration with the Catholic Archdiocese of Chicago and the Episcopal Diocese of Chicago built Lawndale Manor, one of the first inner-city apartment projects to be financed under the National Housing Act of 1968.

By the 1970s John Baird was actively involved in efforts spearheaded by the business community to revitalize Chicago's South Loop. In this period Baird became associated with Harry Weese, an innovative and visionary Chicago architect who was then promoting his notion of rehabilitating buildings in Chicago's historic Printers Row for use as loft apartments and offices. Baird and a group of investors that included Weese and architect Larry Booth organized Community Resources Corporation (CRC) as a vehicle for financing conversion and restoration projects in the dilapidated South Dearborn district.

The Printers Row project was a far greater risk—although a risk of a different sort—for Baird than the federally backed urban renewal projects had been. The South Loop, which in the early years of the twentieth century had thrived as a center for the printing and publishing industry, had been virtually abandoned when both businesses and people departed for new locations in the suburbs after World War II. Many of the fine old buildings erected along South Dearborn Street in the 1890s had long since fallen into decay. The Dearborn Park development to the south, in which Baird and Warner would later become a consultant and partner, was still a gleam in the planners' eyes. The idea that people might actually make their homes in this area was almost unthinkable.

The Printers Row conversions and the Dearborn Park residential development ultimately proved to be remarkably successful. The future, however, was not at all clear when Baird and his partners began their work to convert the 1911 Transportation Building, at Dearborn and Harrison streets (600 South Dearborn), to apartments. Baird recalls that when CRC showed its plans to the Dearborn Park developers, Philip Klutznick said, "You know, you guys are crazy. That will never work out!" Baird now believes that "to a great extent, Dearborn Park may have been successful because of what we did. We created a corridor down to their project, through slums that people would have had to walk through to get to Dearborn Park."[4] CRC followed its 1978 conversion of the Transportation Building with the redevelopment of the Old Franklin Building (525 South Dearborn), the Pontiac (542 South Dearborn), and the Terminals Building (537 South Dearborn). More restorations done by Weese and by other developers followed, bringing new life to a historic district.[5]

John Baird, along with his brother Warner Jr. and other partners, developed many other properties over the years. Some of these projects were done outside the company, some inside. They include 200 East Delaware, built in partnership with McHugh Levin, and the $10.5 million Willow-Dayton Place restoration in the Lincoln Park area. In the late 1980s Baird and Warner entered into a partnership with Elzie Higginbottom, a former Baird and Warner officer, to build 200 North Dearborn, the first residential building in the North Loop redevelopment area. These developments have made an impact on the face of the city, but they don't adequately represent the impact that John Baird himself made in articulating a vision for the central city and the role of planning and participation of the public sector in implementing that vision:

> You cannot house adequately the lowest income groups without public subsidy; you cannot adequately assemble and redevelop blighted properties without the exercise by government of eminent domain and the sale of the property at vacant land cost; you cannot maintain minimum housing and zoning standards without effective governmental action; you cannot efficiently transport people or goods, or begin to do anything without comprehensive city planning.

These were fighting words to some when spoken by Baird in the late 1950s. But they were heeded as a call to action by many more. The results are seen in a resurgent South Loop and a commitment to urban planning and redevelopment that has been unique among American cities.

AUTHOR'S COMMENTARY

1. All of these Baird family members gravitated to Baird and Warner after gaining experience on the outside. Warner G. Baird Sr. went into the building management department in 1908. John Baird started in 1946 in the commercial loan department. Stephen Baird began in the shopping center division in 1980.

2. South Commons was unique among the urban renewal projects of this period in the extent of its commitment to building an integrated community serving a range of incomes and ages, but targeting upwardly mobile professionals and young families in particular. South Commons, characterized in the press as an "Uncommon Urban Renewal," was a planning experiment that for a time was surprisingly successful, but ultimately failed to achieve its goal of creating a stable multiracial neighborhood. John Baird personally backed the project as one of the original investors in the Central South Development Company, the partnership headed by Daniel Levin that developed the South Commons concept and presented the proposal to Chicago's department of urban renewal. Baird and Warner, Inc., served in the early years as exclusive leasing, sales, and management agents for the complex, but the company otherwise had no financial interest in the development.

3. It seems ironic that despite John Baird's personal stand in support of open housing, the Baird and Warner company would become the object of highly publicized civil rights demonstrations in 1966. At that time, the firm's Oak Park office was picketed because building owners represented by Baird and Warner would not show their apartments to black clients. The demonstrations went on for nearly three months and spread to Evanston, where the company had opened one of its first branch offices in 1921.

4. Baird's observation that redevelopment of Printers Row opened a corridor to Dearborn Park, an entirely new development, illustrates an interesting fact of Chicago's evolving philosophy of development and planning. Conventional wisdom holds that developers and preservationists share no mutual interest and may in fact be natural enemies. In a historic sense, this is true. Any given parcel of urban land has a past; it has been used and reused, subjected to successive layers of improvements undertaken over decades, centuries, or even millennia. The developer's role has been to build anew—usually with the goal of creating bigger or bet-

Dearborn Park. [opposite page] John Baird and Baird and Warner joined other Chicago business leaders and developers in creating the Dearborn Park community in the South Loop, providing a new residential center for Chicago's downtown work force. Baird's own efforts in redeveloping the historic Printers Row district on South Dearborn Street opened a vital corridor linking Dearborn Park to the central business district.
[Scott McDonald, Hedrich-Blessing]

Campus Green ground breaking. Ground-breaking ceremonies in 1968 marked the start of Campus Green, a residential urban renewal complex developed by Baird and Warner near the West Side medical complex. Photographed with local students are [from left] Robert L. Friedman, the project's architect; John W. Baird; Mayor Richard J. Daley; Commissioner Lewis Hill, head of the Chicago Department of Urban Renewal; Jack McHugh, president of McHugh Construction; and West Side business leader Oscar D'Angelo.
[John W. Baird]

ter structures and more economically productive and responsive land uses. The preservationist takes a longer and more romantic view of history, seeking to protect a city's structural relics—sometimes without regard to current or future usefulness and sometimes without a clear consensus about social, aesthetic, or architectural value.

The development of Dearborn Park and the redevelopment of Printers Row illustrate a far more permeable picture of the attitudes of both developers and preservationists in Chicago. Dearborn Park was built on railroad lands—a use that had long been obsolete. The old tracks constituted a dramatic barrier between the economic vitality of the central business district and the city's steadily decaying Near South Side. No one mourned their passing. But the Printers Row district, located in the 500 and 600 blocks of South Dearborn Street, had a history. As we have seen, the area played a significant role in the growth of the city in the late nineteenth century. Redevelopment of South Dearborn Street in the 1970s was a logical and creative reuse of this valuable district—one that was entirely consistent with Chicago's development history.

Chicago is in the process of a second great recycling. The first occurred immediately after the devastating fires of 1871 and 1874. As a consequence of these fires, virtually the whole core of the city was destroyed and almost immediately rebuilt. The elevator buildings that went up on South Dearborn Street in the 1880s and '90s recycled a dissolute, derelict, and dangerous quadrant south of the business district into a center for Chicago's thriving printing and publishing industry. The second recycling, in the 1970s and 1980s, reclaimed the old buildings—no longer useful in an era of new printing and publishing technologies—for use as residences and small office units. New uses brought with them ancillary businesses: restaurants, shops, entertainment.

Recycling is a living part of Chicago's development history. Adaptive reuse in the United States is a late-twentieth-century phenomenon that reflects both the city's unique experience and the creativity of its builders. With maturity has come a greater appreciation of the past and an attempt to preserve what has gone before—in some cases for the uses originally intended and in other cases to adapt that use to a new one. Printers Row is but one example. In the last decade, we have also seen the conversion of Clybourn Avenue from assembly and manufacturing uses to residential lofts. A railroad station has become a retail facility. The Merchandise Mart has converted lower floors into a shopping center, and entire districts such as the blocks just north of the Chicago River and west of State Street have been recycled from distribution and manufacturing uses to commercial, office, and residential communities. In all of these cases, as in the case of Printers Row and Dearborn Park, preservation and redevelopment have gone hand in hand, with new buildings providing the vitality and impetus to make preservation work and with preservation sparking new development.

Another accommodation of past and present, more commonly seen in Europe, is striking in Chicago. This is the combination in the central business district of old and new construction—another form of recycling old buildings. We have seen this, for example, in the renovation of Graham, Anderson, Probst and White's 1920s Builders Building as the 222 North La Salle office building, in the reconstruction of the old State of Illinois Building at the corner of La Salle and Randolph streets, and the redevelopment of the office building once occupied by Aaron Montgomery Ward at 20 North Michigan Avenue.

5. Baird's role in South Loop redevelopment was specifically recognized in late 1989 by Chicago *Sun Times* commercial real estate writer Jerry C. Davis. Davis called attention to the ripple effect that bold efforts such as the Printers Row projects may have, noting that "the reversal of decay in that area has encouraged similar activities on the Near North and Near West sides," and adding that "about 10,000 residents, many upgraded buildings and hotel and restaurant facilities testify to the foresight of Baird and other pioneers in the area."

BUILDER AS DEVELOPER

Albert A. Robin

Albert A. Robin.
[Lyal Lauth—Robin Construction Corp.]

Most developers wear several hats, but few have worn as many as Albert A. Robin. Robin is the developer of some of Chicago's best-known residential buildings, including the 2,600-unit Carl Sandburg Village complex, the imposing Imperial Towers on Marine Drive, and the Carlyle on North Lake Shore Drive. He is also an accomplished artist, an ardent collector of twentieth-century art, and the sponsor of a scholarship fund that sends more than one hundred young people from low-income families to college every year. But the hat that seems to fit Robin best—at least the one he has worn the longest— is a hard hat. Although a small number of developers have been architects as well as developers (Benjamin Marshall and Bertrand Goldberg are among these), far fewer of Chicago's significant developers have also been builders. Robin is the outstanding exception.

Over the course of his long career, Al Robin has been involved in almost every phase of real estate development: single-family homes, apartment complexes, shopping centers, office buildings, and nursing homes. But the sign over the door of his Wells Street office still reads "Robin Construction Company", just as it has since he founded the business in 1935 with a contract to build a $125 fence. In a sense, Robin was born into the business. His father, Max Robin, learned the carpenter's trade in Russia before immigrating to America in 1905. But Max was more than a carpenter. He was also a jack-of-all-trades, an indefatigable entrepreneur, and a perennial optimist. He worked on a cattle ranch in the Arizona Territory at the turn of the century and rushed to the scene of the San Francisco earthquake of 1907 hoping to find work as a builder. By 1910 Max had returned to Chicago to marry his Polish-born sweetheart. Their son Albert was born in 1912; three daughters followed in due course. With a growing family to support, Max tried his hand at the bakery business in Iowa and worked in a Philadelphia shipyard, but eventually he came back to Chicago to open a small general store.

During the building boom of the 1920s, Max sold the store to finance construction of a six-flat apartment building in Albany Park. In time he had built half a dozen more, all heavily mortgaged. When the Depression came, the appearance of prosperity went. "By 1930 the six-flat we owned in Albany Park had become a one-flat building," Al remembers. "That's because we were the only ones left living there. Everyone had moved out. It was lonesome!" Eventually, all of Max Robin's properties were foreclosed, and the family moved again. In 1931 Al Robin was attending the Lewis Institute (which later merged with the Armour Institute as the Illinois Institute of Technology) when his father decided to open a shoe store. Reluctantly, Al dropped out of school to run this new Robin enterprise. Just nineteen, he bought merchandise on credit from suppliers in St. Louis and set up shop in a storefront on Lawrence Avenue. When the chain stores undercut his prices, he had to liquidate. Robin recouped his father's investment, but he did not pay his creditors. As a minor, he could not be held responsible. "That's not the best story in the world," he says. "But it was a matter of life and death."

Al then had the idea of seeking his fortune in South America. He spent eight months in New Orleans, working in shoe stores and trying to get a berth on a freighter. "I wanted to get a boat, not just for the job but as a way to get a regular meal," he recalls. Discouraged, he returned to Chicago and fairly quickly found work managing real estate for the Alfred L. Miltenberg firm and knocking on doors seeking tenants for industrial space. He told Miltenberg that he was a married man. "I figured if I said I was married, I'd get a little more salary," Robin recalls. "Which I did. Got $40 a week. Good money. The girls caught on quickly that I wasn't married. But they never said anything." Robin was a resourceful salesman and too good at what he was doing to be satisfied for long working for someone else. In 1935 he rented a desk in a friend's small real estate office, printed up business cards, and opened the Robin Construction Company. His first job was that $125 fence.

His big break came during World War II when the Robin

company was hired by the Neisner Brothers department store chain to help with the modification of the heating systems of their buildings. Soon Robin found himself in demand by retailers for remodeling stores in Chicago and throughout the Midwest. In the process, Robin discovered his own talent as a designer and artist. Admittedly practicing architecture without a license, Robin began designing the storefronts himself and creating showcase window designs and backdrops.

After the war, with FHA financing available and the demand for housing critical, Robin began his development career, building a number of three- and five-story walk-ups in Chicago's West Rogers Park. These were followed by his first high-rise development: an eighteen-story apartment building at Lawrence and Clarendon avenues. In 1960 Robin began to focus his development activities on the luxury high-rise apartments that have become his trademark. The twenty-story Cornelia-Stratford Apartments at 555 Cornelia Avenue cemented Robin's long association with architects Louis Solomon and John Cordwell. A year later Robin and his investment partners announced plans for the twenty-eight-story Imperial Towers apartments at 4250 Marine Drive, designed by L. R. Solomon/ J. D. Cordwell and Associates (now Solomon, Cordwell, Buenz and Associates).

With Solomon and Cordwell deeply involved in the Sandburg Village development on the Near North Side after 1961, Robin began working with architect Martin Reinheimer and a succession of Reinheimer partners on other apartment tower developments. Plans for the Carlyle at 1040 North Lake Shore Drive were announced in the summer of 1964, with Hirshfeld, Pawlan, and Reinheimer as the architects. Overlooking Oak Street Beach and the Drake Hotel near the point where East Lake Shore Drive meets Michigan Avenue, the Carlyle was the first luxury condominium apartment tower to be built in Chicago. Robin and his family moved in, as did Arthur Rubloff—one of Robin's partners at the time in the Sandburg Village development. Work on the 448-unit Pine Point Plaza (now Lake Park Plaza) apartments, located at the southwest corner of Pine Grove Avenue and Irving Park Road and designed by Hirshfeld and Reinheimer, began in 1968. Robin's second luxury condominium apartment building, the Warwyck, at 1501 North State Parkway, was completed in 1974, but due to market conditions was not as successful as the Carlyle.

In all of these apartment developments, Robin let the full range of his imagination come into play, and he had a good time doing it. Each of the buildings was decorated around a theme, or "motif." Imperial Towers was Oriental. Pine Point

Plaza was given a South-of-the-Border decor. In planning the Carlyle, done in an English mode, Robin worked closely with the interior designers on the wood, fabrics, wall coverings, and fixtures. The layout was done in the Robin company workrooms on Wells Street. In planning Imperial Towers, Robin went to Japan and Hong Kong for the lobby furniture. He hired a Japanese architect to design the gardens and (improbably) found a Yugoslavian landscaper who specialized in Japanese gardens to maintain them.

A Near North Side urban renewal project for the area known as the North Clark–La Salle corridor had been a gleam in the eye of city planners since 1953. In 1958 the Chicago Land Clearance Commission made its first purchase in the area, a site bounded by La Salle Street on the west, Division Street on the south, North Avenue on the north, and the alley between Clark and Dearborn streets on the east. By 1961 land purchases, relocation, and clearance were almost complete, and developers were invited to submit bids for the sixteen acres offered for redevelopment. It was the beginning of what would later be judged one of the finest urban renewal developments in the country: Carl Sandburg Village.[1] Robin has a clear memory of the origins of the Sandburg project, and that memory does not include Arthur Rubloff, who would later claim that the development was his idea and his alone. Robin says that the plan originated with Lou Solomon, who brought the concept to Robin with the suggestion that the two of them put together a group of partners to submit a bid on the project. Robin suggested that Solomon bring in mortgage banker George Dovenmuehle as a partner, adding, as he recalls, the comment that he was "sure that Rubloff would also like to be involved in it." So that became the team: four general partners, each with a different field of expertise— Solo-

Sandburg Village [model]. In 1958 the Chicago Land Clearance Commission began the process of acquiring and clearing sixteen acres of decaying residential and commercial properties along what was called the North Clark–La Salle corridor. Three years later a development group that included Al Robin submitted the winning bid—based on this master plan by architect and former city planner John D. Cordwell—for redevelopment of the site as a middle- and upper-income residential complex.
[Lyal Lauth—Robin Construction Corp.]

Sandburg Village. Looking southeast from Schiller and La Salle, the six high-rise towers of Sandburg Village are seen surrounded at their base with groups of town houses and connected by landscaped courtyards and plazas. (Chicago Historical Society)

mon the architect, Robin the builder, Dovenmuehle the banker, and Rubloff the real estate broker and management agent. Solomon's partner John Cordwell, a former director of planning under Chicago mayors Martin Kennelly and Richard J. Daley, became master planner for the project.[2]

While Cordwell worked on the master plan, Robin and Solomon developed the formula they would apply to the bid they would make to the city for the land. Their offer for the sixteen-acre tract would be based on projected development costs of $40 million for the six twenty-seven-story high-rise apartment buildings and low-rise townhouse complexes they proposed. This was keyed to the estimated income from the 1,700 rental units then planned, with allowance for a ten percent return to the investors. "We worked it backwards," Robin says. "We knew what our costs should be, and so we knew what the highest price we could pay for the land would be and still make the ten percent profit based on a $40 to $42 a month rent per room." When Rubloff balked at the proposed price of $10 a square foot, the figure was lowered, more or less arbitrarily, to $9.17 a square foot. Even so, Robin recalls, the bid came in at a figure several hundred thousand dollars over that of the second highest bidder—and three times the figure anticipated by the Chicago Land Clearance Commission. Robin did not mind that. The partners were still getting their ten percent on the surplus. But Rubloff never forgot, and apparently never forgave it, even when the project sold some years later at a great profit.[3]

The relationship between Al Robin and Arthur Rubloff did not improve over time. Nonetheless, from the day in 1963 when the first tenants moved in, Carl Sandburg Village was regarded as a significant accomplishment from every point of view. From the city's perspective, it succeeded in preserving a historically and geographically significant Near North neighborhood for residential use. From the point of view of the Greater North Michigan Avenue Association, which had strongly supported redevelopment of the North Clark–La Salle corridor in the planning stages, it succeeded in protecting North Michigan Avenue and Gold Coast properties from blight encroaching by the back door. From an urban planner's point of view, it sparked, as was hoped, private redevelopment in the blocks between the Sandburg and the Loop and in surrounding neighborhoods.[4]

Al Robin began collecting art at about the same time that he began designing storefronts for the Neisner chain. His first purchase was a Jean Dubuffet that he bought in the late 1940s for $150. His collection today, numbering hundreds of pieces, includes works by such internationally renowned artists as Paul Klee, Juan Miro, and sculptor Abbott Pattison, and reflects a taste that has evolved from French Impressionism to American Pop and Op art. But it also includes the works of lesser known artists, including Robin himself, who studied painting with Chicago abstract painter Rudolph Weisenborn. (Weisenborn's ''The State Street Bridge'' hangs in the entrance to Robin's offices on Wells Street. Robin's own recent work, in crayon and ink—the medium he currently prefers—is more modestly displayed among the collection of dozens of works that fill the walls of the sprawling one-story Robin Construction office from floor to ceiling.) ''My collection is very eclectic,'' Robin explains. I buy what I like. Still, a lot of things that I bought have appreciated twenty times over.''

In recent years, Robin has shared his success through a number of philanthropies, including the scholarship fund and youth work that is of primary importance to him and his family. Still, the artistic talent that revealed itself in his department store windows, in the interior designs he created for his apartment towers, and in his own work as an abstract painter continues to surface. It is not surprising that in 1991, builder-developer-artist Al Robin would endow a new gallery of twentieth-century contemporary art at the Art Institute of Chicago and make a $1 million gift to the construction fund of the Chicago Museum of Contemporary Art.

AUTHOR'S COMMENTARY

1. Robin credits the advertising executive who helped the partners prepare their presentation to the city with the idea of naming the development for Chicago's most renowned

The Carlyle. The Carlyle, 1040 North Lake Shore Drive, which was built in 1965, was Chicago's first luxury condominium building.
[Lyal Lauth—Robin Construction Corp.]

poet. Carl Sandburg had lived in the area in the 1920s when he as a reporter for the *Daily News*, the period when he was writing the Windy City poems that celebrated Chicago as the "City of the Big Shoulders." Sandburg agreed to lend his name to the project, but did not accept the developers' offer to provide him an apartment, rent-free, for life.

2. Rubloff had a quite different version of how Sandburg Village originated, which he related to *Chicago* magazine reporter Iris Krasnow in 1981. When asked "What about your partners? Didn't they help?", Rubloff replied, "Well, originally, when I developed the plan, I didn't need anyone. But I thought I was very smart in asking these men to join me. I felt they were all experts in their various areas. But it didn't turn out that way. It would have been much better for me if I hadn't had any partners."

3. Toward the end of the Sandburg Village construction, I was asked to participate on the development committee of the Latin School of Chicago. I am an alumnus of the school and was at that time a Latin School parent. The school was mounting a fund-raising campaign to develop a new structure at Scott and Stone streets to replace the building that had housed the girls' Latin School of Chicago prior to the merger of the boys' and girls' schools. While attending development committee meetings, it became obvious to me that the group was going to have serious trouble in getting the fund-raising effort off the ground.

After puzzling for some months over how we might launch this campaign, an idea came to me while attending a Cook County Democratic dinner with city planning commissioner Lewis Hill as my guest. In the course of the evening, and while discussing a variety of real estate and planning issues affecting the city, the thought occurred to me that the Latin School might be better served by buying a site at the southeast corner of Clark Street and North Avenue that lay within the North Clark–La Salle redevelopment area. I estimated that the Scott and Stone streets property would generate between $1 million and $1.25 million and that the Clark Street site could be purchased for approximately $250,000, based on the price that the Solomon-Robin-Dovenmuehle-Rubloff group had paid for the adjacent Sandburg Village land.

I contacted Bill Fettridge, then president of the board of trustees of the Latin School, to discuss the concept. I was advised that a number of groups in the school would probably feel that the Clark Street site was undesirable, given the district's reputation—prior to the urban renewal project—as a run-down neighborhood known for its flop houses and bars. I couldn't let go of the idea, however, because it was so apparent to me that the fact of having a building site for the upper school in hand with $1 million already in the campaign fund would provide the impetus needed to raise the additional dollars needed to complete the building.

I met with Lew Hill again and we discussed how to approach the matter. At that time Arthur Rubloff was trying to acquire additional land at the north boundary of the Sandburg Village project, notably the Germania Club land on the west side of Clark Street at North Avenue. Hill and I reasoned that if Rubloff could be persuaded to present our idea to the Latin School community, two purposes would be served. Rubloff's sponsorship of the concept would eliminate any further claim that he might try to make on the southeast Clark and North Avenue site, while at the same time relocation of the Latin School would add appeal and desirability to the Sandburg development.

We worked out the following format: We went to Mayor Daley and suggested the idea to him. He found it more than acceptable. From there, the mayor contacted Rubloff, and the mayor and Rubloff then contacted members of the Latin School board of trustees, including Carl De Voe. De Voe to this day does not realize that it was Lew Hill and I who suggested to Mayor Daley, and in turn Arthur Rubloff, the idea of approaching the Latin School with the concept.

At any rate, with the strong endorsement of the mayor and Rubloff, the Latin School leadership reconsidered the site and eventually gratefully accepted the opportunity. I was by that time a member of the board of trustees of the school and its treasurer. De Voe and I negotiated the sale of the Scott and Stone streets site to Marshall Abraham, a well-known and active developer of high-rise buildings. We acquired the Clark Street site from the land clearance commission and had our first million dollars in the bank for the development of the new school building.

4. In recognizing Sandburg Village as a highly innovative and successful urban renewal project—which it was and is—observers tend to speak of the development as an entity in and of itself—born, so to speak, in a vacuum. It was not. Although there are instances in which communities have reclaimed large areas and initiated successful development, such occurrences are rare. An example might be some (but

by no means all) of the new towns, such as south suburban Park Forest, that were developed as totally planned communities after World War II. But these, I believe, were aberrations arising from a tremendous immediate need and demand at a given time and characterized by a relatively short development cycle. Although Park Forest in its time was a success, later attempts to create new towns have been economic and planning failures.

The North Clark–La Salle project and the subsequent success of Sandburg Village is an example of a perhaps less apparent reality: If planning is to be effective, it must respond to clear market indicators and market movements. The indicators were there in the case of the Sandburg site, and members of the city planning department were alert to the potential for movement in that area in terms of restoring traditional housing patterns to an unfortunately blighted area. Recovery of the Old Town Triangle district, just north of Sandburg Village, had begun as early as the 1930s, as a privately market-driven redevelopment led by a group of artists and intellectuals such as Paul Angle (who later became director of the Chicago Historical Society).

Imperial Towers. Developer Al Robin hired a Japanese architect to design the gardens at the 1961 Imperial Towers apartments at 4250 Marine Drive and then found a Yugoslavian landscaper who specialized in Japanese gardens to maintain them [Robin Construction Corp.]

Continued redevelopment in Old Town after World War II on a private, parcel-by-parcel basis signaled city planners of a movement under way. This awareness of a market trend dictated that something be done about the area of extreme blight that was developing along La Salle Street between Old Town and the Loop. Thus Sandburg Village became a target of opportunity for the city in the early 1950s.

I believe that the success of this redevelopment and the subsequent recovery of the Lincoln Park area east of Old Town provides proof that the most effective planning is done in concert with, and responsive to, free market conditions. Over the period that I served on the Chicago Plan Commission, some of us were prepared to recommend that the market-driven movement begun in Old Town, reinforced in Lincoln Park, and supported by the city's efforts to recover the North Clark–La Salle corridor between Old Town and Division Street through an urban renewal plan might have to be sustained with additional city redevelopment assistance south of Division. As we can now see, the need did not arise.

DESIGNS FOR LIVING

Daniel Levin

Daniel Levin.
[The Habitat Co.]

When Daniel Levin wanted a warmer look for appliances in the kitchens of his Lafayette Towers development in Detroit, he didn't wait for a new color to be developed. He went to the General Electric and Kelvinator companies and asked for it. Copper and gold, the popular colors of the early 1960s were too limiting, Levin felt. White was too sterile. He suggested ''almond,'' and Kelvinator came up with it. Almond-colored appliances quickly became the choice of decorators in kitchens all over America.

Dan Levin's creation of the color almond as a feature for Lafayette Towers is not a singular event in his career. Like many of his late-nineteenth-century counterparts, Levin is the type of developer who becomes intensely involved with the design details of his projects. He is also very productive, having built enough apartments in his career as a Chicago developer to house the population of a small city—well over 25,000 units since the early 1960s. In fact, some of Levin's developments, done with his partner James McHugh, are all but small cities in themselves. From the center of Chicago, McHugh Levin residential high rises can be seen in every direction: Columbus Plaza and the new Cityfront Place on the east and northeast; a host of first-class apartment towers on the Near North Side; the four Presidential Towers buildings on the west; and earlier developments, such as Long Grove House, on the south. The East Bank Club, a health and fitness facility developed by McHugh and Levin in 1980, has become a contemporary landmark in the River North district just north of the Loop.

When Levin earned an undergraduate degree from the University of Chicago in 1950 and a degree from the School of Law there in 1953, there was no doubt that he was on his way to a solid career in the legal profession. He would follow perhaps in the footsteps of his father, a federal district court judge, or even in the footsteps of his uncle, a U.S. senator. By 1954 he had been admitted to the bar in Michigan, Illinois, and the District of Columbia, but chose to return to Detroit, his hometown, to join the family law firm.

In 1956, when Herbert Greenwald landed a major urban renewal project in Detroit, Dan Levin discovered his own interest in development. Greenwald's Chicago partner, Samuel N. Katzin, was related to the Levin family by marriage, and when the Detroit project, Lafayette Park, was launched, the Levin firm took on some of the legal work. "I got interested in the planning, I got interested in the financing, and in the creativity that was involved with what was happening," Levin recalls. "I was impressed with Greenwald's drive and his determination to do things a certain way." Levin also became fascinated by the potential power of site planning to create communities. By 1957, when Greenwald asked him to move to Chicago and work with the Greenwald organization on other projects, Levin was ready. He had been tapped for Greenwald's personal brain trust, a loosely structured cadre of talented men who were at the time reinventing American high-rise residential development and moving rapidly to the forefront of urban planning.

The empire was shattered in 1959 when Greenwald died in an airplane crash. Greenwald had been involved in major urban redevelopment projects not only in Detroit but also in Newark, Brooklyn, and in Manhattan's Battery Park. The debt load at the time of his death was staggering. Levin became part of the legion of lawyers involved over a four-year period in refinancing and resolving the highly leveraged Greenwald estate. Bernard Weissbourd held together the core of the Greenwald team and completed projects then under way in Chicago and Newark under the umbrella of a new company, Metropolitan Structures. Levin took over the Lafayette Park development. "I wasn't financially part of the Metropolitan Structures setup, so I became just me," Levin recalls.

Lafayette Park, designed by Ludwig Mies van der Rohe and land planner Ludwig Hilberseimer, was a source of both pride and, ultimately, disappointment to Levin. Architecturally and from a planning perspective, it was a resounding success. On the financial side, the project was troubled from the beginning—shadowed by the deepening economic cloud over Detroit brought on by the movement out of the city of the au-

South Commons. This innovative residential complex was built along South Michigan Avenue between Twenty-sixth and Thirty-first streets between 1966 and 1972. [The Habitat Co.]

tomobile industries and their management personnel. "Mies's town houses were wonderful, but they were way over budget and there was no good market for them," Levin remembers. "We just had to go in and get them finished, get them sold, and to some extent manage them." Daniel Levin the lawyer had become a developer, with all the headaches and not many of the rewards. A man without a passion for development would have gone on to other things.

Lafayette Park brought Levin into a close working relationship with Greenwald's architect, the famed Mies van der Rohe. Levin was in his early thirties, just beginning his career as a developer. Mies was in his late seventies. The Lafayette Towers Apartments, the last phase of the Detroit project, was Mies's last residential design. Levin found Mies easy to work with, but had a sense that the Miesian "machines for living" were flawed. "There's no question that Mies's taste and his discipline were very important to me, but I accepted too much at that time as dogma." Levin says. "Mies was open to ideas, but I don't think I gave him as much direction as I would today. I accepted the rigidity of his geometry, which was then the ten-foot module: ten-foot bedrooms, twenty-foot living rooms, and very small kitchens and bathrooms. I sensed, from a marketing point of view, that this was just wrong. But I accepted it then. This was what Herb Greenwald thought was true, and I wasn't in a position to be sure it was wrong." Levin later learned to take another approach in his conferences with architects. If he disagrees with a design idea, he says "show me why your idea is right." If the architect cannot prove his point to Levin, Levin turns the question around to prove his point to the architect.

In the mid-1960s, urban renewal and housing projects insured by the Federal Housing Administration offered great opportunities for developers, in terms of both financing and the personal vision that a developer could bring to these large-scale projects. Although Levin had been disappointed by the failure of Lafayette Park to redeem Detroit's inner city, he was not discouraged. He had learned a lot from the development, and hoped to do the same thing—but better—in Chicago. Even while the Lafayette Towers project was under way, Levin, on his own, was seeking out urban renewal and FHA-insured housing projects in Chicago. He syndicated the purchase of a building at 5000 Cornell Avenue in Hyde Park, built a shopping center on the South Side, and entered into a temporary partnership to build ten-flat apartments in Evanston. It was at this time that architect John D. Black, a friend from college days in Hyde Park, introduced Levin to James McHugh, head of a real estate and construction firm founded in 1895 by McHugh's grandfather. McHugh was then building Lincoln Park Towers at 1960 Lincoln Park West, designed by Dubin, Dubin, Black and Moutoussamy. The three—Levin, McHugh, and Black—hit it off and eventually became "a little development team," Levin remembers.

South Commons, a thirty-acre urban renewal site on Michigan Avenue between Twenty-sixth and Thirty-first streets, was McHugh and Levin's first collaboration. The partners organized the Central South Development Company to bid on the project. As urban renewal land, the project had the benefit of FHA Section 223 financing. "For somebody without a lot of capital, it made sense," Levin recalls, explaining his decision to take on the commitment required in developing a proposal. More importantly, he says, "I was challenged by the planning opportunity of it." The site was severely blighted, ringed by some of the city's most intransigent slum neighborhoods.

Levin believed that the South Michigan Avenue location was a good one—close to the city and close to transportation—and that with enlightened planning, the South Commons development could succeed as an economically and racially integrated community.[1]

The developers went to John Cordwell (L. R. Solomon/J. D. Cordwell and Associates—now Solomon, Cordwell, and Buenz), the firm that was designing Sandburg Village, for advice on a development of the scale they contemplated. Cordwell introduced them to Ezra Gordon of Ezra Gordon/Jack Levin Associates, which became the lead architectural firm on the project—and which later designed many of McHugh and Levin's Near North Side apartment towers. Levin also brought in sociologists Morris Janowitz of the University of Chicago and Paul Mundy of Loyola University to advise on the planning features.

In Gordon, Levin found an architect who understood his own feelings about space. "Ezra Gordon happened to be somebody who thought very much in terms of human need, and he was not as rigid as Mies. He believed in having things in a sort of softer scale," Levin says. "I was very pleased with the first phase of South Commons. I felt it was going to be architecturally good—we really created a land-oriented environment." Between 1966 and 1972, more than fifteen hundred rental units and ninety privately owned town houses were built. Young, socially concerned, professional families abandoned the suburbs for new residences in South Commons. McHugh Levin Associates committed enormous energy to the project. They spearheaded an amendment to the National Housing Act (still known as the South Commons Amendment) that enabled them to build a shopping center and bring in a major supermarket chain as a prime tenant. They negotiated with the Chicago Board of Education to establish a primary school within the complex.

South Commons was an inner-city phenomenon, one that quickly attracted national media attention. *House Beautiful* magazine, in a 1971 feature article, described the development as "An Urban Reawakening." The families living there were dubbed "urban pioneers." Lewis Hill, director of the Chicago Department of Development and Planning, described South Commons in its early years as an ideal blend of building types, income levels, ages, and racial patterns. The *Christian Science Monitor*, in a full-page feature, heralded South Commons as "an inner-city success." The development was indeed a planning success, but as a social experiment it could not be sustained. The pressure of the depressed areas that surrounded the community ultimately dimmed the hopes of the early resi-

River Plaza. Located at 405 North Wabash, River Plaza dates from 1977.
[The Habitat Co.]

dents. Levin has since said, "Nothing was as complicated from a planning point of view. I really would have loved it to have been perfect."[2] With South Commons under way in 1966, McHugh Levin Associates began a series of projects with John Black as their architect. These included the Quadrangle House apartments at 6700 South Shore Drive, followed by Long Grove House at 2001 South Michigan Avenue. Long Grove House, which covered a full city block, was the largest single building to be financed under the National Housing Act. Levin handled the development side, including most of the interface with architects. Jim McHugh covered the construction arm of the business.[3]

If the late 1960s can be characterized as the years of the large South Side FHA developments for Levin and McHugh, the 1970s was the decade in which McHugh Levin Associates established themselves as major developers on Chicago's Gold Coast and in the emerging Near North Side residential neighborhoods.[4] In 1972 McHugh Levin, in partnership with John Baird and Warner G. Baird Jr., built 200 East Delaware, a thirty-five-story Gold Coast condominium. This project was followed immediately by the Newberry Plaza apartment and town-house development at 1030 North State Street, a project that remains one of Levin's own favorites. Elm Street Plaza, River Plaza, Huron Plaza, Columbus Plaza, and Asbury Plaza—all on the North Side—came next. In these developments, Levin refined and expressed in clear terms his evolving view of what constitutes livable space. He had long since lost his awe of the Miesian geometry. He discovered—often by their absence—design features that he considered to be both marketable and economically feasible. And he introduced these into his developments.

Levin's affable manner conceals a man of strong opinions who is uncompromising in his expectations. He is dogged and demanding about even the smallest components of his developments, to the extent that he has been perceived as difficult to work with. Differences between architects and developers are often characterized as a battle between the architect's concern for a building's appearance and the developer's concern with a building's cost. Levin is less inclined to see the conflict as a cost issue than as a matter of planning for livability. Here, Levin says, "The developer has to set the standard. I think architects often have a strong direction of what should be done with a piece of property. They are trained in terms of scale, and this kind of planning creativity is very useful to the developer." On the other hand, he believes, the developer may have a stronger feeling for design features that make an environment livable. In the Levin vocabulary, for example, kitchens and bathrooms are bigger than Mies would have allowed. Provide a place in the kitchen where people can sit down for a meal, Levin says. Add a foot more space to the bathroom, he insists, to allow for vanity walls. Place bedroom doors so that they are not visible from the entrance. Garages must be conveniently located for residents entering or leaving through the building lobby—front and back.

The East Bank Club story began in the late 1970s when Levin and McHugh secured an option on a large undeveloped property on the North Branch of the Chicago River, immediately northwest of the Merchandise Mart. No one now would question the value of that location, but at the time Levin acquired the option, the area was seen as not much more than a rundown warehouse district. Levin planned to put up two high-rise apartment towers connected by a small health club, similar to the fitness facilities included as amenities in other McHugh Levin apartment developments. When the developers found they could not get the conventional financing they sought for the project, they considered building housing for the elderly on the site. But the location, still considered to be "isolated" or possibly "dangerous," did not lend itself to senior housing either.

"We gave up trying to finance it and began to think about what else to do with this property," Levin remembers. "I started to think about whether there was something that was very dramatic that could be done with the health club concept—something that no one else had done." The idea he came up with was to combine a first-class sports center with a private club. "We started to plan the East Bank Club, and the ideas just got bigger and bigger," Levin recalls. Raising the equity to meet construction costs remained a problem. McHugh and Levin at the front end found themselves sinking more money into the project than they had planned. At that point, Levin says, "I just didn't want to give up the idea." The East Bank Club opened in 1980, with almost overnight acceptance, if not financial success. That came later.[5] Levin does not consider East Bank to be a "development" in the way that he thinks, for example, of South Commons. He does, however, admit that it is among his favorite projects. "East Bank continues to be the most satisfying because it's there, it's a business, and it has a life of its own," he mused. "It's become an institution in the community, and that's a lot of fun."

A project that has not been fun for Levin is the Presidential Towers complex, even though nowhere else is Levin's consciousness of the relation of structure to site more visible than in these four, forty-nine-story apartment monoliths. Designed by Solomon, Cordwell, and Buenz, and set at an unexpected angle to the grid system of the city's streets, Presidential Towers has created a striking new skyline for the western gateway to Chicago. The two-square-block, 2,400-unit development, at the intersection of Madison and Canal streets, was built on the hope and the promise of an emerging residential commu-

East Bank Club. This fitness facilities complex is situated on the Chicago River at the Kinzie Street Bridge. Sunning on the roof of the club, opened in 1980, is a popular—and sociable—pastime for some Chicagoans.
[The Habitat Co.]

nity in the West Loop—"The City of Tomorrow," the Chicago *Tribune* predicted. However, Presidential Towers has become—for the present at least—a symbol of the failure a well-intentioned effort on the part of the city and private development interests.[6]

McHugh Levin, in partnership with Dan Shannon Associates, acquired the Presidential Towers site in a contract with the city in the early 1980s, but was not able to begin construction until 1985, when the City of Chicago offered $180 million in tax-exempt mortgage bonds for interim financing, backed by a $159 million FHA mortgage insurance commitment. Although the complex was 90 percent occupied in 1990, Presidential Towers was in financial difficulty. As of this writing, the project was in default, and the developers were seeking a financial restructuring with the U.S. Department of Housing and Urban Development.

Reflecting on the successes as well as the adversities of a prolific career, Levin says he cannot imagine himself in any other line of work. "I do it because I am intrigued by all these things that are complicated. If I had really wanted to make money, I probably would have been in a different aspect of the real es-

Presidential Towers. The four monoliths of the Presidential Towers apartment complex, completed in 1985, have given the Near West Side a new skyline.
[Hedrich-Blessing]

tate business. Such as trailer parks, or maybe just putting up a little warehouse and selling it. There's nothing wrong with that. It's a perfectly honorable business. But for me, that's all it would be—just a business.''

AUTHOR'S COMMENTARY

1. The city had designated a thirty-acre South Michigan Avenue site as an urban renewal area in the early 1960s, and by the time the land had been cleared, competition for the project was keen. Some were surprised when the contract was awarded to the group organized by Dan Levin and Jim McHugh. Levin, who represented the development side of

the group, was a relative newcomer to the Chicago real estate and development community. Better-known firms might have been favored for the job. Dan himself believes his group's site plan, with its combination of high-rise, low-rise, and town-house development, was a deciding factor in the bidding war. I think that Levin's commitment to creating a racially integrated community may also have been a factor. His South Commons plan was consistent with the political objectives at that time of the Chicago Department of Urban Renewal, which had been stung by criticism that earlier projects amounted to relocation plans. The South Commons proposal reached out to middle-income families while at the same time offering housing for former residents of the urban renewal land. The family-oriented town houses at the higher end of the scale, for example, were built for sale; the federal 221(d)(3) housing program supported rent subsidies for lower-income families.

2. South Commons is an example of a very well planned and executed project that could not overcome the deficiencies of its location. By the late 1970s, the racial mix of the early years of the development—70 percent white and 30 percent black and other minorities—had reversed itself. As hope for community integration in South Commons collapsed, so did the value of the developers' investment. South Commons, like Levin's Lafayette Park development in Detroit, could not be made profitable. Levin seems not to regret the financial losses nearly so much as he regrets the failure of the dream.

3. These South Side projects are memorable to me for many reasons, not the least of them being that Levin developments in that period so often drew community activists to Chicago Plan Commission meetings—some for, some against, some who didn't know whether they were for or against but who had been provided with a T-shirt and a coach in the front row.

4. McHugh Levin residential developments were under way throughout the city in the 1970s, but the company was not yet involved in property management. John Baird and Baird and Warner had been the leasing agent on Levin's early projects. When the large South Commons, Quadrangle House, and Long Grove House developments came on line, the Baird and Warner firm became leasing and management agents. I remember a number of conversations with Levin in these years when I suggested that he develop

his own management company. I believed, given the number of units he controlled, that he had the potential for a significant profit center, or at least the ability to offset a great deal of his development overhead, by managing the properties he developed. McHugh Levin's decision in 1970 to create The Habitat Company may have been influenced by these discussions.

5. Dan Levin apparently took my advice when I suggested in 1970 that he manage his own developments, and I should have taken his in 1980. I was offered an opportunity to invest at the beginning in the East Bank Club. With customary reserve, I declined the opportunity. This unusual project was a success, although only after some rocky first years. The original East Bank investors, the writer not included, have been well rewarded.

6. The West Loop property, known as the Madison-Canal Project, was identified by the city as its first downtown urban renewal project, preceding even Sandburg Village. It involved the acquisition and clearance over a period of two decades of blocks along Madison Street west of the river that had become a skid row district of deteriorating residential hotels and industrial properties. The expectation was that the land would be sold, without a write-down, for a class of development that would provide a new entry point to the city. To that end, the city entered into a contract to transfer a portion of the property to a development group headed by Kemmons Wilson, founder of Holiday Inns of America; his partner Wallace Johnson; and Charles Swibel, then chairman of the Chicago Housing Authority. Their proposal was to erect two tall office buildings on the site. As it turned out, this group was not able to put together the development package, and did not complete the transaction. The two blocks on Madison between Desplaines and Clinton streets, where Presidential Plaza now stands, were subsequently sold to McHugh Levin; the federal government acquired the block on the north side of Madison between Desplaines and Jefferson as the site for the new General Services Administration (Social Security) building. A third portion of the property had been sold earlier to Tishman Speyer Properties for the development of 10 South Riverside Plaza.

Frederick Henry Prince.
[From the *National Cyclopedia of American Biography*—The Newberry Library]

Marshall Bennett.
[Jim Kahnweiler—Marshall Bennett Enterprises]

BUSINESS AND INDUSTRIAL PARKS

Frederick Henry Prince (1859-1953)
Marshall Bennett
Louis Kahnweiler

Few would argue Chicago's place in the creation of the modern office tower, high-rise residential apartments, and multiuse megadevelopments. A fact less often recognized, but of no less importance to the development history and economic life of the city, is that Chicago also introduced to America the concept of an organized industrial district—the forerunner to today's business and industrial parks.

The industrial district concept originated at the turn of the century when Boston banker Frederick Henry Prince, an investor in the group that bought the Chicago Union Stock Yards Company in 1890, recognized that the small spur rail line—the Chicago Junction Railway—that circled the yards as a service line was definitely underused. Revenues could be increased and the economies of running with full carloads could be realized, Prince reasoned, if industries in addition to the packing houses could be found to use the stockyards' beltline railway as a transfer line. The potential was clear. Although this was a railroad that went nowhere, it nonetheless was connected, like the hub of a wheel, to every major rail line entering and leaving Chicago. The problem was that, other than cabbage farming and, predictably, a sauerkraut factory, there were no other industries to speak of in the neighborhood. Prince's solution was to bring the mountain to Muhammad. In 1902 a syndicate to which Prince was a party began the purchase of 265 acres of farmland in the area known as the "Cabbage Patch" immediately north of the stockyards. (The tract ultimately was bounded by Thirty-fifth and Thirty-ninth streets and Ashland Avenue and Morgan Street.) The partners named the property the Central Manufacturing District (CMD), an apt reference to the fact that the land lay at the exact geographical center of the city. They established a board of trustees to oversee the management of district's newly acquired real estate.[1]

In the beginning, the trustees' principal interest was in selling or leasing parcels of CMD land to industries that would locate there and subsequently use the services of the Chicago Junction Railway. In 1905 the CMD, under Prince's leadership, took the plan a step further to become a developer of industrial real estate. The idea was to create not only business for the railroad but at the same time build a profitable community of diverse industries on properties developed specifically to serve this class of tenants. It was an altogether new concept. In implementing the idea, Frederick Prince created the model for the modern industrial park. The CMD offered expertly designed industrial sites on a variety of terms, including outright purchase, a contract for purchase arrangement, or a long-term lease. By this means, and by making both land and construction financing available on favorable terms, the CMD quickly drew a broad mix of new manufacturing interests to the district—all provided with a range of services that for decades would make the CMD a leader among industrial centers.[2]

In 1915 the CMD purchased a second development site on Thirty-ninth Street (now Pershing Road) extending westward from Ashland Avenue and launched a massive construction and improvement program that included development of a mile-long procession of general-purpose six-story warehouse and loft buildings that were available for government use during World War I.[3] All of the buildings were designed by CMD architect J. Scott Joy, who introduced a unified and aesthetically pleasing master plan for the complex that nonetheless offered tenants maximum flexibility in arranging interior space. His formula has remained a standard for industrial park development for some seventy-five years. In 1919 the CMD expanded again, adding another ninety acres bordered by Forty-seventh and Forty-ninth streets and by Kedzie and Central Park avenues. The CMD doubled its land holdings in 1931 by adding the 400-acre Crawford development site west of the Kedzie development.

Frederick Prince managed CMD operations through its first two decades and continued to serve as one of two district trustees from 1924 until his death in 1953.[4] In this period he nurtured the district's hundreds of resident industries through the dark days of the Depression (only one succumbed to bankruptcy) and the disruptions of World War II, when the CMD again turned the Pershing Road warehouses over to the U.S. Army. Prince lived to see the beginning of the postwar recovery and the explosive growth in light industry and manufacturing that made the industrial park concept pioneered by the CMD a mainstay of the American scene. Considering the legacy of the CMD, it is hardly surprising that Centex Industrial Park, one of the best- planned and best-located of America's postwar industrial parks (and the largest of its time) would be developed in a northwest Chicago suburb.

Marshall Bennett, who is numbered among the most productive corporate and industrial real estate developers of the postwar period, is fully aware of the economic significance of the 2,500-acre Centex complex, which lies between Elk Grove Village and Chicago's O'Hare Airport. It is a virtual city consisting of light-industrial and high-tech enterprises employing 40,000 to 50,000 people that are housed in some 1,500 architecturally compatible buildings and spread over an area of almost four square miles. Centex and the twenty-five other industrial parks that Bennett has built throughout the country seem in retrospect a surprising body of work for a man who in 1941 was preparing for a civil service career in the field of psychometrics. In fact, both pursuits grew out of Bennett's accurate reading of the economic climate of the times.

Marshall Bennett was born on Chicago's South Side in 1921 and raised in Hyde Park, where his father worked as a store fixtures salesman—a business that all but evaporated during the Depression. As an undergraduate at the University of Chicago in 1938, Bennett brooded over his future. Jobs were scarce to nonexistent. A professor suggested a sure-fire career strategy. No matter how bad the economy gets, the government will always be hiring, he said. Get into government administration as a specialist in personnel testing programs, he advised. You'll have a safe berth, and you can rise fast in civil service. But World War II intervened. Bennett enlisted in the U.S. Navy immediately after the attack on Pearl Harbor. He found that duty on a submarine chaser in the Aleutian Islands was not

Central Manufacturing District Pershing Road Headquarters, c. 1950. The Central Manufacturing District, founded by Frederick Henry Prince, turned its Pershing Road warehouses over to the U.S. government during World War I and again during World War II. The easternmost of these buildings is now the administrative center for Chicago Public Schools.
[Chicago Historical Society]

congenial to his efforts to complete his master's thesis in psychometrics, but he did organize a shipboard Great Books of the Western World study group based on his work at the University of Chicago with Mortimer Adler and Robert Hutchins.

Discharged with the rank of lieutenant at the end of the war, Bennett decided he had had enough of government service. He enrolled in the M.B.A. program at the Wharton School of Business and Finance in Philadelphia, confident now that opportunities in the private sector would emerge. But he was impatient to get going, and soon returned to Chicago to launch a serious job search while continuing his graduate studies in business at night at the University of Chicago.

Bennett discovered corporate and industrial real estate development on the way to looking for another career. Over lunch one day, he asked a longtime friend, Louis Kahnweiler, how he might go about getting in to see presidents of large firms so that he could present his credentials in person. Kahnweiler, who was then making his own transition from law school to a career as a broker in industrial real estate, suggested, "Sell them their factories, and you'll get to know them on a very personal basis." The idea paid off, but not in precisely the way Bennett intended. He discovered that he was intrigued with the field of industrial real estate itself. He found a position with Hart and Whetson, specialists in the field, and continued his lunch meetings with Kahnweiler. They formed a partnership of their own, which in 1949 became the firm of Bennett and Kahnweiler.

Bennett had entered the field at a promising time. He caught a wave. The growth of organized industrial districts on the periphery of urban areas would become one of the most significant characteristics of the suburbanization of America in the years following World War II. Just as Frederick Prince had seen the future for industrial development around the Chicago Junction Railway, Bennett saw the strategic advantages for light industry in the area northwest of Chicago where the new O'Hare International Airport was to be built. In the early years of their partnership, Bennett and Kahnweiler bought pieces of vacant land, often with other financial partners, developed them for industrial use, and leased the properties. Kahnweiler handled the brokerage side of the business, and Bennett was the developer. In 1954 Bennett and Kahnweiler developed their first comprehensively planned industrial district, the O'Hare Industrial Park, east of the airport site. They also began looking for more land in the area.

Just as Bennett had come upon industrial real estate while looking for something else, he discovered the Centex (for Central Texas) Construction Company while looking for a town willing to annex a property that the partnership had acquired north of the airport. The principal business of Centex Construction (later called the Centex Corporation) was home building. Owned by the Murchison brothers of Dallas, Centex had come into Illinois on a government contract to build housing at Great Lakes Naval Air Station. After the Great Lakes project, Centex set out to acquire, piece by piece, extensive acreage in Cook and Du Page counties, northwest of Chicago, as a site for the residential community that is now Elk Grove Village. Centex was not interested in the unincorporated land Bennett offered. "We have plenty of our own," they said. But Bennett was very much interested in the possibilities for the largely rural properties being acquired by Centex and bridging the two-mile area between the planned residential development and the new airport. "They didn't even realize what they had," Bennett recalls. "They had a hell of a good piece of property for an industrial park."

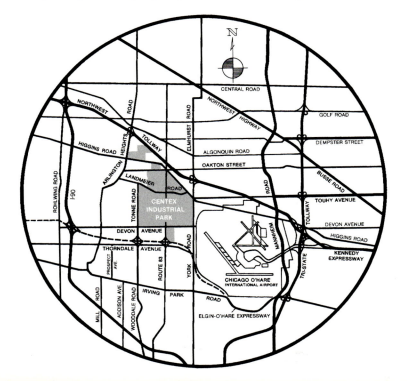

Centex Industrial Park (area map). The 2,500-acre Centex Industrial Park complex, one of the best-planned and best-located of America's postwar industrial parks, was strategically placed adjacent to O'Hare International Airport and is served by major expressways.
[Bennett and Kahnweiler]

Chicago after World War II was the virtual center of the Midwest manufacturing belt and a major node of the nation's rail, highway, and air transportation network. All these elements converged in the vacant Centex tract: The new Northwest (now Kennedy) Expressway, two major railways, and the largest commercial airport in the world were at its doorstep. Chicago's port facilities in the Calumet region were accessible by truck. Whereas Prince's Central Manufacturing District had been linked to the major rail lines, the Centex property, for all practical purposes, was linked to the entirety of the nation's transportation system. Bennett went back to Centex and offered to develop the property for light industry. His strategy was to bring together two large, family-held investment interests: Chicago's Pritzker family and the Texas-based Murchison brothers. It was a brilliant match, both from the standpoint of financing and in the creation of a model for suburban development. Centex Industrial Park happily married the construction of a totally planned residential community with the simultaneous development of an industrial tax base to support city services.

Bennett had known Jay Pritzker, the eldest of the three sons of Chicago businessman Abram Nicholas ("A. N.") Pritzker, since high school days. While Marshall Bennett was serving on his submarine chaser during World War II, Jay Pritzker was a naval aviator. In 1953, when Bennett and Kahnweiler were developing their first industrial park, Jay Pritzker and his brother Robert were forming the Marmon Group, a new cornerstone for the family's far-ranging financial interests.

Pritzker investment in a Bennett and Kahnweiler industrial development of the Centex land was a natural. Clint Murchison apparently agreed. Murchison came to Chicago at Bennett's invitation, met with Jay Pritzker and his uncle Jack Pritzker, and heard Bennett's ideas for the park. "Within half an hour we had cut a deal," Bennett says. But there were second thoughts. The Murchisons had also talked with Chicago broker and developer Arthur Rubloff. A week after the Pritzker-Murchison agreement was sealed, Bennett received the first of what would be many anxious calls from A. N. Pritzker. "He used to call me at two or three in the morning to say 'I can't sleep. How are you doing?'" Rubloff had gotten to A. N. Pritzker and tried to persuade him that the Centex industrial development project was "a lousy deal," Bennett recalls.[5] At the other end of the phone, Bennett would say genially, "Cut it out, Abe. Leave me alone!" Three years later, at a luncheon to celebrate the success of Centex as a major Illinois economic development that was attended by the governor and a constellation of other dignitaries, Pritzker showed a change of heart. "Do you remember," he asked Bennett, "when we started how you used to worry about this thing?"

Bennett himself was not as confident about the project as he pretended to be. "The biggest development I had done was forty acres. Here I saw 675 acres, and I said, 'My God! What am I going to do with it?'" He need not have worried. His instinct for the market and the site was right. "In the first year, it was hard making sales, but the second year was easy, and in the third year, we were deluged," Bennett remembers. The size of the development ultimately quadrupled. "At one point," Bennett recalled, "we were having as many as nine ground breakings a day."

Bennett and Kahnweiler went on develop other state-of-the-art industrial and office parks in Denver, St. Louis, Milwaukee, San Francisco, Atlanta, Southern California, and elsewhere in Chicago. In round numbers, their projects totaled more than 5,000 acres—an area nearly twelve times that of Chicago's central business district. In 1979 Bennett was named Man of the Year by the National Association of Industrial/ Office Parks.

In 1977, Bennett's life had taken an unexpected turn. An avid outdoorsman, he suffered severe head injuries in a kayak accident on the Middle Fork of the treacherous Salmon River in Idaho. He survived four surgeries, but slipped into a deep coma. "No one expected me to come out of it, but I did," Bennett says. "Fooled everybody, including myself." His two-year convalescence included months of exhausting physical therapy. Fully recovered in 1980, Bennett had no intention of retiring, as might well have been expected. He launched another business.

Kahnweiler was by then engaged almost exclusively in brokerage, but Bennett still had development in his blood. The two amicably ended their partnership, and Bennett established Marshall Bennett Enterprises. The firm's specialty has been leasing and development and has included joint venture projects with Miller-Klutznick-Davis-Gray in Boston and in Texas, and redevelopment projects on Chicago's West Side. It is clear that Bennett's kayak accident sapped none of his crackling high energy and persistent good humor. Nor did it dim his passion for outdoor sports. Bennett is back to form as a top-flight skier and is an avid hiker and cyclist. He is a popular figure in Sun Valley, Idaho, where he has a home. People there recognize Marshall Bennett: He's the fellow out there on the slopes in the black crash helmet.[6]

Bennett's heritage—like so many other Chicagoans of his generation, including the Pritzker family—is rooted in the Russian Jewish emigrations of the late nineteenth and early

Planning for Centex Industrial Park. This photo, reproduced from a two-page spread in a Bennett and Kahnweiler portfolio published in the 1960s, groups the key planners of the Centex Industrial Park development in front of one of their modern low-rise industrial buildings. They are [from left] Chicago investor Jack N. Pritzker; Centex chairman Clint Murchison Jr.; developer Marshall Bennett; Frank Crossen, president of the Centex Corporation; and developer-broker Lou Kahnweiler.
[Bennett and Kahnweiler]

twentieth centuries. It is a tradition that he supports with time, talent, and money, including service as a founding director of the Albert Einstein Peace Prize Foundation and a director of the Weizmann Institute in Rehovot, Israel.

Marshall Bennett's contribution to industrial warehouse and business park development springs from a talent for spotting the need for new types of development and tailoring that opportunity to meet rapidly changing geographic and economic conditions. This is a kind of vision that Bennett shares with other highly creative industrial developers who have followed his lead: Men such as William Alter, Milton Podolsky, Ronald Berger, Joseph S. Beale, and others have expanded the concept of the industrial park to the business park, which includes warehouse, office, and high-tech buildings as well as amenities such as hotels, day-care centers, and health clubs. In many respects, Marshall Bennett's success is attributable also to his ability to maintain business and personal relationships with investors such as Chicago's Crown family, the Pritzkers, and Martin Davis from Denver, and to skillfully put together the powerful financial partnerships (such as the Murchison-Pritzker collaboration) that make large-scale industrial park development possible.

Industrial real estate development is not a glamorous field. Generally, it doesn't change the skyline. The outcome of good industrial development is measured in other ways—as a major contributor to the economic health of a city and to the vitality of an entire metropolitan area. Most Chicagoans will never physically see the work of developers such as Frederick Henry Prince and Marshall Bennett. Visitors are not likely to include Centex Industrial Park on a tour of Chicago and its environs. But all experience the results that these developments bring to the everyday life of the city and its suburbs.

AUTHOR'S COMMENTARY

1. John A. Spoor, who had been president of the Chicago Junction Railway and was responsible for many improvements in the infrastructure in 1896, was named a trustee of the Central Manufacturing District, together with another stockyard executive, Frederick S. Winston. Spoor was then president of the Union Stock Yard and Transit Company. Winston would be succeeded in 1909 by Arthur G. Leonard, who had followed John B. Sherman as the general manager of the yards. As founder of the CMD and chairman of the board of the Union Stock Yard and Transit Company, Prince was in charge of all operations.

2. Each site was served by a switch track from the Chicago Junction Railway. Streets and drainage systems were developed, utilities were provided, and landscaping and street lighting were introduced. In 1912 the CMD built its own district office building at 1118 West Thirty-fifth Street, opened the Central Manufacturing District Bank, and built a CMD Club, where district tenants could meet for lunch. The district employed its own security forces and had a district surgeon who visited plants to lecture on industrial safety. A Western Union office, central switchboard, and a traffic bureau were added when the second phase of development began.

   In the strictest sense, the CMD was not the first industrial community in the Chicago area. That distinction would have to be given to Pullman, the manufacturing and residential complex created by George M. Pullman on the shores of Lake Calumet to house the single-industry Pullman railroad car works and its employees. Nor was it necessarily the first industrial district. The Clearing Industrial District established in 1898 by the Belt Railway at Sixty-fifth Street and Central Avenue fell within that category. Clearing, however, did not develop into an organized industrial enclave until World War I—long after the CMD had established itself as an enduring model for the comprehensively planned and masterfully serviced industrial community of the future.

3. When the United States entered World War I, the Commissary Department of the U.S. Army (later renamed the Quartermaster Corps) took over most of the warehouse space in the Pershing Road development as headquarters for provisioning American troops. The buildings first occupied by the army are now the central office headquarters of the Chicago Public Schools. Other tenants in the com-

Louis S. Kahnweiler. Lou Kahnweiler, right, discusses Centex developments with Jay Pritzker, chairman of the Hyatt Corporation, in the late 1950s.
[Bennett and Kahnweiler]

plex were the Montgomery Ward and Spiegel warehouses and the United States Cold Storage Company, which was built for the government.

4. In 1946 William Wood Prince, a distant cousin adopted by Prince in 1944, became a trustee. He later was named president of the Union Stock Yard and Transit Company and served as president of Armour and Company. Today the CMD Corporation, privately held by F. H. Prince and Company, is in its fourth generation of family management.

5. Marshall Bennett was not the only developer in these days who had to deal with Arthur Rubloff's meddling. Al Robin, who had had an uneasy partnership with Rubloff in the development of Carl Sandburg Village, tells the story of how Rubloff did him out of the construction contract for a shopping center planned for development on urban renewal land. Robin Construction Company, one of two firms competing for the project, had been awarded the bid. At the land clearance commission meeting at which the announcement was to be made, Rubloff rose to address the assembly with a suggestion of his own. Mr. Al Robin, Rubloff advised, should withdraw his bid in favor of the other firm—which happened to be minority owned. It would only be the right thing to do, Rubloff argued. "That threw the meeting into a real tizzy," Robin recalled in telling me the story. This was the first anyone had heard of the idea, but once raised, the matter became politically sensitive. To spare Mayor Richard J. Daley any embarrassment, Robin backed away from the project. He also fired off a letter to Rubloff (addressed to "Dear Arthur, old pal, old buddy," a favorite phrase of Arthur's), telling him what he thought of Rubloff's antics. Robin never again communicated directly with Rubloff.

6. Marshall Bennett's accident had a result that Bennett does not mention, one that affects many lives: the establishment of the Arlene and Marshall Bennett Chair in Neurosurgery at Evanston Hospital and the Bennett Research Laboratory in Adolescent Psychiatry at Humana–Michael Reese Hospital. Bennett also serves as a member of the board of governors of the University of Chicago Hospitals, as a trustee of the Brain Research Foundation, and as chairman of the Magnetic Resonance Imagery Center Fund Drive at the University of Chicago.

Marvin Romanek.
[Lynn Romanek Holstein]

IMAGINATION PLUS

Marvin Romanek
Eugene Golub

Eugene Golub.
[Art Wise—Golub + Co.]

When Marvin Romanek decided to try his hand at real estate development in the late 1950s, he had sense enough not to quit his job as an analyst at the Petroleum Gas Association. Eugene Golub, who then made his living manufacturing hats, was equally cautious when he agreed to help Romanek manage his first buildings. Golub continued to tend to the hat business during the day, while he tended the furnaces at night. In this sense, Romanek and Golub were not so very different from hundreds of other entrepreneurial types who caught real estate fever in the postwar years and during the seemingly boundless and bountiful construction boom of the 1950s and early 1960s. But over the long run, they *were* different. While others dabbled in development and dreamed get-rich-quick dreams, Romanek and Golub went into real estate with a passion. It was a precarious business and they stayed with it, through some very lean times—and some good times. In 1981 the former petroleum analyst and the sometime hat maker ranked among the top ten builders and developers in Chicago.

Marvin Romanek and Eugene Golub were both born in 1930 and raised in the neighborhood around Eighteenth

Street and Lawndale Avenue that Golub remembers as "the Jewish ghetto in Chicago." South Lawndale, he says, was a place where a boy growing up during the Depression and war years either "came out a hero or wound up in jail." Gene Golub was the only child of an American-born mother whose family roots were in Riga, Latvia, and a Russian immigrant father who found work in Chicago in the 1920s as an installment collector. "My dad was a pretty sharp guy," Golub recalls. "He didn't have a lot of education. He had native instincts." Good instincts honed with street smarts were traits passed on from father to son. "I had a wayward youth," Golub says with a smile. "There was a time in my life when I would play cards every afternoon on the corner in front of a candy store on Sixteenth Street. I was a hustler. Always out there hustling!" Gene was in his first year at Roosevelt University and anticipating a call from his draft board when his father died at age forty-six. Left as the sole support of the family, Gene dropped out of school and, in his words, "got into business." "I was in action," he says. "Even at a very young age. I never worked for anyone. The only job I ever really had was a job in high school selling shoes." The "action" for Golub in the 1950s including selling used cars, setting up going-out-of-business sales, and eventually going into the hat business with a Lebanese partner.

Marvin Romanek, meanwhile, went on to the University of Illinois. By 1959 he was at the gas association and working as a contributing editor for *Chemical Weekly* and *National Petroleum Gas News*. Although their lives had taken different directions since grammar school days, Golub and Romanek had stayed in touch. Romanek's interest in real estate was piqued, Golub recalls, at a family gathering in the late 1950s when Gene introduced Marvin to his neighbor Ernest Greenberger. Greenberger, a lawyer, had clients looking for a development project to invest in. Although Romanek knew more at the time about petroleum than about real estate, he promised Greenberger that he would keep an eye open for an investment opportunity.

As events unfolded, Romanek continued to work with Greenberger, who became his attorney, but ended up developing his own building and finding his own investors. The project took two years to get off the ground. But the resultant seventeen-story apartment building at 1440 North State Parkway, located at the corner of North State Parkway and Schiller Street in Chicago's Gold Coast neighborhood, turned out to be a good building in a very good location.[1] "Marvin did the entire development process from scratch—through the whole process of getting investors, architects, financing—and he was

Italian Court. The twenty-seven-story 625 North Michigan Avenue building, at the southwest corner of Ontario Street and Michigan Avenue, was built on the site of the old Italian Court, a complex of upscale shops, offices, and studios designed in 1919 by Robert DeGolyer. [Chicago Historical Society]

able to put an apartment building together," Golub recalls. "How he did it, I don't know, but he did it!"[2]

Romanek's next project was the twenty-three-story 25 East Chestnut Apartments, completed in 1963. Gene Golub at this time was spending more and more time at the job site with Romanek, and the two discussed the projects far into the evening. "I was getting an education through Marvin while he was doing this. You get a feel for it," Golub has said. Golub also began studying for his broker's license. In 1961 the first Romanek and Golub partnership, called Parkview Management, was formed. At this time Romanek was masterminding the development side of the business while Golub, in his own words, "did everything else."[3] "Marvin was extremely bright, extremely focused. When he got onto something, he would not let go—which is very, very significant in the development business," Golub says. "He had a terrific sense of finance, a terrific sense of layout. And he had a great style about him. He understood carpentry and how things are put together." Golub, a born salesman, excelled in the marketing and brokerage side of the business.

The development partnership hit its stride in the mid-1960s with the construction of Harbor House, an apartment complex at 3200 North Lake Shore Drive. When Romanek offered Golub a chance to become a partner in the purchase of the land, Golub withdrew the cash he had saved for a down payment on a house and put it up as his stake in the project. His wife was dismayed, but Golub was firm. "I'm going into this deal with Marvin. We're going to buy this land and build this building," he declared. Harbor House, with three towers overlooking Belmont Harbor, was a difficult project, Golub recalls. Money was tight in the mid-1960s, and the sellers had driven a hard bargain on the land. "We probably weren't very sophisticated then," Golub admits. "We were financing here, financing there, selling stuff. But we got it built and leased up." The major part of the equity was provided by the Crown family of Chicago. Harbor House was completed in 1967, and in time became a very successful property. While it was under construction, Romanek-Golub and Company bought the vacant International Harvester Building at 180 North Michigan Avenue and converted it into a commercial office building. Finding financing in those days for a rehab project could not have been easy. "We took the attitude that this was a half-finished building as opposed to a half-empty building," Golub said. It worked. The financing was from Teachers Insurance and Annuity Association of America.

Romanek and Golub were definitely "in action" in the downtown real estate business in the years between 1965 and 1975. They were juggling a lot of balls. They bought and sold property, including the former Blair Building at 645 North Michigan and a shopping plaza in south suburban Flossmoor, and attempted to buy other properties, including 500 North Michigan Avenue. They ventured, with less success, into suburban town-house development, and pursued, with even less success, an idea of turning the old Hampshire House Hotel, at 201 East Delaware Street (then being used as a nurses' residence) into a stylish "boutique" hotel. The Raphael Hotel, as it was named, turned out to be a seven-figure disaster. "We didn't know what we were doing," Golub says. In reality, they probably did know what they were doing. As it turned out, the concept of a small, all-suite hotel was valid; it was just ahead of its time.

To keep things going, Golub often put together financing packages and investment partnerships for other developers, for a fee. Asked how often in the early 1970s the company was on the brink financially, Golub replied, ''All the time! Our profile was being out there, being active. We were young, we were appealing, we had a good line of chatter. We knew how to talk, and we knew how to dress, and we had a style about ourselves.'' Golub describes himself in this period as ''something of a rainmaker,'' getting people to the table and bringing in investors for the development projects. ''Relationships were the way we did deals,'' Romanek noted in a 1991 Chicago *Tribune* interview. ''If we had an idea, we'd call up Continental Bank and talk to a real person who knew us. He'd tell us he'd kick it around and later that day he'd call us back with the OK.''[4] The partners also impressed the First National Bank of Chicago with their can-do style and subsequently formed a solid relationship with the bank, including significant support over the years from Gaylord Freeman and Dick Willer. Romanek-Golub and Company engineered the complex land acquisition leading to construction of the Three First National Plaza building on Madison Street between Clark and Dearborn streets north of the new First National headquarters building. At the same time, Romanek was working on acquiring the companion block south of First National Plaza for another office tower and plaza development.

Romanek-Golub's own first office development was 625 North Michigan Avenue—a project they launched a full two years before the John Hancock Center established that highrise development was Upper Michigan Avenue's destiny. The site was the southeast corner of Michigan and Ontario Street, then occupied by the vintage Italian Court Building.[5] The 625 North Michigan building was characteristic of Romanek and Golub's style in the early days. The project was imaginative, speculative, and pulled together on a shoestring. In late 1967 the real estate press announced the plans for the $14 million, twenty-seven-story office tower, citing the $10.5 million loan negotiated by Heitman Mortgage Company through Teachers Insurance and Annuity. The rest of the story is that Romanek and Golub had bought the site without any certainty that they could put together enough money to complete the transaction. And, in fact, they did come up short at the closing.[6] The 625 project was typical of Romanek's style in another way, in that he worked through the basic layout and design of the building even before giving the concept to his architects to execute. He and Golub both remained involved in every detail of

625 North Michigan Avenue.
The 625 North Michigan
building, completed in 1968,
was Romanek and Golub's first
office development and was
typical of the team's intensive
involvement up to this date in
the design and construction
details of a project.
[Golub + Co.]

the construction process. This, however, was the last building that the team would do without a major architectural firm on board.[7]

In 1973 Romanek-Golub's thirty-eight-story La Salle Plaza building (now Heitman Centre) opened at 180 North La Salle Street. Designed by Harry Weese and Associates, the office tower was the first new building to go up on La Salle Street since the Field Building was completed in 1934. With this building, Romanek for the first time brought in a highly creative architect, and would do so again. La Salle Plaza, however, was typical of the Golub marketing strategy in that he brought in many investors throughout the development process as participants in a succession of tax syndicates.[8]

In the period between 1974 and 1976, Romanek and Golub took their inclination for speculative projects and their talent for marketing one step further: They *created* a tenant for property at 444 North Michigan Avenue that they had acquired for development purposes. Their concept was to establish an Educational Facilities Center (EFC)—Golub called it something like a "Merchandise Mart for Education"—where educators could come from all over the world to see the latest in technology for schools. The EFC, then, would be housed in a building developed specifically for that purpose by Romanek-Golub and Company. An EFC office, headed by a former president of the National Education Association, was in fact set up, and housed temporarily in a nearby building. It was a good idea—one that worked well enough get the Northwestern Mutual Life Insurance Company's commitment to back the project. When it turned out that, although the real estate market was good, there were no funds around for education, the EFC folded. By then, however, construction of 444 North Michigan Avenue, designed by Perkins and Will, was well under way. Romanek-Golub had no trouble converting the project into a successful office tower development.

Romanek and Golub had gained a reputation as a team with the right mix of chutzpah, good luck, and a sense for the market. No truer words than these could have been spoken when, in February 1974, Romanek-Golub and Company acquired twelve major (primarily lakefront) apartment buildings and two important land parcels—the legacy of John Mack and Ray Sher, whose development empire had collapsed with the sale of the Mid-Continental Plaza building. The acquisition of nearly four thousand premium apartment units—on the eve of the wave of condominium conversions that occurred in the mid-1970s and in a period when real estate prices in Cook County were on the verge of doubling—changed the outlook, if not the day-to-day working style, of the company com-

Heitman Centre. [opposite page] Heitman Centre [formerly La Salle Plaza], designed by Harry Weese and completed in 1973, was the first building to go up on La Salle Street after the Field Building was completed in 1934.
[Heitman Properties]

pletely. "It was the first big money we'd made," Golub said. Romanek has called the Mid-Continental deal "a diary of superlatives."[9]

The last downtown office tower that the partners would do together was the award-winning Xerox Centre building (originally called Monroe Centre), designed by Helmut Jahn, who was then with C. F. Murphy Associates. Romanek has spoken of the sleek Xerox Centre as having its beginning as a speculative project, launched in 1977 with a handshake promise of financing from the First National Bank of Chicago. "We were up to the twenty-second floor before all the paperwork finally caught up with us," Romanek has said.[10]

The next project was the Citicorp Plaza complex (originally called Three O'Hare Plaza) near O'Hare International Airport. This development was in another way typical of the Romanek-Golub style. Their decision was to build all three buildings (a total of six hundred thousand square feet) at one time, without any tenants in sight, and in defiance of the fact that the market for suburban office space in the early 1980s was slow. The deciding factors were, first, the economy of constructing three buildings simultaneously, and, second, Romanek's characteristic belief that if he was right in his judgment of the future direction of the market and about the quality of the development, the tenants would come.[11] Citicorp Plaza was finished by 1983—as was the Romanek-Golub partnership. It was an amicable split, both parties say.[12] The partners had one lawyer and one accountant. Assets were divided. (Romanek took Citicorp Plaza; Golub kept 625 North Michigan Avenue; Golub kept the company, buying out Romanek's interest in cash.)

In the decade since the dissolution of the partnership, both have prospered. Eugene Golub changed the name of the firm to Golub + Co. In the mid-1980s he redeveloped and marketed the American Furniture Mart Building at 666 North Lake Shore Drive (the office tower and condominium complex is now known as Lake Shore Place; the address has been changed to 680). By 1990 Golub + Co. was involved in a number of national projects, including the development of the Needham Corporate Center in Needham, Massachusetts, and a two-thousand-acre land development in Snowmass, Colorado, as well as Polish-American joint ventures, including development of the Warsaw Corporate Center and an office highrise in Warsaw to house the National Bank of Poland.

In 1990 Marvin Romanek was back on Michigan Avenue— or close to it—completing another major building in the high-rent district that friends of his once jokingly dubbed "Marvin Gardens." The 633 St. Clair Place office tower, developed by

Romanek Properties, Ltd., designed by Loebl, Schlossman and Hackl, and located on the east side of St. Clair Street between Erie and Ontario streets, was a conversation piece in the community. The building was nearing completion just as the 1990 recession rolled in. Romanek did not have a tenant. This fact did not seem to bother him. Throughout his career as a developer, Romanek had not let the vagaries of business cycles divert his attention from the larger picture. Nor had he ever taken the conservative position of requiring an anchor tenant before beginning construction. No reason to imagine that the 1990s would be any different. When the market rebounds, 633 St. Clair Place will be ready and the tenants will be there, Romanek says. "I built this building for the year 2000, even to the environmental requirements of that decade." He compares his time frame for 633 St. Clair to the ten years it took from land acquisition to the sale of the completed and occupied Xerox Centre building in 1981. "I think we went through three recessions with that acknowledged 'winner.' You must have that decade perspective or you belong in another facet of our business," he says.

AUTHOR'S COMMENTARY

1. It has been said of Romanek's projects that his timing and his sense of the market are impeccable. This certainly was true of his first project. When he began the process of developing 1440 North State Parkway in 1959, the postwar building boom was in full swing and would continue, with brief interruptions, through the 1960s. With his first building, Romanek anticipated the return of a residential market that came to life on the Near North Side in the mid-1960s with the development of Carl Sandburg Village and ultimately the subsequent demand for Near North high-rise apartment units. It has also been said that "good timing" is as much a matter of good luck as it is a matter of timing.

2. Lester Rosenberg, a longtime Romanek-Golub associate, points out that even when the firm grew to include more than two hundred professional employees, Romanek did all the planning on a project himself before involving his advisers. "Marvin never worked on a Friday," Rosenberg told me. "What he did do was take a deal home with him and push his own pencil. He figures it all out himself before showing it to the accountant, the lawyer, or the architect." He describes Romanek as "a great loner. A thinker." Rosenberg has observed a trait that is not un-

common in developers, both historically (I think of Peter C. Brooks's extraordinarily detailed instructions to his Chicago architects) and in current times. Many of the developers that I interviewed for this book spoke of the satisfaction they find in confronting and ultimately mastering the sheer complexity of the projects they undertake, and of their own absorption in detail at every stage. Daniel Levin, who developed the South Commons community, and Richard Stein, the developer of the AT&T Corporate Center, are among those who remarked on this aspect of their own work.

3. In addition to two Romanek apartment buildings, Parkview Management managed the Granville Gardens Apartments, a building that was owned by members of Golub's wife's family and later bought by my family. Gene remembers Granville Gardens as his initiation into the rigors of building management: "I can't tell you how many nights I spent there in the boiler room. But that's what we did in those days."

4. Golub and Romanek's way of doing business essentially related to handshake agreements, based on relationships and trust. Those days may be gone, but they are not forgotten by many developers. In interviews, people such as Ray Sher, Phil Klutznick, Richard Stein, and Gene Golub all commented on the codes of ethics and the value of one's word observed in these transactions. Today, with institutional and pension fund involvement in vastly larger projects that require the expertise of many lawyers, appraisers, accountants, and analysts and that bring together multinational investors, the process requires that everything be spelled out in front.

5. Although I do not believe that all old buildings necessarily should be preserved, it seems surprising in retrospect that the charming Italian Court Building, designed by Robert DeGolyer, should have yielded so easily to a new high-rise office development. This group of buildings had been individual residences, studios, and elegant shops during the 1920s; some were later remodeled as offices. At the time that Romanek-Golub purchased the property, there were more than a dozen offices and shops, including the popular Le Petit Gourmet restaurant, and seventeen duplex apartments and studios in the building. In more recent times, developers have shown a great deal of sensitivity to preservation, but historically, the development mentality has not been consistent with, nor sympathetic to, the

Xerox Centre. (opposite page) For the 1980 Xerox Centre (formerly Monroe Centre), 55 West Monroe, the developers asked architect Helmut Jahn (C. F. Murphy Associates) to provide a nontraditional treatment of a corner speculative office building. (Heitman Properties)

concept of preservation. In the past, the developer typically had a vision of something grander than what had gone before and would be inclined to sweep everything else on a site to the ground in order to realize that vision.

6. Golub recalls that Maynard Wishner, better known as a developer of parking garages, came through with a short-term loan that saved the 625 North Michigan deal at the last moment.

7. For their North State Parkway, East Chestnut Street, and Harbor House apartment buildings, Romanek's architect was the firm of Hausner and Macsai. Gerald Meister and Anthony J. Volpe, both young designers then, were the architects on 625 North Michigan. Volpe later became development director for Romanek Properties.

8. A detail of the design of the La Salle Plaza building provides an interesting insight into different ways in which developers may view the same phenomenon and how their personal perspective may influence the design of a building. While La Salle Plaza was under construction in 1972, Romanek spoke in an interview about the "human scale" of the building, noting that no office window reached from floor to ceiling. Each window, he pointed out, stopped some eighteen inches from the ceiling. "It seems to be a minor point, but the fact is that's the way windows look in your own home," Romanek said. "It's part of the 'human scale' part of putting even the view into a human perspective."

Some twenty years later, in a conversation with me, Richard Stein also commented on the La Salle Plaza (Heitman Centre) windows—but making an entirely different point. He said, "You walk into all of [Stein and Company's] buildings, and the glass goes to the ceiling. . . . And you go into 180 North La Salle Street, done by Harry Weese, and the glass runs to the floor and the header is up at the top." Stein speculated that "this is evidence in my mind that the developer wasn't involved." He explained, "We know that when you walk into a room your eye goes to the high far corner. You run the glass to the top because the ceiling looks higher. Also, people get scared. They don't want to be where glass is at the floor." We know that Romanek was involved, but had a different view than Stein does about what makes people feel comfortable in a steel-and-glass high-rise office building.

9. Although the Mid-Continental Plaza deal took several months to transact, Golub recalls that Romanek-Golub

633 St. Clair Place. [opposite page] Opened in 1990, 633 St. Clair Place brought Marvin Romanek back to the North Michigan Avenue neighborhood, where he began his office development career in the late 1960s.
[Linda Schwartz—Romanek Properties, Ltd.]

was the only firm to make an offer on the properties. John Mack and Ray Sher had sold the Mid-Continental Realty Corporation, whose assets included the Lake Shore Management properties, to Tishman Realty and Construction Company in 1973. (The stock was then sold to Paul Reynolds and the Reynolds Development Company.) For some time prior to the sale, Gene Golub, as broker for Sargent and Lundy, had been negotiating with Mack for at least eleven floors of office space for the engineering consulting firm. The multimillion-dollar lease was concluded six weeks after Mack sold to Tishman. Golub told me that Romanek-Golub's subsequent acquisition of the Lake Shore Management properties was a natural progression of a business relationship that began when the firm acted as brokers for Sargent and Lundy.

10. Xerox Centre was a product of Romanek's drive in the early 1970s to acquire all of the property in the block bounded by La Salle, Monroe, Dearborn, and Adams streets—immediately south of One First National Plaza. His plan was to redevelop the block with office buildings at the southwest corner of Monroe and Dearborn (where Xerox Centre was eventually built) and the northeast corner of Clark and Adams streets, with plazas at the southeast and northwest corners of the block, where the Marquette and Bell Federal Savings buildings were located. He was backed in this project by the First National Bank of Chicago, which in the early 1970s hoped to control the entire environment around its new headquarters building.

   Romanek was successful in acquiring the Westminster Building at Monroe and Dearborn streets, the Monroe Theater at 57 West Monroe Street, and the building at 75 West Monroe. Romanek-Golub was also able to buy the 1894 Marquette Building on Dearborn and Adams streets from Helmsley-Speer in New York, but Romanek was stymied by two forces totally beyond his control. The drive to control the Monroe Street frontage was stopped by the family that owned the narrow Italian Village Restaurant at 71 West Monroe. Plans to level the Marquette Building were checked by the Chicago Commission on Historic and Architectural Landmarks, which dampened the superblock development plans by designating the Marquette a landmark building.

11. An associate explains that Romanek did not seek a tenant before beginning a project because he felt that an anchor

tenant would slow down the development process (and no doubt infringe upon Romanek's sense of autonomy as a developer). The same source recalls that Romanek typically started projects in October, often long before the financing was obtained, because he believed—correctly—that he could do better on construction contracts at that point in the annual building cycle.

12. Business associates agree with the assessment that the Romanek-Golub split was a friendly one. Ten years later, Marvin Romanek and Gene Golub continue to speak highly of one another. It's just that they no longer speak *to* each other.

DOING IT RIGHT

Charles H. Shaw

Charles H. Shaw.
[Kapp Photography—Charles H. Shaw Co.]

In 1991 Charles H. Shaw was photographed on the balcony overlooking the grand lobby of the Chicago Hilton and Towers hotel. He cuts a patrician figure. The Chicago *Tribune* article for which the photo was taken was entitled "The Classics"—a reference to Chicago real estate developments that have stood a dual test of time and quality. In Shaw's case, the term could as easily be applied to the developer as to the environment he created in his $180 million restoration of the venerable Chicago Hilton. The Hilton is among the most successful of the diversified accomplishments of this cerebral and individualistic developer. It seems an unusual accomplishment for a man who was at one time expected to follow a career as a professional baseball player.

Charles Shaw spent his early childhood in Brooklyn; his family moved while he was still in grammar school to the small town of Baldwin on the south shore of Long Island. A long-awaited only child who was brought up during the Depression, Shaw believes he was blessed at birth in many respects. First, he says, "I had wonderful parents who gave me a very basic value system." Second, "We were not poor, but we were right next to it." Third, "I was gifted with good coordination." He explains the connection: "Not having very much materially made me enjoy other things, including baseball, which I played every day. And so in that environment—being a decent student, being poor, and being a good athlete—I was fortunate to have the opportunity to go to college."[1] Shaw had sixteen scholarship offers in his senior year, including the Yale Alumni Award that accompanied his selection as the outstanding high school leader, athlete, and scholar in the Metropolitan New York area. He turned down Yale in favor of Williams College in Massachusetts, largely because Williams was one of the few schools that did not tie its (albeit much smaller) scholarship offer to its athletic program. As a result, Shaw continuously worked three jobs all through college (including a stint as Henry Ford's personal caddie). But he still played three sports: football, basketball, and baseball. He was graduated in 1955 with a degree in English. ("I have no formal training for what I do or what I have done for the last thirty years," he remarks today.) He married his high school sweetheart, and to fulfill his ROTC obligation, signed on for three years with the U.S. Air Force, serving as a navigator-bombardier in a B-47 crew.

Shaw could not have foreseen the Hilton restoration in his college years, but he may have had a sense of things to come. After graduation, he and a friend undertook a hands-on renovation of an aging Brooklyn Heights brownstone. They were years ahead the times. The word "gentrification" was not even in the dictionary in the mid-fifties. The Brooklyn Heights project was an aesthetic success and did good things for the neighborhood, but the young partners were stymied in their efforts to get financing. "The local banks did not recognize what we were trying to accomplish," Shaw recalls. "It taught me a lesson." In 1958 Shaw returned to real estate through more conventional channels. "I was in the service and getting out, we had one child and another on the way, and I didn't have a job." Through a Williams College contact, Shaw found a job as a title insurance salesman. He and his wife Beverly bought a tract house for $13,200 in Levittown, Long Island—one of the first of America's postwar new towns.

In the early 1960s Shaw, characteristically, branched out on his own. Shaw and partner William F. Hartnett formed Hartnett-Shaw and Associates, a real estate consulting firm whose principal client was Alcoa. Shaw had entered the real estate field at the height of the urban renewal period, and his consulting work gave him exposure to urban redevelopment projects in San Francisco, Chicago, Indianapolis, Pittsburgh, Philadelphia, and Washington, D.C. Through Alcoa's association with New York developer William Zeckendorf, he became involved also in the original Century City project in Los Angeles and the first United Nations Plaza multiuse development in New York City. In these years, Shaw says, he gained "a sense of what was happening in the cities" and a conviction that right-minded development can revitalize the central city. In 1966 Shaw was offered the presidency of Alcoa Properties, but reluctantly turned the offer down because he realized that his nature was that of an independent operator. He and his partner were at the time involved in negotiating a lease in Chicago with the Dock and Canal Trust and in seeking financing to develop the Lake Point Tower apartments on a Dock and Canal site.

The remarkable Lake Point Tower was Shaw's first solo development project. The structure was also the first (and still the only) high-rise building to go up east of North Lake Shore Drive north of the Chicago River. At seventy stories, it was the highest reinforced concrete structure in the world at the time of its completion in 1968 and by far the tallest residential building.[2] Lake Point Tower today is one of the most familiar features of the Chicago skyline, but its construction raised issues related to the use and protection of lakefront lands that are as old as the city itself.[3] The height of the building raised questions of another nature for Shaw as the developer. "Lake Point Tower was not exactly the best residential location in 1960," Shaw remembers. "And its seventy stories? Very sophisticated New York bankers said that American people would not live above thirty-five stories. There wasn't an apartment building in New York that tall, so of course it was considered risky."

Shaw speaks of the role of the developer in terms that illustrate the thinking of a man who would undertake a development this large and this unprecedented as his first independent project. "I like to live at the cutting edge of reality. But not on the edge. I'm not a gambler. I don't live at the point where you are going to fall off the cliff. But I don't sit back in a safe place and just do normal things either, especially if there is an opportunity to bring about change." He summarizes: "I like to be as close to the edge as possible, where change is taking place. Effecting positive change—that is what has driven me." The New York bankers' prediction about public acceptance of skyscraper living proved to be unfounded. Lake Point Tower quickly became a prestigious address. And it did serve as an agent for change, although in a sense perhaps not anticipated by Shaw. The development inspired a belated amendment to the Chicago Lakefront Ordinance that had the effect of prohibiting future high-rise developments of its kind east of Lake Shore Drive.[4]

With Lake Point Tower construction under way, Shaw made the decision to move his family and his development activities to Chicago. In the late 1960s he wrapped up his commitments to Alcoa (which included completion of Allegheny Center, an urban renewal project in Pittsburgh, and the restructuring of the Zeckendorf-Alcoa United Nations Plaza de-

velopment) and withdrew from his consulting partnership. In 1968 the Shaws (then with four children born within a five-year span) moved to Chicago's North Shore suburban area.

In 1971 Shaw developed the sleek State National Bank Plaza (now NBD Evanston) in the sedate North Shore community of Evanston. The twenty-story building, with its distinctly Miesian lines, was then the tallest structure in the Chicago suburban area, a distinction that did not endear Shaw to tradition-bound Evanstonians.

In 1974 Shaw, forming the Charles H. Shaw Company, built Williams Center, a $250 million mixed-use development in downtown Tulsa. Center Court Gardens, an apartment complex near the Chicago Near West Side medical complex, followed in 1978. Two years later, in partnership with Jerrold Wexler, he completed the 676 St. Clair office building, now known as the Ogilvie and Mather building.

In 1980 Shaw stepped into the maelstrom of city politics that swirled around the long-delayed and oft-deferred plan for redevelopment of the deteriorating North Loop district. The area, loosely bounded by La Salle Street, Wacker Drive, Wabash Avenue, and Washington Street, had been targeted for urban renewal in 1973 during the last years of Richard J. Daley's administration. After Daley's death in 1976, and after the air had gone out of Arthur Rubloff's much publicized claim to the territory, renewal plans for the seven-block "blighted commercial district" were stalled.[5]

Mayor Jane Byrne opposed North Loop redevelopment when she was elected in 1978, but in the summer of 1979 she reversed her position and revived the North Loop renewal commitment. Mayor Byrne, who had heard about the Shaw company's Museum Tower project in New York City, asked to meet with Shaw. As Shaw recalls the meeting, he discussed his belief that if significant change is to occur in the cities, it has to be activated by local government and business leadership, rather than handed down from Washington. He commented on the North Loop master plan advanced by Rubloff, asking "Is it a promotion or is it a plan? Is it serious or isn't it?" Although it was not his intention at the time, this conversation resulted in Shaw's being named "coordinating planner" for the North Loop project. The understanding was that he would produce a new master plan for the North Loop; recruit other developers; arrange private financing for redevelopment in return for 2 percent of the total development costs; and, if necessary, develop some of the buildings himself.[6] Working with Skidmore, Owings and Merrill, Shaw produced a conceptual plan that was bold and far-reaching. It called for a mix of commercial, residential, and recreational uses. A much-

Lake Point Tower. [opposite page] The remarkable Lake Point Tower apartment building, east of Lake Shore Drive at Navy Pier, was Charles Shaw's first solo development project. At seventy stories, it was also the highest reinforced concrete structure in the world at the time of its completion in 1968 and by far the tallest residential building in the world. [Lake Point Tower Condominium Association]

publicized feature of the plan involved creating a two-and-a-half-acre deck, or "garden level," across the rooftops of four-story base structures that would surround luxury condominium towers and high-rise office buildings. Critics dubbed the plan "Buck Rogers-ish" and, as Shaw had anticipated, claimed that it would put too much housing in the Loop.

Shaw's plan, in this case, was perhaps too far ahead of its time, but the problems were deeper. The North Loop area was mired in political issues that predated Shaw's entry into the project and precluded the kind of sweeping clearance and redevelopment effort that he envisioned. These included Cook County Assessor Tom Hynes's refusal to grant the tax incentives that the city had held out to lure hotel, retail, and residential development into the district. From the beginning, the North Loop renewal plan had hinged on the commitment of the Hilton Hotel Corporation to build a hotel in the block bounded by State, Lake, and Dearborn streets and Wacker Drive. At the height of the controversy over tax abatement for the North Loop site, Hilton withdrew from the fray, deciding instead to restore and renew the stately old Conrad Hilton Hotel on South Michigan Avenue.[7]

Problems created by Mayor Byrne's standoff with Hynes were compounded by city council opposition to Shaw's plan, couched in terms of the concerns of preservationist groups opposed to demolition of older buildings, especially the Chicago, Harris, Selwyn, and Woods theaters located in the district.[8] The city council and the mayor's advisers balked at the 2 percent commission to be paid to Shaw on development he brought into the district and were concerned over Shaw's position as both planner and coordinating developer. The terms were negotiated over the winter of 1980-81 with no mutually satisfactory result. Eight months after his appointment, Shaw formally resigned as coordinator of the North Loop Redevelopment Project. In his resignation statement Shaw said, "Now, it appears that potential conflicts of interest for my company, particularly in the atmosphere that exists today, make it impossible for us to continue in these roles."[9] He later commented, "When Jane Byrne asked me to become involved in the North Loop, many people wiser than me urged me not to do it from the beginning, but I said that maybe it was an opportunity to do something in Chicago that could effect change for generations and create more stability, vitality, excitement in this city. I just couldn't say no."

The North Loop experience was not without a silver lining for Shaw. At the same time he was serving as North Loop planner, he was also Hilton's development partner. When Hilton withdrew from the North Loop, Shaw retained this partnership. He saw the Chicago Hilton and Towers restoration "as an opportunity that comes along only once in a lifetime." The project, which took four years, became one of Charles Shaw's most celebrated achievements and one of Chicago's finest attractions. The renewal enhanced the grandeur of the old Hilton, which, when it was built in 1927 (as the Stevens Hotel) was the largest hotel in the world. But it also modernized the old Hilton with the addition of an internal parking garage, a grand entrance for guests arriving by private auto, and more space for exhibitions and public functions.

The Hilton restoration fit Shaw's development philosophy perfectly. He saw the project both as an anchor for renewal of the declining South Michigan Avenue district and as one of those close-to-the-edge-of-the-cliff commitments that are so attractive to him. A restoration of this scale in a questionable location was an unprecedented undertaking. In planning the Hilton restoration, Shaw may also have had some lingering memory of his hassles with city hall. Speaking of the Hilton's historic but increasingly shabby South Loop neighborhood, Shaw remarked that what it took to begin South Loop rejuvenation "was some people with some courage who were willing to put their own money at stake, because the city was not providing the leadership that the city should. And I told the city this." It was not the first time Shaw had expressed his feelings about the role local government could and should play in redevelopment.

While Shaw was re-creating the Chicago Hilton, his company was completing a series of major projects in New York, including the acclaimed Museum Tower, an award-winning apartment highrise built on air rights over New York's Museum of Modern Art, and Carnegie Hall Tower, a luxury condominium in Manhattan.

In the late 1980s he turned his attention to Chicago's Near West Side medical district, where he built the Inn at University Village hotel and the Garibaldi Square town-house development. He also returned to Evanston as developer of Northwestern University's Evanston Research Park, a twenty-four-acre property dedicated to linking the resources of Northwestern University to both government-sponsored and private-sector research and development. The project was conceived as a highly creative public-private joint enterprise in which underused and undertaxed land owned by the city and by the university would be pooled to create an entirely new type of business center. Shaw, now no stranger to political controversy, weathered a storm of protest against the research park in the planning stages, much of it mounted by Northwestern University students and faculty in concert with the politically active, nuclear-free-zone Evanston liberal community and its representatives on the Evanston City Council. Central to the controversy was heated opposition to potential military applications of research and development activities planned for the installation. The position of the park sponsors was not helped by the fact that the first major building in the park (not a Shaw development) was to be built—with federal funds—to house Northwestern University contract research for the federal government. Peace was bought at the price of an explicit—and politically expedient—agreement wrung from the developers to bar any military-related activities from the park. Shaw does not waste an opportunity to make the point that park facilities he developed house advanced research in the field of artificial intelligence and in the development of biomedical products.

Clearly, Shaw is a developer who is willing to try anything once, and has. His motto is "Do it right and do it well." With the Evanston Research Park successfully launched at the end of the 1980s, Shaw completed the Embassy Suites Hotel in Chicago's River North district (just north of the Loop) and moved on to his next frontier—development of Luther Village, a senior housing community in Arlington Heights.

The size of a project is less important to Shaw than its quality. From the beginning, he has chosen to run a small, tightly-knit organization with a total of no more than thirty employees in the Chicago and New York offices combined. He selects his projects carefully. He has explained that "I like to be in control of things, so I think my personality probably is best suited to a smaller environment, where I make decisions and suffer the consequences." Charles Shaw is serious, intense, and passionate about what he does. His summation of his own perception of the developer's role expresses eloquently the characteristics that he shares with others of his profession. "Entrepreneurial spirit," he says, "involves risk. It involves tremendous dedication, it involves significant effort, and I also think it involves some perception of what hopefully might be a better way of life."

AUTHOR'S COMMENTARY

1. Shaw describes himself as "a baseball nut" to whom "sports came easily." That's an understatement. Charlie Shaw was offered a contract with the New York Yankees even before he finished high school.

2. The 645-foot Lake Point Tower is more than just another of Chicago's cherished "first's" and "biggest's." It is also considered a structural masterpiece. The architects who

designed the building, Schipporeit-Heinrich Associates (with Graham, Anderson, Probst, and White), were students of Mies van der Rohe at the Illinois Institute of Technology. The cloverleaf shape of the building was based on a project designed by Mies in Berlin in 1921. Lake Point Tower was the first actual execution of the Berlin concept.

3. The shoreline of the city of Chicago is among the most beautiful in the world, and its skyline among the most breathtaking. The meeting of lakefront and skyscraper is an unforgettable image. This pairing of natural splendor and human creativity is neither an accident nor is it the result of planning and architectural genius alone. Rather, it is a unique combination of nature and man's intent. When one considers Chicago's beginnings as a frontier town and trading post and reflects on the nature of its early settlers and the speculative character of its economy, it is hard to believe that the city could have succeeded so well in preserving the lakefront in the condition it is today. Of the thirty miles of shoreline within the city's boundaries, more than 80 percent is devoted to public parks and beaches. Of the remaining 20 percent, only one mile, near the Indiana border, has been claimed for commercial or industrial use. This unparalleled feat is the result of zealous commitment on the part of visionary Chicagoans, combined with an entrepreneurial creativity that has been rarely duplicated and seldom bested in the development and planning of American cities.

To be sure, our lakefront is not perfect, and there has been erosion of the promise that it should be retained intact for recreational and cultural use. Many Chicagoans remember the debate and controversy that surrounded the construction of Miegs Field in 1947, two lakefront water filtration plants in the 1950s, and, of course, the McCormick Place exhibition hall, which opened amid great opposition in 1960. In some instances, this erosion has been justifiable, and in other instances, shameful. The miracle of the lakefront as we know it today, however, is all the more apparent when one notes that in the mid-nineteenth century, the waterfront north of Monroe Street was given over entirely to shipping and industrial uses and that the banks of the Chicago River were home to grain elevators, warehouses, and factories.

Chicago *Tribune* editorial page editor and Pulitzer Prize-winning journalist Lois Wille, in her book *Forever Open, Free and Clear,* has described the early history of the city and the history and development of the lakefront with extraordinary clarity and insight. I pause here only to point out that

Chicago Hilton and Towers.
[opposite page] Charles Shaw's
restoration of the 1927
Conrad Hilton Hotel [formerly
the Stevens Hotel] on South
Michigan Avenue took four
years and cost $180 million.
The restoraton preserved a
venerable Chicago building and
provided a firm anchor for
future redevelopment of South
Michigan Avenue.
[Copyright April 3, 1991, Chicago
Tribune Co., all rights reserved, used
with permission]

this city of speculators and entrepreneurs nurtured a vision that both created the skyscraper and, despite driving greed, also became one of the very few cities in this country (or in the world, for that matter) that managed to preserve the frontage and use of its most significant natural asset: its magnificent shoreline.

4. The pledge first made in 1836 by Gordon Saltonstall Hubbard and others among the city's founding fathers that the Chicago lakefront was to be "public ground—a common to remain forever open, clear and free of any buildings, or other obstruction whatever" has been unevenly observed in the course of Chicago development history. The completion of Lake Point Tower in 1968 raised the fear that a wall of similar highrises might rise up on Chicago Dock and Canal lands and along the Illinois Central Railroad right-of-way, barring the lakefront and lake views from public access.

There was a great deal of concern in the early 1960s over the fact that the Lake Point Tower project had been allowed to go forward, in apparent disregard of the 1948 Chicago Plan Commission Lakefront Resolution affirming that the lakefront should be used for recreational and cultural purposes—a position that was reaffirmed in the 1964 "Basic Policies for the Comprehensive Plan of Chicago" drafted by the city planning department. The loophole was this: The 1948 lakefront resolution made an exception of the few blocks on both sides of the mouth of the Chicago River, between Grand Avenue and Randolph Street, which it said might be used for essential "harbor or terminal facilities." The 1964 Comprehensive Plan retained the "exception" for that area, but omitted the language limiting development there to harbor or terminal facilities. The proposed Lake Point Tower development, located just south of Grand Avenue, was thus considered to fall within the category of an allowable "exception." The planning department and the Chicago Plan Commission, on which I served, responded by drafting an amendment to the Lakefront Ordinance banning multistory buildings east of Lake Shore Drive. The amendment was too late to prevent the Lake Point Tower development, but in time to prevent construction of additional high-rise apartment buildings to be built by the Texas-based Centex Home Corporation on land leased from the Chicago Dock and Canal Trust lands between the Ogden Slip and the river.

The important question, I believe, is our understanding of the promise that the lakefront be preserved as "a common, forever open, clear and free." The issue involves the extent to which the area is devoted to public purposes and is preserved for public use. I think of the controversy in the mid-1960s when the location of the Grant Park band shell, built in 1932, was moved from a small, noisy, and undesirable site at the south end of the park to its present site. The

Chicago Park District plan to construct a new music bowl that would accommodate the thousands of people who gathered for Grant Park concerts generated a great deal of opposition involving a number of effective and responsible civic groups such as the Metropolitan Housing and Planning Council and the Midwest Open Lands Association.

Their objection was to the creation of a permanent structure on Grant Park land. I was at that time serving as vice chairman of the plan commission and as chairman of its lakefront subcommittee. We held a number of hearings on the question, and eventually reached a compromise. The new band shell was built, but it was designed as a demountable structure, meaning that it could be disassembled and moved. So far, it has not been demounted.

Does a strict interpretation of "forever open, clear and free" really mean that there should have been, for example, no McCormick Place, notwithstanding the fact that this is a public facility of monumental economic importance to the city of Chicago? Should there have been no band shell—or a merely temporary bandshell—notwithstanding the fact that hundreds of thousands of people enjoy the concerts in Grant Park every year? These are the trade-offs. I appreciate that there is a point at which you are trading too much off for the sake of the now and the here. We've tried to keep the balance, and on the whole, I believe we have succeeded.

5. Implementation of North Loop redevelopment plans was to some extent slowed by Mayor Richard J. Daley's technique of stonewalling Arthur Rubloff's persistent efforts to commandeer the project as his own. Rubloff did not take the hint. Contrary to Rubloff's later statements, I have no doubt that had Daley lived, in time and in his own way he would have disposed of the Rubloff problem. Development of the North Loop properties could then have proceeded without the loss of momentum and further politicization of the issues that arose in the mayoral administrations of Michael Bilandic and Jane Byrne.

6. Inducements to developers who committed to build in the North Loop and within the planning guidelines included write-downs on the cost of land, city-funded public works improvements, and a property tax incentive to be given in return for contributions to amenities such as parks and theaters.

7. The political issues that emerged in the vacuum following the death of Mayor Daley in 1976 escalated sharply when Mayor Byrne came into office. North Loop renewal plans became a lightning rod for the inevitable conflict between old-time Daley regulars and the new administration. This climate of open conflict offered fertile ground for assessor Tom Hynes in his opposition to North Loop tax abatements. As a result, the tax question swelled to an issue of monumental proportions. Tom Hynes is and should be

recognized as a serious public servant. He believed that North Loop tax abatements amounted to a potential give-away disproportionate to the return. I believe that had Daley lived, given his stature and commitment to the project, the proposed tax abatement would have been enacted, and the Hilton would have been built.

8. By 1990 North Loop redevelopment was virtually in place. The only properties not redeveloped were a portion of Dearborn Street between Lake and Randolph streets and the now-famous Block 37. There is something of a sad irony in this, in that the preservationists' battle to protect some venerable buildings involved resulted ultimately in a lose-lose situation for all parties concerned. And I acknowledge some responsibility for the outcome. When I became involved in early 1981 in moving the North Loop development process forward, we attempted to protect the Woods, Selwyn, and Harris theater buildings, and several of the Block 37 buildings, especially the McCarthy Building. I questioned the architectural merit of some of these structures, but nonetheless that was the deal we struck with the preservationists.

   Subsequently, the agreement was renegotiated—despite the fact that a commitment had been made—with the result that the preservationists lost everything except the now-vacant Selwyn and Harris buildings (the Cinestage and Michael Todd) at 170 and 190 North Dearborn Street. Block 37 was cleared to make way for a $500 million development planned as a joint venture of Metropolitan Structures, the Levy Organization, and JMB Realty. A redevelopment agreement was reached for the Woods Theater block with Miller-Klutznick-Davis-Gray. Unfortunately, much time had been lost. The economic downturn that hit the real estate industry in late 1990 forced both development groups to put their plans on hold for an indefinite period. At this writing, Block 37 lies fallow, although there was some discussion in 1991 of developing it under private ownership for public use as additional municipal offices or using the property as a park or public plaza.

9. My own direct involvement in the North Loop Redevelopment Project came about in a circuitous fashion. When Mayor Byrne came into office, my term as vice chairman of the Chicago Plan Commission had expired. She did not renew it. I was off the commission. Shortly after she assumed office, however, she began a series of communications with me. I was reappointed to the plan commission, as chairman, at the end of her first year in office. When Mayor Byrne

realized the extent of the conflict that Charlie Shaw faced in his dual role as planner on behalf of the city and as a private developer in a public development project, she removed him from the position and appointed me, as the newspapers put it, to act as "czar of the North Loop." In reality, I became the coordinator for the city in my capacity as chairman of the plan commission. My job was to work with the city department of planning to see that a new North Loop plan was devised and to facilitate, insofar as possible, continued movement of the development process.

Charlie Shaw is extremely capable and probably could have done an excellent job in both capacities. The problem is, that is not the way our system works. Not only is avoidance of privileged access the law, it is also an essential tenet of the democratic political system. Mrs. Byrne managed to overlook this point initially. As she became aware of the conflict, she withdrew her support for Shaw, a fact that was in no way a reflection on either his integrity or his ability to execute the plan.

NEW BREED

John A. Buck

John A. Buck.
[David R. Barnes—John Buck Co.]

When John Buck decided in the late 1970s that he wanted to build an office tower, he had a few dollars in borrowed capital, an architect who agreed to do preliminary design work for nothing, and a free option on an odd-shaped piece of land on the South Branch of the Chicago River. Within a decade, the name of John Buck was attached to some of the city's most important new office towers and to a score of other developments in Chicago and elsewhere. Buck's Chicago buildings include 200 South Wacker Drive, his first project; 190 South La Salle, one of the most publicized and admired buildings of the 1980s; and 35 West Wacker Drive (codeveloped with the Leo Burnett Company), the first major structure to go up in the North Loop redevelopment area after the State of Illinois Building.

The John Buck Company's joint-venture participation in the late 1980s in development of the American Medical Association's new headquarters building, and a host of related properties in the Near North Side "billion-dollar" development corridor firmly established the ten-year-old firm's place among the ranks of the city's megadevelopers. This may sound like a Horatio Alger story, but it isn't. Don't be fooled by Buck's boyish appearance, his leisurely West Texas drawl, or stories of his upbringing on a farm southwest of Amarillo. Buck represents the best and the brightest of a new breed of developers—highly trained, professional specialists in commercial real estate and finance.[1] It is true that John Buck grew up

200 South Wacker Drive.
Architect Harry Weese did the designs for John Buck's first development, at 200 South Wacker Drive [1981], on speculation. The agreement was that Weese's fee would be paid only if Buck were able to get financing. Weese's innovative pairing of two right triangles maximizes both floor space and light on a small site. [Hedrich-Blessing]

on a farm near Hereford, Texas, but that was no small operation either. The Buck family farm encompassed six sections of West Texas dryland, which Buck's father, a lawyer, transformed into 3,800 acres of wheat, corn, and soybeans by tapping underground streams for irrigation. John A. Buck came

200 South Wacker Drive lobby.
[Jon Miller, Hedrich-Blessing—John Buck Co.]

into the arena of Chicago real estate development very well prepared. He had a bachelor's degree from the University of Notre Dame, a law degree from the University of Texas at Austin, and an M.B.A. from Philadelphia's Wharton School of Business and Finance, seat of one of the country's leading academic real estate programs. Buck's nine years of higher education (a period that he describes as his "work-deferral program") were followed by seven years of on-the-job experience with the Chicago office of Cushman and Wakefield.

When Buck joined Cushman and Wakefield in 1971, he was offered a choice among openings in the firm's New York, Los Angeles, and Chicago offices. He chose Chicago, reasoning that there was less competition in Chicago than in New York and that the city had more of a business atmosphere than did Los Angeles. In Chicago he was assigned by Cushman and Wakefield to the team charged with leasing the Sears Tower. The task of finding tenants for two million square feet of space in what would become the world's tallest building was exactly the kind of challenge Buck relished. He recalls that when he started on the Sears project in 1972, he was something of an "errand boy." When the Sears Tower opened in 1974 he was comanager of leasing for the building.[2] By 1978 he had become a senior vice president at Cushman and Wakefield.

Buck was eager to try his hand at development. The opportunity was tantalizingly near, in the form of a property at the southwest corner of Wacker Drive and Adams streets, directly across from the Sears Tower. "I used to walk by this site going to and from work every day, and I thought I'd like to take a stab at getting an option," he says. The story of how John Buck created 200 South Wacker Drive, one of the first major office buildings to join the Sears Tower in the new South Wacker district, reveals something of the tenacity with which developers embrace their projects. The property that he had his eye on was owned by the Continental Insurance Company of New York. Buck, with nothing to offer but himself and a great idea, went to New York to request an option and, in his words, "almost got laughed out of the office." He returned to Chicago and in six months managed to raise $350,000— enough, he hoped, to get him the option with some money left over for predevelopment. Back at Continental, he found himself meeting with the same group that had shown him the door on his first trip—except this time the chairman of the company was present. "The chairman had a drink of Wild Turkey before lunch—a chairman can do this—and I had a drink of Wild Turkey. We hit it off quite well," Buck remembers. "So I launched into my argument, and the same people started shooting me down again—saying that I had never done a building, that I was too young, that I was undercapitalized. The long and the short of it is that at the end of the meeting the chairman stands up and says 'Aw, let's give it to the boy. I kinda' like him.' And so that was it. I had a free option."

Buck came home with his nest egg intact but soon found that even that would not buy him much in the way of architectural services. "I secured proposals from the Skidmores of the world," he recalls, and cringed when he found that the cost of schematic drawings alone could decimate his budget. A friend suggested that he talk to Harry Weese, a highly original and multifaceted Chicago architect. Buck liked Weese's ideas very much, and Weese liked the challenge of the site and the opportunity to build across from the Sears Tower. The two men, developer and architect, made a deal. Weese would do the designs on speculation. Weese's fee would be paid when, and if, Buck got financing. "I didn't want him to think I was cheap, so I gave him a thousand bucks," Buck smiles. "And he came up with some very interesting plans." Now, Buck had a one-year option, he had an architect, and he had enough money left to launch a preleasing campaign. That was critical. Without a major tenant, Buck would have no financing and no building.

Seven months passed, and Buck began to lose sleep. Good

thing, too, because it was during one of those sleepless nights that the solution to the anchor tenant problem came to him. The Continental Insurance Company had a Chicago office just around the corner from the Wacker Drive property, on Jackson Street. The company was considering a move to the suburbs. Suddenly, the pieces fell into place in Buck's mind: "I woke up literally in the middle of the night and said 'Dammit! Your tenant is Continental Insurance!'" As it turned out, he was right. Buck flew back to New York—with Weese's designs under his arm—and had lunch and another sip of Wild Turkey with the Continental chairman. When asked if he had found a major tenant yet, Buck replied, "Yes, and it's you." It took some negotiating, but Buck came home with Continental's agreement to lease nearly 50 percent of the space in 200 South Wacker Drive. But even though he had a major tenant, he still needed help to get a construction loan. He went to Tom Klutznick at Urban Investment and Development Corporation, and Urban entered the project as an equity partner. The Prudential Insurance Company provided the permanent financing.[3] Ground was broken in 1978, and the forty-story office tower was completed in 1981. Buck had become a developer. He was then thirty-four years old.

John Buck is thoughtful and articulate in discussing his chosen profession. Take, for example, his view of the respective roles played by the developer and the architect in the design process. In 200 South Wacker Drive, Harry Weese had come up with a configuration of triangular masses that produced both maximum floor space and maximum natural light in a building that would otherwise have been limited by the irregularly shaped site. Visually, the building was a blockbuster. As a rental property, it was a great success. Buck clearly was very pleased by the collaboration on this project between architect and developer. "One of your jobs as a developer is to translate the market as best you can to the architect," he explains. "You want the architect to lend his full creativity to a project, but the architect also must confine that creativity to market needs. Some architects are prone to do that and some are not." Buck discovered that truth when he interviewed architects for the preliminary design work on 200 South Wacker. "It was very clear to me that some were going to tell me what it was that I needed. And some were going to listen to me explain what I needed. Harry Weese did the latter, and it worked out very well."[4]

Buck's views on the developer's role in the design process have not limited his ability to attract internationally renowned architects to Chicago to work with him: Philip Johnson and John Burgee to do 190 South La Salle Street, Kevin Roche for

190 South La Salle Street lobby.
[Hedrich-Blessing—John Buck Co.]

190 South La Salle Street.
[opposite page] John Buck turned to internationally known architects John Burgee and Philip Johnson to design the highly publicized 190 South La Salle building, opened in 1986.
[Hedrich-Blessing—John Buck Co.]

35 West Wacker, and Kenzo Tange to design the thirty-story AMA headquarters building at 515 North State Street. Buck has an equally clear view of why he became a developer. "People have their inclinations," he explains, noting that some people in the real estate field are good financiers. Others—the real estate entrepreneurs—are interested in the transactions. Buck's definition of a developer is more comprehensive. In his own case, Buck said, "I am not a financial wizard, I am not a building manager. And I've outgrown the leasing job. I am attracted to the development process because it encompasses all of the above. It's interdisciplinary. It's true that the end product can be financially rewarding—but not without risk. It's the complexity of the process that absorbs me." The secret of the development business, Buck believes, is to know what you are going to do before you start, and then do what you can to minimize risks in construction, financing, and leasing. "Know what you need, design what you need, and build it. Don't change your mind eighteen times." Buck's answer to the vicissitudes of the market is to take a lesser equity position himself—as he has in the AMA developments—and share a larger part of the leasing risk with deeper-pocket partners.

Although in the 1980s John Buck was a leader among those

developers who were forging larger, more global, and more diversified development companies, Buck also continued to study at the feet of the masters. He admired Arthur Rubloff. "I met him only two or three times, but what I learned was that he had a dream," Buck remembers. "I studied him intensely, and I was attracted to him. If you look around the Loop, his buildings represent quality. Quality sells, and quality, I think, adds value." Buck learned lessons about risk from New York developer William Zeckendorf, who wrote candidly in his 1970 autobiography of the consequences of overextension. "I reread that book every few years or so just to reconfirm what not to do," Buck said. "You take Zeckendorf, one of the greatest property promoters and developers of his time, and he died almost broke. How did that happen? By his own admission, he took too many risks."

Buck takes a sensible position toward risk, but that doesn't mean he doesn't relish a challenge. The challenge he faced in developing 200 South Wacker was persuading people that he could do it. The challenge of the 190 South La Salle Building was putting together the land. The site, at the northwest corner of La Salle and Adams streets, had been occupied by the old Exchange National Bank Building. The major part of the property was held by seventeen descendants of a turn-of-the-century owner; the other section needed for the development was in a family trust. "That was a very interesting job for me," Buck said. "It was a very complex land acquisition." It was also the kind of business that he likes best.

Buck faced another kind of challenge when he tackled the North Loop, an area that had long been promoted by the city for redevelopment but where progress had been stymied by political conflict, turnovers in the city administration, and a shifting cast of interested developers. Construction of the fifty-story 35 West Wacker building began in August 1986. The Chicago *Tribune*, recalling that thirteen years had passed since the block had been designated for redevelopment, declared that the John Buck Company-Leo Burnett ground breaking "was met with a collective sigh of relief from city planners on hand."[5]

In 1988 the Buck Company entered into its biggest development project to that date—a joint venture with Miller-Klutznick-Davis-Gray and Company to develop three of the four city blocks owned by the AMA between State Street and Michigan Avenue north of the Chicago River. The first phase of the project was the AMA headquarters, followed by a fifty-story apartment tower at 440 North Wabash.

As successful as John Buck has been in putting together very big deals, he dreams of another project—one that could be completed at a fraction of the cost of his major developments. Since the mid-1980s, Buck has been a leader in the effort to beautify West Wacker Drive between Lake Street and Van Buren and create a "river walk" of shops, arcades, and parks interspersed among the wall of office buildings at the riverfront. "Wacker Drive and the riverfront are important to the city as a whole," he says, "and I'm confident we'll see this done." With John Buck behind the idea, it probably will be.

AUTHOR'S COMMENTARY

1. Development will always be an art, but increasingly, it is also a science. The individual, seat-of-the-pants capitalist is a thing of the past. Today's developers, men like John Buck, put together projects that carry price tags of $100 million or more. Their specialties include sophisticated and complex skills in fields such as market analysis, property acquisition, consortium financing, brokerage, construction, consulting, and real estate asset management. There are no nine-day wonders in the business today.

2. John Buck's involvement with the Sears Tower did not end with his job as leasing agent when the building opened. Twenty years later, in 1991, his company was selected to re-develop and re-lease the building after Sears, Roebuck and Company announced the move of its Merchandise Group to new offices in suburban Hoffman Estates. The Sears Tower may well be the best-known example in the world of a corporate development—a major building erected by a company for its own use. Certainly, at 110 stories, it is the most visible. From the day the project was conceived, the building has generated its own catalog of Chicago statistical superlatives: first, biggest, most. At 1,454 feet, the Sears Tower has been secure for nearly two decades as holder of the "world's tallest" title. The assembly and sale of the land itself was heralded at the time as "the world's greatest real estate deal." Albert Rubenstein, Bernard Feinberg, and Philip Teinowitz of Fleetwood Realty Corporation began to acquire the property in the block bounded by Wacker, Jackson, Quincy, and Franklin in 1964, banking on their belief in a future for the West Loop. Rubenstein recalls that there were more than a hundred owners involved in transactions for the block. Sears became interested in the property, but only if the Fleetwood partners could also deliver a second block immediately north of Quincy Street, fronting on Adams Street. They had six months to do it, and at one time had $1 million in option

money outstanding on properties in the second block, Rubenstein recalls.

Although some redevelopment of the old textile and loft-building district along South Branch of the Chicago River was under way in the late 1960s, the construction of the Sears Tower had the effect of opening up the southwest quadrant of the Loop to a new era of office tower development—in much the same way that Peter Brooks's Monadnock Building had opened the area south of Jackson to development a century earlier. Buck's 200 South Wacker Drive was the first of the new skyscrapers to go up in the shadow of the Sears Tower, followed by One South Wacker Drive, Gateway IV, 10 and 30 South Wacker Drive (Chicago Mercantile Exchange), and 311 South Wacker Drive. The designers of these buildings constitute a roster of some of Chicago's leading architects, beginning with the Skidmore, Owings and Merrill team headed by Bruce Graham and head engineer Fazlur Kahn, who did the Sears Tower; and including Harry Weese and Associates; Murphy/Jahn; Fujikawa, Johnson and Associates; and Kohn Pedersen Fox Associates.

3. The first time I met John Buck was when he came in to discuss financing for 200 South Wacker Drive with Norman Perlmutter, chairman of Heitman Financial Services, and me. Buck did not select Heitman as the mortgage banker, but he reminded me in 1990 when I interviewed him for this chapter that I had chaired the 1978 Chicago Plan Commission meeting at which he presented his plans for the building. Had Heitman been the mortgage holder, I would, of course, have disqualified myself from sitting on the panel that reviewed his application. Similar situations arose from time to time in my early years on the commission. This might happen when someone I represented in an appraisal or counseling matter would come before the commission on other business. On these occasions, I would abstain from voting, and in one instance, withdrew from the hearing altogether.

Management of the perception—not the fact—of potential conflict of interest is a difficult call to make for a volunteer in public service. As a member of the commission, I found it sufficient to abstain from voting in any case where I had some business relationship, however remote, with the petitioner. When I became chairman of the commission in 1980, I reluctantly decided that in order to avoid any question of conflict I should sell my interest in Mid-America Appraisal and Research Corporation, the com-

Leo Burnett Building. The 35 West Wacker Drive headquarters building for the Leo Burnett Company, completed in 1989, was the first private development in the North Loop Redevelopment District. [George Kufrin—John Buck Co.]

pany that I cofounded in 1957. My separation from the company was an arm's-length sale severing all financial involvement with Mid-America or any of its affiliates. While considering this step, I asked three different law firms to research existing law. They came to the conclusion that there was enough law and precedent in Illinois to suggest a conflict should I retain an interest in Mid-America's business. Although I had been willing to divest myself of my interest in a company I had helped to create, I feel that to ask the same of any volunteer in public service goes far beyond the intention of the law. Public advisory bodies need the judgment and insights of competent people who are willing to share the benefit of their years of professional experience, but by exercising an overly broad interpretation of the word "conflict," we may exclude from service on public boards the very individuals whose judgment could be most valuable.

4. The kind of interaction between developer and architect that Buck found so productive on the 200 South Wacker building is certainly not the exception, but neither is it the rule. Buck mentioned in conversation that in the European tradition, "the architect is king, the architect tells the client what he wants." He added his opinion that "there are some current examples of that here in Chicago."

5. I agree that city planners were greatly relieved when North Loop redevelopment finally got under way. In the more than twenty years that I served on the Chicago Plan Commission, the most difficult and most politically frustrating episodes swirled around plans for the North Loop. The area had been designated an urban renewal site in 1973. There were several promising beginnings, but by 1983 the initiative had been all but buried in the transition from the Jane Byrne to the Harold Washington mayoral administrations. In 1985 a team of developers led by John Buck and Jerrold Wexler offered the city $12 million for the block bounded by Wacker Drive and State, Dearborn, and Lake streets, along with their guarantee to undertake $250 million in new development, which was to include a six-hundred-room hotel, a shopping mall, and an office tower. It was a promising prospect for all concerned. Unfortunately, the city administration began layering costly conditions onto the projects, such as set-asides, "linked development" contributions, and rent reductions to minority tenants. Under these circumstances, the hotel and retail developers dropped out of the project in 1986, but Buck and the Burnett company stayed.

SCALING THE HEIGHTS

Lee Miglin
J. Paul Beitler

Lee Miglin and J. Paul Beitler.
[Miglin-Beitler, Inc.]

When Lee Miglin and J. Paul Beitler revealed their plans to build the world's tallest building—a delicate spire that would pierce the sky at 125 stories—Chicagoans were alternately stunned, amused, amazed, and skeptical. The reaction was curious, coming as it did from a city that has taken great pride in its role as the birthplace of the modern skyscraper and the home—since the first tall building went up on West Monroe Street in 1881—of a succession of "world's tallest," including the current title-holder, the 110-story Sears Tower. Chicagoans love the tallest, largest, busiest, and biggest, but they also love their role as sidewalk superintendents. Critics claimed the proposed Miglin-Beitler Tower, with its small floor areas, would be unrentable. They questioned the site, a narrow corner lot paralleling elevated train tracks. They assailed the developers' motives, calling the plan an act of "colossal egotism" and a "publicity ploy" hatched to call attention to the Miglin-Beitler company and its other projects.

The factor that the skeptics failed to take into account was the unique mentality that has characterized Chicago developers for more than 150 years. Historically, Chicago developers have been bold, innovative risk takers, driven often by a highly personal vision.

Miglin and Beitler are in that tradition. Were they not, they would still be building personal fortunes as superstar brokers at Rubloff Inc. Miglin and Beitler are absolutely serious about the tower, which they liken to a slender rocket rising from the Loop. And they are known for their ability to deliver what they promise, as can be seen in the shimmering Madison Plaza and 181 West Madison buildings they developed on corners opposite the site chosen for the new tower. "Chicago needs something new and exciting in architecture," Miglin explains. "We have no really tall building that is beautiful. The Sears Tower is not beautiful. People don't feel about it in the way, for instance, that they feel about the Chrysler Building in New York. We want to do something for Chicago that is not only the tallest but the most beautiful building."

Although the publicity and controversy surrounding the announcement of the Miglin-Beitler plan made Lee Miglin's name something of a household word in Chicago in the late 1980s, Miglin is no newcomer to Chicago development. He was born in Westville, Illinois, a small coal mining community south of Danville near the Indiana border. His father was a miner who worked double-time to support a family of nine by running the Westville ice cream parlor and a local tavern—businesses that he lost during the Depression. Lee graduated from the University of Illinois in 1947 with a degree in journalism. He turned down a job in marketing with Procter and Gamble to become a Chicago sales representative for premixed pancake batter, one of the intriguing convenience foods that delighted American housewives in the postwar years.[1] Miglin soon turned to marketing another—far more successful—postwar product: television sets manufactured under patents held by Lee De Forest, the inventor of the vacuum tube.

In the mid-1950s Miglin took a year off and went to Europe to think about his future. He had done very well in sales, but was looking for more opportunity. Two fields, he believed, were open to a young man willing to work hard to make big money: oil and real estate. The smell of the oil fields had little attraction to a man who remembered his childhood in a coal-mining town. The scent of the boardroom was more alluring. "There were more millionaires in the real estate business than in the oil business, and that work involved dealing with people on a different level. So I decided to come back to Chicago and try real estate," Miglin recalls. He tried showing homes to pro-

Presidents Plaza Three. This building, dating from the early 1980s, was later renamed Triangle Plaza.
[Bob Harr, Hedrich-Blessing— Miglin-Beitler, Inc.]

spective buyers, but quickly realized that was not the type of real estate career he had in mind. "Arthur Rubloff and Company was then the hottest name in town, so that's where I went." Miglin showed the kind of initiative that was to make him one of the Rubloff's top executives in the way he went after the job. Brushed off on two successive days in his request for an interview with Rubloff executive vice president Abel Berland, Miglin arrived at Berland's office on the third day at eight a.m., an hour before Berland's secretary began work. As he had anticipated, Berland was already at his desk and was willing to talk. Lee Miglin was hired on the spot.

Miglin joined Rubloff at an opportune time. Population movement out of the city in the 1950s and '60s, accompanied by a rapid expansion of light industry into suburban areas, had created a market for the development both of industrial sites and new corporate headquarters buildings. This was particularly true in the sector northwest of the city, which was anchored by the opening of the O'Hare International Airport in 1955 and linked to the downtown by the completion in 1958 and 1960 of the Northwest Expressway (now the Kennedy Expressway).

After little more than a year, Miglin began to think about developing industrial/warehouse properties on his own, mindful of the Rubloff policy that the company be offered an equity position in any property that a Rubloff broker bought or developed on his own. In his years with Rubloff, Miglin was responsible for the development of more than five million square feet of industrial buildings and industrial parks, built either as speculative ventures or for major corporations and private and institutional investors. Miglin became a senior vice president at Rubloff and served on the board of directors, but

Madison Plaza. This forty-five-story structure at 200 West Madison Street was completed in 1983. [Scott McDonald, Hedrich-Blessing— Miglin-Beitler, Inc.]

continued to follow his own instincts as a developer. Arthur Rubloff and Company chose not to participate in most of Miglin's projects, considering them to be either too small or too risky. As of 1990 Miglin himself still owned more than two dozen of these industrial properties.

Miglin's first office building was a six-story headquarters building built for the National Tea Company at Cumberland Avenue and the Kennedy Expressway, followed by a ten-story building at the same intersection that was leased to the National Can Corporation as its world headquarters. When Miglin acquired an eighteen-acre site in Oak Brook in the late 1970s and began planning the Commerce Plaza office building complex, the Rubloff company finally decided to come in with him as a partner in a major project.[2] The company also participated in the early 1980s in the first two of Miglin's three Presidents Plaza office developments near O'Hare. (These three developments, totaling 1.5 million square feet of office space, were later named Sperry Univac Plaza, Presidents Plaza Two, and Triangle Plaza.) During this period, Miglin acquired his present partner.

J. Paul Beitler was an aggressive young broker at Rubloff who had tried his hand in several other enterprises before discovering real estate. Beitler is a Detroit native, a graduate of Michigan State University, and a Vietnam veteran trained as a helicopter and turbojet pilot. He came to Chicago as a franchise salesman for a company called Lease-A-Plane, operating out of Sky Harbor Airport in Northbrook. When the company went out of business in 1973, Beitler gravitated to office leasing as a broker for Helmsley-Spear of Illinois. In 1977 Beitler joined Arthur Rubloff and Company, becoming the company's top leasing broker in four of the five years he was there.

Miglin was not surprised when Beitler asked to come in with him as a development partner—many brokers had done the same. But he didn't expect Beitler's enthusiasm for development to last. Miglin set three requirements. "First," he told Beitler, "you have to be willing to see your income cut in half. Second, you have to agree to be at all meetings with architects or contractors, even if it means losing a commission. Third, you have to spend whatever time it takes—weekends, evenings, all day every day if necessary." Their first experience working together was on Presidents Plaza One. As Miglin found out, Beitler had no problem with the requirements. "He was a very, very persistent guy," Miglin remembers. Beitler usually started work on the project at five or six a.m. Miglin often was still at it long after midnight. But the two had no trouble communicating, Miglin says. "When he couldn't get me, he'd leave messages on my wall, stuck there with pins. I quickly found out why he'd won the top producer award for four years in a row."

Lee Miglin and Paul Beitler seem to have happened into the perfect partnership. Miglin—urbane, elegantly tailored, soft-spoken, unassuming in manner—moved easily through the higher reaches of Chicago's business and social worlds. Beitler, twenty years younger and relatively new in town, was perceived as brash, aggressive, ambitious—a hard driver and a fierce competitor. But their talents were highly complementary. Miglin had twenty-five years' experience behind him as a developer of high-quality but generally low-profile buildings.

Beitler had a talent for promotion and the willingness and ability to learn from his partner. Both were wearied by the paralysis in management at the lumbering Rubloff organization—a business climate that they believed inhibited creative development. And both had a drive to build memorable office buildings.

When the second phase of the O'Hare Presidents Plaza complex was under way, Beitler suggested that it was time to undertake a development project in the Loop. Miglin agreed. Drawing on his experience in creating corporate office centers and innovative industrial space, Miglin believed that their niche should be high-identity, prestige office buildings. "It has to be something important," he said. Beitler agreed. After making an unsuccessful bid for the property at Wacker Drive and Madison Street now occupied by the Chicago Mercantile Exchange, they acquired the northwest corner of Madison and Wells streets and—perhaps unknowingly at the time— established a Miglin and Beitler claim to the Wells and Madison intersection. The forty-five-story Madison Plaza Building (200 West Madison) at the northwest corner was their first project there, completed in 1982. This was followed by the fifty-story 181 West Madison Building diagonally across the street at the southeast corner, completed in 1990. And this was followed by planning for the 125-story "Chicago Skyneedle" on the southwest corner.[3]

Madison Plaza precipitated the final split with Rubloff, surfacing problems that had more to do with the internal operations at Rubloff than with Miglin and Beitler's individual relationships with the firm. Miglin and Beitler had bought the land at the Wells and Madison corner on their own, had secured the loan for the $100 million project (a joint venture with the AT&T pension fund), and had begun construction. The usual equity split was offered to the company, but Rubloff, which at the time was opening branch offices in other cities, chose not to participate. The Rubloff company then came back and claimed the right to manage the building, built at great risk to Miglin and Beitler themselves but at no risk to Rubloff.[4] At this point the two decided, in Miglin's words, that "we really had nothing in common with them, so we might as well have our own company." Miglin-Beitler Developments (later renamed Miglin-Beitler, Inc.) was incorporated in 1982. As a new company—although in no way a new team—the partners completed Presidents Plaza, Madison Plaza, 181 West Madison, the La Salle National Service Center (for La Salle National Bank), and the Chicago Bar Association Building, designed by Chicago architect Stanley Tigerman (Tigerman McCurry). The two had decided early in their partner-

181 West Madison Street.
The fifty-story building, opened in 1990, was the second structure at the Wells-Madison intersection developed by Miglin and Beitler.
[Jon Miller, Hedrich-Blessing—Miglin-Beitler, Inc.]

Miglin-Beitler Tower (model).
If built as planned the
Miglin-Beitler Tower, at the
southwest corner of Madison
and Wells streets, would be, at
125 stories, the world's tallest
building.
[Kenneth Champlin—Miglin-Beitler, Inc.]

ship to link their vision to that of nationally recognized architects. Chicago's Helmut Jahn was selected to design the thirty-one story, glass-clad Oakbrook Terrace Tower. They commissioned Cesar Pelli, the architect of New York's World Financial Center, to design the fifty-story white granite and silver reflective glass office building at 181 West Madison Street. Pelli is also the architect for the proposed Miglin-Beitler Tower.

Miglin and Beitler are clear about what they want in a building and are committed to their concept of creating prestige office space. But they are also committed to following their architects' vision. Beitler explains, "Whenever you come together as a developer with an architect, there has to be a synergy that exists between the two of you. On the one hand, the architect does not want to feel that he is constrained by economics. And on the other hand, the developer is totally constrained by economics." He adds, "We ask architects to design their dream, to paint a picture for us. And what we do is try our very, very best to articulate that dream, as far as the economics will allow us to go."

Miglin's style in developing industrial/warehouse space was to make the space special, either in the design or in the use of materials. "You have to do something a little different," he says. "You may think, How can I do anything different with a warehouse? It's just square walls." His solution was to "add something—vary the ceiling heights, create an L shape, provide berming, spend three times more than you normally would on landscaping." He carried the same philosophy into office building development. In Miglin's view, developers of many of the downtown buildings constructed in the 1980s built the warehouse equivalent of square boxes. "They just built office space," he says. "When we build a building, we build an environment. People are going to live here." Miglin and Beitler believe in monumental lobbies, exemplified by the soaring five-story lobby at 181 West Madison. "It has to be a grand entrance," Miglin says. They also believe in monumental sculpture, and have treated the public spaces of Miglin-Beitler buildings as settings for art they commission from contemporary American artists, including Abbott Pattison, Jerry Peart, Nancy Graves, Louise Nevelson, and Frank Stella.

Ground breaking for the $440 million Miglin-Beitler Tower, originally scheduled for fall 1990, was delayed by a downturn in the economy and retrenchment in sources of development capital. Miglin, however, remained confident that Chicago's new world's tallest building would go up as planned. The building's architect, Cesar Pelli, expresses the vision behind this development in more universal terms. "These aspirations appear in all cultures," he observes. "For humanity to lift itself on its tiptoes and reach for the clouds. It's a very, very deep-seated aspiration, and an achievement that we can all share in." In the case of the Miglin-Beitler Tower, Pelli says, "It will be a great achievement of engineering and logic, but, most important, it will be a great poetic gesture on the skyline of Chicago."[5]

AUTHOR'S COMMENTARY

1. Miglin soon discovered that the product he was representing, Gridl-Redi pancake batter, not only sold itself but also reproduced itself when not kept under perfectly controlled refrigeration. He tells the story of the happy consumer who used half a quart for a Sunday breakfast, returned the carton to her refrigerator, and found to her surprise the following weekend that the quart was full again. The downside of that phenomenon was that in the spring and summer, Gridl-Redi also tended to ooze out of its packaging into the grocer's dairy cases, leaving Miglin to chip away a residue that quickly assumed the density of concrete.

2. In an interesting turn of events, Arthur Rubloff and Company officers were able later to take over control of the Rubloff company by selling half of their share in the Commerce Plaza project to Arthur Rubloff in exchange for his stock in the company. In this way, Arthur Rubloff himself became Miglin's partner for the first and only time in Miglin's long career with the company.

3. The 125-story tower is not the project that Miglin and Beitler originally intended for the southwest Wells and Madison corner. In 1985 the partners announced plans to build "Madison Plaza II," a twin to Madison Plaza I, creating, in their words, "a gateway to the Loop." Land for the second Madison Plaza was cleared, but the project did not proceed to the construction stage.

4. Madison Plaza was built in the early 1980s, a time to try men's souls if they happened to be in the development business. Interest rates were running to 20 percent. A mild recession was under way, and in the early stages of this development, no prime tenant had committed for the space.

5. A new world's tallest building sounded like a good idea at the time, but for now, the time has passed.

Charles R. Gardner.
[David Wagenaar—Chicago Dock and
Canal Trust]

William Butler Ogden.
John Carbutt—Chicago Historical
Society]

OGDEN'S LEGACY

Chicago Dock and Canal Trust

In the years after 1910, when Daniel Burnham's Plan of Chicago was given final endorsement by the city, Chicagoans were hard at work implementing many of the plan's provisions: a broad, new Upper Michigan Avenue; the Michigan Avenue Bridge; the completion of Grant Park; and the graceful sweep of a double-decked Wacker Drive along the south bank of the Chicago River west of Michigan Avenue. By the mid-1920s plans for a new business district to be built over the Illinois Central tracks east of Michigan Avenue had been approved by the city. These plans were checked by the construction hiatus of the Depression and World War II years, but they were not forgotten. The plan was recreated in modern form with the development of Illinois Center in the 1970s.

In marked contrast, the north bank of the river east of Michigan Avenue seemed for the better part of this century to be a land that time forgot. Even as elegant highrises began to appear in the area north of the river and east of Michigan Avenue, the river's north bank remained much as it had been at the turn of the century—a shabby and somewhat inaccessible riverfront district of warehouses and nondescript low-rise industrial buildings.

The dockside properties along the river had become such a familiar sight that Chicagoans in the late 1980s were surprised by a sudden surge of construction activity on north bank properties where for decades they had seen only aged warehouses and the familiar advertising displays for Baby Ruth and Butterfinger candy bars surmounting the old Curtiss Candy Company building. The dramatic change taking place was the birth of Cityfront Center—sixty acres of twenty-first-century real estate going up on one of the longest-held, most valuable, and, for the better part of this century, most underused pieces of land in the history of a city otherwise known for relentless development and redevelopment of its downtown area.

The story of the Chicago Dock and Canal Company land—bounded roughly by the Chicago River, the lakefront, Grand Avenue, and Michigan Avenue—begins with William B. Ogden, one of the most energetic and diverse of Chicago's nineteenth-century real estate entrepreneurs. It is a saga of a property secured in the best traditions of the early capitalists, but a holding that became mired in inactivity in a family trust until—like Sleeping Beauty—it was awakened for development in the 1980s. The story began with the arrival of William B. Ogden in Chicago in the 1830s.

Ogden made his way to Chicago from his home in western New York state in 1835 and reported back to his family that he saw scant promise in the little settlement on the lake and even less of a future for the boggy land his brother-in-law had bought in a speculative fever a few years earlier. When the land sold at a profit, Ogden had a change of heart and decided to stay. Within two years he became one of the town's top real estate promoters, was elected Chicago's first mayor, and was well on his way to amassing his first million in a staggering array of other enterprises. There were few activities in early Chicago that did not attract Ogden's attention. He bankrolled a young inventor by the name of Cyrus McCormick. He built a brewery on Goose Island, ran a thriving lumberyard fed by timber from forest lands he bought in Peshtigo, Wisconsin, and was a member of Chicago's first Board of Trade.

Ogden, who had been elected to a term in the New York state legislature as an early advocate for the Erie Canal, had trade and transportation on his mind from the beginning. He was a prime mover behind the 1848 completion of the Illinois and Michigan Canal, which linked the Great Lakes to the Mississippi. He built Chicago's first railroad, the Galena and Chicago Union, and eventually owned or operated several more, including the Chicago and North Western and the Union Pacific, which in 1869 joined with the Central Pacific Railroad at Promontory Point, Utah, to become part of the first transcontinental railroad.

By the mid-1850s the area at the mouth of the Chicago River had become a clamorous industrial area and bustling marketplace. The McCormick Reaper Works dominated the north bank of the river at Pine Street (now Michigan Avenue); opposite, on the south bank, were massive grain silos and the great Illinois Central train shed that served the tangle of new railway yards on the lakefront. It is not surprising that William B. Ogden would cast a covetous eye on the river and on the lakefront shoals to the north of it. He wanted a Lake Michigan harbor for his lumber shipments and a terminal for his Galena railroad, which by then was shipping harvesting machines south and west as fast as McCormick could make them. In 1857, with a little help from his friend Mayor ''Long John'' Wentworth, Ogden both bought and seized land in the notorious ''Sands'' district along the shore of Lake Michigan north of the river. The story of Ogden's siege of the Sands and the rout of the squatters who inhabited the district is one of the more colorful episodes in the lore of early Chicago.

With the lakefront land at the mouth of the river in his control, Ogden formed the Chicago Dock and Canal Company, with the avowed purpose of improving the harbor and building a series of piers, breakwaters, and slips along the lakeshore and on the north bank of the river. He enlisted the help of a savvy lawyer from Springfield by the name of Abraham Lincoln to lobby the state legislature for a special act that both ratified the company's charter and enabled Ogden to condemn the additional land along the river deemed necessary for its purposes. When title to the lakefront lands acquired earlier was challenged, Lincoln (just a month before his nomination for president) was again called in to resolve the dispute, which was decided in Ogden's favor. The company leased lots along the riverfront profitably, but the harbor improvements promised by Ogden never quite materialized, nor did the slips and docks. Only one was built, the L-shaped Ogden Slip two blocks north of the river.

In 1866 William Ogden retired to his country estate in New York (where he died in 1877), leaving his brother Mahlon Ogden in charge of the Chicago Dock and Canal Company. Responsibility for managing the property was left in the hands of Ogden, Sheldon, the Chicago real estate firm that Ogden and his brother-in-law had established in 1836. Whatever Ogden's intentions were at the outset, for fifty years after the

Chicago River and S-curve bridge. The Curtiss Candy Company display at North Pier Terminal was a familiar sight to Chicagoans for decades following the 1937 construction of the S-curve linking the north and south portions of Lake Shore Drive with a bridge.
[Hedrich-Blessing—Chicago Historical Society]

grant of its charter, the company did little to fulfill the major purpose for which its charter was granted: the development of a harbor. In 1911 a legislative investigative committee declared that "the history of the Chicago Dock and Canal Company shows conclusively that what was intended to be a great public harbor enterprise merely became a cloak for one of the greatest land grabs recorded in modern history."[1]

Although harbor improvements languished, development of some of the Chicago Dock land had begun at the turn of the century, when a quarter-mile-long string of six- and seven-story warehouses known as the Chicago North Pier were built by the company for lease to James A. Pugh, one of the town's all-time great promoters. Pugh saw the warehouse development as a magnet for an international furniture trade. The North Pier Terminal Building became the centerpiece for a complex billed by Pugh as the largest combined warehouse and docking facility in the world. The enterprise was short-lived, however. Pugh's declaration of bankruptcy in 1918 brought Chicago Dock construction to a precipitous end, even as the new Michigan Avenue Bridge heralded the development boom of the 1920s that took place across the river along Wacker Drive. The company roused itself only briefly in the Depression and war years when it leased a parcel of land on Peshtigo Court to the Kraft-Phenix Cheese Corporation for construction of a headquarters building. The warehouse buildings nearest the lake were torn down when the "boulevard link" connecting the north and south portions of Lake Shore Drive with a bridge was completed in 1937. Any fleeting impulse Chicago Dock might have had to promote further development west of Lake Shore Drive was dampened by long-term leases to industrial tenants and to the Tribune Company, which leased some Chicago Dock land for its own newsprint warehouses.

In 1960 the century-old Chicago Dock and Canal Company was jolted by a takeover bid mounted by the University of Chicago, one of the company's largest shareholders. The takeover failed, but members of the Ogden family, who were the majority stockholders, responded by naming a new board of directors and replacing the Ogden, Sheldon firm with more aggressive property managers. In 1962 the company reorganized itself as the Chicago Dock and Canal Trust, a real estate investment trust (REIT). The trust remained closely held by the Ogden family and heirs but still numbered the University of Chicago among its stockholders.

If the reorganization of the early 1960s signaled a new direction, however, the change was all but imperceptible. Another twenty years went by with but one significant modification in the use of the trust's land. In 1967 the company leased three acres on the lakefront to a development partnership headed by Charles H. Shaw that built Lake Point Tower. Efforts to develop additional property were checked, following the construction of Lake Point Tower, by amendments to the 1919 Lakefront Ordinance that had the effect of banning construction of new multistory buildings east of Lake Shore Drive.[2]

Chicago Dock had been long captive to a conservative management whose risk-avoidance policies would have sent shudders through the dignified frame of the company's entrepreneurial founder. But it also had become a captive of its own geography. Access to the property from the central city and from the west was limited to lower Michigan Avenue, Illinois Street, and Grand Avenue. The tract was inaccessible from the east, because Lake Shore Drive soared right over the top of it. Through the 1960s and '70s, the trust could do little but sit back and watch a bustling, modern city rise up around it.

The breakthrough, when it came, came fast. The completion in 1982 of the $33 million Columbus Drive Bridge and extension unlocked the Chicago Dock tract to through north-south traffic and opened the land at last to development. The reconstruction of Lake Shore Drive, eliminating the "S-curve" south of the river and providing new access from streets on both sides of the river, provided solid linkages between the Chicago Dock properties and the surrounding city.

In 1981 Chicago Dock hired Charles R. Gardner to take over the leadership of the company. Gardner, a professional real estate executive and developer, had been a senior vice president for Canada's giant Oxford Development Group, and brought valuable experience in joint-venture projects into the mix. A former professional basketball center who is six feet eight inches tall, Gardner has a commanding presence and is a decisive executive, with a talent for seeing the big picture and moving on it. Graduated from the University of Colorado in 1968 with a degree in mathematics, he played basketball with the Denver Rockets before returning to graduate school in 1972 to earn an M.B.A. degree. Gardner worked as a senior accountant with Arthur Andersen and Company before joining the Oxford Development Group in 1977 as treasurer for a Colorado joint-venture project. He became senior vice president for marketing for the parent company in 1979 and was named senior vice president for corporate development soon after that.

In 1983, under Gardner's leadership, the Chicago Dock and Canal Trust—land-rich but cash-poor—formed a joint venture with a deep-pockets investor, the Equitable Life Assurance Society of the United States, which owned the Equitable Building immediately west of the Chicago Dock property. The trust was given responsibility for development of the area east of Columbus Drive and Equitable responsibility for the western portion. Together the partners brought in former New York planning commissioner Alexander Cooper to consult on a plan for a riverfront megadevelopment. Cooper, Robertson, and Partners (formerly Cooper Eckstut Associates) was later commissioned (with Skidmore, Owings and Merrill) to develop a master plan for the sixty-acre site.

The planned development ordinance for Cityfront Center was approved by the city council in November 1985. City planners were actively involved as partners-in-spirit in the new development. The key was a master plan that protected the riverfront for public use, assured access to a lakefront Du Sable Park, and consolidated open space requirements to produce larger, more usable park areas and green space than had been the case in the Illinois Center development just across the river. The city worked hand in hand with the developers to establish density and height limitations for the area. The plan-

Lake Point Tower. In 1967 the Chicago Dock and Canal Trust leased three acres of lakefront land to a development partnership headed by Charles H. Shaw that built the Lake Point Tower apartments. This was the first new use of Chicago Dock property since the 1920s. The Chicago Dock warehouses seen in the foreground of this photograph have been removed, and the fifty-acre property west of Lake Point Tower has become the site of the Cityfront Center megadevelopment.
[Hedrich-Blessing—Chicago Historical Society]

ning had gone forward with an energy and oneness of purpose that would have astonished Abe Lincoln himself. Implementation became the work of many hands and several development and design teams.[3] Chicago Dock and Equitable amicably separated their interests in the project after 1985. Equitable continued the primarily commercial development west of Columbus Drive, including Cityfront's signature building, the striking NBC Tower, designed by a team headed by Adrian Smith of Skidmore, Owings and Merrill and completed in

Cityfront Place [Cityfront Center]. This apartment complex was ready for occupancy in 1991. [David Clifton—The Habitat Co.]

1989. Chicago Dock continued to shepherd the slower development of the residential complex and hotel and retail facilities east of Columbus Drive.

The inaugural structure of the Cityfront Center complex was the Broadacre Development Company's North Pier Terminal building, which opened in 1988 as an office, retail, and entertainment center. In the North Pier project, Chicago architects Laurence Booth and Paul Hansen (Booth/Hansen and Associates) created an adaptive reuse that retained the original wood and brick character of the old Pugh Warehouse buildings, even to the point of salvaging the original steel flooring material. A new upper Illinois Street, linking the western portion of the Cityfront Center project to Michigan Avenue, was dedicated with drum rolls and a parade of dignitaries in 1989. Centennial Fountain, commemorating the 100th anniversary of the Metropolitan Water Reclamation District (formerly the Metropolitan Sanitary District) and celebrating the Chicago riverfront, was also dedicated in 1989. Even as the 1980s rolled over into the 1990s, the park spaces, hotels, and high- and low-rise residential complexes of Cityfront Center were taking shape and fanning new life into the area.

The structures that were so rapidly creating the new cityscape on the old Dock and Canal lands met the specifications of the master plan but allowed for the creative diversity of several teams of architects and developers. Broadacre Development's sixty-one-story North Pier Apartment Tower, designed by Dubin, Dubin and Moutoussamy with Florian-Wierzbowski, was completed in 1989. The Cityfront Place apartment complex, developed by McHugh Levin and designed by Gelick Foran Associates Ltd., was ready for occupancy in 1991. The thirty-three-story, 1,215-room Sheraton Chicago Hotel and Towers, designed by Solomon, Cordwell, Buenz and Associates, opened in March 1992.

The Chicago Dock and Canal land suffered from the beginning from a split personality. Was it a great public harbor project—or a land grab? Did the North Pier warehouses herald Chicago's future as a center for the international furniture industry or were they dinosaurs from the beginning? Would the verdict of history see Chicago Dock as last holdout of private ownership on a downtown lakefront long since promised to the people, or had Chicago Dock, in the end, played its role well as a placeholder, protecting the riverfront for public-private development in its time and in its season?

It has been all of those things. The final reckoning could not have been foreseen. As recently as 1973, Chicago art historian and professor of urban affairs Carl W. Condit cast a worried eye on both the Chicago Dock and the Illinois Central

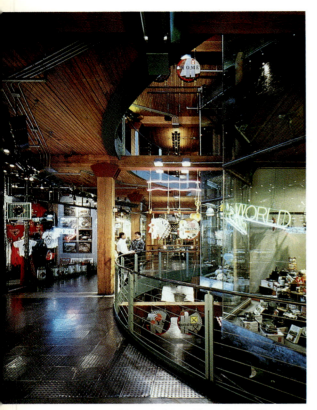

North Pier Terminal. The adaptive reuse of the old Pugh warehouse at North Pier as a riverfront retail, museum, entertainment, and restaurant complex was based on designs by Laurence Booth and Paul Hansen [Booth/Hansen Associates] and has provided a lively new public space on the north bank of the Chicago River.
[Broadacre Management Co.]

lands at the mouth of the Chicago River, noting that these properties constituted "a gap of about half a mile in which the riparian land has remained in the hands of private owners." As such, Chicago Dock represented a real and present danger to a last, crucial link in the preservation of the downtown lakefront for public use. Condit recalled that "it was the intention of the Chicago Plan Commission under the Burnham proposals to acquire this property for public recreational and harbor uses," and predicted that in the absence of effective city controls "this prime area for the construction of high-rise luxury apartments will eventually be drastically overbuilt and the lakefront at the river will be blocked from public access."

And so it might have been. In 1989 Howard Decker, an architect and president of the Landmarks Preservation Council of Illinois, stepped back and looked at the product of the public-private collaboration that galvanized around the Cityfront Center plan in the 1980s—ten years after Condit's dire prophecy. He suggested another ending to the story. Decker said, "Here's a development that can do something important for the river. It can make a blank part of the city come alive and connect the city to its lakefront; it can connect the city to Navy Pier. It can do so many things right, and there are not that many good opportunities left."

Cityfront Center as envisioned in the master plan will not be completed until some two decades into the twenty-first century, but Chicago Dock President Charles Gardner is not concerned about the time frame. After all, says Gardner, "We've been doing it for 130 years."

AUTHOR'S COMMENTARY

1. The proposed dock and harbor improvement plan may have been tainted with politics, but it must also be pointed out that shortly after Ogden acquired the land and established the Chicago Dock and Canal Company, events intervened that commanded a greater share of the city's attention than the implementation of the harbor improvement plan: the Civil War, a national financial crisis, the opening of Calumet Harbor south of the city in 1869, and recovery from the Great Chicago Fire of 1871.

2. The concern for protection of lakefront access that emerged in the 1960s during construction of Lake Point Tower and the planning for the Illinois Center development was followed in the 1970s by a similar concern for protection of the Chicago River. In early 1981, Joanne Alter, who was then a commissioner of the Metropolitan Sanitary District,

**North Pier Apartment
Tower (Cityfront Center).**
Broadacre Development
opened this sixty-one-story
structure in 1989.
[Don du Broff, Christopher Hinds—
Broadacre Management Co.]

met with me in my role as chairman of the plan commission to advise me of the work of the Friends of the Chicago River organization. At that time they were lobbying for a development ordinance similar to the lakefront ordinance that would protect the river and create a vehicle for reclaiming the river and the river bank. She told me that Mayor Jane Byrne had initially indicated support for such an ordinance but that somehow, in the translation, the city department of planning and the Friends of the Chicago River were beginning to find themselves in conflict. This was not surprising to me. Historically, citizens' groups had not fared well in the interface with city planning agencies. The suspicions and concerns of elected and administrative officials were in some instances well founded and in other instances totally unjustified. The climate of conflict nonetheless had the effect of putting a cloud over efforts to establish public-private partnerships.

I met with the principals of the Friends of the Chicago River to see what I could do to relieve the situation and head off impending conflict. Their position was reasonable and legitimate and their involvement, I believed, could contribute in a significant way to the planning process. I then went to Mayor Byrne and shared with her my thoughts and my perception that the difficulty was a communications problem and nothing more. Mayor Byrne responded immediately, directing me to talk with planning commissioner Martin Murphy about the issue and assure him of her continuing support for the ordinance. After Murphy and I met, he gave direction to his staff to work with the Friends organization in a conciliatory and cooperative manner. Shortly thereafter, Mayor Byrne reiterated her support for the ordinance in a major public address. I urged leaders of the Friends organization to be constructive in their dealings with the department of planning; to avoid confrontation and public airing of differences; and, where there were differences, to try to work them out so that all parties would feel a sense of participation and cooperation.

In 1983 an amendment to the Chicago zoning ordinance was adopted that addressed the riverfront issues and was satisfactory both to the planning department and to the Friends group and other community organizations that had joined in the discussions. This amendment, the first legislation ever passed by the city focused on riverfront development, recognized existing problems and property rights along the river and at the same time recognized the great possibilities for the development of the Chicago River in the years ahead. The ordinance provided for review of projects along the river and established flexibility in the zoning ordinance that would allow the city and developers to negotiate public improvements. There was almost no confrontation in the final process of adoption of the ordinance; rather, to the very end there was a great spirit of cooperation. The results can be seen in the riverfront improvements and the maintenance of public access that was written into the Cityfront Center master plan. This experience, I believe, helped to establish the climate for the spirit of public-private mutual effort that proved to be so successful in the Cityfront Center development.

3. Teams working on the Cityfront Center project included, among others, Lohan Associates, which became master planner for the Chicago Dock and Canal Trust in 1985; Tishman Realty and Construction Company; Broadacre Development Company; Broadacre Apartments; and the Habitat Company.

TEAMWORK

Robert Wislow

Robert Wislow. [At the 840 North Michigan Avenue job site.]
[Ron Gordon—U.S. Equities, Inc.]

Robert Wislow discovered the stock market at the age of fifteen and began trading pork bellies at the Chicago Mercantile Exchange as his first job out of college. He could not have foreseen the day that as the codeveloper of a new home for the Midwest Stock Exchange and the Chicago Board Options Exchange he would be instrumental in opening up La Salle Street south of Van Buren as a new financial center. These aspects of Wislow's career—commodities trader and developer of the striking One Financial Place—may seem related. They are not. His early aptitudes in the financial markets notwithstanding, the road to Wislow's role in the development of One Financial Place grew out of far broader interests—including a sense of Chicago history, an artistic orientation, and a tenacity and tough-minded approach to business that carried him through years of negotiation over the One Financial Place site.

As chairman of U.S. Equities Realty, the company he founded in 1978, Wislow is accustomed to dealing with large and very visible projects. He headed the development group that designed and built the Harold Washington Library Center. U.S. Equities was also responsible for the historically sensitive rehabilitation of Chicago's stately Union Station and has been selected to supervise the redevelopment of Navy Pier. Wislow was named Chicago *Sun-Times* developer of the year for 1991 in recognition of the library and Union Station projects, which were cited in the award as ''public works that will benefit the city for decades.''

Wislow is a first-rate developer who seems not to fit the image of a man at the top of this profession. Soft-spoken, ducking the limelight, seemingly without the ego that people think developers should exhibit, he is insistent on speaking of U.S. Equities projects not as personal accomplishments but as team efforts. Similarly, while Chicago exults in its innovative architecture, Wislow seems far more excited about projects that blend old and new. The library, for example, echoes nineteenth-century designs; One Financial Place re-creates Daniel Burnham's vision of Congress Parkway as a gateway to the city; Union Station is a monument to the grand era of Chicago railroading.

Bob Wislow was born in Chicago and would never think of living anywhere else. His grandparents on his father's side were Russian immigrants and on his mother's side, Serbo-Croatian. Wislow describes his own father as a "self-educated engineer" who carved out a career as a consultant specializing in the redesign of tools and machinery for factory production lines. The nuts and bolts of the developer's trade are a second language to Wislow. Bob grew up working summers and weekends in his father's third-floor walk-up studio in the Humboldt Park area, surrounded by a revolving cast of designers, engineers, and architects. He attended Chicago public schools, but received a more relevant education in the company of his step-grandmother, who was the founder of the costume design department at the Art Institute of Chicago and from his godmother, who was a makeup artist for screen stars and an ardent art collector. "They gave me that kind of touch with a different world, and that kicked off my interest in art," he says. In hindsight, Wislow says that he probably would have liked to have studied architecture, but in fact he went into premed at the University of Illinois, where he had a track scholarship. "I was the first kid in the family to go to college, so they thought maybe I should be a doctor." After two dutiful years, Bob left school to work for a semester and think things over. While attending the Illinois Institute of Technology at night, he sat in on a lecture series by Milton Friedman and discovered economics. Following a professor he admired, he transferred to North Central College in Naperville, where he went out for football and track and traded on the stock market. He graduated in 1967 with a degree in business and economics.

Just as things mechanical are in the Wislow family's blood, so, to an unusual degree, are athletics. Bob's mother was a champion weight lifter and a member of the underwater and acrobatic swimming team at the 1933 Century of Progress world's fair. His father was a six-day bike racer and a member

Union Station waiting room at Christmas in the 1930s.
[Frank C. Zak—U.S. Equities, Inc.]

of the U.S. speed skating team. His brother Len was an All-American football player, and his sister, Nancy Kronenfeld, is a professional racquetball player. Wislow is an avid skier, bypassing established slopes to ski the Continental Divide. Not to be outdone, the Wislow parents—in their seventies—were among the first adult Chicagoans to take up roller-blading.

An entrepreneurial spirit also runs deep in Bob Wislow. While he was at North Central, Wislow got into business for himself—several businesses. He bought land in northern Michigan and built rental A-frame ski chalets, which he still owns ("The only thing my mortgage has been paid off on, ever," he says). He rehabbed a condemned house near the campus and rented it out to students. He invested in a small fleet of station wagons and started a limousine service. He also arranged his classes so that he always had a seat near the door, close to the pay phone so that he could keep in touch with his Chicago stock broker. After graduation, it was not a big leap from trading stocks to trading pork bellies and live hogs, and later, plywood futures, for the Packers Trading Company at the Chicago Mercantile Exchange. In 1969 he was poised to buy his own seat but, on a tip from a ''wise old guy on the exchange,'' withdrew his bid at the last moment. Three days later, the market crashed. Wislow, newly married, decided, ''I can't do this anymore. I've got to get a job with a salary.''

He went to work for IBM's Chicago distribution office as a marketing representative selling on-line computer installations to large Chicago corporations. It was experience that would prove invaluable in Wislow's later career as a developer of office space for major financial and trading institutions. In 1971 Wislow's entrepreneurial instincts and independent nature got the better of his interest in job security. He left IBM to join Texas-based IDC Real Estate, where he was charged with helping open a Chicago office and establish a leasing and marketing division. When IDC later moved its headquarters to Chicago and changed its name to La Salle Partners, Wislow was a principal and stockholder. As a member of the IDC office properties group that developed One Woodfield Place in suburban Schaumburg and the Gould Center world headquarters complex in Rolling Meadows, Wislow became hooked on development. ''I was bitten by the bug,'' he says.

The Woodfield project exposed Wislow to the full range of the development process. Although his primary role was marketing and management, he also became involved in land acquisition and architect selection. The architect he selected turned out to be Thomas Beeby, who would team up with Wislow again in the design of the Harold Washington Library Center. One Woodfield Place was Wislow's first development experience; it was also Beeby's first independent office building project after leaving the C. F. Murphy firm to form a partnership with Jim Hammond (now Hammond, Beeby and Babka). ''We were all kids; we were new at this,'' Wislow says.

''I became very involved in the architecture,'' Wislow says. Perhaps too involved from Tom Beeby's point of view. At one meeting, Wislow recalls, Beeby pointedly remarked that ''people who aren't architects shouldn't be allowed to express architectural opinions.'' Wislow continues the story by way of describing how creative interactions between developer and architect may mature over the course of working together, as happened with Beeby and Wislow on the library project: ''Tom and I were in Connecticut on a cold Saturday morning, lying on the ground, looking up at this huge scale model of the

Union Station projected redevelopment. [opposite page]
[James C. Smith—U.S. Equities, Inc.]

exterior of the library. He said, 'Do you think we should tilt this owl out a little bit?' Then we both laughed, remembering those meetings over Woodfield Place. We had come from this very tough relationship of businessman and architect to the point where we were lying on the ground together figuring out how to do it.''

In the sixty-acre Gould Center complex, Wislow's perspective from the leasing and marketing side of the business precipitated another confrontation between developer and architect, in this case the Holabird and Root firm, which was hired for the project before La Salle Partners came in. The design called for tall, very narrow windows. "I perceived that the market wanted big, open, floor-to-ceiling windows," Wislow says. La Salle Partners had a mock-up made on the site to demonstrate their concept and persuade the client to support the change. "It was a huge problem architecturally with the Holabird office," he recalls. "But we came up with a compromise that worked real well. That building was a great success."

Wislow gathers his team as he goes along. Just as he had met Beeby on the Woodfield Place project, the Gould Center project—which included an impressive sports facility—brought Wislow into a relationship with Roland Casati, the first Chicago area developer to make a health club part of a corporate facility. Casati and Richard Heise (Casati-Heise Partnership) would later become codevelopers with U.S. Equities of One Financial Place.

In 1976 Robert G. Bicek, who had been with Wislow at La Salle Partners, recruited Wislow to Fidinam (U.S.A.). Wislow's job was to establish a United States operation for the massive Swiss-based real estate and development organization. After two years with Fidinam, Wislow and Bicek left and established U.S. Equities. They were able to persuade Camille Julmy, a Swiss national and career executive with Fidinam, to join them. Although Bicek would leave the company in 1983, the Wislow team by this time was gathering mass. The separation from Fidinam, however, was traumatic. "We had a tough settlement," Wislow says. In the course of that settlement, the partners found themselves left holding promises they had made on behalf of Fidinam to buy the 840 North Michigan building (where they eventually set up their offices) and the old La Salle Street Station, then owned by the Rock Island Railroad. "So we started our company to pursue those projects," Wislow says. "We had stars in our eyes" he says, stars that were in no way dimmed by two very fortuitous deals: the sale of the 3440 Lake Shore Drive apartment building just months before the bottom dropped out of the condo market, and the sale to an international corporation of a large tract of

One Financial Place. [opposite page] The 400-440 South LaSalle Street building opened its doors in 1984.
[Hedrich-Blessing—U.S. Equities, Inc.]

development land and a shopping center in Maryland. That transaction provided the seed money to complete the acquisition of 840 North Michigan Avenue and the La Salle Street Station.

The Wislow-Bicek renovation of the original seven-story 840 North Michigan Avenue began a series of renovation and redevelopment projects that stamped U.S. Equities as specialists in Michigan Avenue properties.[1] Wislow's Michigan Avenue developments came full circle in 1991 with the announcement of the redevelopment of the 840 North Michigan site in a joint venture with Marshall Holleb and Robert H. Gerstein as a low-rise retail center. Architect Lucien Lagrange's design for the four-story building won praise on the editorial pages of the Chicago *Sun-Times* as "the first [building] in a long time to restore some of the street's appealing old scale."

U.S. Equities' vision for the district south of the La Salle Street Station was anything but small-scale. Wislow and his partners began a land acquisition program in 1979 that consolidated 150 acres of Rock Island and Penn Central railroad land, extending from Van Buren Street south as far as Sixteenth Street, through a series of options extending over a twenty-year period. "We were trying to do an Illinois Center. That was our dream. It was such a unique opportunity for the South Loop. It would have been an amazing development," Wislow says. The plan was shelved when the bankruptcy court handling the Rock Island dissolution denied the twenty-year options. U.S. Equities retained control of the La Salle Street Station block, which extended from Van Buren through to the south side of Congress Parkway, at the point where the Eisenhower Expressway enters the city. Wislow saw a significant opportunity to add new office space to the city's financial district, which for the past century had been defined as ending at the Board of Trade Building at the foot of La Salle Street. "We knew that there were no modern offices in the South Loop and that the world was changing," he explains. "We had worked with financial firms around the country securing office space, so we knew they needed large amounts of open floor space with higher amounts of electricity than could be provided in older buildings. They were also looking at extended hours of operation, so they needed efficient mechanical systems for running overtime."

The La Salle Street Station property, located as it was immediately south of the Board of Trade Building and Addition, was ideal for the state-of-the-art financial complex that Wislow and his good friend and then-partner Bob Belcaster envisioned. This could be a development that would, in effect, extend La Salle as a pedestrian corridor south to Congress Parkway, opening up the financial district and creating a bridge to the South Loop, he thought. Wislow spent the next two-and-a-half years in negotiations that at various stages involved the Board of Trade, the Chicago Mercantile Exchange, the Midwest Stock Exchange, the Chicago Board Options Exchange, the Penn Central and Rock Island railroads, the Re-

20 North Michigan redevelopment. The former John M. Smyth furniture store was rehabbed in 1983. [Hedrich-Blessing—U.S. Equities, Inc.]

gional Transportation Authority, and the courts.

When the $100 million One Financial Place development opened in 1984, it was anchored at the north by the Chicago Board Options Exchange Building (developed on land sold to the CBOE by U.S. Equities) and on the south by the Midwest Stock Exchange Building, suspended over Congress Parkway. Centering the exchanges is the forty-story 440 South La Salle

office tower, a building that offers so many amenities that it has been described by the real estate press as "the Rolls Royce of office towers." Wislow says that the demonstrable elegance of the building is in part a by-product of the facts that the land—which other developers had considered undesirable—was cheap and that construction costs in the early 1980s were down. One Financial Place codevelopers Roland Casati and Richard Heise and the U.S. Equities team agreed that money saved should be poured back into the building. Wislow and architect Lucien Lagrange suggested that the windows of the Midwest Stock Exchange Building, which creates a memorable new gateway to the city, be framed as double arches reminiscent of the arches of Chicago's landmark Auditorium Building. Casati backed the idea with the $400,000 needed make the construction changes—over the strong objections of design architect Bruce Graham. Casati also supported Wislow in his request that the exterior of the building be of polished red granite and concurred in the concept of a landscaped plaza designed to human scale. "This is a man just embedded in detail," Wislow says of Casati. "He really made a very special building out of it."

If the public was not yet aware of the role that U.S. Equities was playing in the recovery of Chicago's South Loop, that awareness came quickly in 1988 when the development team led by U.S. Equities triumphed in the hard-fought competition to design and build Chicago's new central library at State and Van Buren streets.[2] The winning design by architect Tom Beeby was straightforward in its intention to blend into its South Loop site both architecturally and historically. The neoclassical, ten-story granite and brick library block looks and feels, in Beeby's words, "like other buildings you see in Chicago . . . the Auditorium, City Hall, the Cultural Center, the Art Institute." Considering Wislow's determination to incorporate arches inspired by the nineteenth-century Auditorium into the twenty-first-century Midwest Stock Exchange Building, it is not hard to imagine the collaboration that occurred between developer, builder, and architect in the library design.

U.S. Equities' experience working on the Near South Side and the firm's manifest commitment to architectural preservation served the company well in the 1987 competition for the job of redeveloping Chicago's historic Union Station on South Canal Street. U.S. Equities was selected over eighteen major U.S. and Canadian developers, because, Wislow believes, the firm did its homework—or this case, its field work. Wislow and Lagrange were aware that lurking in the history of the 1925 structure was a "Daniel Burnham building that didn't get built"—specifically, a twenty-story office tower envisioned

Harold Washington Library Center. [opposite page] The neoclassical ten-story building, opened in 1991, blends well with its surroundings. [U.S. Equities, Inc.]

by Burnham to top the old four-story ''headhouse'' west of Canal Street. The plan was abandoned when the site for the waiting room was shifted after a long construction delay forced on the project by World War I. Wislow and Lagrange began a search for the Burnham firm's original plans. Lagrange found them, with the assistance of a long-time employee in the railroad plan department. They then employed archaeolo-

Plaza Escada. This low-rise retail center at 840 North Michigan Avenue was scheduled to open in 1992. [Gilbert Gorski—U.S. Equities, Inc.]

gists who discovered that the caissons for the original Burnham plan were actually in place. The resulting design presented by U.S. Equities to the Chicago Union Station Company included the $37 million reconstruction of the railroad's passenger facilities completed in 1991 and restoration of the skylighted, vaulted ''Great Hall'' and original four-story facade. But they included as well the addition (yet to be built) over the old structure of twin twenty-six story towers of commercial office and retail space, replicating, Wislow believes, Daniel Burnham's original concept for a building that has long been an unofficial Chicago landmark.

Wislow is tolerant of the delay in the completion of the Union Station redevelopment brought on by the 1990 recession, just as he is tolerant of the lack of progress toward development of a thirty-six-acre site controlled by U.S. Equities south of the Roosevelt Road, which had at one time been the site selected for the new White Sox stadium. Tolerant, but impatient. "I like building things, whether it's taking a watch apart and putting it back together, or doing a new development." U.S. Equities' real estate services, built to a large extent on commercial property management, are diverse and successful. But Wislow hasn't shaken off the development bug. "It's bothersome when something is not under construction," he admits.

AUTHOR'S COMMENTARY

1. The first 840 North Michigan Avenue project, done in 1980 by architect Lucien Lagrange, transformed the dilapidated but historic building into a home for the Michigan Avenue Crate and Barrel store. In 1981, with architect Patrick Shaw, U.S. Equities redeveloped the seventy-year-old 300 North Michigan building, with the Handmoor Company as anchor tenant. In 1983 the firm renovated the John M. Smyth furniture store building at 20 North Michigan Avenue, which had been the original Montgomery Ward Building. In this project architect James Nagle of Nagle and Hartray restored the 1885 facade and roof line to its original appearance but cut a dramatic eight-story atrium through the center of the building to bring light into the mid-block structure. In 1989 U.S. Equities co-developed the striking new four-and-half-story Crate and Barrel building at 646 North Michigan Avenue, designed by John Buenz of Solomon, Cordwell, Buenz and Associates. Redevelopment of the 840 North Michigan Avenue site as a thirty-story tower, with a Park Hyatt hotel occupying the top twenty-six floors, was planned in the late 1980s. Given the economic conditions of late 1991, the project was scaled back to a four-story retail component housing an FAO Schwarz store; Plaza Escada, the first American outlet for Escada, a German-based women's clothing line; and Waterstone's, a British bookseller.

2. The SEBUS Group Design/Build Team selected over four other teams by the city and Chicago Public Library for the $144 million library project included U.S. Equities, developer; Hammond, Beeby and Babka, architects; Schal Associates and M. A. Mortenson, general contractor; and A. Epstein and Sons International, engineers. Although the

Harold Washington Library Center was in many ways a unique project, Wislow has said that the role of the developer—with the exception of long-term financing responsibilities—was no different from what it is in privately sponsored projects. "Our user is the library. Our owner is the city. We are the developer, who coordinates between the user and the owner, works with the architect, and oversees the contractor, all the while making sure that it all comes in at budget cost." A difference, Wislow commented, was that the building was "100 percent preleased!"

HIGH TECH, OLD WAYS

Richard A. Stein

Richard A. Stein.
[Stein and Co.]

People are still talking about the time in 1985 that Richard A. Stein, with only one downtown office tower in his portfolio, bested a field of first-class developers to win what some called the "Super Bowl" of development contracts: the 2.7 million-square-foot AT&T Corporate Center/USG Building complex in Chicago's West Loop. Since then Stein and Company has launched one pacesetting development after another, including award-winning suburban office sites, Chicago's new federal office building, and the $675 million contract to expand Chicago's lakefront McCormick Place convention center. This whirlwind of headline-making activity in the years between 1985 and 1992 may leave the impression that Stein is a newcomer to the Chicago development scene and a Johnny-come-lately to success. By no means. Stein is a highly professional, multifaceted developer who began at the bottom and worked his way one step at a time to the top of the heap. Richie Stein is a high tech developer with the style of an old-timer. He grew up in a colorful era in Chicago history among larger-than-life characters who played the ponies and still remembered Eliot Ness. Stein's recollections—delivered in a torrent of words that can leave even the listener breathless—are rich with street smarts and good humor.

Even while surveying the city from his suite of offices on the thirty-fourth floor of the AT&T Corporate Center, Stein does not lose sight of the fact that he began his development career remodeling two-flats on Chicago's West Side. "I'll tell you this," he says. "I was always afraid I would go broke. And I still think, every time, that it's my last big deal—that I'll never do anything bigger. Every year I'm going broke. Every year is my last deal." The attitude has kept Stein humble, but it has also made him both cautious and smart. "You can't hold back the tides of the ocean or the sun in the morning," he says. "A recession's a recession. But you can reduce your exposure by bringing professionalism and control to a project."

Stein was born in Chicago's Edgewater neighborhood in 1939 and raised in the North Shore suburb of Highland Park. After an undistinguished freshman year at the University of Colorado, he transferred to the school of hotel administration at Cornell University in Ithaca, New York. This was not an unlikely career choice at this point in Stein's life. In a sense, hotels were the family business. Stein's father, Joe Stein, had worked his way through law school during the Depression and helped a brother through medical school before he gravitated into the business of buying leaseholds on apartment hotels. One of these was the New Michigan Hotel at Twenty-second Street and South Michigan Avenue, better known as the old Lexington Hotel, home of Chicago gangland figure Al Capone. Stein's thought in studying hotel management had been that he would come home and help his father manage the apartment hotels. But by 1961, when Stein graduated, his father had lost all but one of the properties and had suffered a series of heart attacks. Hotels gone, Richie enrolled at the University of Chicago School of Law, figuring that corporate law might put him on a fast track into the business world. "I never wanted to be a lawyer," he recalls, noting that it didn't take long to be sure of that fact. Two weeks into the first semester, he went into the registrar's office and asked if he could get a tuition refund if he quit. The answer was yes. "There must have been an asterisk next to my name—I must have been marginal to begin with," he laughs. "All my money back, that was terrific!"

Even before he enrolled at the University of Chicago, Stein had taken over management of the Cedar Hotel, at 1118 North State Street, which his father still owned and where both parents then lived. But the hotel wasn't bringing in enough to pay the bills. Richie took a second job with Lee Gould, another hotelman and friend of Stein's father whose main line of work was his coal and oil business. While peddling fuel oil to apartment owners in 1963, Richie Stein met Ray Klein, a builder who was then renovating and reselling small apartment buildings in the district known as Little Italy on the Near West Side. The two hit it off immediately. Over a workingman's lunch—on the very day they met—Klein invited Richie to come in with him in his business, Littlestone and Company. "He said he'd give me half of anything he had. Turns out he owed $20,000 to the Exchange National Bank. So I took on a debt of $10,000," Stein says with a twinkle.

Klein and Stein scraped by doing remodeling work on the West Side, working one project at a time, hands on, and often as moonlighters while juggling other jobs. (Even while developing such major projects as the AT&T Corporate Center, Stein has stayed close to the hands-on construction side of the business. Typically, he visits a job site daily, greeting construction workers by name.) They concentrated on Little Italy streets such as Flournoy, Miller, Taylor, May, and Halsted; this area is now a fashionable enclave known as University Village (for its proximity to the Chicago campus of the University of Illinois). In the late 1960s, with urban renewal money flowing into the pipeline, Littlestone expanded its rehab operations into the up-and-coming Old Town district on the Near North Side.

When Stein and Klein met, Klein was camping out in an office at the original Carriage House hotel, which was owned by Jack Galter, an investor whose fortune was built on the Spartus Clock Company. The three fell into the habit of meeting at the hotel for breakfast at 6 a.m., and Galter eventually became the principal backer for Littlestone's projects—helping the partners, Stein recalls, "with ten thousand here, ten thousand there" to buy two-flats and four-flats for renovation. When Galter discovered that the Carriage House was losing money, he fired the manager and hired twenty-three-year-old Richie Stein to run it.

At this point, Stein's career took a another brief detour. He became part owner (with Klein) of a storefront hay, feed, and grain business located under the El tracks at Halsted and Lake streets. Stein and Klein had persuaded Galter to buy a building one door in from the northeast corner, thinking it would be a good site for a parking lot. The tenant, the Lev Hay, Feed, and Grain Company, came with the deal. It was the 1960s, and Lake and Halsted was scarcely an agricultural heartland, so the partners diversified. They purchased surplus paper on credit, shredded it, and then baled it for sale, using a fifty-year-old McCormick baling machine. They had just two groups of steady customers for their products: statuary companies, which bought the shredded paper for use as a packing material, and Hasidic Jewish peddlers, who still used horse-drawn wagons in traveling their West Side trade routes. It was a precarious operation.

Klein and Stein did far better in the Old Town rehabilitation projects of the late 1960s than they had in the paper and ani-

203 North La Salle Street.
Located in the North Loop
Redevelopment District, the
building opened in 1985.
[David Clifton—Stein and Co.]

mal feed business. From Old Town they expanded into apartment house development in the north and west suburbs, specializing in FHA-financed moderate income housing. By 1971, the year they were approached by a New York broker offering to sell the business, Littlestone had completed more

203 North La Salle Street east atrium.
[David Clifton—Stein and Co.]

than twenty-six hundred units. When Klein and Stein met in the broker's New York offices to close the sale of the company to a subsidiary of Wheelabrator-Frye, the construction conglomerate, Stein found it hard to believe that the deal would actually go through, much less that someone was willing to pay them money for their company. ''I felt like the thief who thinks his hat's on fire,'' he remarks, paraphrasing a Yiddish proverb. With the business sold (for $1.2 million), Klein moved to Santa Barbara, California, and Stein formed Stein and Company, entering first into an unhappy partnership that he ended after two years. (He suggests the nature of the problem by drawing a deft analogy to the hunter who would prefer to shoot one goose out of season than a dozen in season.) "So I left it," he says, "and I left everything behind. I had zero."

"You have to be smart or lucky," says Stein in describing the turns that his career has taken. He considered it lucky when, with nothing else going, he ran into Jim Otis, an architect and good friend, who asked Stein if he might be interested in working on the conversion to condominiums of an apartment building in the Lincoln Park neighborhood. The condo market was gathering steam in 1974, and the project was a success. "Because of that, I floated into condominium conversions," Stein says. It was scarcely an uncharted drift. Between 1976 and 1984, Stein and Company masterminded $500 million in condominium conversions in nineteen complexes in Chicago and elsewhere. The Chicago projects included some well-known addresses, such as the famed 900-910 North Lake Shore Drive apartments designed by Mies van der Rohe; 2800, 2900, and 3900 North Lake Shore Drive; and Hemingway House, at 1825 North Lincoln Plaza. Only one, 2970 North Lake Shore Drive, did not repay the investors. Stein wrote a personal check for $290,000 to State Mutual Investors to cover the loss—much to that company's surprise. The action was unusual, but would not be surprising to people who know Stein and who have done business with him.

During the period that the condominium conversions were under way, Stein and architect Jim Loewenberg were fighting a protracted zoning battle to develop the Village Center senior housing complex in north suburban Skokie. Village Center was successfully completed in 1980, but Stein spent years in court getting the project through. He also moved into the field of suburban office development. With a nudge from Jim Otis and good advice from Stein's longtime friend and lawyer Perry Snyderman, Stein and Company developed the Combined Centre complex in Northbrook for Clement Stone's Combined Insurance Company. When Combined Centre, designed by Otis Associates, was sold to the Prudential Insurance Company in 1984, Stein cast his eye on a large tract of undeveloped land on Lake-Cook Road at the Tri-State Tollway in north suburban Deerfield, visualizing the property as a site for other low- and medium-rise office developments in a campus setting. It took a year's time and a lot of lunches for Stein to close the deal with the single owner of the acreage. The result was the twenty-four-acre Lake Cook Office Centre and the thirty-eight-acre ArborLake Centre office and hotel complex, completed in 1987. Both complexes were designed by Skidmore, Owings and Merrill.

Stein and Company's 203 North La Salle building, begun in 1982 and completed in 1985 at the northeast corner of Lake and La Salle streets, was a first in a number of respects: It was the first downtown high-rise office building that Richie Stein had done, it was Stein's first experience with the Skidmore architectural colossus, and it was the first private development project to go up in the slumbering North Loop redevelopment district. Myron C. Warshauer, president of General Parking Corporation, had approached Stein in 1980 with the idea of bidding on the Lake and La Salle corner being offered by the city as part of the North Loop Redevelopment Project. The concept for the site was innovative, combining a parking garage topped by an office tower and linked at a lower level to the city's rapid transit lines. In August 1981 the city's commercial district development commission selected the Stein and Warshauer proposal over those of two other development teams. Stein and Company had become a high-rise developer.[1]

Stein remembers his first meeting with Bruce Graham, then senior designer at Skidmore: "I know I need a big-time architect. I call Perry. He says, go see Bob Diamont at Skidmore. Perry's never met Bob Diamont, he's just heard the name. Diamont takes me in to see Bruce Graham. I say, 'Mr. Graham, your reputation precedes you. You dominate the work in this city.' He says, 'We certainly do. We dominate the work in this country.' I looked at Bob Diamont and said, 'You got anybody else here?'" So that was how Richie Stein met Adrian Smith, who has since replaced Graham at the top of the Skidmore, Owings and Merrill hierarchy in Chicago. Smith took on the 203 North La Salle project and stayed with Stein as designer of the AT&T Corporate Center and USG buildings.[2]

Recalling the beginnings of the 203 North La Salle building, Stein suggests that he was a babe in the woods. "All of a sudden we're doing a twenty-seven-story building. The biggest I'd ever done was five stories. It's just more floors, but it gets complicated—working below grade, bringing in gas pumps, expansion in the engineering work needed. I learned a whole lot, but I needed help." He considered a partnership with another downtown developer. The discussions were protracted, perhaps because the prospective partner insisted that if he came aboard he would have to be "captain of the ship." Stein became impatient. "Got fed up with him at one meeting and said, 'You're either on or off. No more "captain of the ship." We're out to sea.'" Engineer Mike Oppenheim, who would become a close associate and who Stein describes as "clearly one of the construction geniuses of our time," had by then come into the picture. Stein had no regrets about saying goodbye to the captain.

If Stein was bold in bidding against better-known developers for the North Loop redevelopment site, he was consid-

AT&T Corporate Center.
The 2.7 million-square-foot
building, at 227 West Monroe
Street, became Chicago's
fourth tallest building when it
was completed in 1989.
[David Clifton—Stein and Co.]

ered absolutely audacious when he decided to go up against the titans of the development industry in a bid to develop the AT&T Corporate Center headquarters in Chicago. "This is the brass ring," Stein told his team when he heard in 1985 that AT&T was putting out a request for proposals on a development project that would be cited as one of the largest real estate deals in the city's history. "We're going to go for this job," Stein promised. Stein and Company was one of twelve firms receiving a request for proposal, but even then the RFP was contingent on the respondent's having control of the site being proposed for the development. AT&T set a three-week deadline from the date of the issuance of the RFP to the date

AT&T Corporate Center Lobby.
[Gary Knight—Stein and Co.]

for submission of a proposal. "Can you imagine?" Stein shakes his head in amazement even now. "Twenty-three days. They issued it on April 1 and the thing was due at noon on April 23!" The Stein team worked around the clock in their offices at 208 South La Salle Street.

Stein's site was an excellent one, the east side of Franklin Street, between Monroe and Adams streets, diagonally across from the Sears Tower. Stein had the south parcel on Adams Street, owned by M&J Wilcow, under option. The north parcel was owned by the University of Chicago and was occupied by a parking garage. "It's tough getting the University of Chicago to do anything in two-and-a-half weeks," Stein says (perhaps not recalling his own two-and-a-half-week career in the law school). With $300,000 in costs and his entire staff committed to preparing the proposal—but without assurance that he would have land control—Stein must have had a few anxious moments. Three days before the deadline, Stein got the signature he needed from the University of Chicago. Three months after the submission of the proposal—and three months before the contract was awarded—Stein scribbled a note to his partner Richard Hanson on a scrap of lined paper torn from a pocket-sized note pad. He predicted the outcome: "July 17, 11:27 a.m., AT&T, Stein and Company transaction, 99.9% confidence." Today, Stein keeps that note tacked to a bulletin board behind his desk, surrounded by photos of his wife and two daughters and snapshots from the annual fishing trips he takes in Alaska.

Stein believes his company won out in the competition because of its thoroughness and attention to the details of the client's needs. "While other developers were working with the chairman of the board, we worked through the people at the lower levels and built up their confidence in us." He recalls that one week into the preparation of the proposal, Stein and Company had asked so many questions that AT&T had to put out an addendum to the RFP. "We did our homework," he says. He recalls seeing a matrix after the deal was completed in which the competitors were rated on a scale of one to three on factors such as finance, security, aesthetics, etc. A category called "guts" had been added by hand. In that column, Stein and Company had been awarded three points.

The sixty-story glass-and-granite AT&T Corporate Center opened in 1989 to rave reviews from critics who admired Adrian Smith's elegant design and Stein and Company's commitment to creating a building that, even by Chicago standards, was a truly class act, carried off in the tradition of excellence of the Art Deco skyscrapers of the 1920s. Topped with two 100-foot spires, the AT&T Corporate Center became the fourth

USG Building. Under construction at the northeast corner of Monroe and Adams, the building was scheduled to open in 1993. [Rael D. Slutsky and Associates—Stein and Co.]

tallest building in Chicago—after the neighboring Sears Tower, John Hancock Center, and the Amoco Building. Phase 2 of the project, the thirty-five-story USG Building, which will serve as the international headquarters for the United States Gypsum Corporation, was scheduled for completion in 1993.

Stein readily admits that he doesn't win them all. Stein and Company entered the 1988 design competition for the new Harold Washington Library Center—a competition in which his firm, he acknowledges, was the first to be eliminated in a field of five. "We had the best inside. It was magnificent," he says. "But the exterior was a compromise."[3] Stein reflects on the disappointment. "Do I feel bad that I didn't get it? Sure. Would I have loved to get it? Sure. Was there ego involved? Show me a developer who doesn't have an ego," he says. "But what you learn, then, is you can't put your heart on the line with every deal. You can't lay your soul out there on these competitions because it's too tough, too subjective. These things you live and learn, and that's that."

Stein rebounded quickly from the experience of the library competition. In December 1988 the federal General Services Administration selected Stein and Company to finance, build, own, and lease back to the government a new federal office building in the Chicago Loop. The "lease-to-own" arrangement made between Stein and the GSA, the first of its kind in the country, has set a precedent for similar partnerships in the future between government and the private sector. The twenty-seven-story Ralph H. Metcalfe Federal Building at the southeast corner of Jackson Boulevard and Clark Street was delivered to the government in the summer of 1991, ahead of schedule and ahead of budget, and with the enviable record of having employed more women tradespeople in its construction than any job in the United States.[4]

Stein and Company's aggressive affirmative action policies, honed over the years by chief administrative officer Julia Stasch (who was named president in 1991), made the difference when the $675 million contract for design and construction of a third exhibition hall and connecting concourse at McCormick Place was awarded in the fall of 1991. In awarding the contract to the construction team dubbed "Mc3D" and headed up by Stein and Company,[5] Chicago Metropolitan Pier and Exposition Authority chairman John Schmidt noted the authority's goal of awarding 30 percent of contracts to minority and women-owned firms. "And Richard Stein," Schmidt said, "is recognized as Chicago's leader in orchestrating minority participation." The Mc3D development, said to be the largest public-works contract in Chicago's history, is part of the $987 million McCormick Place expansion program approved by the Illinois General Assembly in July of 1991 after two years of political wrangling. The legislation provides for financing through a thirty-year bond issued by the state to be repaid through new taxes on hotels, rental cars, and some taxi fares. But the project is not without risk. The contract requires that cost overruns be borne by the developers. A $60 million overrun on a 1986 McCormick Place expansion notwithstanding, Stein does not appear to be worried about completing the present project on time (mid-1996) and on budget. His record on the Metcalfe Federal Building seems to justify his confidence.[6]

When asked why he became a developer, Stein has a simple answer. "What else could I do?" he says. "Some guys are on the board of trade. They like the excitement. A lot of guys bet on the horses. That's exciting. For a developer, there's excitement in creating a new project, in those great meetings in the architect's offices, telling the architect what you want and seeing what he brings you back and shaping it back and forth." He adds that there is also a lot of satisfaction in seeing the impact that a project such as the hard-won Skokie senior housing complex can make in the life of individuals and in the life of the city. He begins to formulate another thought on the subject. "Being a developer is very analogous to being a movie producer. No different than producing a movie. It's an art form. It's a way to influence people's thinking," Stein says.

AUTHOR'S COMMENTARY

1. Completed in 1986, 203 North La Salle was designed and marketed as a Loop transporation center, a concept that for the most part has been realized—notwithstanding the fact that city promises made in the planning stages to renovate elevated and subway stations to create a Chicago Transit Authority station on the street level floor of the building did not bear fruit. The building is linked under Lake Street to the rapid transit line that terminates at O'Hare International Airport, making it a convenient departure and arrival point for business travelers. Ground- and mezzanine-level retail facilities are tailored for travel-related businesses such as airline ticket offices, car rental services, and travel agencies. A ten-floor parking garage above the retail level is topped by fifteen stories of high-rise office space lighted by deep atriums on the east and west sides of the building.

2. The 203 North La Salle project, in fact, brought together the informal Stein and Company brain trust that moved

McCormick Place expansion.
[opposite page] Plans for the
$675 million McCormick Place
expansion include a towering
glass-walled "galleria"
connecting a new exhibit hall
with the 1986 McCormick
Place Annex.
[Rael D. Slutsky and Associates—Stein
and Co.]

the company into the front ranks of Chicago high-rise developers in the 1980s. In addition to Julia Stasch, who joined Stein in 1976 as one of four employees, the team included Stein's partner Richard A. Hanson and construction engineer Mike Oppenheim. Stein and Hanson met over the financing for 203 North La Salle project, when Hanson was heading up the national real estate group at Coopers and Lybrand, the accounting firm that became the lead tenant at 203 North La Salle building. Oppenheim was with Herbert Greenwald when he was pioneering Miesian design and construction in Chicago in the 1950s and stayed on as a partner in Metropolitan Structures, the successor to Greenwald's firm headed by Bernard Weissbourd, the developer of Illinois Center.

3. To meet the intent of the "international competition" announced by the city, Stein had sought out Mexican architect Ricardo Legoretta for the project. In his words, in doing so he had to go "toe to toe" with Adrian Smith. Stein and Company's "Library '88 Partnership" entry carried the names of four architectural firms: Skidmore, Owings and Merrill; Legoretta Arquitectos; William E. Brazley and Associates; and Solomon, Cordwell, Buenz and Associates.

4. The Metcalfe Federal Building, named for former Olympic star and U.S. Representative Ralph Metcalfe, completes a triad of Federal Center buildings oriented to Dearborn Street between Jackson and Adams. The design for the plaza was established with the construction of the thirty-story Dirksen courthouse and office building designed by Ludwig Mies van der Rohe in the early 1960s. Accordingly, Stein selected Fujikawa, Johnson and Associates, the firm that carried out Mies's designs at Illinois Center, as architects for the new federal building.

5. In addition to Stein and Company, partners in the Mc3D team include A. Epstein and Sons International, which heads the engineering group, and the Atlanta-based architectural firm of Thompson, Ventulett, Stainback and Associates as design architects.

6. The plan for the McCormick Place expansion will add nearly one million square feet of exhibition-hall and meeting-room space. It features a towering glass-walled "galleria" connecting the new exhibit hall with the 1986 McCormick Place Annex and the original site on the lakefront. The state's plan also includes $60 million for rerouting northbound lanes of South Lake Shore Drive to the

west of Soldier Field. This relocation of Lake Shore Drive reflects a welcome revival of urban planning and city commitment to enhancing and opening up the lakefront south of the Loop. The extent of this commitment was evident in the 1990 guidelines prepared by the city's department of planning for the portion of the Central Station develop-

ment that will be built immediately west of Lake Shore Drive between Grant Park and McCormick Place. Named for a downtown rail terminal demolished in 1974 and built on land and air rights purchased from the Illinois Central Gulf Railroad, the seventy-two-acre Central Station project is planned as a megadevelopment on the order of Illinois Center and Cityfront Center. The project will break through the old rail lines that have constituted a formidable barrier between the South Loop and the lakefront. The first phase of the project, which will include a long-awaited extension of Roosevelt road through to Grant Park at Indiana Avenue, was launched in late 1991.

BIBLIOGRAPHY

Principal sources for building histories and details regarding location, ownership, financing, and technical and architectural features have been the contemporary accounts of real estate and construction activity provided by the many newspapers, news magazines, and architectural journals that—each in its own time—have flourished in Chicago over the 150 years of the city's development history.

Primary among these are the Economist (volumes 1-115; 1888-1946) and its successor publication Realty and Building. Other valuable sources include the Chicago Daily News, Chicago Daily Tribune, Chicago Evening Post, Chicago Herald, Chicago Herald-American, Chicago Inter Ocean, Chicago Record-Herald, Chicago Sun Times, Chicago Tribune, Construction News, Engineering News, Inland Architect and Builder, Inland Architect and News Record, Land Owner, and Metro Chicago Real Estate.

Adler, Dankmar. "The Chicago Auditorium." Architectural Record 1 (April-June 1892), 415.

Aldis, Graham. "Fifty Years in Twenty Minutes." Proceedings of the Annual Convention of the National Association of Building Owners and Managers. Chicago, 1952.

Aldis, Owen F. Correspondence, World's Columbian Exposition. University of Illinois at Chicago, the Library.

[Aldis, Owen F., and Peter C. Brooks.] "Narrative Summary of Correspondence, 1879-1920." Archives and Manuscript Department of the Chicago Historical Society.

Andreas, A. T. History of Cook County, Illinois, from the Earliest Period to the Present Time. Chicago: A. T. Andreas, 1884; reprint ed., Evansville, Ind.: Unigraphic, Inc., 1976.

Andreas, A[lfred] T[heodore]. History of Chicago from the Earliest Period to the Present Time. 3 vols. Chicago: A. T. Andreas, 1884-86; reprint ed., New York: Arno Press, 1925.

"Arthur Rubloff: Giant of Real Estate." The Magazine of Success 6 (12 November 1963): 2-7.

Bach, Ira J., ed. Chicago's Famous Buildings: A Photographic Guide to the City's Architectural Landmarks and Other Notable Buildings. 3rd ed. rev. Chicago: University of Chicago Press, 1980.

Baird & Warner, Inc., 1855-1980: Celebrating 125 Years in Real Estate. Chicago: Baird and Warner, 1980.

"Ben Marshall's Villa." In: Wilmette's Nautical Heritage. Wilmette (Ill.): Sheridan Shore Yacht Club, 1982.

Biographical Sketches of the Leading Men of Chicago, Written by the Best Talent in the Northwest. Chicago: Wilson and St. Clair, 1868.

Block, Jean F. Hyde Park Houses: An Informal History, 1856-1910. Chicago: University of Chicago Press, 1978.

Bloomfield, Craig. "Golub's Eclectic Activities." Commerical Property News, 16 February 1992.

Bluestone, Daniel. Constructing Chicago. New Haven and London: Yale University Press, 1991.

The Book of Chicago: 1911. Chicago: Chicago Evening Post, 1911.

"Brooks Estates in Medford, 1669-1927." Medford Historical Register. Medford, Mass.: Medford Historical Society, March 1927.

Bross, William. History of Chicago. Chicago: Jensen, McClurg and Co., 1876.

Bruegmann, Robert. "Holabird and Roche and Holabird and Root: The First Two Generations." Chicago History 9 (Fall 1980): 130-65.

Bryan, I. J. Report of the Commissioners and a History of Lincoln Park. Chicago, 1889.

"Builder Greenwald Views Relations with Architects." Construction News 9 (7 May 1954): 1.

Burnham, Daniel H. Papers. Burnham Library, Art Institute of Chicago.

Burnham, Daniel H., and Edward H. Bennett. Plan of Chicago. Chicago: Commercial Club, 1909.

Burrows, George S. "The Builders of Chicago: An Intellectural History of the Wealthy Class in Chicago in the 1890s." Senior thesis, Yale University, 1942; reprinted, 1991, Lake Forest, Ill.

The Central Manufacturing District: A Book of Descriptive Text, Photographs and Testimonial Letters. Chicago: Central Manufacturing District, November 1911.

Chaddick, Harry F. Chaddick! Success Against All Odds. Chicago: Harry F. Chaddick Associates, 1990.

Chappell, S. A. "Early History of River Forest." Oak Leaves [Oak Park, Ill.], 28 November 1914: 40.

Chatfield-Taylor, H. C. Chicago. Boston and New York: Houghton Mifflin, 1917.

Chicago Central Area Committee. Chicago 21: A Plan for the Central Area Communities. Chicago: September 1973.

Chicago City Directory and Business Advertiser. 1888 through 1920 editions.

Chicago Commercial District Development Commission. North Loop Guidelines for Conservation and Redevelopment. Chicago: 1981.

Chicago Commission on Historical and Architectural Landmarks. Landmark Neighborhoods in Chicago. Chicago: 1981.

Chicago Department of Development and Planning. The Riveredge Plan of Chicago. Chicago: December 1974.

Chicago Department of Development and Planning. Illinois Central Air Rights Development: Guidelines for Development of the Randolph Terminal Properties. Chicago: May 1968.

Chicago Department of Development and Planning. The Comprehensive Plan of Chicago. Chicago: December 1966.

Chicago Department of Development and Planning. Historic City: The Settlement of Chicago. Chicago: 1976.

Chicago Department of Development and Planning. Summary of Information on the Reliance Building. Chicago: November 1971.

Chicago Department of Development and Planning. "Illinois Center Development." Typescript, December 1982. Municipal Reference Library.

Chicago Department of Development and Planning. Near West Development Area. Chicago: January 1967.

Chicago Department of Development and Planning. South Loop New Town: Guidelines for Development. Chicago: August 1975.

"Chicago Frame-Up:...Illinois Center." Architectural Forum 140 (January-February 1974): 74.

Chicago Land Clearance Commission. Michael Reese-Prairie Shores Redevelopment Project, Final Project Report. Chicago: 1962.

Chicago Landmarks Recording Project. Manhattan Building. Typescript. Historic American Buildings Survey, Chicago Project II: Manhattan Building, 1964.

Chicago Office Building Directory. Chicago: Chicago Office Building Directory Company, 1892.

Chicago Plan Commission. The Outer Drive. Chicago: 1929.

Chicago Plan Commission. Chicago Land Use Survey. Vol 1: Residential Chicago. Vol 2: Land Use in Chicago. Chicago: 1942 and 1943, respectively.

Chicago Plan Commission. The Chicago Plan in 1933. Chicago: 1933.

Chicago Plan Commission. Forty-four Cities in the City of Chicago. Chicago: April 1942.

Circuit Court of Cook County. 1430 Lake Shore Drive Corporation vs. W. C. Bannerman. Bill of Complaint filed 23 June 1930; Response filed 30 July 1931; Decree entered by Judge William V. Brothers on 30 July 1931; Master's Report of Sale and Distribution and for Deficiency filed 11 September 1931.

Circuit Court of Cook County. June Catherine Martin vs. The First National Bank of Chicago, as Trustee under the Will of Otto Young [for his heirs]. Bill of Complaint filed 19 June 1936. Exhibit "A"—Last Will and Testament of Otto Young.

City of Chicago. The Lakefront Plan of Chicago. Chicago: December 1972.

City of Chicago. Proceedings of the Chicago City Council. For the municipal years 1880 through 1913. Municipal Reference Library.

City of Chicago. Chicago Dock-Equitable Venture: Development Guidelines. Chicago: 11 April 1985.

City of Chicago. Chicago 1992 Comprehensive Plan: Goals and Policies and Ten-Year Capital Development Strategies. Draft for Discussion. Chicago: May 1982.

Commercial and Architectural Chicago. Chicago: G. W. Grear, 1887.

Commercial Club of Chicago. Plan for a Boulevard to Connect the North and South Sides of the River on Michigan Avenue and Pine Street. Chicago: R. R. Donnelley and Sons, 1908.

Commission on Chicago Historical and Architectural Landmarks. The Rookery. Chicago: n.d.

Commission on Chicago Historical and Architectural Landmarks. "Waller Apartments." Preliminary Staff Summary, December 1987. Municipal Reference Library.

Commission on Chicago Historical and Architectural Landmarks. Monadnock Block. Chicago: 1975.

Commission on Chicago Historical and Architectural Landmarks. Robert W. Roloson Houses. Chicago: August 1979.

Commission on Chicago Historical and Architectural Landmarks. "Proposed Designation of the

Waller Apartments District as a Chicago Landmark." Typescript. Municipal Reference Library.

Commission on Chicago Historical and Architectural Landmarks. Seven Houses on Lake Shore Drive: Preliminary Staff Summary of Information. Chicago: June 1989.

Condit, Carl. Chicago 1910-29: Building, Planning, and Urban Technology. Chicago: University of Chicago Press, 1973.

Condit, Carl. Chicago 1930-70: Building, Planning, and Urban Technology. Chicago: University of Chicago Press, 1974.

Condit, Carl. The Chicago School of Architecture: A History of Commercial and Public Building in the City Area, 1875-1925. Chicago: University of Chicago Press, 1964.

Council on Buildings and Urban Habitat. Lynn S. Beedle, ed. Second Century of the Skyscraper. New York: Van Nostrand Reinhold, 1988.

Crawford, Mary Caroline. Famous Families of Massachusetts. Vol 2. Boston: Little, Brown, 1930.

Cromie, Robert. The Great Chicago Fire. New York: McGraw-Hill, 1958.

Cross, Robert. "Can New Towns Save Old Cities?" Chicago Tribune Sunday Magazine, 10 September 1972.

Crump, Joseph. Less is Skidmore. Chicago [magazine], February 1991.

Currey, J. Seymour. Chicago: Its History and its Builders: A Century of Marvelous Growth. 5 vols. Chicago: S. J. Clarke, 1912.

Cutler, H.G. The World's Fair: Its Meaning and Scope. Chicago: Star Publishing Co., 1892.

Davenport, E. A. "River Forest: Its Party Government and a Little of Its History." Typescript, 28 November 1932. River Forest Public Library, River Forest, Ill.

Dean, C. The World's Fair City, and Her Enterprising Sons. Chicago: United, 1892.

Dedmon, Emmett. Fabulous Chicago: A Great City's History and People. New York: Random House, 1953.

Dedmon, Emmett. Great Enterprises: 100 Years of the YMCA of Metropolitan Chicago. Chicago: Rand McNally, 1957.

Doty, Mrs. Duane. The Town of Pullman: Its Growth with Brief Accounts of Its Industries. Pullman, Ill.: T. P. Strusacker, 1893; reprinted by Pullman Civic Association, 1974.

Drury, John. Dining in Chicago. Chicago: John Day Co., 1931.

Drury, John. Old Chicago Houses. Chicago: University of Chicago Press, 1941.

Eaton, Leonard K. Two Chicago Architects and Their Clients: Frank Lloyd Wright and Howard Van Doren Shaw. Cambridge: MIT Press, 1969.

Ebner, Michael H. "Many Twists to Sheridan Road's History." Crain's Chicago Business, 30 May 1988: 56.

Edes, Grace Williamson. Annals of the Harvard Class of 1852, s.v., Brooks, Peter Chardon. Cambridge: 1922.

Edgerton, Michael, and Kenan Heise. Chicago: Center for Enterprise. Vol. 2: The Twentieth Century. Chatham, Calif.: Windsor Publications, 1982.

England, Merelice K. "Before and After. . .In a Core City" [South Commons]. Christian Science Monitor, 23 April 1971.

"Enterprise of Chicago Land Men." Land Owner 4 (January 1872): 12.

Ericsson, Henry, with Lewis E. Myers. Sixty Years a Builder: The Autobiography of Henry Ericsson. Chicago: A. Kroch and Son, 1942.

Farr, Finis. Chicago: A Personal History of America's Most American City. New Rochelle, N.Y.: Arlington House, 1973.

Farr, Finis. Frank Lloyd Wright. London: Jonathan Cape, 1962.

Fields, Jeannette S., ed. A Guidebook to the Architecture of River Forest. River Forest, Ill.: Architectural Guidebook Committee, 1981.

Flinn, John J. Chicago, the Marvelous City of the West: A History, An Encyclopedia, and a Guide. Chicago: The Standard Guide Company, 1892.

Flinn, John J. The Standard Guide of Chicago. Chicago: Standard Guide Co., 1893.

[Forbes, Abner.] The Rich Men of Massachusetts. Boston: Redding and Co., 1852.

Frazier, Nancy. Louis Sullivan and the Chicago School. New York: Crescent Books, 1991.

Friendly, Alfred Jr. "Mies at 77 Explains." Chicago Scene 5 (February 1964): 29-32.

Furen, Howard B. Chicago: A Chronological and Documentary History 1784-1970. Dobbs Ferry, N.Y.: Oceana Publications, 1974.

Gage, Lyman J. Report of the President to the Board of Directors of the Columbian Exposition. Chicago: Rand McNally, 1898.

Gage, Lyman J. Memoirs of Lyman J. Gage. New York: House of Field, 1937.

Gale, Edwin. Reminiscences of Early Chicago and Vicinity. Chicago: Fleming H. Revell, 1902.

Gallup, Donald C. "Aldis, Foley, and the Collection of American Literature at Yale." In: Papers of the Bibliographical Society of America. Vol. 42. New York: Bibliographical Society of America, 1948.

Gilbert, Paul T., and Charles L. Bryson. Chicago and Its Makers. Chicago: F. Mendelsohn, 1929.

Gill, Brendan. Many Masks: A Life of Frank Lloyd Wright. New York: G. P. Putnam's Sons, 1987.

Goff, Lisa. "Saving the Reliance: Beneath the Grime, a Loop Jewel." Crain's Chicago Business, 24 August 1987: 69.

Gordon, Sarah, ed. All Our Lives: A Centennial History of Michael Reese Hospital and Medical Center, 1881-1981. Chicago: MRHMC, 1981.

Grant, Bruce. Fight For a City: The Story of the Union League Club of Chicago and Its Times— 1880-1955. Chicago: Rand McNally, 1955.

Gross, Lisa. End Game [Cityfront Center]. Forbes, 26 April 1982.

Hall, Albert L. History of River Forest. River Forest, Ill.: Forest Publishing, 1937.

Hansen, Harry. The Chicago. [Rivers of America Series]. New York: Rinehart, 1942.

Harrison, Carter H. Stormy Years: The Autobiography of Carter H. Harrison. Indianapolis: Bobbs-Merrill, 1935.

Harrison, Carter H. II. Growing Up With Chicago. Chicago: Ralph Fletcher Seymour, 1944.

Harrison, Mrs. Carter H. II. "Strange To Say—": Recollections of Persons and Events in New Orleans and Chicago. Chicago: A. Kroch and Son, 1949.

Hauser, Philip M., and Evelyn M. Kitagawa. Local Community Fact Book for Chicago, 1950. Chicago: Chicago Community Inventory, University of Chicago, 1953.

Hayner, Don, and Tom McNamee. Streetwise Chicago: A History of Chicago Street Names. Chicago: Loyola University Press, 1988.

Henn, Roger E. "Our Neighbor to the East, the Monadnock Building," Union League Men and Events 47 (March 1955): 15.

Hilliard, Celia. "Rent Reasonable to the Right Parties: Gold Coast Apartment Buildings 1906-1929." Chicago History 8 (Summer 1979): 66-77.

Hines, Thomas S. Burnham of Chicago: Architect and Planner. New York: Oxford University Press, 1974.

History of Chicago: Its Men and Institutions. Chicago: Inter Ocean, 1900.

Hoffman, Donald. The Architecture of John Wellborn Root. Baltimore: Johns Hopkins University Press, 1973.

Hofmeister, Rudolf A. The Germans of Chicago. Chicago: Stipes Publishing Co., 1976.

Horowitz, Helen Lefkowitz. Culture and the City: Cultural Philanthropy in Chicago from the 1880s to 1917. Lexington: University Press of Kentucky, 1976.

Hoyt, Homer. According to Hoyt: 53 Years of Homer Hoyt. Washington, D.C.: Homer Hoyt Associates, 1970.

Hoyt, Homer. One Hundred Years of Land Values in Chicago, 1830-1933. Chicago: University of Chicago Press, 1933.

Hutchinson, William R. "Disapproval of Chicago: The Symbolic Trial of David Swing." Journal of American History 59 (June 1972): 30-47.

Ibata, David. "Buying Into Retail." Chicago Tribune, Commercial Real Estate supplement, 5 April 1989.

Industrial Chicago. 4 vols. Chicago: Goodspeed, 1891.

Ingersoll, John H. "Chicago's South Commons: An Urban Awakening." House Beautiful 113 (October 1971): 109-11.

Jannot, Mark. "Off the Drawing Board. . . And Onto the Streets" [Cityfront Center]. Chicago [magazine], January 1989.

Jensen, Elmer. "The World's First Skeleton Building." Paper read to the Chicago Chapter of the Newcomen Society, 9 November 1944.

Karp, Richard. "The Age of the Megaproject." Real Estate, August 1988.

Kay, Beatrice Lorranine. "History of River Forest." Typescript, n.d. River Forest Public Library, River Forest, Ill.

Kelly, Jeffrey. "The Village: America's First Planned Community Enters Middle Age." Chicago Tribune Sunday Magazine, 5 May 1985.

Kerch, Steve. "Extras Aren't Extra Anymore." Chicago Tribune, Commercial Real Estate supplement, 5 April 1989.

Kerch, Steve. "The Classics: Architecture, History Combine with Economics to Build Successes." Chicago Tribune, Commercial Real Estate supplement, 3 April 1991.

Kirkland, Caroline, ed. Chicago's Yesterdays: A Sheaf of Reminiscences. Chicago: Daughaday, 1919.

Kirkland, Joseph. The Story of Chicago. 3 vols. Chicago: Dibble, 1892-94.

Klutznick, Philip M. Angles of Vision: A Memoir of My Lives. Chicago: Ivan R. Dee, 1991.

Kogan, Herman and Lloyd Wendt. Lords of the Levee: The Story of Bathhouse John and Hinky Dink. Indianapolis: Bobbs-Merrill, 1943.

Krasnow, Iris. "Arthur the Magnificent." Chicago [magazine], April 1981.

Laine, Christian K. "The Harold Washington Library Center." Metropolitan Review 1 (September-October 1988): 5-51.

Lake Geneva Estates, Aloha Lodge. Papers. Lake Geneva Public Library, Lake Geneva, Wis.

Lakeside Annual Directory of the City of Chicago. 1874/75-1917.

Lewis, Lloyd, and Henry Justin Smith. Chicago, the History of Its Reputation. New York: Harcourt, Brace, 1929.

Lind, Alan R. Limiteds Along the Lakefront: The Illinois Central in Chicago. Park Forest, Ill.: Transport History Press, 1986.

Lindberg, Richard. Chicago Ragtime: Another Look at Chicago, 1880-1920. South Bend, Ind.: Icarus, 1985.

Linn, James Weber. "Hosts of Chicago: An Account of Certain Keepers of the Public Houses." The Chicagoan 7 (13 April 1929): 11-13.

Lovering, Frank W. "Peter Chardon Brooks [I]." Typescript, n.d. Medford Public Library, Medford, Mass.

Lowe, David. Lost Chicago. Boston: Houghton Mifflin, 1975.

Mabee, Bessie A. "History of Villa Park." Typescript, 1936. "Some of the Early History of Villa Park." Typescript, 1964. Villa Park Historical Museum, Villa Park, Ill.

Mack, Edwin F. Old Monroe Street: Notes on the Monroe Street of Early Chicago Days. Chicago: Central Trust Company of Illinois, 1914.

Manson, Grant Carpenter. Frank Lloyd Wright to 1910: The First Golden Age. New York: Reinhold, 1958.

Marshall, Benjamin H. "Architecture of an Expanding Metropolis and Some of Its Towers." In: Chicago: The World's Youngest Great City. A. G. Becker and Co., ed., 53-58. Chicago: American Publishers, 1929.

Masters, Edgar Lee. The Tale of Chicago. New York: G. P. Putnam's Sons, 1933.

Mayer, Harold M. "Centex Industrial Park: An Organized Industrial District." In: Thoman, Richard S., and Donald J. Patton, eds. Focus on Geographic Activity. New York: McGraw Hill, 1964.

Mayer, Harold M., and Richard C. Wade. Chicago: Growth of a Metropolis. Chicago: University of Chicago Press, 1969.

Melichar, Ernie. "Charles H. Shaw Forecasts How Hilton Renewal Will Affect Chicago." Real Estate Magazine 73 (18 April 1986).

Mendelsohn, Felix. Chicago Yesterday and Today. Chicago: F. Mendelsohn, 1932.

Metropolitan Housing Council. Records [1930s]. University of Illinois at Chicago, the Library.

"Michigan Square Building, Chicago, Ill.: Holabird and Root, Architects." Architectural Record 70 (October 1931): 257-62.

Miller, Ross. American Apocalypse: The Great Fire and the Myth of Chicago. Chicago and London: University of Chicago Press, 1990.

Monroe, Harriet. John Wellborn Root: A Study of His Life and Work. Boston: Houghton Mifflin, 1896.

Montgomery, Royal E. Industrial Relations in the Chicago Building Trades. Chicago: University of Chicago Press, 1927.

Moore, Charles. Daniel H. Burnham: Architect, Planner of Cities. 2 vols. Boston: Houghton Mifflin, 1921; reprint ed., New York: De Capa, 1968.

Moses, John, and Joseph Kirkland, eds. History of Chicago, Illinois. 2 vols. Chicago and New York: Munsell, 1895.

Mundie, William B. "Skeleton Construction." Microfilm Project, Art Institute of Chicago. n.d.

Museum of Science and Industry, Chicago. A Guide to 150 Years of Chicago Architecture. Chicago: Chicago Review Press, 1985.

Newman, M. W. "Soaring Twenties." Architectural Forum 140 (January-February 1974): 48.

Newton, Joseph Fort. David Swing: Poet Preacher. Chicago: Unity Publishing, 1909.

North Michigan Avenue Association. Papers. Chicago Historical Society.

Notable Men of Chicago and Their City. Chicago: Chicago Daily Journal, 1910.

Official Proceedings, Board of Commissioners, Cook County, Illinois. Chicago: J. M. W. Jones Stationery and Printing Co., for the years 1880 through 1888.

Osman, James. "Chicago Society." Harper's Weekly 49 (28 October 1905): 1568.

"Otto Young." American Jeweler 27 (January 1907): 1-2.

Pacyga, Dominic A., and Ellen Skerret. Chicago: City of Neighborhoods. Chicago: Loyola University Press, 1986.

Palmer, Herman L. Prominent Citizens and Industries of Chicago. Chicago: German Press Club of Chicago, 1901.

Pegg, Betsy. Dreams, Money, and Ambition: A History of Real Estate in Chicago. Chicago: Chicago Real Estate Board, 1983.

"The Phenix Insurance Company Building." Inland Architect 10 (September 1887): supplement.

Pierce, Bessie L. A History of Chicago. 3 vols. New York: Alfred A. Knopf, 1937-56.

Pierce, Bessie L. As Others See Chicago: Impressions of Visitors. Chicago: University of Chicago Press, 1933.

"Planning in Chicago." American Society of Planning Officials Newsletter 15 (March 1949): 1.

A Portfolio of Fine Apartment Homes. Chicago: Baird and Warner, 1928.

Rand, John C., ed. One of a Thousand: One Thousand Representative Men Resident in the Commonwealth of Massachusetts A.D. 1888-'89. Boston: First National Publishing Co., 1890.

Rand McNally. Bird's-Eye View and Guide to Chicago. Chicago, 1893.

Randall, Frank A. History of the Development of Building Construction in Chicago. Urbana: University of Illinois Press, 1949.

"Re-Opening Chicago Building Height Problem." Western Architect 32 (January 1923): 1.

"Report of the Architect's Committee, North Michigan Avenue Development of the North Central Association, Chicago. Submitted November 1, 1918." American Architect 114 (December 11, 1918): 690-94.

Root, John W. "A Great Architectural Problem." Inland Architect and News Record 15 (June 1890): 67-71.

Root, John Wellborn. "Architects of Chicago." Inland Architect and News Record 16 (January 1891): 91.

Ross, Ishbel. Silhouette in Diamonds: The Life of Mrs. Potter Palmer. New York: Harper and Brothers, 1960.

Rottenberg, Dan. "Who's Building What: The Top Ten for the Eighties." Chicago [magazine], April 1981.

Rubloff, Arthur. Papers. Chicago Historical Society.

Saliga, Pauline A., et al, eds. The Sky's the Limit: A Century of Chicago Skyscrapers. New York: Rizzoli, 1990.

Saltenstall, H. M. Papers. [Viz., Owen F. Aldis letters to Peter C. Brooks.] Art Institute of Chicago.

Schopp, Mary D. "Fifty Golden Years." Central Manufacturing District Magazine 39 (June-October 1955).

Scully, Vincent Joseph. Frank Lloyd Wright. New York: G. Braziller, 1960.

Selfridge, Harry Gordon. "Selling Selfridge." The Saturday Evening Post, 27 July 1932.

Selz, Jay H. "The Elegant Drake." Chicago Magazine 4 (Autumn 1967): 122-28.

Seymour, Ralph Fletcher. The Origin of the Skyscraper, Report of the Committee Appointed by the Trustees of the Estate of Marshall Field for Examination of the Structure of the Home Insurance Building. Chicago: Alderbrink Press, 1939.

Shultz, Earle, and Walter Simmons. Offices in the Sky. Indianapolis: Bobbs-Merrill, 1959.

Silver, Deborah. "Long-Dormant South Loop." Crain's Chicago Business, 3 January 1983.

Sinclair, Upton. The Jungle. New York: Doubleday Page, 1906.

Siry, Joseph. Carson Pirie Scott: Louis Sullivan and the Chicago Department Store. Chicago: University of Chicago Press, 1988.

Smith, Michael J. P. "Buildup." Inland Architect, January-February, 1990.

Soloway, Elaine M. "South Commons: A Study of a Planned Community." Master's thesis, University of Illinois, 1977.

South Park Commission, Annual Report, 1 December 1875 to 1 December 1876.

Spaeth, David. Mies van der Rohe. New York: Rizzoli, 1985.

Stamper, John W. Chicago's North Michigan Avenue. Chicago and London: University of Chicago Press, 1991.

Stamper, John W. "Patronage and the City Grid: The High-Rise Architecture of Mies van der Rohe in Chicago." Inland Architect, March-April 1986.

Stead, William T. If Christ Came to Chicago: A Plea for the Union of All Who Love in the Service of All Who Suffer. Chicago: Laird and Lee, 1894.

Storrer, William Allen. The Architecture of Frank Lloyd Wright: A Complete Catalogue. 2d ed. Cambridge: MIT Press, 1978.

Strahler, Steven R. "Rubloff: How a Great Name in Real Estate Lost Its Way." Crain's Chicago Business, 29 October 1990 (Part 1); "Rubloff in the '80s: Upheaval Tears Apart a Stumbling Firm," 5 November 1990 (Part 2).

Stribling, Dees, and Kevin Deany. "The John Buck Company: Major League Developers." Metro Chicago Real Estate 75 (20 May 1988).

Stribling, Dees, and Kevin Deany. "The First Ever Full-Length Interview with Miglin-Beitler." Metro Chicago Real Estate 75 (22 July 1988).

Stribling, Dees. "U.S. Equities Embarks on Its Second Decade in Real Estate." Metro Chicago Real Estate 76, 27 January 1989.

Sullivan, Louis H. Kindergarten Chats and Other Writings. New York: Wittenborn, Schultz, 1947.

Sullivan, Louis H. The Autobiography of an Idea. New York: Press of the American Institute of Architects, 1922.

Tallmadge, Thomas E. Architecture in Old Chicago. Chicago: University of Chicago Press, 1941.

Thimmesch, Nick. "The Builder: How Philip Klutznick Helped Change the Face of Chicago." Chicago Tribune Sunday Magazine, 5 May 1985.

Thomas, Dana L. Lords of the Land. New York: G. P. Putnam's Sons, 1977.

Thompson, Richard A., ed. Du Page Roots. Ann Arbor: Dupage County Historical Society, 1985.

Turak, Theodore. William Le Baron Jenney: A Pioneer of Modern Architecture. Ann Arbor: UMI Research Press, 1986.

Twombly, Robert. Louis Sullivan: His Life and Work. New York: Viking, 1986.

United States Census Office. Records. 1860, 1880, 1900.

Villa Park 75th Anniversary Commission. Villa Park 75th Anniversary, 1914-1989 [commemorative collection]. Villa Park Library, Villa Park, Ill.

Waterman, A. N. Historical Review of Chicago and Cook County and Selected Bibliography. 3 vols. Chicago and New York: Lewis, 1908.

Weiner, Steve. "Everything's Negotiable: Chicago's Construction Frenzy." Forbes, 19 March 1990.

Weissbourd, Bernard. "An Urban Strategy." The Center Magazine, September 1968.

Weissbourd, Bernard. "Satellite Communities." Urban Land Magazine, October 1972.

Weissbourd, Bernard. "Survival Tactics for the Year 2000." Chicago [magazine], January 1984.

Wendt, Lloyd, and Herman Kogan. Give the Lady What She Wants! The Story of Marshall Field & Company. Chicago: Rand McNally, 1952.

Wille, Lois. Forever Open, Clear and Free: The Struggle for Chicago's Lakefront. Chicago: Henry Regnery, 1972.

Williams, Kenny J. In the City of Men: Another Story of Chicago. Nashville, Tenn.: Townsend Press, 1974.

Wirth, Louis and Eleanor H. Bernert, eds. Local Community Fact Book, 1938. Chicago: Chicago Recreation Commission, 1938.

Witherspoon, H. W. Men of Illinois. Chicago: Halliday W. Witherspoon, 1902.

Witom, T. R. "A Constructive Mind" [Charles H. Shaw]. North Shore, November 1987.

Wolfmeyer, Ann, and Mary Burns Gage. Lake Geneva: Newport of the West, 1870-1920. Lake Geneva, Wis.: Lake Geneva Historical Society, 1976.

Wolper, Gregg. The Chicago Dock and Canal Trust: 1857-1987. Chicago: Chicago Dock and Canal Trust, 1988.

Wooley, Edward M. "Otto Young's Odd Boyhood; Lived in London and New York." Chicago Tribune, Worker's Magazine supplement, 23 December 1906.

Wright, Frank Lloyd. Frank Lloyd Wright: An Autobiography. New York: Duell, Sloan and Pearce, 1943.

Wright, Frank Lloyd. Genius and the Mobocracy. New York: Duell, Sloan and Pearce, 1949.

Wright, John Lloyd. My Father Who Is On Earth. New York: G. P. Putnam's Sons, 1946.

Yearbook of the Friday Club: 1887-1937. Chicago: [1937].

Ziemba, Stanley. "Coupling Old, New: Owner Plans to Restore the Grandeur of Union Station." Chicago Tribune, Commercial Real Estate supplement, 26 September 1990.

Zimberoff Bayard, Aleen. "The Ascendance of Robert Wislow." Crain's Chicago Business, 5 May 1986.

CHICAGO AREA PROJECTS BY SELECTED DEVELOPERS

1868-1930

DEVELOPER	ARCHITECT	BUILDING	DATE	LOCATION
Aldis, Owen (with Bryan Lathrop)	Holabird and Roche	Caxton	1890	500 South Dearborn
Aldis-Brooks (with E. C. Waller) (Central Safe Deposit Company)	Burnham and Root	Rookery	1886	209 South La Salle
Aldis-Brooks (Chicago Real Estate Trust)	Burnham and Roche	Venetian	1892	15 East Washington
Aldis-Brooks (Trust) (Chicago Leasehold Trust)	Holabird and Roche	Champlain, first	1894	State and Madison, northwest corner
Aldis-Brooks (Marquette Safety Deposit Co.)	Holabird and Roche	Marquette	1895	140 South Dearborn
Aldis-Brooks (Chicago Real Estate Trust)	Holabird and Roche	Hamilton	1904	Clark and Van Buren, southeast corner
Brooks, Peter C.	William Le Baron Jenney	Portland Block, second	1872, 80	Dearborn and Washington, southeast corner
Brooks, Peter C.	Burnham and Root	Montauk Block	1882	West Monroe, between Dearborn and Clark
Brooks, Peter C.	Burnham and Root	Monadnock - North	1891	53 West Jackson
Brooks, Peter C. (Shepherd Brooks, owner)	Holabird and Roche	Pontiac	1891	542 South Dearborn
Brooks, Peter C.	Holabird and Roche	Yukon	1898	Clark and Van Buren, southeast corner
Brooks, Peter C.	Holabird and Roche	Brooks Building	1911	223 West Jackson

Brooks, Shepherd		Sydenham	1888	Michigan and Monroe, southwest corner
Brooks, Shepherd (Boulevard Music Hall Corp.)	Holabird and Roche	Cable Building	1889	Jackson and Wabash, southeast corner
Brooks, Shepherd	Holabird and Roche	Monadnock - South	1893	53 West Jackson
Brooks, Shepherd	Holabird and Roche	Monroe Building	1912	Monroe and Michigan, southwest corner
Clark, Wallace G. (Clark and Trainer)	A. R. Clark Builders	Hyde Park/Kenwood/Lake View Houses	1892-1905	Ellis/Greenwood/ Vincennes/Prairie/ Forrestville Avenues; Pine Grove and Waveland
Clark, Wallace G. (Clark and Trainer)	T. Bishop and Co.	Kenwood/Garfield Park area apartment buildings	1897-1913	Kenwood/Garfield Park
Clark, Wallace G. (Michigan Avenue Trust Estate)	Jarvis Hunt with Holabird and Roche	Michigan Boulevard Building	1914	30 North Michigan Avenue
Clark, Wallace G. (Riverside Plaza Corporation; Wacker-Wabash Corporation)	Thielbar and Fugard with Giaver and Dinkelberg	35 East Wacker Drive (Jewelers/Pure Oil Building)	1926	35 East Wacker Drive
Drake, John and Tracy (Blackstone Hotel Co.)	Marshall and Fox	Blackstone Hotel	1909	South Michigan Avenue at East Balbo Avenue
Drake, John and Tracy (Blackstone Co.)	Marshall and Fox	Blackstone Theater	1911	60 East Balbo Avenue
Drake, John and Tracy (Whitestone Hotel Co.)	Marshall and Fox	Drake Hotel	1920	Lake Shore Drive, Michigan Avenue and Walton

434

DEVELOPER	ARCHITECT	BUILDING	DATE	LOCATION
Field, Marshall		Field and Leiter Wholesale Store	1872	Madison and Market (South Wacker), northeast corner
Field, Marshall	Henry Hobson Richardson	Marshall Field Wholesale Store	1885-87	Adams/Quincy/Wells/Franklin
Field, Marshall	D. H. Burnham and Co.	Merchants Loan and Trust (later Standard Trust) building	1900	West Adams and Clark, northwest corner
Field, Marshall	D. H. Burnham and Co.	Marshall Field "River" Warehouse	1905	Polk and Ellsworth
Field, Marshall, and Field Estate	D. H. Burnham and Co.	Marshall Field Retail Store rebuilding and expansions (1892, 1902, 1907, 1914)	1892-1914	Washington/Randolph/State/Wabash
Field Estate	D. H. Burnham and Co.	Conway Building (Chicago Title and Trust)	1913	111 West Washington
Field Estate	Graham, Anderson, Probst and White	Pittsfield Building	1927	55 East Washington
Field Estate	Graham, Anderson, Probst and White	Merchandise Mart	1928-30	222 West North Bank
Field Estate	Andrew J. Thomas and Ernest Graham	Marshall Field Garden Apartments	1929-30	Hudson/Sedgewick/Blackhawk/Evergreen
Field Estate	Graham, Anderson, Probst and White	Field Building (La Salle National Bank)	1931-34	135 South La Salle
Gross, Samuel E.		Subdivisions	1883-1904	Chicago Area
		Including: Gross Park (1883); Brookhaven (1886); Calumet Heights (1887); Avondale (1888); Humboldt Park (1888); Under Linden (1888); Grossdale (1889); Dauphin Park (1889); West Grossdale (1891); Hollywood (1893); Alta Vista Terrace (1900-1904); University Park (1900-1904)		
Hale, William E.	E. S. Jenison	Hale building, first	1870	State and Washington, southeast corner

Hale, William E. (with Lucius G. Fisher)	E. S. Jenison	Hale building, second	1872	State and Washington, southeast corner
Hale, William E.	Burnham and Root	Kenwood Observatory	1890	4545 Drexel Avenue
Hale, William E.	Burnham and Root; D. H. Burnham and Co.	Reliance Building	1891-94	32 North State
Hale, William E. (with Oakland Music Hall Association)	Thomas and Rapp	Oakland Music Hall	1895	Cottage Grove and 40th, northeast corner
Heisen, Charles C.	John M. Van Osdel	Temple Court	1886	Dearborn and Quincy, northeast corner
Heisen, Charles C.	John M. Van Osdel	Como	1887	443 South Dearborn
Heisen, Charles C.	Jenney and Mundie	Manhattan	1890	431 South Dearborn
Heisen, Charles C.	John M. Van Osdel	Monon	1890	440 South Dearborn
Heisen, Charles C.	F. B. Abbott	Heisen home	1891	1250 North Lake Shore Drive
Heisen, Charles C.	Jenney and Mundie	Star Accident Insurance Building (Morton Building)	1896	538 South Dearborn
Heisen, Charles C.	Fred V. Prather	Transportation Building (Heisen Building)	1911	600 South Dearborn
Heisen, Charles C.		Villa Park homes	1912	Villa Park, Illinois
Marshall, Benjamin H.	Wilson and Marshall	Hyde Park homes	1896-1900	Ellis and 49th; Grand Boulevard
Marshall, Benjamin H.	Benjamin Marshall	Raymond Apartments	1900	920 North Michigan Avenue
Marshall, Benjamin H.	Marshall and Fox	1100 North Lake Shore Drive	1906	1100 North Lake Shore Drive
Marshall, Benjamin H. (joint ownership)	Marshall and Fox	49 Cedar Place	1908	36-40 Cedar Street

(Marshall continued on next page)

(Marshall continued from previous page)

DEVELOPER	ARCHITECT	BUILDING	DATE	LOCATION
Marshall, Benjamin H.	Marshall and Fox	Stewart Apartments	1912	1200 North Lake Shore Drive
Marshall, Benjamin H.	Marshall and Fox	1550 North State Parkway	1913	1550 North State Parkway
Marshall, Benjamin H.	Marshall and Fox	199 East Lake Shore Drive (The Breakers)	1915, 1916, 1927	199 East Lake Shore Drive
Marshall, Benjamin H.	Marshall and Fox	Edgewater Beach Hotel	1916, 1924	5349 Sheridan Road
Marshall, Benjamin H.	Marshall and Fox	Wilmette Villa	1921-24	612 Sheridan Road, Wilmette, Illinois
Marshall, Benjamin H. (with Dake Building Corp.)	Marshall and Fox	Lumber Exchange Building	1924	Adams and Clinton, Northeast corner
Marshall, Benjamin H. (with Ogden McClurg and 209 Building Corp.)	Marshall and Fox	209 East Lake Shore Drive	1926	209 East Lake Shore Drive
Marshall, Benjamin H.	Benjamin Marshall	202 East Walton	1927	202 East Walton
Marshall, Benjamin H. (Drake Tower Building Corp.)	Benjamin Marshall	Drake Tower Apartments	1929	179 East Lake Shore Drive
Marshall, Benjamin H.	Benjamin Marshall	Edgewater Beach Apartments	1929	5555 North Sheridan Road
Nixon, Wilson K.		Smith and Nixon Building (concert hall)	1864	Clark and Washington, southwest corner
Nixon, Wilson K.	Otto H. Matz	Nixon Building	1871	La Salle and Monroe, northeast corner
Nixon, Wilson F.		St. James Flats	1873	East Illinois Street
Nixon, Wilson K.	Burnham and Root	Commercial Bank Building (Mohawk Building)	1884	Dearborn and Monroe, southeast corner
Nixon, Wilson K. Northwestern Safety Deposit Co.)	Burnham and Root	Insurance Exchange (Continental Bank)	1885	La Salle and Adams, southwest corner
Nixon, Wilson K. (Illinois Vault Co.)	Burnham and Root	Illinois National Bank	1886	21-29 North Dearborn

Name	Architect	Building	Year	Location
Nixon, Wilson K. (Chicago Deposit Vault Co.)	Burnham and Root	Rialto Building	1886	148 West Van Buren at La Salle
Nixon, Wilson K.	Burnham and Root	Chemical Bank Building	1889	115-121 North Dearborn
Nixon, Wilson K. (Abstract Safety Deposit Co.)	Burnham and Root	Williams Building, second	1889	111 North Dearborn
Nixon, Wilson F.	D. H. Burnham and Co.	Edison Building, first	1898	120 West Adams
Palmer, Potter	John M. van Osdel	Field, Leiter and Company Store	1868	State and Washington, northeast corner
Palmer, Potter		State Street Retail District 32 Structures, pre-fire	1867-71	State Street, Lake to Adams
Palmer, Potter	John M. Van Osdel	Palmer House, first ("The Palmer")	1869-71	State and Quincy, northwest corner
Palmer, Potter	W. W. Boyington	Inter-State Industrial Exposition Building	1873	Michigan Avenue between Monroe and Jackson
Palmer, Potter	John M. Van Osdel and C. M. Palmer	Palmer House, third (second rebuilt)	1871-74	State and Monroe, southeast corner
Palmer, Potter	Henry Ives Cobb and Charles H. Frost	Palmer home	1882-85	1350 North Lake Shore Drive
Palmer, Potter	C. M. Palmer	"Palmer houses" (300 residences)	1885-1902	Gold Coast/Streeterville
Palmer Estate	Holabird and Roche	Palmer House, fourth	1923-27	State and Monroe, southeast corner

438

DEVELOPER	ARCHITECT	BUILDING	DATE	LOCATION
Peck, Ferdinand W. (with Central Church of Chicago subscribers)	Dankmar Adler	Central Music Hall	1879	State and Randolph, southeast corner
Peck, Ferdinand W. (Peck family)	Adler and Sullivan	La Salle-Water building	1886	La Salle and South Water (La Salle and Wacker Drive)
Peck, Ferdinand W. (Chicago Auditorium Association)	Adler and Sullivan	Auditorium Building and Theater	1886-89	South Michigan Avenue and Congress, northwest corner
Peck, Ferdinand W. (Chicago Auditorium Association)	Clinton J. Warren	Auditorium Annex (Congress Hotel)	1893	South Michigan Avenue and Congress, southwest corner
Peck, Ferdinand W. (Peck family)	Adler and Sullivan	Chicago Stock Exchange Building (30 North La Salle)	1894	Washington and La Salle, southwest corner
Waller, Edward C.	William Le Baron Jenney	Home Insurance Building	1885	La Salle and Adams, northeast corner
Waller, Edward C.	Burnham and Root	Rookery	1886	La Salle and Adams, southeast corner
Waller, Edward C.	Burnham and Root	Phoenix	1887	Jackson and Clark, southwest corner
Waller, Edward C.	Frank Lloyd Wright	Waller Apartments	1895	2840-2858 West Walnut
Waller, Edward C.	Frank Lloyd Wright	Francisco Terrace apartments	1895	253-257 Francisco Avenue
Waller, Edward C.	Frank Lloyd Wright	Lexington Terraces apartments	Proposed	Lexington and Homan
Waller, Edward C.	Frank Lloyd Wright	Rookery lobby remodeling	1906	209 South La Salle
Waller, Edward C.		North Woods subdivision	1912 -	River Forest, Illinois
Waller, Edward C.		River Forest State Bank	1912	River Forest, Illinois
Waller, Edward C. Jr.	Frank Lloyd Wright	Midway Gardens	1914	Cottage Grove Avenue and 60th

Name	Architect	Building	Date	Location
Waller, Robert A. (James B. Waller family)	George W. Maher, William Le Baron Jenney, and others	Buena Park subdivisions	1887 -	Broadway/Irving Park Road/Kenmore/Marine Drive
Waller, Robert A. (Ashland Block Association)	D. H. Burnham and Co.	Ashland Block, second	1892	Clark and Randolph, northeast corner
Waller, Robert A. (Merrimac Building Corp.)	D. H. Burnham and Co.	Stewart Building	1897	State and Washington, northwest corner
Wolbach, Murray	L. M. Mitchell	Hyde Park houses	1905	Ellis Avenue and 54th
Wolbach, Murray	Philip B. Maher	545 North Michigan (Jacques)	1929	545 North Michigan Avenue
Wolbach, Murray	Philip B. Maher	669 North Michigan (Saks)	1930	669 North Michigan Avenue
Wolbach, Murray	Holabird and Root	Michigan Square	1930	540 North Michigan Avenue
Young, Otto (with E. J. Lehmann)	Jenney and Mundie	The Fair Store	1891-97	State/Adams/Dearborn
Young, Otto (with Gorham Manufacturing and Benjamin Allen)	D. H. Burnham and Co.	Silversmith Building	1897	10 South Wabash
Young, Otto (with Lawrence Heyworth)	D. H. Burnham and Co.	Heyworth Building	1905	Madison and Wabash, southwest corner
Young, Otto	D. H. Burnham and Co.	Carson Pirie Scott 1906 Addition	1906	State between Madison and Monroe

1945-1992

DEVELOPER	ARCHITECT	CHICAGO PROJECTS	DATE	LOCATION
Baird, John W. (partnership)	Harry Weese	227 Walton redevelopment	1956	227 Walton
Baird, John W. (with Interaction, Inc.)	Seymour Goldstein	Lawndale Manor	1969	18th and Kostner
Baird, John W. (with Interaction, Inc.)	Seymour Goldstein	Lake Park Manor	1970	3601-3645 South Lake Park
Baird, John W. (Baird and Warner)	Robert L. Friedman Associates	Campus Green apartments and town houses	1968-72	Ashland, Taylor, Polk, Laflin
Baird, John W. (With McHugh Levin)	Dubin, Dubin, Black and Moutoussamy	200 East Delaware apartments	1972	200 East Delaware
Baird, John W. (Baird and Warner with Community Resources Corp.)	Harry Weese, Laurence Booth	Transportation Building redevelopment	1978	600 South Dearborn
Baird, John W. (Baird and Warner)	Aubrey Greenberg	Willow-Dayton Place redevelopment	1976-80	Halsted and Willow
Baird, John W. (Baird and Warner with CRC)	Harry Weese, Laurence Booth	Franklin Building redevelopment	1984	525 South Dearborn
Baird, John W. (Baird and Warner with CRC)	Harry Weese, Laurence Booth	Pontiac Building redevelopment	1986	542 South Dearborn
Baird, John W. (Baird and Warner with CRC)	Harry Weese, Laurence Booth	Terminals Building redevelopment	1986	537 South Dearborn
Baird, John W. (Baird and Warner with Elzie Higginbottom)	Lisec and Biederman	200 North Dearborn apartments	1989	200 North Dearborn

441

Name	Architect	Building	Year	Address
Buck, John (John Buck Company)	Harry Weese and Associates	200 South Wacker	1978-81	200 South Wacker Drive
Buck, John (JBC)	John Burgee with Philip Johnson	190 South La Salle	1983-86	190 South La Salle
Buck, John (JBC with Leo Burnett Co.)	Kevin Roche-John Dinkeloo and Associates	Leo Burnett Building	1986-89	35 West Wacker Drive
Buck, John (JBC with Miller-Klutznick-Davis-Gray)	Kenzo Tange with Shaw and Associates	American Medical Association headquarters	1990	515 North State
Buck, John (JBC with Miller-Klutznick-Davis-Gray)	Solomon, Cordwell, Buenz and Associates	440 North Wabash apartments	1991	440 North Wabash
Greenwald, Herbert	Mies van der Rohe	Promontory Apartments	1947-49	5530 South Shore Drive
Greenwald, Herbert (Trust)	Holsman, Holsman, Klecamp and Taylor	Sherman Gardens Apartments	1948-49	1616 Chicago Avenue, Evanston
Greenwald, Herbert	Harold A. Stahl	Foster-Hoyne apartments	1950	2100 Foster Avenue
Greenwald, Herbert (with Robert Hall McCormick)	Mies van der Rohe	860-880 Lake Shore Drive apartments	1949-52	860-880 North Lake Shore Drive
Greenwald, Herbert (with Sam Katzin)	Pace Associates	Algonquin apartments	1950-52	50th and Cornell Avenue
Greenwald, Herbert	Friedman, Alschuler and Sincere	Chippewa apartments	1950-52	5050 East End Drive
Greenwald, Herbert	A. Epstein and Sons	Twin Towers apartments	1950-52	5000 South Lake Shore Drive
Greenwald, Herbert	Loebl, Schlossman and Bennett	The Darien apartments	1953	3100 North Lake Shore Drive
Greenwald, Herbert (with Sam Katzin)	Mies van der Rohe	Commonwealth Promenade apartments	1954-57	330 Diversey Parkway
Greenwald, Herbert (with Sam Katzin)	Mies van der Rohe	900 Esplanade apartments	1955-57	900-910 North Lake Shore Drive

DEVELOPER	ARCHITECT	CHICAGO PROJECTS	DATE	LOCATION
Klutznick, Philip (American Community Builders)	Loebl and Schlossman	Park Forest (new town)	1946-49	Park Forest, Illinois
Klutznick, Philip (ACB)	Loebl, Schlossman and Hackl	Old Orchard (shopping center)	1956	Skokie, Illinois
Klutznick, Philip (KLC)	Loebl, Schlossman and Hackl	Oakbrook Center (shopping center)	1962	Oak Brook, Illinois
Klutznick, Philip (KLC)	Loebl, Schlossman and Hackl	River Oaks (shopping center)	1966	Calumet City, Illinois
Klutznick, Philip (Urban Investment and Development Corporation)	Loebl, Schlossman and Hackl	New Century Town (Hawthorn Center)	1973	Vernon Hills, Illinois
Klutznick, Philip (UIDC)	North Architectonics	Fox Valley Villages (Fox Valley Center)	1975	Aurora, Illinois
Klutznick, Philip (UIDC)	Gerald Meister and Associates	River Oaks West	1975	Calumet City, Illinois
Klutznick, Philip (UIDC)	Loebl, Schlossman, Dart and Hackl with C.F. Murphy Associates	Water Tower Place	1975	845 North Michigan Avenue
Klutznick, Philip (UIDC)	Skidmore, Owings and Merrill	Orland Square (shopping center)	1976	Orland Park, Illinois
Klutznick, Philip (UIDC)	RTKL Associates	Stratford Square (shopping center)	1981	Bloomingdale, Illinois
Klutznick, Philip (Dearborn Park Corporation)	Skidmore, Owings and Merrill; Gordon-Levin and Associates; Booth, Nagle and Hartray; Dubin, Dubin, Black and Moutoussamy; Hammond, Beeby and Babka.	Dearborn Park Phase I	1977-88	8th to Roosevelt Road between Clark and State
Kramer, Ferd (Draper and Kramer)	Loebl, Schlossman and Bennett	Faculty Housing, University of Chicago	1949	55th and Dorchester
Kramer, Ferd (Draper and Kramer)	Loebl, Schlossman and Bennett	1350-1360 North Lake Shore Drive	1950	1350-1360 North Lake Shore Drive

Kramer, Ferd (New York Life Insurance Company)	Skidmore, Owings and Merrill	Lake Meadows complex	1952-60	King Drive between 31st and 35th
Kramer, Ferd (Draper and Kramer)	Loewenberg and Loewenberg	4800 Beach Drive apartments	1961	4800 Chicago Beach Drive
Kramer, Ferd (Draper and Kramer with Prairie Shores Development Corporation)	Loebl, Schlossman and Bennett	Prairie Shores complex	1957-62	King Drive between 28th and 31st
Kramer, Ferd (Draper and Kramer)	Skidmore, Owings and Merrill	Faculty Housing, University of Chicago	1964	58th and Dorchester
Kramer, Ferd (Draper and Kramer)	Loewenberg and Loewenberg	2626 North Lakeview apartments	1965	2626 North Lake View
Kramer, Ferd (Draper and Kramer)	Loewenberg and Loewenberg	1130 South Michigan apartments	1967	1130 South Michigan Avenue
Kramer, Ferd (Draper and Kramer with Slough Estates Ltd.)	Skidmore, Owings and Merrill	33 West Monroe	1980	33 West Monroe
Kramer, Ferd (Draper and Kramer with Slough Estates Ltd.)	Sidney H. Morris and Associates	Riverview Plaza shopping center	1981	Western Avenue at Roscoe
Kramer, Ferd (Dearborn Park Corporation)	Skidmore, Owings and Merrill; Gordon-Levin and Associates; Booth, Nagle and Hartray; Dubin, Dubin, Black and Moutoussamy; Hammond, Beeby and Babka	Dearborn Park Phase I	1977-88	8th to Roosevelt Road between Clark and State
Kramer, Ferd (Dearborn Park Corporation)	Skidmore, Owings and Merrill	Dearborn Park phase II	1988 -	Roosevelt Road to 15th between Clark and State
Kramer, Ferd	Skidmore, Owings and Merrill (Redevelopment plan)	North Kenwood redevelopment plan	Proposed	Drexel between 39th and 42nd
Levin, Daniel (McHugh Levin Associates)	Dubin, Dubin, Black and Moutoussamy	Quadrangle House	1969	6700 South Shore Drive

(Levin continued on next page)

444

(Levin continued from previous page)

DEVELOPER	ARCHITECT	CHICAGO PROJECTS	DATE	LOCATION
Levin, Daniel (McHugh Levin)	Dubin, Dubin, Black and Moutoussamy	Long Grove House	1969	2001 South Michigan Avenue
Levin, Daniel (McHugh Levin with Baird and Warner)	Dubin, Dubin, Black and Moutoussamy	200 East Delaware apartments	1972	200 East Delaware
Levin, Daniel (McHugh Levin)	Ezra Gordon/Jack Levin Associates, with L.R. Solomon/J.D. Cordwell	South Commons community	1964-72	South Michigan Avenue between 26th and 31st
Levin, Daniel (McHugh Levin)	Gordon and Levin	Newberry Plaza	1973	1030 North State
Levin, Daniel (McHugh Levin)	Gordon and Levin	Kenmore Plaza	1974	5225 North Kenmore Avenue
Levin, Daniel (McHugh Levin)	Gordon and Levin	Elm Street Plaza	1976	1130 South Dearborn
Levin, Daniel (McHugh Levin)	Gordon and Levin	River Plaza	1977	405 North Wabash Avenue
Levin, Daniel (McHugh Levin)	Environment Seven	West Point Plaza	1978	300 South Damen
Levin, Daniel (McHugh Levin)	Fujikawa, Johnson and Associates	Columbus Plaza	1980	233 East Wacker Drive
Levin, Daniel (McHugh Levin)	Gordon and Levin; Gelick Foran Associates	East Bank Club	1980	500 North Kingsbury Court
Levin, Daniel (McHugh Levin)	Gordon and Levin	Huron Plaza	1980	30 East Huron
Levin, Daniel (McHugh Levin)	George Schipporeit and Associates	Asbury Plaza	1981	750 North Dearborn
Levin, Daniel (McHugh Levin with Stewart Grill and Stuart Kaplan)	Booth/Hansen and Associates	540 Lake Shore Drive redevelopment	1983	540 North Lake Shore Drive
Levin, Daniel (McHugh Levin)	Swann and Weiskopf	Pines of Edgewater	1980-83	18 rehabilitated buildings, scattered sites
Levin, Daniel (McHugh Levin)	Environment Seven	Paul G. Stewart apartments	1975-84	South Side, 41st street area

445

Developer	Architect	Building	Date	Address
Levin, Daniel (McHugh Levin with Madison-Canal Company)	Solomon, Cordwell and Buenz	Presidential Towers	1985	555, 575, 605, 625 West Madison
Levin, Daniel	Gelick Foran Associates	Cityfront Place apartments	1991	400, 440, 480 McClurg Court
Mack, John, and Ray Sher	Shaw, Metz and Dolio	3101 Sheridan Road apartments	1951	3101 Sheridan Road
Mack, John, and Ray Sher	Shaw, Metz and Dolio	3121 Sheridan Road apartments	1951	3121 Sheridan Road
Mack, John, and Ray Sher	Shaw, Metz and Dolio	350 Oakdale apartments	1951	350 Oakdale
Mack, John, and Ray Sher	Shaw, Metz and Dolio	201 East Walton apartments	1952	201 East Walton
Mack, John, and Ray Sher	Philip B. Maher	2909 Sheridan Road apartments	1952	2909 Sheridan Road
Mack, John, and Ray Sher	Shaw, Metz and Dolio	3950 North Lake Shore Drive apartments	1955	3950 North Lake Shore Drive
Mack, John, and Ray Sher	Shaw, Metz and Dolio	3130 North Lake Shore Drive apartments	1956	3130 North Lake Shore Drive
Mack, John, and Ray Sher	Shaw, Metz and Dolio	3180 North Lake Shore Drive apartments	1956	3180 North Lake Shore Drive
Mack, John, and Ray Sher	Shaw, Metz and Dolio	3150 North Lake Shore Drive apartments	1957	3150 North Lake Shore Drive
Mack, John, and Ray Sher	Philip B. Maher	1445 North State Parkway apartments	1958	1445 North State Parkway
Mack, John, and Ray Sher	Hausner and Macsai	1150 North Lake Shore Drive apartments	1959	1150 North Lake Shore Drive
Mack, John, and Ray Sher	Shaw, Metz and Dolio	1550 North Lake Shore Drive apartments	1959	1550 North Lake Shore Drive
Mack, John, and Ray Sher	Shaw, Metz and Dolio	1325 North State Parkway apartments	1960	1325 North State Parkway
Mack, John, and Ray Sher	Shaw, Metz and Dolio	3600 North Lake Shore Drive apartments	1960	3600 North Lake Shore Drive
Mack, John, and Ray Sher	Loewenberg and Loewenberg	3550 North Lake Shore Drive apartments	1962	3550 North Lake Shore Drive
Mack, John, and Ray Sher	Shaw, Metz and Associates	777 North Michigan Avenue apartments	1963	777 North Michigan Avenue
Mack, John, and Ray Sher	Shaw, Metz and Associates	Westin Hotel (the Continental)	1963	160 East Delaware Place
Mack, John, and Ray Sher	Hausner and Macsai	1240 North Lake Shore Drive apartments	1969	1240 North Lake Shore Drive
Mack, John, and Ray Sher	Loewenberg and Loewenberg	Park Place apartments (Frontier Towers)	1973	655 West Irving Park Road
Mack, John, and Ray Sher	Alfred Shaw and Associates	Mid-Continental Plaza	1969-73	55 East Monroe

DEVELOPER	ARCHITECT	CHICAGO PROJECTS	DATE	LOCATION
Miglin, Lee		Sky Harbor Airport redevelopment (office and business park)	1968 -	Northbrook, Illinois
Miglin, Lee	Otis Associates	Talman Home Building	1970	8303 West Higgins Road
Miglin, Lee	Otis Associates	8101 Higgins Building	1972	8101 West Higgins Road
Miglin, Lee	Patrick Shaw Associates	Commerce Plaza	1972	Oak Brook, Illinois
Miglin, Lee, and Paul Beitler (Miglin-Beitler Developments)	Patrick Shaw Associates	Sperry Univac Plaza (Presidents Plaza One)	1980	8600 West Bryn Mawr
Miglin, Lee, and Paul Beitler (Miglin-Beitler Developments)	Patrick Shaw Associates	Presidents Plaza Two	1983	8700 West Bryn Mawr
Miglin, Lee, and Paul Beitler (Miglin-Beitler Developments)	Skidmore, Owings and Merrill	Madison Plaza	1980-83	200 West Madison
Miglin, Lee, and Paul Beitler (Miglin-Beitler Developments)	Patrick Shaw Associates	Triangle Plaza (Presidents Plaza Three)	1985	8770 West Bryn Mawr Avenue
Miglin, Lee, and Paul Beitler (Miglin-Beitler, Inc.)	Helmut Jahn (Murphy/Jahn)	Oakbrook Terrace Tower	1986-88	Oak Brook, Illinois
Miglin, Lee, and Paul Beitler (Miglin-Beitler, Inc.)	Patrick Shaw Associates	La Salle National Services Center	1989	5515 North East River Road
Miglin, Lee, and Paul Beitler (Miglin-Beitler, Inc.)	Cesar Pelli and Associates	181 West Madison (PaineWebber Tower)	1990	181 West Madison
Miglin, Lee, and Paul Beitler (Miglin-Beitler, Inc. with Chicago Bar Association)	Stanley Tigerman/ Tigerman McCurry	Chicago Bar Association building	1991	321 South Plymouth Court
Miglin, Lee, and Paul Beitler (Miglin-Beitler, Inc.)	Cesar Pelli and Associates	Miglin-Beitler Tower	Planned	201 West Madison
Robin, Albert A.	Solomon/Cordwell and Associates	Cornelia-Stratford apartments	1960	555 Cornelia Avenue
Robin, Albert A.	Solomon/Cordwell and Associates	Imperial Towers apartments	1962	4250 Marine Drive
Robin, Albert A. (with Sandburg Village general partnership)	Solomon/Cordwell and Associates	Carl Sandburg Village complex	1961-65	North Clark and La Salle between Division and North Avenue

Name	Architect	Building	Year	Address
Robin, Albert A.	Hirshfeld, Pawlan and Reinheimer	The Carlyle	1966	1040 North Lake Shore Drive
Robin, Albert A.	Hirshfeld and Reinheimer	Pine Point Plaza apartments	1969	3930 Pine Grove Avenue
Robin, Albert A.	Martin Reinheimer and Associates	The Warwyck	1974	1501 North State Parkway
Romanek, Marvin	Hausner and Macsai	1440 North State Parkway apartments	1960	1440 North State Parkway
Romanek, Marvin	Hausner and Macsai	25 East Chestnut apartments	1963	25 East Chestnut
Romanek, Marvin, and Eugene Golub	Hausner and Macsai	Harbor House apartments	1967	3200 North Lake Shore Drive
Romanek, Marvin, and Eugene Golub	Meister and Volpe	180 North Michigan redevelopment	1968	180 North Michigan Avenue
Romanek, Marvin, and Eugene Golub	Meister and Volpe	625 North Michigan	1967-70	625 North Michigan Avenue
Romanek, Marvin, and Eugene Golub	Harry Weese and Associates	Heitman Centre (La Salle Plaza)	1973	180 North La Salle
Romanek, Marvin, and Eugene Golub	Perkins and Will	444 North Michigan	1974	444 North Michigan Avenue
Romanek, Marvin, and Eugene Golub	Helmut Jahn (C. F. Murphy Associates)	Xerox Centre (Monroe Centre)	1977-82	55 West Monroe
Romanek, Marvin, and Eugene Golub	George Schipporeit and Associates	Citicorp Plaza (Three O'Hare Plaza)	1983	8410-8430 West Bryn Mawr
Golub, Eugene (Golub + Co.)	Himmel/Bonnes	Lake Shore Place	1990	680 North Lake Shore Drive
Romanek, Marvin (Romanek Properties)	Loebl, Schlossman and Hackl	633 St. Clair Place	1990	633 North St. Clair
Shaw, Charles H. (Hartnett-Shaw)	Schipporeit-Heinrich Associates; Graham, Anderson, Probst and White	Lake Point Tower	1968	505 North Lake Shore Drive
Shaw, Charles H.	Schipporeit-Heinrich Associates	State National Bank Plaza (NBD Evanston)	1971	Evanston, Illinois

(Shaw continued on next page)

(Shaw continued from previous page)

DEVELOPER	ARCHITECT	CHICAGO PROJECTS	DATE	LOCATION
Shaw, Charles H.	Solomon, Cordwell, Buenz and Associates	Center Court Gardens apartments	1978	Congress Parkway, Ashland, Harrison, Loomis
Shaw, Charles H.	Skidmore, Owings and Merrill	676 St. Clair	1980	676 St. Clair
Shaw, Charles H. (with Hilton Hotel Corporation)	Solomon, Cordwell, Buenz and Associates	Chicago Hilton and Towers redevelopment	1986	720 South Michigan Avenue
Shaw, Charles H. (with Research Park, Inc.)	Perkins and Will	Northwestern University/ Evanston Research Park	1988 -	Evanston, Illinois
Shaw, Charles H.	Nagle, Hartray and Associates	The Inn at University Village	1988	625 South Ashland Avenue
Shaw, Charles H.	Nagle, Hartray and Associates	Garibaldi Square town houses	1989	610-618 Laflin
Shaw, Charles H.	Solomon, Cordwell, Buenz and Associates	Luther Village	1989 -	Arlington Heights, Illinois
Shaw, Charles H.	Solomon, Cordwell, Buenz and Associates	Embassy Suites Hotel	1991	600 North State
Stein, Richard (Stein & Company)	Otis Associates	Combined Centre	1980	Northbrook, Illinois
Stein, Richard (Stein & Company)	Loewenberg/Fitch Partnership	Village Center	1980	Skokie, Illinois
Stein, Richard (Stein & Company)	Skidmore, Owings and Merrill	Lake-Cook Office Centre	1985	Deerfield, Illinois
Stein, Richard (Stein & Company)	Skidmore, Owings and Merrill	ArborLake Centre office and hotel complex	1986	Deerfield, Illinois
Stein, Richard (Stein & Company with General Parking Corp.)	Adrian Smith/ Skidmore, Owings and Merrill	203 North La Salle (Transportation Center)	1982-86	203 North La Salle
Stein, Richard (AT&T/Stein Partnership)	Adrian Smith/ Skidmore, Owings and Merrill	AT&T Corporate Center	1985-89	227 West Monroe
Stein, Richard (Stein & Company)	Fujikawa, Johnson and Associates	Ralph H. Metcalfe Federal Building	1991	536 South Clark
Stein, Richard (AT&T/Stein Phase II Limited Partnership)	Skidmore, Owings and Merrill	USG Building	(1993)	222 West Adams

Name	Architect	Building	Year	Address
Stein, Richard (Mc3D, Inc.)	Thompson, Ventulett, Stainback & Associates, with A. Epstein and Sons International	McCormick Place Expansion	(1996)	2301 South Lake Shore Drive
Weissbourd, Bernard (Metropolitan Structures, and Herbert Greenwald Estate)	A. Epstein and Sons, Inc.	Essex Motor Hotel	1961	800 South Michigan Avenue
Weissbourd, Bernard (Metropolitan Structures)	Mies van der Rohe	2400 Lakeview apartments	1963	2400 Lake View Avenue
Weissbourd, Bernard (Metropolitan Structures)	Skidmore, Owings and Merrill	DeWitt-Chestnut apartments	1965	260 East Chestnut
Weissbourd, Bernard (Metropolitan Structures with IC Industries)	Fujikawa, Conterato, Lohan and Associates (coordinating architects)	Illinois Center complex	1967	Wacker Drive, Columbus Drive, Michigan Avenue, East Randolph
Weissbourd, Bernard (Metropolitan Structures)	Mies van der Rohe	One Illinois Center	1970	111 East Wacker Drive
Weissbourd, Bernard (Metropolitan Structures)	Mies van der Rohe	Two Illinois Center	1973	233 North Michigan Avenue
Weissbourd, Bernard (Metropolitan Structures)	A. Epstein and Sons	Hyatt Regency Chicago (West Tower)	1974	151 East Wacker Drive
Weissbourd, Bernard (Metropolitan Structures)	Fujikawa, Conterato, Lohan and Associates	Three Illinois Center	1979	303 East Wacker Drive
Weissbourd, Bernard (Metropolitan Structures)	A. Epstein and Sons	Hyatt Regency Chicago (East Tower)	1980	151 East Wacker Drive
Weissbourd, Bernard (Metropolitan Structures)	Fujikawa, Conterato, Lohan and Associates	Boulevard Towers-North	1982	225 North Michigan Avenue
Weissbourd, Bernard (Metropolitan Structures)	Fujikawa, Conterato, Lohan and Associates	Buckingham Plaza apartments	1982	360 East Randolph
Weissbourd, Bernard (Metropolitan Structures with The Walken Company)	Helmut Jahn (Murphy/Jahn)	One South Wacker	1983	One South Wacker Drive

(Weissbourd continued on next page)

(Weissbourd continued from previous page)

DEVELOPER	ARCHITECT	CHICAGO PROJECTS	DATE	LOCATION
Weissbourd, Bernard	Fujikawa, Johnson and Associates	Boulevard Towers-South	1985	205 North Michigan
Weissbourd, Bernard (Metropolitan Structures and JMB Realty)	Fujikawa, Johnson and Associates	Mercantile Exchange Center	1983, 88	10 and 30 South Wacker Drive
Weissbourd, Bernard (Metropolitan Structures)	Hellmuth, Ohata and Kassabaum	Fairmont Hotel	1987	200 North Columbus Drive
Weissbourd, Bernard (Metropolitan Structures)	Fujikawa, Conterato, Lohan and Associates	North Harbor Tower apartments	1988	175 North Harbor Drive
Weissbourd, Bernard (Metropolitan Structures)	Harry Weese and Associates	Swiss Grand Hotel	1988	323 East Wacker Drive
Wislow, Robert (U.S. Equities Realty)	Lucien Lagrange and Associates	840 North Michigan Avenue redevelopment	1980	840 North Michigan Avenue
Wislow, Robert (U.S. Equities)	Patrick Shaw Associates	300 North Michigan redevelopment	1981	300 North Michigan Avenue
Wislow, Robert (U.S. Equities)	Nagle and Hartray	20 North Michigan redevelopment	1983	20 North Michigan Avenue
Wislow, Robert (U.S. Equities, with Casati-Heise)	Skidmore, Owings and Merrill	One Financial Place	1984	400-440 South La Salle
Wislow, Robert (U.S. Equities)	John Buenz/Solomon, Cordwell Buenz	Crate and Barrel building	1989	646 North Michigan
Wislow, Robert (U.S. Equities with SEBUS Group)	Hammond, Beeby and Babka	Harold Washington Library	1991	400 South State
Wislow, Robert (U.S. Equities Realty with Chicago Union Station Realty)	Lucien Lagrange and Associates	Union Station renovation and restoration	1991 -	210 South Canal
Wislow, Robert (U.S. Equities)	Lucien Lagrange and Associates	Plaza Escada	(1993)	840 North Michigan Avenue

INDEX